AGENCY AND AUTONO[...]
KANT'S MORAL THEORY

Agency and Autonomy in Kant's Moral Theory

ANDREWS REATH

CLARENDON PRESS·OXFORD

OXFORD

UNIVERSITY PRESS

Great Clarendon Street, Oxford OX2 6DP

Oxford University Press is a department of the University of Oxford.
It furthers the University's objective of excellence in research, scholarship,
and education by publishing worldwide in

Oxford New York

Auckland Cape Town Dar es Salaam Hong Kong Karachi
Kuala Lumpur Madrid Melbourne Mexico City Nairobi
New Delhi Shanghai Taipei Toronto

With offices in

Argentina Austria Brazil Chile Czech Republic France Greece
Guatemala Hungary Italy Japan Poland Portugal Singapore
South Korea Switzerland Thailand Turkey Ukraine Vietnam

Oxford is a registered trade mark of Oxford University Press
in the UK and in certain other countries

Published in the United States
by Oxford University Press Inc., New York

© Andrews Reath 2006

The moral rights of the author have been asserted
Database right Oxford University Press (maker)

First published 2006

All rights reserved. No part of this publication may be reproduced,
stored in a retrieval system, or transmitted, in any form or by any means,
without the prior permission in writing of Oxford University Press,
or as expressly permitted by law, or under terms agreed with the appropriate
reprographics rights organization. Enquiries concerning reproduction
outside the scope of the above should be sent to the Rights Department,
Oxford University Press, at the address above

You must not circulate this book in any other binding or cover
and you must impose the same condition on any acquirer

British Library Cataloguing in Publication Data

Data available

Library of Congress Cataloging in Publication Data

Reath, Andrews.
Agency and autonomy in Kant's moral theory / Andrews Reath.
p. cm.
Includes bibliographical references and index.
1. Kant, Immanuel, 1724–1804. 2. Act (Philosophy) 3. Agent (Philosophy)
4. Autonomy (Philosophy) I. Title.
B2799.A28R43 2006 170.92—dc22 2005026642

Typeset by Newgen Imaging Systems (P) Ltd., Chennai, India
Printed in Great Britain
on acid-free paper by
Biddles Ltd., King's Lynn, Norfolk

ISBN 0–19–928882–8 978–0–19–928882–3
ISBN 0–19–928883–6 (Pbk.) 978–0–19–928883–0

1 3 5 7 9 10 8 6 4 2

For Blandine

Preface

I was lucky to have become interested in Kant's moral philosophy at a time when work on this area of his thought had begun to flourish, following the lead of several talented philosophers who, because they grasped the complexity and depth of Kant's moral thought, understood what a powerful approach to moral theory it provided. I have learned from many people, both from their written work and in conversation. I would especially like to thank Henry Allison, Steve Engstrom, Hannah Ginsborg, Barbara Herman, Tom Hill, Pierre Keller, Chris Korsgaard, and Onora O'Neill. To John Rawls, with whom I had the very great fortune to study, I owe a different kind of debt that is described in the last note of Chapter 6.

Some of these essays were written with the support of the National Endowment for the Humanities and the National Humanities Center, both of which I thank.

Finally, I am grateful to my wife, Blandine Saint-Oyant, for putting up with me while I wrote the individual essays and completed the volume, which in each case took too long. She provided the cover art, and this book is dedicated to her.

Contents

Translations and Abbreviations

Translations

Citations of Kant's works are to the volume and page number in the Royal Prussian Academy of Sciences edition of Immanuel Kant, *Gesammelte Schriften* (Berlin: Walter de Gruyter, 1902–), except for references to the *Critique of Pure Reason*. The latter cite the page number of the B Edition. I use the following abbreviations and translations:

G   *Groundwork of the Metaphysics of Morals*, tr. Mary J. Gregor, in Immanuel Kant, *Practical Philosophy* (New York: Cambridge University Press, 1996).

KpV   *Critique of Practical Reason*, tr. Mary J. Gregor, in Immanuel Kant, *Practical Philosophy* (New York: Cambridge University Press, 1996).

KrV   *Critique of Pure Reason*, tr. Paul Guyer and Allen W. Wood (New York: Cambridge University Press, 1998).

KU   *Critique of Judgment*, tr. Paul Guyer and Eric Matthews (New York: Cambridge University Press, 2000).

MdS   *The Metaphysics of Morals*, tr. Mary J. Gregor, in Immanuel Kant, *Practical Philosophy* (New York: Cambridge University Press, 1996).

MP-C   *Moral Philosophy: Collins*, tr. Peter Heath, in Immanuel Kant, *Lectures on Ethics*, ed. Peter Heath and J. B. Schneewind (New York: Cambridge University Press, 1997).

Rel   *Religion within the Boundaries of Mere Reason*, tr. George di Giovanni, in Immanuel Kant, *Religion and Rational Theology*, ed. Allen Wood and George di Giovanni (New York: Cambridge University Press, 1996).

VRL   'On a Supposed Right to Lie from Philanthropy', tr. Mary J. Gregor, in Immanuel Kant, *Practical Philosophy* (New York: Cambridge University Press, 1996).

Other works of Kant cited are:

'Conjectural Beginning of Human History', in *On History*, ed. Lewis White Beck (Indianapolis: Bobbs-Merrill, 1975).

'An Answer to the Question: What is Enlightenment?' and 'What is Orientation in Thinking?' tr. H. B. Nisbet, in *Kant: Political Writings*, ed. Hans Reiss (New York: Cambridge University Press, 1991).

Abbreviations

I use the following (now standard) abbreviations to refer to the different formulae of the Categorical Imperative:

FUL   The Formula of Universal Law, first introduced at *G* 4: 421—'act only in accordance with that maxim through which you can at the same time will that it become a universal law'.

FLN   The Formula of the Law of Nature, first introduced at *G* 4: 421—'act as if the maxim of your action were to become by your will a universal law of nature'.

FH   The Formula of Humanity, first introduced at G 4: 429—'so act that you use humanity, whether in your own person or in the person of another, always at the same time as an end, never merely as a means'.

FA   The Formula of Autonomy, first introduced (in truncated form) at G 4: 431— 'the idea of the will of every rational being as a will giving universal law'.

FRE   The Formula of the Realm of Ends, first introduced at G 4: 436—'all maxims from one's own law-giving are to harmonize with a possible kingdom of ends as with a kingdom of nature'.

I treat the FLN as a variant of the FUL, and the FRE as a more complete statement of the idea expressed by the FA. For the most part I am concerned in these essays with the FUL, the FA, and the connections between them. In Chapter 5 I argue that Kant regards the FUL and the FA as strictly equivalent, since he thinks that both can be derived from the concept of a practical law.

Sources

I am grateful to the original publishers for permission to reprint the following essays:

'Kant's Theory of Moral Sensibility', *Kant-Studien*, 80/3 (1989), 284–302. Reprinted with permission of the publisher.

'Hedonism, Heteronomy, and Kant's Principle of Happiness', *Pacific Philosophical Quarterly*, 70/1 (1989), 42–72. © University of Southern California 1989. Reprinted with permission.

'The Categorical Imperative and Kant's Conception of Practical Rationality', *The Monist*, 72/3 (1989), 384–410. Copyright © 1989, *THE MONIST: An International Quarterly Journal of General Philosophical Inquiry*, Peru, Illinois 61354, USA. Reprinted with permission.

'Legislating the Moral Law', *Nous*, 28/4 (1994), 436–64. Reprinted with permission of the publisher.

'Legislating for a Realm of Ends: The Social Dimension of Autonomy', in Andrews Reath, Barbara Herman, and Christine M. Korsgaard, eds., *Reclaiming the History of Ethics: Essays for John Rawls* (New York: Cambridge University Press, 1997), 214–39. Reprinted by permission of Cambridge University Press.

'Duties to Oneself and Self-Legislation', in Mark Timmons, ed., *Kant's Metaphysics of Morals: Interpretive Essays* (Oxford: Oxford University Press, 2001), 349–70. Reprinted by permission of Oxford University Press.

'Agency and the Imputation of Consequences in Kant's Ethics', *Jahrbuch für Recht und Ethik* 2 (1994), 259–82. Reprinted with permission of the publisher.

Introduction

The essays in this collection are attempts to understand various features of Kant's moral psychology, his conception of rational agency, his conception of autonomy, and related areas of his moral theory. They were written over a period of years as independent essays, but there are connections between them and the topics that they address. Certain of the essays led to others, or draw on an idea developed elsewhere. Several of the essays circle around a common set of themes and explore them from differing angles. Almost all the essays are driven initially by some point of interpretation—a question raised by a remark that is puzzling, unclear, or troubling in some other way, or by an obscure transition in a text—mainly in the *Groundwork* and the *Critique of Practical Reason*. I try to come to terms with the interpretive question by reconstructing a philosophical conception or an argument that can be seen to underlie what Kant says, and that explains it in a satisfactory way. For the most part I do not ask whether the views that I ascribe to Kant, or to which I claim that he is committed, are true, though I devote effort to reading views into the texts that are plausible and worth taking seriously. Not much is gained by saddling a great philosopher with a philosophical view that has little to recommend it.

The first three chapters take up issues that arise in connection with Kant's moral psychology and his conception of rational agency. Chapter 1, 'Kant's Theory of Moral Sensibility', and Chapter 2, 'Hedonism, Heteronomy, and Kant's Principle of Happiness', develop an interpretation of Kant's understanding of motivation and choice. Chapter 3, 'The Categorical Imperative and Kant's Conception of Practical Rationality', shifts the focus to his conception of practical rationality and its role in his derivation of the universal law formulation of the Categorical Imperative. One common theme, developed in the first essay, is the claim that Kant thought that all rational choice is guided by considerations that an agent regards as good and sufficient reasons for action. That is, I suggest that for Kant it is a constitutive feature of free, rational choice that it is guided by considerations that an agent takes to have normative force for others, as well as himself, and that an incentive motivates through the judgment that it provides a sufficient reason for action.

'Kant's Theory of Moral Sensibility' analyzes Kant's account of respect for morality as the distinctive form of moral motivation in the *Critique of Practical Reason* ('The Analytic of Pure Practical Reason', Chapter III), and uses his account of respect as a way into his general conception of rational motivation and choice. Kant refers to respect both as the immediate recognition of the authority of the moral law and as a distinctive moral feeling. I try to show how these are connected aspects of a single phenomenon. Properly speaking, what motivates is the recognition of the authority of the moral law; the feeling of respect—its affective dimension—is the way in which we experience the authority and motivating influence of moral considerations. In order to understand how respect for morality counteracts the influence of inclination and non-moral interests, as Kant thinks that it can, one needs an appropriate understanding of the motivating influence of the latter. I argue that since moral considerations motivate through an agent's recognition of their authority, non-moral desires likewise get their purchase on the will when an agent takes them to provide sufficient reasons for action. Their motivational influence can then be undercut when moral scrutiny shows that these reasons are insufficient and that their claims to validity do not stand up.

'Hedonism, Heteronomy, and Kant's Principle of Happiness' extends this account of motivation to argue that Kant did not accept a crude hedonistic picture of non-moral motivation, as is widely assumed. In the *Critique of Practical Reason*, Kant claims that non-moral choices are all of a kind because they make 'pleasure in the reality of an object' or expected 'feelings of agreeableness' the 'determining ground of choice' (*KpV* 5: 21–2). The standard interpretation of these passages has Kant saying that all non-moral choice is motivated by the desire for pleasure as its end. Kant's critics have often taken him to task for holding this view, arguing that central elements of his moral theory are undermined because they presuppose a crude and mistaken conception of non-moral motivation. But read in light of a proper understanding of Kant's conception of action, the 'determining ground of choice' is the principle on which the agent acts, not the end at which the action is directed. Thus Kant's point is that non-moral choice takes expected satisfaction or strength of desire as a sufficient reason for adopting an action or an end. What unifies non-moral choices is not a common end of pleasure, but rather a shared structural feature that is consistent with their being directed at the normal range of different ends. My larger point in this essay is that the real import of what Kant terms the 'principle of happiness' is that it represents the shared structure or common form of non-moral choice, which can be contrasted with the form of moral choice (as represented by the Categorical Imperative). The hedonistic reading of Kant's conception of non-moral motivation misunderstands the significance of this principle.

These two essays try to preserve Kant from a simple dualistic picture of motivation that, according to many critics, deforms his moral psychology. On the interpretation that I support, his conceptions of motivation and choice remain dualistic, since the principles of happiness and morality represent fundamentally different forms of choice. But moral and non-moral considerations motivate in essentially the same way, through an agent's judging that an incentive provides a good reason and freely adopting it into a maxim of action. Chapter 3 further develops this normative conception of choice as based on reasons whose normative force extends to the point of view of others. This essay shows how this conception of rational choice figures in Kant's attempt to derive a statement of the Categorical

Imperative from a conception of practical reason in the first and second sections of the *Groundwork*.

Chapters 4 through 6 develop what I hope is a distinctive approach to one of the centerpieces of Kant's moral theory—his conception of autonomy. Kant famously argues that a proper philosophical understanding of the conception of morality found in ordinary thought must present the basic principle of morality as a principle of autonomy. The special authority that moral requirements carry, according to ordinary thought, can be explained and can be substantiated only if moral principles originate in our rational will, or to use Kant's preferred locution, if we are, in some sense, their legislators. The first moment, as it were, of moral experience is subjection to duty—subjection to requirements that apply with necessity and limit the force of reasons based in desire and subjective interest. But Kant argues that subjection to duty presupposes, indeed is just another aspect of, the autonomy of the will, which he characterizes as 'the property of the will by which it is a law to itself (independently of the property of any objects of volition)' (*G* 4: 440). Kant's conception of autonomy has many elements and different strands. Prominent among them is his view that the will has the power to legislate moral law, that it is subject only to its own legislation, and that the agents who are bound by categorical moral requirements are the legislators from whom they receive their authority. Moral requirements are based on principles that we will for ourselves.

These essays articulate a reading of Kant's conception of autonomy and address some questions that it raises. What is the autonomy of the will? In what sense, or senses, do rational agents legislate the moral principles to which they are subject, or impose them through their willing? While Kant stresses that the principle of morality is a principle of autonomy and that the autonomy of the rational will is the ground of its dignity, at the same time he regards moral principles as objective and universally valid principles that apply with necessity. How is the autonomy of the moral agent consistent with subjection to universally valid moral law? One feature of my treatment of these issues is to take seriously the political and juridical metaphors that provide the framework underlying much of Kant's moral theory. The vocabulary of 'law', 'legislation' or 'lawgiving', and 'subject' versus 'sovereign' are prominent in Kant's writing, especially in the *Groundwork*, and his account of the authority of moral principles draws on the idea that laws get their authority from the will of a lawgiver. 'Autonomy' in its origin is a political concept applied to sovereign states with the power of self-rule. We might expect that attention to Kant's use of such concepts and to their inner logic will provide insights into various elements of his moral theory and help us make headway with some of its puzzling features. Furthermore, the power to create reasons through one's willing—willing laws for oneself or others, taking on obligations, assuming commitments to a principle or to an end—seems to require a structured act of volition. One way to make sense of that structure is to refer to a deliberative procedure governed by a constitutive principle, and the political and juridical spheres provide models of such procedures.

In this spirit I suggest that Kant's conception of autonomy is modeled on a conception of sovereignty and should be understood as a kind of legislative power. I argue that autonomy is best interpreted not primarily as a psychological or motivational capacity, but as the rational agent's sovereignty over himself or herself. Roughly, in regarding moral agents as autonomous, Kant regards them as a kind of sovereign legislator not bound to any external authority, with the power to give law through their willing. This reading of autonomy requires a companion interpretation of the Categorical Imperative as a formal principle that sets out a kind of legislative procedure. I take the Formula of Universal Law to be the principle that is constitutive of autonomy in the sense that it is the principle that one must follow in order to exercise this normative power. Here I suggest that there are instructive parallels between the Formula of Universal Law and a political constitution: the Formula of Universal Law sets out a legislative procedure analogously to the way in which a constitution sets out a process through which a legislature creates civil law. In this way the Formula of Universal Law may be understood as a power-conferring rule that enables rational agents to create law through their willing. That the Formula of Universal Law can be understood in this way is one reason why it may be restated as the Formula of Autonomy. This general understanding of autonomy provides a framework for resolving various questions within Kant's moral theory. For example, viewing the Formula of Universal Law as a power-conferring rule that defines a kind of legislative process explains how autonomy is consistent with subjection to universal law: if autonomy is the power to give law through one's will and the Formula of Universal Law is the constitutive principle of this activity, then one exercises this power by guiding one's will by the Formula of Universal Law (i.e., by acting from universalizable maxims). So understood, the Formula of Universal Law is not a restriction of autonomy, since it is the principle that confers the power with which autonomy is identified.

There is some overlap among these three essays, but they focus on different aspects of this complex conception of autonomy. Chapter 4, 'Legislating the Moral Law', spells out two distinct senses in which the rational will legislates moral requirements, one that holds for the Categorical Imperative and a different sense that holds for particular categorical imperatives or moral requirements. The Formula of Universal Law is a law that Kant derives from the nature of rational volition or rational choice. In this sense, it is a law that the rational will legislates or gives to itself. Roughly, the will is a law to itself since the nature of rational volition leads to a principle that governs its own exercise, namely the Categorical Imperative. To understand the sense in which rational agents legislate particular moral requirements, it is important to bear in mind that Kant is led to this idea by considering how such requirements get their normative authority. Kant appears to claim that the agents who are subject to moral law must be the 'legislators' from whom these requirements receive their authority, because only then can we explain their unconditional authority as categorical imperatives. The view that

I ascribe to Kant is that the reasons to comply with moral requirements are given simply by the reasoning that establishes them as requirements, from which it follows that moral agents are bound to moral requirements in such a way that they model the source of their authority. This capsule statement of my reconstruction of Kant's view does not convey much on its own, but I develop the idea initially in Chapter 4, and at greater length in Chapter 5. In both I draw on the idea that the Formula of Universal Law is a kind of legislative procedure that may be used to generate moral principles that agents can apply to their maxims of action.

Chapter 5, 'Autonomy of the Will as the Foundation of Morality', was the first of these essays to be drafted but the last to be completed. It aims to distinguish and to explain the different elements that go into Kant's claim at the end of the Second Section of the *Groundwork* that autonomy of the will is the foundation of the commonly accepted conception of morality (*G* 4: 445). In doing so it explores the parallels between moral autonomy and sovereignty (while acknowledging that these parallels give out at a certain point). Much of this chapter is an extended reading of a move in the *Groundwork* that is arguably a turning point in the history of modern ethics, where Kant argues that moral agents are not just subject to moral requirements, but are subject to them in such a way that they must be regarded as their authors, or source of their authority (*G* 4: 431). This claim, which I call the 'Sovereignty Thesis', follows analytically from Kant's conception of a practical law or categorical imperative. It marks the transition from subjection to duty to autonomy that drives the later portions of the argument of the Second Section of the *Groundwork* and it is a component of the argument in the Third Section that the moral law is the law of a free will. Kant's argument for the Sovereignty Thesis is obscure, but I take it to go roughly as follows. Since moral requirements (practical laws) apply unconditionally, without reference to an agent's desires and subjective interests, the reasons to comply with them cannot come from desire, but must instead be based on the rational procedure that makes them requirements. In other words, one is bound to moral requirements by the reasoning that makes them laws. The agent who complies with moral requirements as such thus goes through the same rational process as a legislator would in willing them as law. The upshot is that moral requirements bind rational agents in a way that collapses the distinction between subject and sovereign.

Chapter 6, 'Legislating for a Realm of Ends', picks up certain themes in the previous two essays. One is the connection between autonomy and governance by norms. I argue that the apparent tension between autonomy and subjection to universally valid principles dissolves when we consider how autonomy depends upon and is made possible by the capacity to reason in ways that can make claims to universal validity. A second theme is the idea that autonomy is a power exercised in relation to other rational agents with equal capacity to give law—in other words that its exercise presupposes the community of rational agents that Kant terms a 'Realm of Ends'. This line of thought brings out a social dimension to Kant's conception of autonomy which I try to highlight in this essay.

The idea that the agents who are subject to moral principles must be regarded as their legislators (the Sovereignty Thesis) has implications throughout Kant's moral thought, two of which I explore in Chapters 7 and 8. 'Agency and Universal Law' focuses on the interpretation of the Formula of Universal Law and its role in the overall argument of the *Groundwork*. The main thesis is that Kant's Formula of Universal Law relies on a conception of autonomy to generate substantive moral judgments—specifically that a conception of agents as having autonomy plays a role in generating the contradictions that result from the universalization of certain maxims, by which they are judged impermissible. I show how the Formula of Universal Law, so understood, can give an account of prototypical violations of duty such as deception, coercion, and violence. But, one might ask, what licenses reading a conception of autonomy into the Formula of Universal Law? Here I draw on the previous chapters. According to the Sovereignty Thesis, the agents subject to moral principles must be regarded as their legislators, and thus as agents with autonomy. But then moral principles should be understood as addressed to and intended to govern the conduct of agents with the legislative capacities that go into Kant's conception of autonomy—they are laws willed by and for agents with autonomy. Since this conception of agency is presupposed by the concept of a moral requirement or practical law, it is implicit in the Formula of Universal Law and should guide its application.

Chapter 8, 'Self-Legislation and Duties to Oneself', begins by using the Sovereignty Thesis to fill out a missing element in Kant's foundational remarks about duties to oneself in the *Doctrine of Virtue*. It then articulates certain features of Kant's general model of duty that are implicit in his remarks about self-regarding duties. The idea is that duties are generated by a form of interaction among agents which has a structure defined by various positions that agents can occupy (such as 'legislator', 'subject', and agent to whom a duty is owed or the 'source' of a claim). With this model in hand, one can see that both duties to oneself and self-legislation are perfectly coherent notions because a single agent can occupy multiple positions within this structure. However the model also shows that duties to oneself and self-legislation involve different forms of self-constraint, since the 'legislator' and 'source' of a duty represent different positions within this structure.

Chapter 9, 'Agency and the Imputation of Consequences in Kant's Ethics', takes up a somewhat different topic, but in a way that is shaped by ideas in the earlier chapters. In his infamous essay, 'On a Supposed Right to Lie from Philanthropy', Kant relies on a principle of responsibility for consequences, according to which all the consequences of an action contrary to duty may be imputed to the agent. This principle has been given little critical attention, perhaps because it is overshadowed by, though as troubling as, the rigoristic position that he takes on lying. I argue here that this principle can be defended in modified form. The basic idea is that the subject to whom an action or its consequences are imputed is the agent on whose authority the action is undertaken. Since an agent who violates a moral requirement acts 'on his own authority', the bad consequences of such an action are imputable to that agent. Even unforeseeable or accidental consequences of a violation of duty are fairly imputed because, given the moral requirement, the agent had compelling reason to refrain from the action that led to them. This essay fills out his conception of agency in certain respects, for example by developing a normative understanding of the relationships between agents and the consequences of their actions.

Chapters 1–4, 6, and 8–9 have been previously published. Chapters 5 and 7 are published for the first time in this volume. I have made minor changes to all the previously published essays—updating translations, updating footnotes, and editing the text for consistency. I have made more substantial changes to Chapters 1 and 2, including revisions to a section of each, some new endnotes, and the addition to each of an appendix. These essays have elicited some critical discussion. In some instances I found the criticisms persuasive and have modified the essays accordingly, while in others I have offered a brief response—mainly in notes and the appendices. Any modifications to the original text that verge on being substantial are flagged with an endnote.

1

Kant's Theory of Moral Sensibility: Respect for the Moral Law and the Influence of Inclination

This essay is concerned with two parallel topics in Kant's moral psychology—respect for the moral law as the motive to moral conduct and the influence of inclinations on the will. I explain some of Kant's views about respect for the moral law and its role in moral motivation, and this leads to a consideration of the sensible motives that respect for the law limits, as well as the more general question of how Kant thinks that inclinations affect choice. It turns out that these two topics are best understood in relation to each other. When we look at the motives that respect for the law must oppose, certain facts emerge about how it determines the will. By the same token, when we consider how respect limits the influence of inclinations, we are forced to articulate a clearer picture of how inclinations influence the will. In considering these questions together, one can begin to outline an interpretation of Kant's general theory of motivation and choice which provides the common ground between sensible and rational motives that is needed to explain how they interact. I begin in Section I with some background, and in Section II turn to Kant's account of respect.

I. MORALITY AS INCENTIVE

Kant's most complete discussion of respect occurs in the third chapter of the *Critique of Practical Reason*, entitled 'On the Incentives of Pure Practical Reason'.[1] To place it in context, we should recall that a central aim of the second *Critique* is to show that pure reason is practical, and that in this work Kant employs a strategy for establishing the authority of the moral law that differs from that seen in the *Groundwork*. The first two chapters of the latter simply derive a statement of the moral law from the concept of practical reason; its validity for us is not established until the Third Section, where Kant argues that any agent with a free will is committed to the moral law and offers non-moral grounds for thinking that we are free in the relevant sense. In the second *Critique* Kant tries to establish the authority of the moral law by arguing directly for the claim that pure reason is practical. If pure reason can provide a 'ground sufficient to determine the will, then there are practical laws'—that is, laws that have authority for us (*KpV* 5: 19). This issue, in turn, is resolved through the doctrine of the Fact of Reason. Kant holds that our ordinary moral consciousness shows us that we do recognize the authority of the moral law and can act from its principles.[2] Since the moral law is an expression of pure practical reason, this suffices to show that pure reason is practical.

By the third chapter of the *Critique*, Kant has established that the moral law can influence the will, or in his phrase, functions as an 'incentive' (*Triebfeder*). One purpose of this chapter is to explore the effects of moral consciousness on the faculty of desire. Here Kant outlines what might be called a theory of moral sensibility, in that he is led to a set of topics that concern the interaction between practical reason and our sensible nature, which marks out the experience of the moral law peculiar to us.[3] This includes, first, the account of respect both as the moral incentive, and as the feeling that arises when the moral law checks the inclinations. Second, there is a discussion of virtue as a condition in which one successfully masters motives that are contrary to duty. Kant closes by considering the elevating side to the experience of respect, which leads us to see certain elements of our nature as worthy of esteem. The very fact that the moral law can check the inclinations and 'humiliate' the pretensions of our sensible nature reveals our responsiveness to rational principles, and independence from the natural order. Respect points out certain of our limitations; but when we realize that this law has its source in our own reason, it also reveals the 'higher vocation' which is the source of our dignity.[4]

Since the concept of an incentive is a technical term for Kant, it deserves comment. He defines it as 'a subjective determining ground of the will of a being whose reason does not by its nature necessarily conform with the objective law' (*KpV* 5: 72). It is a subjective determining ground of the will in the sense that it is the motivational state of the subject that is operative on a particular occasion. Thus, an incentive must be a kind of determining ground of the will, or a kind of motivation from which human beings can act. The sense of the concept, as understood by Kant, presupposes a contrast between different kinds of motivation that may be effective at different times. Though incentives are 'subjective' in the above sense, they can include reasons that are objectively valid: respect for the law is the operative incentive in morally worthy conduct, and hence its 'subjective determining ground'.[5]

II. TWO ASPECTS OF RESPECT

In a footnote to the *Groundwork*, Kant offers apparently different characterizations of respect, all of which reappear in the second *Critique*. First, it is a 'feeling self-wrought by means of a rational concept'. Second, it is 'the immediate determination of the will by means of the law and consciousness of this [determination]'. And third, Kant calls it 'the representation of a worth that infringes upon my self-love'.[6] The second remark conveys what I shall view as the primary notion of respect as the proper moral incentive, or form of moral motivation. Respect for the moral law, in this sense, is the immediate recognition of its authority, or the immediate determination of the will by the law. To be moved by, or to act out of, respect is to recognize the moral law as a source of value, or reasons for action, that are unconditionally valid and overriding relative to other kinds of reasons; in particular, they limit the force of and outweigh the reasons provided by one's desires. Respect is the attitude that it is appropriate to have towards a law, in which one acknowledges its authority and is motivated to act accordingly. I will refer to this attitude as the 'intellectual' or 'practical' aspect of respect.[7] One can also display this attitude towards individuals. This could be in an honorific sense, as when one respects a person's merits or accomplishments by acknowledging the value of what he or she has achieved. Or one can show respect for humanity in the broadly ethical sense defined by the second formula of the Categorical Imperative, the Formula of Humanity. Here it involves the recognition that humanity (in oneself or in others) has an absolute value that places limits on how it is permissibly treated.[8] But in addition to its practical aspect, Kant also makes it clear that respect has an 'affective' side: it is a feeling or emotion that is experienced when the moral law checks the inclinations and limits their influence on the will.[9]

Though the practical and the affective aspects of respect at first seem quite different, Kant does not keep them apart. In fact he seems to devote effort to showing that they are the same thing. An understanding of the phenomenon in question requires that we first distinguish them, and then see how they are related and why Kant thinks that they coincide in us. The existence of the affective aspect of respect also raises special questions in the context of Kant's theory. How can there be a 'moral feeling' and what is its role in moral motivation? We will see that it is the practical aspect that is active in motivating moral conduct, while the affective side, or feeling of respect, is its effect on certain sensible tendencies. I will begin by looking at what Kant says about the moral feeling of respect.

This feeling is most easily explained as the experience of constraints that the moral law imposes on our inclinations. Thus, Kant stresses that it originates as a 'negative effect' of our moral consciousness. When the moral law determines the will, it frustrates the inclinations, and 'the negative effect on feeling . . . is itself feeling' (*KpV* 5: 73). In short, the feeling of respect is an emotion that is the effect of, and follows from, the determination of the will by the moral law, when the latter limits the inclinations. Kant also tries to spell out a sense in which this feeling is an incentive in moral conduct by showing how this originally negative effect is at the same time a positive source of motivation. In us the inclinations present obstacles that we must control, or overcome, when we act morally. Respect promotes the satisfaction of our moral interests by counteracting these obstacles. Kant holds that it is an incentive toward good conduct in that it offsets the influence of contrary motives, and thus moves us toward something that we must at some level find good. This point is made in the following passage:

For whatever diminishes the hindrances to an activity is a furthering of this activity itself . . . Therefore, respect for the moral law must be regarded as also a positive but indirect effect of the law on feeling insofar as the law weakens the hindering influence of the inclinations by humiliating self-conceit, and must therefore be regarded as a subjective ground of activity—that is, as the incentive for compliance with the law . . . (*KpV* 5: 79. Cf. also 5: 75)

Some of Kant's attempt to show how the feeling of respect is an incentive can be somewhat misleading. Strictly speaking, it is not this feeling that weakens the influence of inclinations. Since, as we shall see, the feeling of respect is the experience one has when the inclinations are weakened by a superior motive, it presupposes that the inclinations have already been weakened. This point emerges from a clarification which Kant himself adds to his discussion of the moral incentive. In attempting to explain how the feeling of respect is an incentive in good conduct, he stresses that there is 'no antecedent feeling in the subject that would be attuned to morality' (*KpV* 5: 76). In other words, Kant is careful to make it clear that he is not adopting any sort of moral sense theory. Since his aim is to show that the will is directly responsive to practical reason, and thus that pure reason is practical, he must avoid a view which makes use of a natural desire, or disposition, that moves us toward moral conduct, and provides morality with its content. He cannot explain our ability, or interest, in acting morally as a feature of our psychological constitution, or by introducing any motivational factor beyond the recognition of the authority of the moral law. Such a view would in effect grant that pure reason is not practical. Thus, respect can be neither a source of motivation, nor a standard of moral judgment, which is independent of our recognition of the moral law.[10]

Such considerations underlie the following important, if obscure, remark: 'And so respect for the law is not the incentive to morality; instead it is morality itself subjectively considered as an incentive inasmuch as pure practical reason, by rejecting all the claims of self-love in opposition with its own, supplies authority to the law, which now alone has influence' (*KpV* 5: 76). Here Kant means to say that respect is not an incentive that exists prior to, or independently of, our recognition of the moral law, but is simply this recognition itself as it functions as an incentive in us.[11] All of this suggests that the *feeling* of respect is an incentive only in an attenuated sense. It is indeed the inner state of a subject who is moved by the moral law, but the active motivating factor is always the recognition of the moral law. Thus the moral incentive, properly speaking, is what was distinguished above as the practical aspect of respect. The affective aspect is the experience of one's natural desires being held in check by the moral consciousness, and as such, an effect that occurs after, or in conjunction with, the determination of the will by the moral law. At times a subject may feel as though these sensible motives are being overpowered by a higher-order emotion, which, so to speak, clears the way for one to act morally—so that a specifically moral emotion would be operative as a motive force. But this is not correct, on the model Kant means to propose. One's inclinations are held in check simply by the recognition of the moral law (the practical aspect of respect), and this interaction between practical reason and sensibility gives rise to the feeling of respect (the affective aspect). The resulting moral emotion ends up being something like the way in which we experience the activity of pure practical reason.[12]

It turns out that there is a tight connection between these two aspects of respect, due to certain facts about our nature, and this explains why Kant tends to treat them as identical. Our sensible nature is a source of motives that conflict with the moral disposition—specifically, because it includes the tendencies to give priority to our inclinations which Kant terms self-love and self-conceit. Kant thinks that these motives and tendencies are always present to some degree. Thus, whenever the moral law is effective, it must overcome contrary motives that originate in sensibility, and will thus produce some feeling. The determination of the will by moral law will always be accompanied by an affect. Moreover, though distinguishable, these aspects of respect need not be phenomenologically distinct, but would be experienced together. As a result, the immediate recognition of the moral law and the feeling that it produces represent connected aspects of what is in us a single phenomenon.

This discussion brings out a further point of some importance: Kant does not think that the moral law determines the will through a quasi-mechanical or affective force.[13] Such a view is implied by his remark that respect is not an 'incentive to morality', but the moral law itself regarded as an incentive. This qualification to the account of respect is added to make it clear that moral motivation does not require, or occur, through any feeling that exists independently of moral consciousness. In addition, we saw that, while an affect is produced when the moral law determines the will, it is not this affect that motivates. The picture underlying these ideas is that, in acting from respect, the simple recognition of an obligation determines or guides one's choice. This is to be opposed to a model that would understand the moral motive to operate by exerting a force on the will.[14]

More general grounds for this interpretation are supplied by Kant's conception of the freedom of the will. In the *Religion* Kant makes the following important claim, which has come to be known as the Incorporation Thesis:

. . . freedom of the power of choice has the characteristic, entirely peculiar to it, that it cannot be determined to action through any incentive *except so far as the human being has incorporated it into his maxim* (has made it a universal rule for himself, according to which he wills to conduct himself); only in this way can an incentive, whatever it may be, coexist with the absolute spontaneity of the power of choice (of freedom). (*Rel* 6: 23–4)

Kant claims here that an incentive never determines the will directly, but only through a spontaneous judgment or choice made by the individual that can be expressed as the adoption of a maxim.[15] This conception of free agency rules out the idea that the choice is determined solely by the force that an incentive might have, or that actions should be understood as resulting from the balance of forces acting on the will. It indicates that Kant's conception of choice should not be understood on the analogy of a sum of vector forces (or of mechanical forces acting on an object). Kant can allow an incentive to have an affective force of some sort, but the role assigned to such force in motivation and the explanation of action must be limited so as to leave room for the notion of choice. Thus, we may think of respect for the law as one incentive in competition with others, against which it sometimes wins out. But rather than prevailing against its competitors by exerting the greater force on the will, its influence comes from providing (and being taken by the agent to provide) a certain kind of reason for choice.

This is a point of interpretation, but there are deeper reasons for thinking that it should be Kant's view. If the moral law determines choice by exerting a force that is stronger than the alternatives, moral conduct will result from the balance of whatever psychological forces are acting on the will. The issue is whether this model permits us to sustain the idea that such conduct is the outcome of volition. To see this, we might first consider why Kant cannot turn to a moral sense theory to explain moral motivation. If the moral motive were based on a natural desire or disposition that could be directed and refined in various ways, moral conduct would be the result of different drives and natural desires that are present in our psychology. Morality would then become an empirically explainable natural phenomenon; and one would lose the notion that pure reason is practical, since one could account for moral conduct entirely in terms of natural desires. (Whatever the merits of this view, Kant certainly wants to avoid it.) Furthermore, it is not clear that this model leaves room for any real notion of volition or choice. The determination of action rests on the ways in which competing forces support each other, or cancel out, so that individuals act morally when the desires moving in the direction of moral conduct are stronger than the alternatives. Now consider a model on which the recognition of the moral law motivates by exerting a force on the will. Reason might still determine the will, but it is difficult to see how it does so through a choice by the individual. The moral motive would still be one psychological force among others, which is effective when it is the strongest, or when favored by the balance of psychological forces. What is missing from this model is the idea that the subject's action stems ultimately from a choice made on the basis of reasons.

The concerns raised in this section lead to two further lines of inquiry which I will pursue in the remaining sections. First, we have seen that our experience of the activity of pure practical reason has a subjective character, due to the sensible motives with which it interacts. This suggests that we can broaden our understanding of respect by exploring the character of the motivational tendencies that it offsets (Section III). Second, to fully understand how the moral law functions as an incentive, one must see how it limits the influence of inclinations. But we will not understand that until we see how inclinations influence the will. At this point

Kant's views about specifically moral motivation begin to have implications for his general theory of motivation. Once we grant that the moral law does not become an incentive by exerting a force on the will, it becomes harder to see how it can counteract inclinations, though Kant surely thinks that it does. Asking how this can occur leads us to look for an account of how inclinations influence the will that allows for this possibility. In short, on the assumption that respect for the moral law does counteract the influence of inclination, we need a model of both that explains how this is possible (Section IV).

III. SELF-LOVE AND SELF-CONCEIT

In the following passage Kant provides a catalogue of different kinds of motivational tendencies that respect for the law counteracts:

All the inclinations together . . . constitute self-regard (*solipsismus*). This is either the self-regard of *love for oneself* [*Selbstliebe*], a predominant *benevolence* toward oneself (*philautia*), or that of *satisfaction with oneself* (*arrogantia*). The former is called, in particular, *self-love* [*Eigenliebe*]; the latter, *self-conceit* [*Eigendünkel*]. Pure practical reason merely *infringes upon* self-love . . . But it *strikes down* self-conceit altogether. (*KpV* 5: 73)

Here self-regard (*Selbstsucht*) refers to the rationally guided interest in the satisfaction of one's inclinations, which is indifferent to the interests of others.[16] In this section I will offer an interpretation of the two kinds of motivational tendencies that it comprises: self-love (either *Selbstliebe* or *Eigenliebe*), on the one hand, and self-conceit (*Eigendünkel*).[17] Self-conceit in particular is pertinent to an understanding of respect. The points to bear in mind are that self-love is a 'predominant benevolence [*Wohlwollens*] towards oneself', while self-conceit is termed 'satisfaction [*Wohlgefallens*] with oneself' and later, the 'opinion of personal worth' (*KpV* 5: 78). Furthermore, the moral law or pure practical reason responds to these attitudes in different ways. It 'merely *infringes* upon self-love [*die reine praktische Vernunft tut der Eigenliebe bloß Abbruch*], inasmuch as it only restricts it, as natural and active in us even prior to the moral law, to the condition of agreement with this law . . .'. In that case it is called 'reasonable self-love' (*KpV* 5: 73). But it 'strikes down' and 'humiliates' self-conceit. Or as Kant later says, the moral law 'excludes altogether the influence of self-love on the highest practical principle', but 'forever infringes upon self-conceit' (*tut dem Eigendünkel . . . unendlichen Abbruch*) (*KpV* 5: 74). The influence of self-love needs to be controlled, but self-conceit involves 'illusion' (*KpV* 5: 75). While one may act on self-interested inclinations when properly constrained, this is never true of self-conceit, and this difference requires an explanation.

The distinction between self-love and self-conceit is mentioned briefly in the discussion in the *Doctrine of Virtue* of *love* and *respect* as different kinds of concern that one can have (or fail to have) toward others.[18] The object of love is a person's welfare (*Wohl*) or the satisfaction of a person's ends, where such concern for another's well-being could be based either in feeling for or attachment to the person ('delight' (*Wohlgefallen*) in the person or pleasure in the person's perfections), or in the duty of benevolence. Respect, by contrast, is concerned with worth, esteem, dignity, or how a person is regarded by others. As self-love and self-conceit are forms of these attitudes directed at the self, we may interpret the distinction as follows. Self-love is a love of oneself that manifests itself as interest in one's own welfare and in the satisfaction of one's own desires. It comprises inclinations directed at ends outside the self, such as goods and activities that produce satisfaction or well-being, the means to such ends, and so on, as well (as we shall see in a moment) as the disposition to regard such inclinations as reasons for action. On the other hand, the object of self-conceit is best described as personal worth or esteem, or importance in the opinions of others. It is a desire to be highly regarded, or a tendency to esteem oneself over others. It should be stressed that it is a natural inclination, specifically for a kind of esteem that depends on the opinions either of oneself or of others, and on one's standing relative to others, and which operates independently of one's moral consciousness. It turns out for this reason to be a comparative form of value that one only achieves at the expense of others—for example, by surpassing them, or by being perceived to surpass them in certain qualities. Briefly, the object of self-conceit is a form of esteem or personal importance that you can only achieve when you deny it to some others.[19]

A further dimension to this distinction appears in the following passage:

This propensity to make oneself, on subjective determining grounds of choice [*Willkür*], into the objective determining ground of the will [*Wille*] in general can be called *self-love*; and if self-love makes itself lawgiving and the unconditional practical principle, it can be called *self-conceit* . . . [S]elf-conceit . . . prescribes the subjective conditions of [self-love] as laws. (*KpV* 5: 74)[20]

Provisionally we may take self-love as a tendency to treat one's inclinations as objectively good reasons for one's actions, which are sufficient to justify them to others. In making self-love 'lawgiving', self-conceit goes a step further in being a tendency to treat oneself or one's inclinations as providing reasons for the actions of *others*, or to take one's desires as sources of value to which they should defer. To put the point another way, self-love tends toward a form of general egoism: I take my inclinations as sufficient reasons for my actions, but can view the inclinations of others as sufficient reasons for theirs, so that all would be permitted to pursue their own interests as they see fit. In contrast, self-conceit would produce a form of first person egoism, in which I act as though *my* inclinations could provide laws for the conduct of *others*: it expresses a desire that they serve or defer to my interests.[21]

People naturally place a special importance on themselves, and often make a concern for others conditional on its congruence with their own interests. Kant's remarks suggest that, when moved by self-conceit, you act as though others should accord your interests the same priority that you give them, and you put your desires forward as conditions on the satisfaction of theirs. Though self-conceit aims at increasing one's welfare, it does so by claiming a certain kind of value for one's person relative to others. How could you possibly get other rational individuals, with desires of their own, to treat your desires as reasons for their actions? Self-conceit attempts to get others to defer to your interests by claiming a special value for your person and by ranking yourself higher. In this way, it seeks a kind of respect that moves in one direction. When you treat a person with respect, you attribute a value to his or her person which limits how you may act. Self-conceit would have others act as though your interests outweigh theirs, and refuses to return the respect that it demands. This indicates that it is at root a desire to dominate others. It is an outgrowth of self-love in that those who are able to manipulate others in this way both protect their own interests, and increase the means available for getting what they want.

We can now say why the moral law only restricts self-love, but strikes down self-conceit. Self-love is a concern for well-being which modifies an inclination only when it conflicts with one's overall happiness. It is opposed to the moral disposition, not due to the inclinations involved, but because it recognizes no moral restrictions. The inclinations may be good in that they can ground morally permissible ends, when properly limited. But in recognizing no moral restrictions, self-love makes the moral law a subordinate principle. In the language of the *Religion*, by reversing the moral ordering of incentives, it is a propensity to evil.[22] It follows that what is bad about self-love can be corrected when restricted by moral concerns. In this case, many of the original inclinations may be retained and their ends adopted, though now on different grounds. It is in this sense that the moral law need only 'infringe upon' (limit) self-love, and 'exclude altogether the influence of self-love on the highest practical principle'. When it does so, self-love can become good.

In contrast Kant claims that inclinations for personal importance can never be made acceptable. He says that 'all claims to self-esteem for oneself that precede accord with the moral law are null and quite unwarranted' and that any presumption to personal worth that is prior to the moral disposition is 'false and opposed to the law' (*KpV* 5: 73). The view to consider is that no claims to self-esteem are acceptable unless grounded in the consciousness of one's moral capacities. As Kant says, the moral law opposes 'the propensity to self-esteem so long as it only rests on sensibility' (*KpV* 5: 73).

First we should clarify when a morally grounded claim to self-esteem, or demand that others respect you, is acceptable. One could claim what we earlier called honorific respect, out of a belief that one has acted well in some significant way, and some people might think this would entitle one to preferential treatment. Or one could claim broadly ethical respect from others—that is, demand that one be treated as an end. It is hard to see how one could legitimately make a claim of the former kind on one's own behalf.[23] Others may offer you this form of respect; but you cannot demand it, and it would not entitle you to special treatment. But it is certainly acceptable to demand ethical respect from others when it is being denied, and to think that one's interests ought to be regarded as important. This is an example of a claim to be worthy of respect that is grounded in one's moral consciousness; it is justified simply by one's possession of rational and moral capacities, and not by anything in particular that one has done with them.[24] Of course, this form of respect is mutual and reciprocal: giving it to one person, or claiming it for oneself, will not be prejudicial to the interests of anyone else.

Self-conceit is a claim to deserve priority (resembling a demand for honorific respect) that implicitly treats your inclinations as special sources of reasons or value. It seeks a form of personal worth attainable only at the expense of others, which is oriented toward domination and manipulation. Since such desires seek to use others as a means, they are incompatible with ethical respect for others. They are bad inclinations, unacceptable in all forms, and for this reason, the moral law opposes claims to self-esteem based on inclination. It is interesting to note how the moral flaws of self-conceit can be located in certain features which it very nearly shares with the proper moral attitude. It is as a distortion of a moral attitude that it is fundamentally opposed to true respect. Self-conceit is a desire for a kind of respect that claims something like an absolute value for oneself. But this is thought to ground preferential treatment or deference from others; it is not reciprocal; and its aim is to further the satisfaction of one's inclinations.[25] It is as though you take your inclinations to confer a value on your person that sets you above others. This prevents you not only from recognizing their humanity, but your own as well, in that you have taken inclinations, rather than rational nature, as the ultimate source of value in your person.

IV. HOW INCLINATIONS INFLUENCE CHOICE

The preceding section discussed different kinds of inclinations and motivational tendencies that respect for the law must counteract. In this section I will turn to the more general question of how inclinations influence the will. I have interpreted self-love as the tendency to treat one's inclinations as sufficient reasons for one's actions, and, following Kant's usage, have freely referred to the 'claims' made by both self-love and self-conceit. The interpretation of Kant's understanding of motivation and choice that I develop should make it clear why this language is appropriate.

In Section II, I argued that the moral incentive does not influence choice by exerting a quasi-mechanical or affective force on the will. Among other reasons, this was supported by the fact that the motive to moral conduct is the practical aspect of respect, or the immediate recognition of an obligation, rather than any feeling that it produces, or which exists independently. This interpretation is also required by the model of free choice seen in Kant's Incorporation Thesis. As Kant's view is that no incentives (including sensible incentives) determine the will directly except through a choice by the individual, similar considerations should apply to actions done from inclination. That is, while inclinations can have an affective force, it is not through this force that they ultimately influence the will. Furthermore, if inclinations could determine the will solely by their affective force, it is hard to see how they could be offset by respect for the moral law, as Kant clearly wants to hold is possible. Consider for a moment that counteracting an inclination consisted only of setting up an opposing psychological force that cancels it out. That leaves no way to explain how respect for the law limits the influence of inclinations, since it exerts no such force. This indicates the need for a different account of how inclinations influence choice. There must be enough common ground between motivation by inclination and moral motivation to show how the moral incentive can limit the influence of non-moral incentives. Here we can see how Kant's views about specifically moral motivation have important implications for his overall theory of motivation. If the moral incentive does not operate by exerting a force on the will, then it seems that, in general, a 'balance of forces model' of the will is not appropriate to Kant's theory of motivation.

How then do inclinations influence choice? Kant's view, I want to argue, is that one chooses to act on an incentive of any kind by regarding it as providing a sufficient reason for action, where that is a reason with normative force from the standpoint of others, not just that of the agent. Simply stated, inclinations influence choices by being regarded as sources of reasons that can be cited in some form to justify your actions. Their influence on choice comes not simply from their strength or affective force, but from the *value* that the agent supposes them to have. This view needs certain qualifications. First, it does not suppose that inclinations do provide sufficient or justifying reasons for actions. It is enough that the individual is prepared to regard them in this way, and here lies the appropriateness of referring to the 'claims' made by self-love. Typically the person moved by self-love claims a value, or justifying force, for the inclinations that they do not have; yet it is by being viewed in this way that they provide grounds for choice. Second, it is not necessary for the agent to view his inclinations as sources of reasons that will make the action acceptable to *all* others, or to those most directly affected by the action. Rather, they must be viewed as reasons that would justify or explain the action from a point of view which individuals other than the agent can take up (e.g. the members of some community). Thus, the interpretation proposed is that all choice occurs on quasi-moral grounds, or proceeds from reasons that resemble moral reasons in form, in the sense that they provide justification for the action in question. How the moral law checks inclinations may be explained roughly as follows. Since inclinations influence the will through the value that the agent supposes them to have, the moral law can limit their influence by showing that they do not have this value, and by presenting a higher form of value. This is not a question of countering one kind of affective force by another that is stronger. The appropriate metaphor is rather that of a struggle between two parties for something like legal authority or political legitimacy.[26]

This conception of choice presupposes that all rational action carries an implicit claim to justification.[27] To explore its ramifications, we should bear in mind that the Incorporation Thesis characterizes choice as the adoption of a maxim: all action proceeds from maxims that the agent in some sense adopts or decides to act on. How does this conception apply to action done from inclination? Schematically, we can say that inclinations are produced as sensuous affections (that we experience as potential reasons) and that, in response, an agent formulates a maxim of acting in a certain way—for instance, performing the action that will best satisfy the inclination. Here the role of the maxim is to express the reason for action in a form that can be assessed and cited to others. I would argue that the Incorporation Thesis implies further that a maxim is only adopted if it is regarded as a principle with justifying force that the agent endorses. It is a constitutive feature of free choice that it involve regarding one's action as good at some level. If incentives become effective through the adoption of maxims, then maxims are always chosen on the supposition that they express sufficient reasons for action. As well as being objects of choice, they carry the burden of justification, and serve as principles that explain your actions to others. To put the point another way, we always choose maxims that we suppose carry some form of universal validity.

This feature of action can be taken as an aspect of the Fact of Reason—that is, of our recognition of the authority of the moral law in everyday life. One element of ordinary moral consciousness is a readiness to submit your actions to public scrutiny and to supply reasons and explanations of a certain kind. On Kant's view, this procedure is initiated by citing the maxim of your action, which commits you to view it, at least initially, as a sufficient explanation for what you did. The presumption is that someone who understands your maxim can at some level accept your way of acting. Such dialogue might have the structure of rudimentary universality arguments. Others might agree that if they were in the same situation, they might have done the same thing, or acted from your principle. This acknowledgement on their part might lead them to view your action as one that you had good reason to choose, and might bring them to some sort of understanding with you. But if individuals do acknowledge the burden of accounting to others, this will not occur only after choices are made, but must inform the procedure of choice itself. Choice and action must occur within some framework of sufficient reasons from the start.

The direct textual support for attributing to Kant the view that all action carries an implicit claim to justification is limited. But it can be seen in the characterization of self-love discussed above, and in a passage from the *Groundwork*. Regarding the first, Kant writes that

we find our pathologically determinable self, even though it is quite unfit to give universal law through its maxims, nevertheless striving antecedently to make its claims primary and originally valid, just as if it constituted our entire self. This propensity to make oneself, on subjective determining grounds of one's choice, into an objective determining ground of the will in general can be called self-love . . . (*KpV* 5: 74)

Here self-love is described as the tendency to treat subjective grounds of choice as objective reasons. That is, one's inclinations, which may provide reasons valid for the agent, are treated as reasons that are valid for anyone or that anyone can recognize as valid, and could thus provide justification for the action. The context permits the reading that the agent, when acting from a sensible motive, views the maxim as carrying some form of justifying force or universal validity (whether or not it actually does). The passage from the *Groundwork* claims that even in 'transgressions of duty' we acknowledge the validity of the categorical imperative. In such cases, he suggests that we view the action as a permissible exception to a principle that we otherwise hold valid. This could be done by regarding one's action as a departure warranted by exceptional circumstances; or by restricting the principle so that it will not apply to this case.[28] Thus he is claiming that the agent will continue to regard the action as consistent with principles acceptable to others, and as a maxim with justifying force.

These passages bring out the fact that this model of choice applies equally to actions that are not morally acceptable. The claim is not that maxims based on inclination do provide sufficient reasons for action, but only that they are adopted by regarding them in this way. It is in this sense that the model conceives all rational choice to occur on quasi-moral grounds, or to proceed from reasons that resemble moral reasons in form in the sense that they are regarded as providing some kind of intersubjective justification.[29] This model assigns a significant role to rationalization in Kant's conception of choice.[30] It is central to his moral doctrine that we always act with some recognition of the requirements of the moral law. But this assumption leaves the problem of what to say about conduct that is contrary to duty—specifically about conduct in which we ignore our duty, or act against our better judgment. While Kant generally says only that conscience condemns one on such occasions, his theory is better served by taking stock of the distorted forms in which moral consciousness can surface in public behavior. A recognition of the need to account to others is exemplified as much as anywhere in the rationalizations and disingenuous explanations that individuals are prone to engage in. One can acknowledge the propriety of public scrutiny through the pretense of submitting to it, and this occurs in many ways. Individuals often skew the perceptions of their circumstances so as to favor their private interests, or protect their reputations. Nor is it unusual for people to support their actions with principles that they do not really accept, and would not accept from others. These are everyday forms of dissemblance and self-deception in which the appearance of moral dialogue lends the impression of legitimacy to self-interested motives. Such behavior reveals an underhanded recognition of the authority of moral concerns. How else are we to understand these particular forms of dishonesty?

In self-regarding conduct, individuals make the principle of self-love their highest maxim, and act from reasons that are only subjectively valid (valid only for the subject). But this fact must be obscured if choice proceeds from reasons taken to justify their actions. In short, on Kant's view subjectively valid motives must be viewed as though they were objective reasons if they are to influence choice. In this way, self-regarding conduct seems to require a discrepancy between an individual's actual maxim and avowed maxim, or between the actual value and the value claimed for the maxim. There are numerous forms that this could take, some disingenuous, others more straightforward. Where individuals recognize that self-love by itself cannot count as a principle with justifying force, they will hide or disguise their motives. The result will be to act under the guise of a principle that is acceptable, but which may have little bearing on, or will tend to obscure, their actual motive. In such cases, subjective motives are treated as objective reasons by disguising them. On the other hand, self-love is sometimes cited as a principle with justifying force—for example, out of an impoverished view of the self, or confusion about the nature of moral reasoning. Someone who believes that the will is moved exclusively by empirically given motives will view self-interest in some form as a justifying reason, simply because there are no alternatives. Here it is not a question of disguising one's motives, but of attributing a value or normative force to them that they do not have. In cases where individuals make a permissible exception for themselves from a principle that they otherwise accept, they need not be treating self-interest as a generally sufficient reason. But they may claim that special circumstances obtain, so that in this case it counts as a reason with something like moral (i.e., fully justifying) force.

When Kant refers to treating the subjective grounds of choice as objective reasons, there need be no single phenomenon that he has in mind. But the different tendencies that this description fits might share the feature of being sustained by some set of false or impoverished beliefs. These could range from beliefs about one's motives or the relevant features of one's situation, to beliefs about practical reason or the moral capacities of the self. For this reason it seems appropriate to say that the influence of self-love on the will is sustained by an ideology of sorts, which enables individuals to view their maxims as objectively acceptable reasons. In the passage just cited, Kant says that 'we find our pathologically determinable self . . . striving antecedently to make its claims primary and originally valid, just as if it constituted our entire self' (*KpV* 5: 74). Beliefs to the effect that our practical and motivational capacities are limited to empirical practical reason support the view that our sensible capacities are the only source of value in the self, or that all reasons are based on sensible needs and desires. In a similar way, disguising or misdescribing a maxim of self-love allows the individual to claim to be acting from a maxim that is a good reason. In all of these cases, some false or impoverished beliefs serve to hide the gap between the actual value of one's maxim and its asserted value, and prevent the individual from openly assessing his motives. This seems particularly noteworthy. The claims to value made by self-love can only be sustained in the absence of any comparison of its maxims with the moral law. Ideological beliefs support the influence of self-love in this way: they enable the individual to regard inclinations as sources of sufficient reasons by obstructing any comparison of their value with the value of the moral law.[31]

V. CONCLUSION

We can now add a few details to our account of respect. Respect for the law limits the influence of inclinations by exposing the claims of self-love and undermining its pretensions to being a source of sufficient reasons. Perhaps the main point to be made is that it operates by effecting a devaluation of the inclinations in the eyes of the agent. It shows that maxims of self-love do not have the value, or justifying force, that they are initially taken to have. Given what we have seen, we might distinguish two aspects to this process. Some analysis seems needed to expose any discrepancies between the actual value of the agent's maxim and the value that the agent takes it to have. Roughly, the overall process is initiated by bringing the actual maxim into the open, so that it can be seen for what it is. Second, the texts indicate that this leads up to a comparison of the value of the maxim with the value of the moral law that had previously been obstructed by the agent's beliefs and rationalizations. At one point Kant says that 'the moral law unavoidably humiliates every human being when he compares the sensible propensity of his nature with it' (*KpV* 5: 74). His view is that when maxims of self-love are placed side by side with moral maxims, we cannot help but acknowledge the superiority of the latter. The moral law always presents a higher form of value that diminishes the value of inclinations in comparison, so that they can no longer appear to be sources of sufficient reasons. When this occurs, maxims of self-love will be withdrawn, because the condition of their adoption is seen not to hold.

Kant says that the moral law becomes an object of respect when it limits self-love and strikes down self-conceit. We have seen that these are tendencies to exercise the power of choice that, in different ways, give priority to the inclinations. Kant thinks that these motivational tendencies are so deeply rooted in our nature that they are always present, and must be held in check whenever one acts from a moral motive. Thus the immediate recognition of the moral law is always the recognition of a form of value that entails a devaluation of the inclinations. As Kant says in the *Groundwork*, respect is 'the representation of a worth that infringes upon my self-love' (*G* 4: 401 n).

The model of choice outlined in the previous section should explain how interaction between sensible and rational motives is possible, as well as making clear the arena in which it takes place. Even though these kinds of motives may originate in different parts of the self, they affect choice within the same framework of reasons (in each case, by being regarded as sources of sufficient reasons). Here we should note that the 'sensible tendencies' which respect for the law checks are tendencies to view inclinations as providing certain kinds of reasons, and to value a certain part of the self. This fact has a bearing on the character of the feeling of respect. We can now see that this is the feeling that results when the agent recognizes that inclinations are not sources of justifying reasons, and represent only a subordinate form of value. We underestimate this experience if we understand it simply as the frustration that might result from electing to leave certain inclinations unsatisfied. More than anything, respect is thought to show that claims about the value of the inclinations that the agent is prepared to advance are unwarranted. In many instances what is at stake here will be one's conception of one's self-worth and ability to view one's actions as justified from the point of view of others. It is for this reason that Kant often associates respect for the law with a lowering of the agent's self-esteem. It may be most interesting to consider this point in relation to self-conceit. Respect for the law is thought to have an intimate connection with the negation of self-conceit, which Kant specifically describes as a form of humiliation. Self-conceit attempts to place a kind of absolute value on one's person, that sets one apart from and above others. Respect produces humiliation in striking down this tendency, because it denies an excessive esteem or personal importance that one seeks for oneself. It effects a devaluing not just of particular desires, but of a part of your person. It seems particularly appropriate that Kant should tie respect to the feeling that results from the frustration of this particular tendency. And as Kant suggests, it is the capacity to strike down self-conceit that makes the moral law an 'object of greatest respect' (*KpV* 5: 73).[32]

APPENDIX: SELF-LOVE AND SELF-CONCEIT.[33]

It is fairly clear that Kant understands self-conceit as a desire-based demand for personal worth or esteem, where the grounds of such worth are found in one's standing relative to others along some dimension. It is a conception of personal worth that is formed independently of moral consciousness in the sense that it is not based on one's moral standing as a person, one's virtue, and so on. Self-conceit manifests itself in an inflated conception of one's personal worth relative to others, of one's accomplishments, of one's degree of virtue, or in certain vices such as arrogance or the tendency to take pleasure in the faults of others. However, the basic distinction that Kant draws between self-love and self-conceit at *KpV* 5: 74 points to a dimension of self-conceit that remains puzzling and open to alternative interpretations. In Section III above I read into this passage the claim that self-conceit leads to a form of first person egoism and the desire that others serve one's interests; this interpretation now seems to me to overstate the distinction. Henry Allison reads Kant simply as saying that self-love is 'the tendency to find a reason to act in what promises satisfaction'. Since reasons of this kind can be limited by moral concerns, this tendency can be transformed into 'reasonable self-love'. By contrast, self-conceit makes the satisfaction of one's desires into 'a matter of principle or right' and inflates the tendency to regard desire satisfaction as a reason for action 'into an unconditional principle or "law" capable of overriding all other claims'. Since self-conceit, so understood, rejects any moral constraints on the demands of inclination, it is inherently opposed to the moral law.[34]

An interpretation of this distinction must make sense of Kant's claim that self-conceit goes beyond self-love and therefore cannot merely be limited by moral concerns, but must be 'struck down'. Self-conceit involves a valuing of oneself that is based on 'illusion'

(*KpV*5: 75). To cite the full passage again:

Now, however, we find our nature as sensible beings so constituted that the matter of the faculty of desire . . . first forces itself upon us, and we find our pathologically determinable self, even though it is quite unfit to give universal law through its maxims, nevertheless striving antecedently to make its claims primary and originally valid, just as if it constituted the entire self. This propensity to make oneself, on subjective determining grounds of choice, into the objective determining ground of the will in general can be called *self-love*; and if self-love makes itself lawgiving and the unconditional practical principle, it can be called *self-conceit* . . . [S]elf-conceit . . . prescribes the subjective conditions of [self-love] as laws. (*KpV*5: 74)

Self-love is a tendency to make *oneself* into an objective determining ground of the will (independently of moral concerns and for purely subjective reasons), and becomes self-conceit when it makes itself *lawgiving*. That is, Kant says that self-love becomes self-conceit when out of love for oneself one makes oneself, or the interests that comprise the material of self-love, into a source of laws. The distinction between self-love and self-conceit will depend both on the distinction that Kant intends between objective determining grounds of the will in general and laws and on the kind of normative force that he assigns to a law in this context. Objective determining grounds are presumably objectively valid reasons—considerations that anyone can recognize as good reasons in some sense. Absent conflicting reasons with deliberative priority, they are sufficient to justify action; but they can be overridden by reasons with higher priority. Laws, by contrast (as Allison points out), are sources of reasons that are unconditional and overriding. But offhand it seems that laws could be understood in different ways that would lead to slightly different interpretations of self-conceit. A law could provide overriding reasons simply for the agent—so that self-conceit would be the tendency to treat oneself or one's interests as sources of unconditional reasons *for oneself* that override all other claims on oneself (including, e.g., claims made by the interests of others or other kinds of moral claims). Or a law could provide overriding reasons for anyone, in which case self-conceit is a tendency to treat oneself and one's interests as an authoritative source of *reasons for anyone*. According to the second reading, self-conceit is a disposition to accord oneself a standing that is necessarily denied to others.

Both readings lead to a conception of self-conceit that is incompatible with respect for humanity as an end in itself. I favor the latter view of self-conceit as a tendency to value oneself that leads one to act as though one's interests were sources of laws in the second sense. While self-conceit need not manifest itself as a desire or expectation that others serve you, it does involve placing a superior value on oneself and acting as though others ought to defer, both to one's sense of self-worth and to one's interests.

The passage suggests that Kant regards self-love as a natural concern for oneself that emerges independently of moral consciousness. It is a (pre-moral) love for or attachment to oneself that is the basis of a concern for the satisfaction of one's desires and manifests itself as a disposition to take one's desires and needs as sources of objectively valid reasons for action. Out of love for yourself, you take the fact that an action would satisfy your desires, fulfill your needs, or in some way benefit you as an objectively justifying reason for action, or as the basis of some kind of 'claim' to action. That is, you treat a consideration that is merely subjectively valid for you as having some objective weight, for example, as a consideration that could justify your acting on that desire. The sense in which self-love here treats subjective considerations as *objective* or *justifying* reasons is quite weak. As described so far, your self-love and the subsequent disposition to treat your desires and interests as objective reasons for action does not preclude your recognizing that others have the same self-concern and that they likewise treat their subjective considerations as objective reasons. This recognition will not lead you to think that their subjective concerns are reasons that make claims on you, but only that each person treats his or her subjective concerns as reasons. Thus self-love, so understood, allows that each individual is moved to treat his or her own desires as objective justifying reasons for action—that I take my desires to provide sufficient reasons for me, while you take yours to provide sufficient reasons for you. Here they treat their desires as justifying reasons in the sense that they each take themselves to have standing to treat their subjective concerns as reasons and to have the liberty to act so as to satisfy their desires and needs. Since each agent treats his or her own subjective considerations as objective reasons and recognizes that others do the same, I cannot complain when your actions and plans interfere with mine. But neither do I have reason to yield to you, nor to pursue my interests less vigorously than you, when our plans conflict. The considerations that you count (and that I recognize) as reasons for you don't have that kind of normative weight for me.

Individuals moved by self-love, then, can recognize that each person has, as it were, the same standing to, out of love for oneself, treat one's subjective concerns as though they were objective reasons for action, though without regarding them as reasons that make claims on anyone else. If so, in what way does self-conceit make itself lawgiving and go beyond self-love? Kant regards self-conceit as a tendency to treat oneself and one's subjective interests as a source of reasons whose authority is unconditional in some sense. One way to understand this is as follows: self-conceit is a disposition to assign oneself a standing to treat oneself and one's subjective concerns as objective reasons that one does not and cannot acknowledge in others. That is, it is a disposition to accord oneself a special standing to make claims on one's own behalf in virtue of one's superior personal worth—again, out of love for oneself. In self-love you love yourself more than you love others. But in self-conceit you love yourself as better; you express your love for yourself by taking yourself to have greater personal worth. If your standing to make claims is based on your superior personal worth, then you take yourself to have standing to make claims that others do not possess, and you cannot acknowledge that others have standing to make even the limited claims of self-love just described. You act as though you are the only one who can put claims on the table. But if only you and your interests are the basis of claims—if only your demands count as 'claims'—then you are treating them as laws or overriding reasons to which you expect others to defer. (If you are the only one with the standing to make claims, the claims that you advance will, in your view, have no legitimate rivals; being the only claims on the table, you will regard them as sources of unconditional reasons to which others should defer.) This kind of self-conceit could be manifested in various forms—in certain kinds of disregard for others where one acts as though one has privileges that others lack, in the (tacit) expectation that others defer to one's interests or to one's conception of one's superior self-worth, in the vices of disrespect, and so on.

NOTES

1. Though Beck laments that this is 'the most repetitious and least well-organized chapter of the book', he stresses its importance, and I have drawn on his treatment. See *A Commentary on Kant's Critique of Practical Reason*, 209–36.

2. See *KpV* 5: 31, 42, 47, and 91 ff. For discussion of the Fact of Reason, see John Rawls *Lectures on the History of Moral Philosophy*, 'Kant, Lecture VII'. See also Beck's *Commentary*, ch. X.

3. Kant suggests that this discussion be called the 'aesthetic of pure practical reason' (*KpV* 5: 90).

4. Cf. *KpV* 5: 86–9.

5. Beck makes this point in his *Commentary*, 217. See also pp. 90 ff., and generally, pp. 215–25. It is not immediately obvious why Kant holds that 'no incentives at all can be attributed to the divine will' (*KpV* 5: 72), since incentives can include objectively valid reasons. The explanation as to why human conduct is characterized by incentives must be that, in us, reason and sensibility provide different grounds for choice. Since human beings do not by nature act from the moral law, those occasions when an individual does must be due to some fact about his or her state at that time. Since a divine will acts only from objectively valid motives, there is no variation in the character of its choices, and thus no sense to talking about the kind of motivation from which it acts. Thus, the idea of a 'subjective determining ground'—one that is effective due to its state at a particular time—is out of place in a description of its will.

6. *G* 4: 401 n. For a discussion of the role of respect in the *Groundwork*, see Nelson Potter's 'The Argument of Kant's *Groundwork*, Chapter 1', 45–7. For some older commentary on the notion of respect, see, for example, Bruno Bauch, *Immanuel Kant*, 317–19; and Hans Reiner, *Pflicht und Neigung*, 22–8.

7. I intend 'immediate recognition of the authority of the moral law' to be roughly equivalent to and an explication of Kant's phrase 'immediate determination of the will by the law'. Perhaps it would be clearer to say that one determines one's will by the moral law when one recognizes the overriding authority (or deliberative priority) of moral considerations and is motivated accordingly, that is, one adopts the relevant considerations into one's maxim of action. An agent who recognizes the authority of moral considerations regards them as sufficient and overriding reasons for action, and in so far as he or she responds rationally, will be motivated to act from them. (An agent who recognizes a consideration as a sufficient reason for action in some situation but is not motivated to act on it displays a form of irrationality.) One acts out of respect for the moral law when one adopts and acts on a maxim that gives moral considerations deliberative priority over competing reasons for action. In the original version of this paper, I referred to the recognition of the authority of morality as the 'intellectual' aspect of respect, but I now prefer to call it the 'practical' aspect of respect. It is a cognitive state, because it is the result of practical reasoning. It is the acceptance of a set of principles and value priorities that involves the judgment or belief that one has certain reasons for action, and it admits of rational support. But as a belief about what one has reason to do (in particular about what sorts of reasons should be given deliberative priority), it is a state with motivational implications. I am inclined to say that it is a motivational state, and one that is effective in action in so far as an agent responds rationally. The term 'practical' seems to me to better capture this idea of a cognitive attitude with motivational implications. I wish to distinguish the 'practical' aspect of respect, so understood, from the 'affective' aspect of respect, which is the feeling that results when one limits the influence of certain tendencies of inclination (specifically self-love and self-conceit, as explained in the next section). However, I should also stress that, as I read Kant, they are connected aspects of a single complex phenomenon.

8. Kant discusses 'honorific respect' for individuals (my terminology) at *KpV* 5: 76 ff. He explains it as respect for their moral qualities and accomplishments (a '*tribute* that we cannot refuse to pay to merit'), and thus as respect for the principles that they exemplify—'strictly speaking to the law that [their] example holds before us' (*KpV* 5: 78). For a discussion of 'broadly ethical respect' see, of course, *Groundwork* 4: 428–31, among other places. There is also a brief reference to ethical respect for humanity in this chapter of the second *Critique*; see *KpV* 5: 87.

9. The honorific attitude toward merit will also have an affective aspect, which Kant describes as the experience of feeling humility before the talents of another, or the example that he or she has set. This is a distinctive moral emotion, whose explanation will be the same as for the feeling of respect for the moral law.

10. Cf. *KpV* 5: 76.

11. Kant makes the same point in an equally obscure discussion of the 'predisposition to personality' in the *Religion*, 6: 27–8.

12. Kant may create an unnecessary difficulty for himself in these passages (cf. *KpV* 5: 75 ff., 79 ff.). He seems concerned to explain how the feeling of respect can be a legitimate moral incentive which moves us in some positive direction by winning out against competing motives (but without viewing it as an impulsion that would end up being heteronomous). In doing so he may have had the following schema in mind. The recognition of the moral law produces the feeling of respect; this feeling then neutralizes opposing non-moral motives, thereby allowing the original recognition of the moral law to become practical and take effect. The need for such a model might rest on the assumption that the affective obstacles posed by inclinations can only be controlled by a greater affective force—an assumption that one might find in Hume or Spinoza. If this was how Kant reasoned in certain passages, then it seems to me that he was not completely clear about the distinctive force of his own account of motivation, as I shall try to show. Kant does want to say that inclinations pose obstacles that must be controlled, and indeed that this involves controlling their affective force. But this would be accomplished through our recognition of the authority of the moral law, and not by an emotion that this recognition produces. This is a part of the force of claiming that pure reason is practical in us—in fact, it is what it is to have a will, on Kant's view. Thus, it adds an unnecessary step to say that a morally produced emotion is necessary to offset the influence of inclinations, as in the model just sketched.

13. I occasionally refer to the concept of an 'affective force' (or an 'affect'), by which I mean the force (or excitation) carried by a psychological state such as a desire, emotion, or drive, which provides a stimulus to action in a subject. It is appropriate to think of an affective force as moving or inclining the subject toward a course of action. I trust that an intuitive characterization of this notion will suffice.

14. Richard McCarty has objected to the interpretive claim that Kant thought that recognition of the authority of moral considerations is sufficient to motivate moral conduct, citing as evidence Kant's characterization of moral weakness or frailty in the *Religion*. There Kant says that the morally frail person 'incorporates the good (the law) into the maxim of [his] power of choice; but this good, which is an irresistible incentive objectively or ideally (*in thesi*), is subjectively (*in hypothesi*) the weaker (in comparison with inclination) whenever the maxim is to be followed' (*Rel* 6: 29). McCarty argues that the morally frail person recognizes the authority of morality

(regards the moral law 'as providing an all sufficient reason for action'), but lacks the motivation to act morally in the face of contrary inclinations; therefore Kant did not hold that recognition of the authority of morality suffices as a moral motive. On his reading, the strength of moral feeling produces moral motivation and determines whether it is effective. See McCarty, 'Kantian Moral Motivation and the Feeling of Respect', 426–9; cf. also McCarty, 'Motivation and Moral Choice in Kant's Theory of Rational Agency'. The phenomenon of moral weakness, in which an agent acts contrary to values that he accepts or professes to accept, or acts contrary to his judgment of what he has reason to do, deserves more discussion than I can give here. But it does not undermine the interpretive claim that Kant regarded the recognition of the authority of moral concerns as the proper moral incentive (and was right to have done so). The frail person does not recognize the authority of the moral law in the requisite sense of adopting a maxim that gives deliberative priority to moral considerations. I understand the passage from the *Religion* as follows: the frail person at some level accepts the priority of moral concerns (and in that sense 'incorporates the law' into his maxim), but gives insufficient weight to that commitment 'whenever the maxim is to be followed'. That is to say that he acts on a different maxim, one that subordinates morality to self-love; and that is why Kant classifies frailty as a degree of evil. The fact that frailty is a form of evil suggests that Kant would trace the motivational failure of the frail person to his failure to fully and consistently acknowledge the authority of moral concerns.

15. The term 'Incorporation Thesis' was introduced by Henry Allison in *Kant's Theory of Freedom*. In the original version of this essay, I referred to this claim as the 'principle of election', a term that I took from Rawls. I understand the 'incorporation of an incentive into a maxim' as the normative judgment that an incentive is a good or sufficient reason for action, thus as the endorsement of an incentive or consideration as a reason for acting. For further discussion, see Allison, *Kant's Theory of Freedom*, 39–41.

16. In the second *Critique*, Kant tends to treat all inclinations as self-regarding, in a way that suggests an egoistic conception of happiness. Cf. his 'Theorem II', which holds that all action from inclination falls under the principle of 'self-love' (*Selbstliebe*) (*KpV* 5: 22 ff.). But this seems inconsistent with his recognition that we can have sympathetic inclinations, directed at the welfare of others. I discuss these issues in Chapter 2, where I argue, among other things, that the 'principle of self-love' is simply the principle of acting from the strongest desire, and that action done from 'self-love' need not be egoistical.

17 Kant's distinction between *Eigenliebe* and *Eigendünkel* seems to derive from Rousseau's distinction between *amour de soi* and *amour propre*, of which he was certainly aware. However, space does not permit me to explore the precise relationship in any detail. In Rousseau see *Discourse on the Origin of Inequality*, in *The Discourses and Other Early Political Writings*, 151–2, 218 (n. XV) (*Discours sur l'Origine de l'Inégalité*, in *Oéuvres Complètes*, III, 154 and n. XV). For an excellent discussion of Rousseau's conception of *amour propre* as an inherently inegalitarian form of self-regard, see Joshua Cohen, 'The Natural Goodness of Humanity'.

18. Cf. *MdS* 6: 448–68.

19. This can be seen in specific examples of self-conceit, such as the vices of arrogance, defamation, and ridicule. All attempt to gain esteem for oneself by trying to improve one's standing relative to others—either by soliciting the honor of others and

demanding that they think less of themselves in comparison with oneself (arrogance), or by exposing the faults of others and making fun of them so that one will look better in comparison (defamation, ridicule) (*MdS* 6: 465–7). In general, self-conceit is connected with the failure to give others the respect that they are due. Thus, in the *Doctrine of Virtue*, Kant calls it a 'lack of modesty in one's claims to be respected by others', or what amounts to the same thing, the failure to limit one's self-esteem by the dignity of others (*MdS* 6: 462, 449). See also *KpV* 5: 76–7, where Kant writes that the example of the 'humble common man in whom I perceive uprightness of character in a higher degree than I am aware of in myself' strikes down my self-conceit because it undermines my high opinion of myself based on my superior social position. Here it is clear that Kant views self-conceit as a desire for personal worth or a tendency to value oneself based on comparative and non-moral qualities. Allen Wood stresses the fact that self-conceit is based on comparative (and therefore morally unsustainable) judgments of personal worth; see 'Self-Love, Self-Benevolence, and Self-Conceit', 147–56.

20. 'Man kann diesen Hang, sich selbst nach den subjektiven Bestimmungsgründen seiner Willkür zum objektiven Bestimmungsgrunde des Willens überhaupt zu machen, die Selbstliebe nennen, welche, wenn sie sich gesetzgebend und zum unbedingten praktischen Prinzip macht, Eigendünkel heißen kann . . . Eigendünkel die subjektiven Bedingungen der ersteren [Selbstliebe] als Gesetze vorschreibt . . .' (*KpV* 5: 74). Mary Gregor renders 'nach' into 'as having': 'This propensity to make oneself *as having* subjective grounds of choice into the objective determining ground of the will in general can be called self-love . . .' (emphasis added). Gregor's translation suggests that Kant understands self-love as a tendency to make oneself into an objective ground of volition simply in virtue of having subjective grounds of choice (presumably inclinations and desire-based interests)—implying that beings with such incentives have a tendency to treat themselves and their interests as objectively valid reasons for action. A somewhat more natural reading of the passage, it seems to me, is that self-love is the tendency to make oneself into an objective ground of the will on, or according to, subjective grounds of choice, that is, to treat oneself as an objective ground of the will for reasons that are merely subjectively valid. The differences between these two readings may not be significant.

   I am indebted to both Stephen Engstrom and Pierre Keller for discussions of this passage and how best to translate it.

21. The distinction between general egoism and first person egoism is discussed by Rawls in *A Theory of Justice*, 107–8. I have added an appendix to this essay in which I discuss this passage further and amend some points in this and the next paragraph.

22. Cf. *Rel* 6: 30, 36.

23. This is for a variety of reasons. One is Kant's view that, in general, we cannot know when an individual has acted with true moral worth, and that, in particular, one is a bad judge of one's own case on this matter. There is also the question as to whether one would lose title to the honorific form of respect by trying to claim it publicly. I am indebted in this paragraph to a comment by a referee for *Kant-Studien* which led me to clarify my initial analysis.

24. Cf. *G* 4: 440.

25. This is to suggest that if self-conceit were made universal, reciprocal, and focused on rational nature, it would develop into true ethical respect.

26. Some readers may reject this interpretation on the grounds that Kant often discusses motivation in terms that suggest the metaphor of mechanical force. For example, Kant says that through respect 'the relative weightiness of the law . . . is produced in the judgment of reason through the removal of the counterweight' (*KpV* 5: 76). For other instances of the image of opposing physical forces, see, for example, *KpV* 5: 78, 88, and *MdS* 6: 216, 380.

    However such metaphors are consistently embedded in discussions in which the dominant theme is a struggle for authority, sovereignty, superiority, and so on, in which it is claims or pretensions that are being opposed to each other. This holds even for the remark just quoted, in that the 'counterweight' is removed 'in the judgment of reason' through a 'representation of the superiority [*Vorzug*] of its objective law over the impulses [*Antriebe*] of sensibility' (*KpV* 5: 75). I believe that a close reading of this chapter of the second *Critique* shows that legal and political metaphors dominate.

27. This must be understood in light of the qualifications introduced in the previous paragraph. The 'claim to justification' need only be something that the agent is prepared to advance, and need not be universal in scope.

28. *G* 4: 424. Cf. also *G* 4: 405.

29. Questions of interpretation aside for a moment, while many people find this view plausible, others find it extremely implausible. However it is harder to find clear exceptions to this model than those not initially inclined to accept it might realize. While it is not my aim to fully endorse this conception of choice here, I will indicate briefly how it might handle difficult cases. One such case is weakness of the will, of which one might distinguish two versions. In the first, weakness is accompanied by rationalization. One acts against one's considered judgment, but constructs a rationalization that allows one to view the action as consistent with one's principles and ongoing ends, and thus as permissible under the circumstances. For example, one might be drawn toward some action whose immediate appeal is a reason for choosing it, but judge that it is best to refrain. One then constructs a rationalization—for example, that there is no harm in doing it 'just this once' or that one will refrain on the next occasion. Though the rationalization would not stand up on reflection, it permits one to view the action as supported by sufficient reasons under the circumstances and is the maxim on which one acts. In the second kind of weakness an agent performs an action that, at the time, he judges he has no reason to do and does not in any sense endorse. Perhaps the agent thinks that the action is without value and condemns himself for doing it (in which case he may wonder why he is doing it). Here it is not clear that the agent acts on a maxim, since there is no rationale under which the agent views the action as choiceworthy at the time. In such cases, what the agent does is less than an action, because there is a failure to exercise the capacities for rational control and self-governance that are standardly employed in rational action. (The agent may still be responsible for the action, since one can be held responsible for failing to exercise capacities that one possesses.) But the thesis that I am ascribing to Kant is that (rational) action carries an implicit claim to justification and is motivated by reasons that provide justification in some form. Cases in which what an agent does is less than an action are not counter-examples to this thesis. A second difficult kind of case includes those of harm to another, in which an action seems clearly wrong from the public point of view, and unacceptable to the recipient. Here one would look for a rationalization to attribute to the agent that might make the action seem acceptable to

some, though not all others—perhaps to a special community of which the agent, but not the recipient, is a part. As an example, the agent might view the action as forced on him by his circumstances, and claim that the recipient might be forced to the same action in similar circumstances. Here it should be noted that it is consistent with the view being proposed that often the agent can expect at best a limited understanding with others through his rationalization of the action. After understanding the agent's rationale, the recipient might still resist the action. ('You've got your reasons, but I have mine too.') Or observers who understand the agent's rationale need not approve of, or see the action as something they would have done. But this is to be expected when the principle used to justify an action is one of self-interest.

30. A similar interpretation is developed by Alexander Broadie and Elizabeth Pybus in 'Kant and Weakness of the Will', where they discuss the role that self-deception might play in actions contrary to duty. For a general discussion of this idea see T. M. Scanlon, 'Contractualism and Utilitarianism', 115–19, esp. 117.

31. I have modified some of the language in this section in response to Henry Allison's comments in *Kant's Theory of Freedom*, 268. Legitimate questions can be raised about the conception of action that I read into Kant in this section, according to which all action carries an implicit claim to justification and proceeds from reasons that resemble moral reasons in form in that they are taken to provide justification for the action in question. However, I do want to attribute to Kant the view that in adopting a maxim, one regards the relevant incentive as a reason or the basis of a principle that provides a justification of an action that is intersubjective. I believe that strong support for this interpretation is found in the long paragraph at *KpV* 5: 74 and surrounding discussion. The 'pathologically determinable self' strives to make the 'claims' of self-regard 'primary and originally valid, just as if it were the entire self', and Kant makes it clear that self-love and self-conceit are tendencies to treat certain kinds of subjective concerns as objective reasons—as 'objective determining grounds of the will in general' or as 'laws'. The language of 'laws', 'claims', and 'validity' suggest an operative inter-subjective arena. The implication is that subjective concerns are treated as though they have some kind of normative force from the standpoint of others and not just for the agent, as though they have normative force for anyone. Kant's remark that the sensible self acts 'as if it were the entire self' suggests a way to understand how one can regard the reasons and claims of self-love as having intersubjective normative force. If the 'pathologically determinable self' were all there is to the self, the concerns advanced by self-love and self-conceit would be the only kinds of reasons. In that case they would be sufficient reasons by default, and the basis of justifications that would have force for other agents. Granted, the resulting conception of justification would be defective because it would not lead to truly shared evaluations of action. My reasons would not fully justify my actions *to you* or lead *you* to accept them *as good*. But if they were the only kinds of considerations that count as reasons, you would still have to grant that they were sufficient reasons for my action.

32. I would like to thank Christine Korsgaard for discussion and many helpful comments during the writing of this essay. I am also indebted to the referee for *Kant-Studien*, whose comments led to several changes in the essay when originally published. Versions of this essay were presented to the departments of philosophy at the University of Chicago (October 1984) and at the University of Massachusetts at Amherst (October 1986). I also had the opportunity to discuss the paper with the

members of the Center for Philosophy and Public Policy at the University of Maryland, and with the department of philosophy at Mount Holyoke College. More recently I benefited from discussions of the distinction between self-love and self-conceit with Amy MacArthur.

33. Added 2005.
34. *Kant's Theory of Freedom*, 124, 267–8.

2

Hedonism, Heteronomy, and Kant's Principle of Happiness

It is widely assumed that Kant adopted a hedonistic view of non-moral motives and choice.[1] According to this interpretation, Kant takes inclinations to be desires for pleasure, or desires for objects in virtue of the pleasure that they will afford, and therefore holds that actions done from inclination are motivated by an interest in the pleasure that the agent believes will result. Many commentators find support for this interpretation in various remarks that Kant makes about inclinations. But in addition, there are some well-known passages in the *Critique of Practical Reason* that on the surface seem almost certainly to indicate a hedonistic view. Here Kant opposes moral conduct to conduct motivated by what he terms 'the principle of self-love or one's own happiness' (*KpV* 5: 22). Moreover, he seems to say that what unifies the actions that he brings under the principle of happiness is that they are aimed at pleasurable feeling in the agent, and can be ranked by the amounts of pleasure that they offer. I shall refer to this view as the adoption of a 'hedonistic psychology of non-moral choice', or simply as a hedonistic psychology.

This essay addresses the issue of whether Kant was a psychological hedonist about natural desires and the actions for which they are the motives. My intention is to call that interpretation into question. I will argue that Kant did not adopt a simple hedonistic psychology of non-moral choice, and that nothing in his moral theory, in particular the central distinction between autonomy and heteronomy, depends on such a psychology. The heart of my argument is an alternate reading of those passages in the second *Critique* often taken to provide decisive support for the hedonistic interpretation. This discussion leads to an account of Kant's 'principle of happiness' which shows that what this principle expresses is both different and more complex than one might initially suppose. But more is at issue than deciding whether Kant held what most people will regard as a crude and mistaken psychology of motivation. Seeing why he did not provides insight into a cluster of issues that are central to our understanding of his moral theory; here I include his general theory of motivation, the meaning of the principle of happiness and, in consequence, the proper understanding of the distinction between morality and happiness, and the difference between autonomy and heteronomy. Furthermore, a hedonistic psychology is a reductive view since it asserts that a variety of apparently different actions and motives are really alike in some fundamental respect. Asking whether such a view figures in Kant's theory offers an opportunity to explore the issue of whether a moral view that attempts to provide insight through very general distinctions and high-level organizing principles must be reductive.

Section I of this essay introduces some of the issues that a hedonistic psychology would raise for Kant's moral psychology and moral theory. Sections II to IV take up the relevant texts and show why they do not indicate a crude hedonistic psychology. Among other things, I argue that the principle of happiness does not express a hedonistic theory of motivation, but a principle of choice in which actions are evaluated in terms of expected satisfaction or the strength of the desires they will satisfy. Finally, Section V considers how the proposed interpretations of Kant's views bear on the broader issues raised in the introduction.

I. INTRODUCTION

The presence of a hedonistic view of non-moral conduct has been viewed as a weakness in Kant's empirical psychology, and many writers have argued that it undermines certain elements of his moral theory. They have claimed that Kant adopts a crude hedonistic psychology that threatens the coherence of his picture of motivation and choice, and vitiates his distinction between autonomy and heteronomy, as well as its normative significance. Thus T. H. Green writes:

Kant ... [seems to hold] that human motives are reducible either to desire for pleasure on the one side (in which case the will is 'heteronomous') or desire for fulfillment of the moral law on the other (in which case alone, according to him, it is 'autonomous') . . . Kant's error lies in supposing that there is no alternative between the determination of desire by the anticipation of pleasure and its determination by the conception of a moral law.[2]

In distinguishing autonomous from heteronomous choice, Kant intends a contrast between different ways in which people can be moved to act that has evaluative implications. In heteronomous conduct, actions in some sense follow from the laws of our psychology, while in autonomous conduct, we act from laws that we give to ourselves.[3] Autonomy represents an ideal of conduct in which actions are fully self-determined, and express our rational nature. The insight that only moral conduct expresses our autonomy is to provide a deeper understanding of the nature of morality, strengthening its motivational base by revealing the ideal of the person that it realizes. Presumably the distinction is intended to be exhaustive, so that all actions must fall under one of these headings. Green's point is that if it rests on a hedonistic view of non-moral conduct, it would oppose acting from laws that one gives for oneself to action explainable in terms of the desire for pleasure. But it is certainly wrong to think that all actions must fall into one of these categories, or to think that all non-moral motivation is hedonistic.

If this is all that this distinction boils down to, it is far from being exhaustive, and seems to leave out an important range of actions and motives. Furthermore, it is unclear why this distinction (acting from the moral law versus acting from the desire for pleasure) should provide an important criterion for valuing actions.

Several contemporary writers echo the concerns raised by Green, and the issues go beyond the correctness of Kant's psychology.[4] The source of the dissatisfaction shared by Kant's critics is that a hedonistic psychology appears symptomatic of a deeper reductivism. Philosophical theories tend to seek insight by showing that what appear on the surface to be a heterogeneous set of phenomena are the same in some fundamental respect, and thus to introduce general distinctions and classifications that attempt to assimilate this diversity to a single model. One trend in contemporary moral philosophy stresses the importance of fine-grained distinctions, and has criticized this approach for leading to distortions in our understanding of human conduct and moral experience. It is thought that the general distinctions to which it leads are reductive in that they are unable to capture, and even obscure, the significance of certain kinds of details. A moral view structured around a set of general distinctions will be forced to oversimplify the phenomena to fit into its theoretically motivated categories, and in collecting many different actions, motives, and attitudes under one heading, will lack the resources for making needed evaluative discriminations among them.

One way to bring out the force of this critique against Kant is to consider the wide variety of personal ends that we would normally see as neither moral in intent nor hedonistically motivated. As construed by Green and others, Kant's scheme appears to leave no room for ends of personal importance to the agent, whose originating motive is not the sense of duty: activities and goals of personal interest, career interests, friendships and personal relationships, devotion to family, and so on.[5] If we do try to fit such ends into this classification, we must take them to be motivated by the desire for pleasure. Here Kant would seem to face two unattractive alternatives. Either his scheme ignores many ordinary activities that give value and substance to life, in which case it seems radically incomplete. Or it includes them by forcing them into a hedonistic mold that is inappropriate. The notion of heteronomy would then involve a kind of leveling that fails to acknowledge differences in the value and importance of the many different kinds of activities grouped together. In either case, its plausibility as an evaluative classification would be undermined. Why should we place a special value on autonomous conduct when so many actions of importance to an individual's life fall under the category of heteronomy?

In light of these considerations, there is cause to ask whether a hedonistic psychology is what enables Kant to mark out the distinction between autonomous and heteronomous conduct as he does and supports its evaluative implications. One might be led to this question by the following line of thought. In distinguishing autonomy from heteronomy, Kant attempts to show that an enlightening division can be made in what we would ordinarily regard as a heterogeneous set of phenomena. To do this he must provide an organizing principle that divides actions and motives into two categories, and assimilates those in each to a single model. Kant's analysis will succeed only if it can isolate a shared feature that gets us to see many different actions as alike in salient respects. In particular, the similarities to which it draws attention must seem more significant than various differences to which we would otherwise attend. Thus, pre-theoretically we might distinguish actions in terms of their aims, or their motivating desires. We regard actions done for personal gain or reputation differently from those aimed at the good of another, and actions motivated by sympathy differently from those motivated by concern with one's own needs. But Kant's analysis is supposed to lead us to see these differences, while not unimportant, as having less overall weight than a feature shared by all—namely, that they are motivated by desires that arise contingently in individuals via various psychological mechanisms. Furthermore, the analysis must draw on some intuitive notions of self-determination (or free and rationally governed conduct), and show that only moral conduct meets the conditions that these notions imply when fully articulated. Actions based on other kinds of motives do not meet these conditions, and the features which get us to see these actions as being of a kind are what get us to see this. With these tasks accomplished, the distinction between autonomous and heteronomous conduct would not only seem a plausible way of dividing up human conduct; if we value self-determination (or rationality or freedom), we would also see why we should value the actions in one category more highly than those in the other.

When we reflect on the diversity of the actions grouped together as non-moral, or heteronomous, we must wonder whether they could convincingly form a unified category. Any such classification is bound to rest on considerations that are largely formal and thus artificial. However, if much human conduct can be explained hedonistically, that would provide a rationale for bringing such actions under a single category. That they are all moved by a desire for pleasure would be a feature which gets us to see them as being fundamentally alike; at the same time, it would give content to the notion of heteronomy by explaining why they are not fully self-determined. Moral conduct would then provide the avenue by which we avoid being determined by the desire for pleasure, and assume control over our actions. In this way a hedonistic psychology might lend support to the distinction between autonomy and heteronomy, by providing a way of looking at the non-moral which makes it seem a natural and more unified category, and explains why only moral conduct is autonomous.

The next three sections take up the straightforward interpretive issue of whether Kant adopted a hedonistic psychology and of whether any such view plays a role in his theory. It is important to see why the views that Kant holds do not amount to a crude hedonistic psychology, and clarity about what they represent instead will indicate why they are not reductive in the way that many critics have assumed. There are two things that lead people to interpret Kant as a psychological hedonist about non-moral conduct (discussed in Sections II and III to IV respectively).

First, the way in which Kant connects inclinations with feelings of pleasure has led many readers to assume that Kant thought that inclinations are always directed at pleasure, or have pleasure as their object. Second, his classification of all non-moral conduct under the principle of happiness, or self-love, seems to rest on the belief that all such actions are alike in being done for the sake of pleasure or satisfaction—that is, that they are motivated by the desire for pleasure and have pleasure as their aim. In each case I will show why the hedonistic interpretation is mistaken and what it overlooks, with one qualification that is added at the end of Section IV.

II. INCLINATIONS AND FEELINGS OF PLEASURE

Psychological hedonism is a thesis about the objects of desires which leads to a theory of motivation. It holds that all desires are desires for pleasure in the agent, or for the means thereto, where pleasure is construed as a definite feeling or experience. Alternatively it is the thesis that the only object desired for its own sake is pleasure. Thus it makes the desire for pleasure the primary motive to human action, to which all other motives can be reduced. The standard rebuttal is that psychological hedonism confuses the object of a desire with the satisfaction that will result when that object is attained. The fact that you gain satisfaction from acting on a desire does not mean that the feeling of satisfaction was your aim, or that you were acting for the sake of that satisfaction. Rather, the satisfaction occurs because you already had that desire. The desire may have a cause that is independent of the satisfaction that results in its fulfillment, and may be directed at an end outside of the self.[6]

Kant did think that there is a connection between inclinations and feelings of pleasure and displeasure, and he does think that we can distinguish a form of motivation by the role of such feelings in its operation. But this does not amount to psychological hedonism as just defined. In this section, I will argue that when Kant discusses the relation of inclinations to feelings of pleasure, he is not adopting a view about the objects of inclinations, but about their origin. He thought that feelings of pleasure play a role in the processes by which inclinations are generated. But that is not what is generally meant by psychological hedonism.

In the introduction to the *Metaphysics of Morals*, Kant claims that there are two ways in which a motive can be related to feelings of pleasure or satisfaction, and that this relationship enables us to distinguish two models of motivation and choice. Kant holds that pleasure is always connected with desire (motivation), but he says that such 'practical pleasure' may be either 'the cause or the effect of the desire [*Begehren*]' (*MdS* 6: 212). What Kant has in mind is this. Sometimes a feeling of pleasure will precede a desire and will figure in the process by which it is caused. The experience of something as pleasurable may create a desire to experience it again, or the judgment that an object would give satisfaction might give rise to a desire for it in the present. Desires of this sort arise in a subject according to psychological laws, as the result of feelings and experiences with external causes. When they become 'habitual', they are termed inclinations.[7] Kant's views about the connection between inclinations and feelings of pleasure are stated in the following passage: 'As for practical pleasure, that determination of the faculty of desire [*die Bestimmung des Begehrungsvermögens*] which is caused and therefore necessarily *preceded* by this pleasure is called *desire* [*Begierde*] in the narrow sense; habitual desire is called inclination [*Neigung*]' (*MdS* 6: 212).[8]

The important claim here is that feelings of pleasure which an individual has experienced play some causal role in the processes by which natural desires arise. The feature that Kant singles out is that inclinations are caused by some previously experienced satisfactions. But none of this implies that pleasure is the object of such desires.[9] Further, actions motivated by inclinations fall under heteronomy because their underlying motives are produced by causal processes that do not involve the will. The fact that feelings of pleasure play a role in these processes is not essential.

This relationship is contrasted with cases in which the pleasure taken in an action follows from the prior determination of the will on rational grounds. Here the judgment that an action is morally good, or that there are objectively good reasons for performing the action, motivates the subject to act. Given such motivation, a feeling of satisfaction will then be experienced upon the successful execution of the action.[10] Both the motivation to act and the satisfaction that may result presuppose a prior judgment of objective goodness, which the agent recognizes as providing a sufficient reason for acting. The resulting pleasure or satisfaction is thus the effect of the desire or motivational state [*Begehren*], and follows from the judgment that an action is objectively good.

Thus the view about inclinations that Kant adopts is that feelings of pleasure and displeasure figure in their causal history.[11] This is a thesis about the origin of inclinations, rather than their objects, and is fairly open-ended in that it does not commit Kant to thinking that the feelings of pleasure, or their causal role, fit into a uniform pattern. To illustrate how the object of a desire need not be identified with the experiences of satisfaction that figure in its formation, it may help to introduce some examples. Consider an attachment to baseball. Perhaps your interest is initially sparked when you find playing or watching the sport exciting, or engaging, and these enjoyable experiences motivate you to continue playing or watching, and so on. (That is, these experiences attach you to certain specific activities.) Over time you form an attachment to the game. You come to appreciate the subtleties of a game; you become committed to a team, take an interest in the development of its players, share in their successes and failures; and may develop a sense of community with others who care about the sport. In short, you become a fan. Here feelings of satisfaction experienced in a variety of contexts are responsible for the growth of your attachment, but the objects of your attachment are different aspects of the game of baseball, and not these experiences of satisfaction.

The formation of a friendship may follow a similar pattern. You begin to like someone because you enjoy the person's company or conversation, and these experiences create a desire for further association. Eventually a friendship forms, which by itself motivates certain attitudes and actions on your part. You care about the friend's well-being and interests and act on their behalf, seek opportunities to spend time with the friend, and now enjoy his or her company because you are friends. At this point you are attached to the person, and the existence of this attachment is what explains the satisfaction you derive from continued association and action on the friend's behalf. (Indeed what you initially found engaging might no longer be the basis of the friendship; certainly you are not associating with the friend simply to repeat those experiences.)

These examples suggest plausible patterns by which desires are formed, and Kant's view that feelings of pleasure and displeasure figure in the causal history of inclinations is flexible enough to accommodate them. In this regard, there are two general points worth making in order to bring out how much Kant's model allows. First, the feelings of pleasure and displeasure that go into the formation of a desire could themselves have a complex history, and the causal chain between these feelings and the resulting desires need not be simple or direct. What an individual finds satisfying can be shaped by a range of experiences, and can depend on the acquisition of various tastes and values. Accordingly, inclinations and desires can arise through the interaction of several experiences, emotions, and other desires, all of which could require complex cognitive activity as well as involvement in a social context.[12] Second, it is not necessary that the feelings of pleasure that give rise to a desire be identical with the satisfaction that results when its object is attained. In simpler cases the experience of a certain pleasure may create a desire to repeat that same pleasure, and such desires would be hedonistic. But more often the satisfactions that result from successfully acting on a given desire are a function of the fact that the individual has that desire. They may largely be shaped by the character of the desire and the experiences that give rise to it, or by the activities in which the individual is led to engage. It seems plausible to hold that a complex of experiences and feelings gives rise to a desire, but that at a certain point, the desire takes on a life of its own, depending on how it fits in with an individual's other desires and ends, or temperament. In such cases there is no simple relationship between the feelings of pleasure that figured in the causal history of the desire and the satisfaction that is eventually experienced. My only point here is that none of this common-sense psychology is made unavailable to Kant by any of the views about inclinations examined so far.[13]

The examples of inclinations that Kant cites throughout his writings also indicate that he did not intend to view them either hedonistically or exclusively egoistically. While some inclinations appear to have pleasure as their object, most are directed at ends outside of the self.[14] Kant recognizes a category of inclinations that develop from a natural 'aptitude for culture', whose objects include pursuits in the arts and sciences or the increase of one's knowledge, as well as social values or goods.[15] Many of the latter are indeed self-regarding. Early in the *Groundwork*, for example, in addition to referring to inclinations for power, wealth, and health, Kant mentions the 'inclination to honor' (*G* 4: 398).

However, Kant clearly did not believe that all inclinations are self-regarding, since he recognizes the existence of benevolent inclinations, as we see (among other places) by the example of natural sympathy in *Groundwork*, I, and his discussions of sympathy elsewhere. He does not think that such inclinations constitute a genuine moral disposition, but he acknowledges that they are an aid to its development and there is no doubt that he views them as a normal part of our psychology.[16] In closing this section, it is worth stressing that Kant understands the 'friend of humanity', or person of sympathetic temperament, to be moved by a direct inclination for the welfare of others (*G* 4: 398). The fact that Kant distinguishes the 'prudent merchant' from the friend of humanity, and his way of doing so, have an important bearing on the issue. Kant assumes that the merchant has no 'immediate inclination towards his customers' and that he does not charge fair prices 'out of love [for them]'; rather he aims to serve them honestly because it is good for his business, that is, from motives of self-interest. By contrast, the friend of humanity does have an immediate inclination toward the welfare of others, which leads him to care about and act on their behalf with no further aim in view ('without any other motive of vanity or self-interest'). The object of his concern and the motive of his actions is their happiness. When Kant says that such people 'find an inner satisfaction in spreading joy around them and can take delight in the satisfaction of others so far as it is their own work', we must understand this as outlined above. The satisfaction which such a person takes in making others happy is to be explained by, or is an indication of, the presence of the sympathetic desire, not vice versa. (That's why this agent loses the motivation to help when this desire is 'extinguished'.)[17,18]

III. THE PRINCIPLE OF SELF-LOVE, OR ONE'S OWN HAPPINESS

Kant's remarks about inclinations do not indicate a simple hedonistic psychology. However, some well-known passages in the second *Critique* appear to undermine this interpretation, and have led many commentators to the view that Kant is a hedonist about all non-moral motives. In this section I turn to these passages, and will offer an alternate interpretation of what goes on there.

The passages in question are the first and second 'Theorems' of the first chapter of the second *Critique* and the accompanying 'Remarks', in which Kant tries to distinguish 'material practical principles' from 'practical laws' ('merely formal laws of the will'). This is a distinction between practical principles that give reasons for action in different ways, that Kant thinks captures the distinction between non-moral and moral principles of choice. A material practical principle is defined, roughly, as one that determines the will, or gives a reason for action, through a desire that arises according to natural psychological laws: its normative force presupposes already existing desires. Since one's desires depend on contingent facts about one's psychology and past experience that differ from one person to another, principles of this sort cannot serve as practical laws. A practical law must provide reasons that are necessary and universally valid; they hold in virtue of interests that are constitutive of rationality, that all rational beings can be assumed to share. The larger aims of this chapter are to show that material practical principles form a recognizable class of reasons by which we can be motivated; that all actions proceed from one or the other kind of reason or principle; that the normative force of reasons provided by practical laws does not depend on given desires and inclinations, but comes instead from the fact that they have the form of lawgiving; and that it is only in acting from reasons of this sort that one acts autonomously.

Kant's 'Theorem II' reads:

All material practical principles as such are, without exception, of one and the same kind and come under the general principle of self-love, or one's own happiness. (*KpV* 5: 22)

It depends on Kant's claim that when you act from such a principle (a non-moral motive), the 'determining ground of choice' is 'pleasure [*Lust*] in the reality of an object' or the 'feeling of agreeableness [*Annehmlichkeit*] that the subject expects from the reality of an object' (*KpV* 5: 21, 22). The argument for the 'Theorem' defines happiness as 'a rational being's consciousness of the agreeableness of life uninterruptedly accompanying his whole existence'. To make expected satisfaction the 'supreme determining ground of choice' is to act from the 'principle of self-love, or one's own happiness' (I will abbreviate this as the 'principle of happiness'.) Since material practical principles place the determining ground of choice in the satisfaction expected from an object, they and the actions in which they result all exemplify this more general principle of choice. Kant concludes that they 'are wholly of the same kind [*gänzlich von einerlei Art*] in so far as they belong without exception to the principle of self-love or one's own happiness' (*KpV* 5: 22). Here, and in related passages, Kant seems to be saying that non-moral actions are alike in being hedonistically motivated, and this seems to be his rationale for including them all under the principle of happiness. Presumably this would also figure in our understanding of why they fall under heteronomy.

This impression is reinforced by the ensuing discussion of the 'lower faculty of desire' ('Remark I', *KpV* 5: 23). Kant claims that no interesting distinctions can be drawn among choices made on the basis of expected satisfactions by looking at the origins of the feelings of satisfaction, or at the kind of object from which satisfaction is expected. However different the objects of the desire may be, the only relevant concern in such choices is what will give most satisfaction. Moreover, the feeling of pleasure by which the subject measures the value of an object, and compares alternatives, is 'of one and the same kind'. He writes:

> . . . it affects one and the same vital force that is manifested in the faculty of desire, and in this respect can differ only in degree from any other determining ground. Otherwise how could one make a comparison in *magnitude* between two determining grounds quite different as to the kind of representation, so as to prefer the one that most affects the faculty of desire? (*KpV* 5: 23 f.)

Here the view that a single feeling of pleasure provides the ground of choice in all such instances is cited as a further rationale for classifying such choices together.

In bringing all material practical principles under the 'principle of happiness', Kant is attempting to articulate a shared structural feature that will lead us to see all non-moral motivation and choice as the same in an important respect. They will then be seen to embody one form of motivation, or model of choice, that can be contrasted with another (i.e., moral choice which realizes autonomy). As most people read this passage, the structural feature elicited is that such actions are done for the sake of pleasure or satisfaction. But this misses Kant's point, and does not capture what is at issue in the principle of happiness. The 'principle of happiness' is a principle of choice that leads to a specific model of deliberating about actions and ends. It should be understood as the rather unproblematic notion of acting from one's strongest desires on balance (doing what one desires most strongly), or acting so as to maximize individual satisfaction. This, rather than being hedonistically motivated, is the basis of the classification that occurs in Kant's 'Theorem II'. The proper interpretation turns on how one understands the key phrase, 'the determining ground of choice'. The best reading of this phrase indicates that it does not imply the adoption of a hedonistic psychology, and that nothing Kant wants to establish depends on his so doing. But before arguing for these conclusions, a few observations about the text are in order.

Beginning at 'Theorem I', Kant's aim is to establish the idea of a material practical principle, and to show that such principles do not yield practical laws. Initially the only psychological conception that he appears to draw on is the 'causal history thesis'—the view that feelings of pleasure and pain play a role in the generation of inclinations.[19] The desires that result in this way, and the reasons which they provide, will depend on an individual's 'subjective condition of receptivity to a pleasure or displeasure' (*KpV* 5: 21). Some pleasurable experience is required to give rise to the desire, and anticipated feelings of pleasure or satisfaction may also be needed to sustain it, or to confirm that it continues to provide a reason to act. This establishes a model of motivation in which reasons depend on past experiences (of satisfaction and dissatisfaction), and the desires they have created. From this it follows that material practical principles are not candidates for practical laws. The reasons that they give depend on one's susceptibility to pleasure and pain (what one desires or finds satisfying), which differs from one individual to another, and thus lack the necessity and universality required for a practical law.

But in addition, Kant says that feelings of pleasure or expected satisfaction are the 'determining ground of choice' in such cases. Such remarks give the impression that he believes that pleasure provides the motive to the actions in question.[20] This certainly creates an ambiguity as to whether the text relies on the causal history thesis, or on the thesis of psychological hedonism. But clearly the causal history thesis is all that Kant needs to carry out his immediate aims. It offers an account of the origin of desires that helps to distinguish a specific form of motivation; and it shows how material practical principles lack the grounding in a conception of rational agency that is needed for a principle to serve as a law. A hedonistic theory of motivation would serve this purpose, but it is not needed to establish a contrast between a form of motivation in which prior feelings of satisfaction and the 'subjective susceptibility' of agents play an essential role and one in which they do not. Thus, even if there are elements in the text that suggest a hedonistic account of non-moral motivation, that could not be the point of his 'Theorem II'. And as I shall now argue, there are reasons to prefer the non-hedonistic interpretation.

What does Kant mean when he says that maxims that place the determining ground of choice in expected satisfaction fall under the principle of happiness? How should we understand the 'determining ground of choice'?

In Kant's conception of action as guided by reasons, the determining ground of choice is not the object of an action, or the end at which it is directed; rather, it is the principle from which the agent acts. Kant thought that all actions proceed from maxims, and (following the Incorporation Thesis) that no incentive can determine the will except by being incorporated into a maxim that the agent freely adopts (cf. *Rel* 5: 24). Among other things, this involves the view that choice is guided by considerations that the agent takes to provide justifying reasons. These are expressed in the maxim, which is best understood as a principle that states the reason for one's action in a form that can be cited and explained to others. What motivates the agent is the normative force of the reasons expressed in the maxim.[21] With this in mind, the 'ground of choice' must be a maxim of some kind, or a reason that can be stated in the form of a principle. Thus it is not the object of one's action (that for the sake of which one acts), but the principle from which one acts, or the reason that motivates one's choice. Accordingly, where Kant says that the ground of choice is pleasure or expected satisfaction, he does not imply that such actions are done for the sake of the pleasure they will bring. His point instead is that one takes the fact that an action will produce satisfaction as a reason that supports its performance; one is motivated by the judgment that it will produce satisfaction and by one's taking that to be a good reason for acting. This means that expected satisfaction becomes the feature that is relevant in assessing the value of an action, and that one chooses by judging what one will find most satisfying on balance—or what seems equivalent, what one desires most strongly. In this sense, one acts so as to increase individual satisfaction, or does what one desires most strongly on balance; this is the force of the principle of happiness, simply put.

This will be one's fundamental principle of action in such cases, which describes what one is doing at the most general level, and what one takes to provide reasons for action. The significance of the principle of happiness is that it is a distinctive principle of choice, by which one decides how to act.

This point can be developed as follows. We have seen that material practical principles take reasons for acting from desires that arise according to psychological mechanisms in which pleasure and pain play a role. The decision to act on such a maxim follows from the judgment that doing so will satisfy various existing desires, or desires that one foresees one will have in the future. The stronger are the desires that it fulfills, or the more it advances one's aims—in short, the greater the satisfaction one can expect—the stronger are the reasons provided by the maxim. Here expected satisfaction, or the strength of one's desire for the outcome, becomes the standard or criterion by which one evaluates the action or its end, and decides whether to pursue it. This is most evident when one faces a deliberative problem—for example, choosing between conflicting desires, or courses of actions that exclude each other. The natural way to rank desired alternatives is to compare the satisfaction expected from each, or the strengths of competing desires. Kant gives a series of examples that illustrate this point when he notes that an individual can return an instructive book unread in order not to miss the hunt, leave in the middle of a fine speech in order not to miss a meal, or 'even repulse a poor man whom at other times it is a joy for him to benefit, because he now has only enough money in his pocket to pay for his admission to the theater' (*KpV* 5: 23). His examples illustrate a principle of choice in which expected satisfaction, or the strength of one's desires, serves as the criterion for ranking alternatives. But the general point is that one is measuring the value of an end by its contribution to one's overall happiness. When choosing in this way, expected satisfaction is the determining ground in that one decides what to do by judging what will be found most satisfying, what one desires most on balance.

On the interpretation that I propose, your ultimate reason for choosing an action over alternatives can be the fact that it yields most satisfaction, without feelings of satisfaction being your aim. To make this distinction appear less of a subtlety, let me state the contrasts between the hedonistic and the non-hedonistic interpretation of the principle of happiness more explicitly. I will then add further detail about the deliberative procedures entailed by the principle of happiness.

According to the hedonistic interpretation, it is a shared feature of non-moral choice that we are attracted to a course of action by the pleasure we expect. The desire for pleasure would then be the fundamental motive from which such actions result, and presumably the underlying cause by which they are to be explained. This interpretation errs on two counts: both by holding that non-moral conduct is motivated by the desire for pleasure, and by implying that this desire is the proximate cause of the relevant actions (or that some determination thereof leads directly to the action). To begin with, the second overlooks the fact that, according to Kant's view of rational conduct, actions originate in a judgment on the part of the agent, and are never caused directly by a desire. An agent acts from reasons that she takes to support acting in a certain way, or by taking an end to be of value—in short, by judging an action or end to be good in some respect. Such judgments are grounded in general principles that determine what sorts of particular considerations count as reasons, or confer value on an end. Thus Kant thinks that rational conduct originates in an agent's application of general principles to her circumstances.[22]

These general considerations about action supply some of the main reasons for rejecting the hedonistic interpretation. We may take Kant to hold that when one acts on a desire, one sees the existence of the desire, or the satisfaction expected from acting on it, as providing a reason, or as conferring value on its object. In the kind of conduct that Kant includes under the principle of happiness, we take certain sorts of substantive considerations to be reasons because of the desires that we have, which determine what we find satisfying. ('Let's work through the summer, and then take off in September. August will be unpleasant, but September weather is great for traveling, and we'll avoid the tourists.') That an action will produce satisfaction in the agent is taken to be a reason for choosing it, which makes it good, and its contribution to one's overall satisfaction is what one looks at in weighing it against alternatives. The principle of happiness states the general form underlying reasoning of this sort, and is the principle that determines what sorts of considerations count as reasons within it. Moreover, someone who accepted happiness as a final aim might cite this principle in the course of justifying certain choices to others. In the context of this picture of rational conduct, when expected satisfaction is understood as a standard or criterion by which the value of an action is assessed, there is no reason to conclude that Kant has adopted a hedonistic theory of non-moral conduct. More generally, there appears nothing reductive about the picture of non-moral conduct that he does accept. This framework acknowledges a diversity among the objects of our desires, the aims of our actions, and the kinds of substantive considerations that we recognize as reasons. Indeed there is nothing exceptional about this aspect of Kant's theory. He does not hold that such conduct is directed at a single aim or manifests a single fundamental motive, but rather that it shares a common underlying form. And such a view would appear to leave in place the ordinary distinctions that we want to draw.

Though Kant does not develop this point, we would expect the principle of happiness to be associated with specific deliberative procedures and techniques for resolving practical problems. Deliberation according to this model starts from existing desires and aims, and involves estimates and comparisons of the strengths of one's desires or expected satisfactions. Beyond that, it would include such techniques as trading off gains and losses in expected satisfaction; finding plans that will combine the satisfactions of different desires, or schedule them over time; evaluating specific desires by their compatibility with other desires, and with aims to which one gives greater weight; or simply determining what one wants most.[23] Though these procedures might be quite complex, their general aim will be to order one's desires to determine what will contribute most to one's overall satisfaction, and to use expected satisfaction as a criterion for assessing the value of any particular desire, action, or end.

In referring to a conception of happiness as an 'ideal of imagination', Kant suggests that imagination will play an important role in this model of deliberation.[24] Often you determine which of two things you prefer, or how strongly you actually desire an end, by imagining what it would be like to attain it. Similarly, an ordinary deliberative problem is to determine what would count as the realization of an end desired under a vague or very general description, or to decide on a concrete activity that will satisfy a desire not yet specified (e.g., what would count as a good career, or a good vacation).[25] One approach to such a problem is to imagine the available possibilities and see how they strike you, or what further possibilities they suggest. In both cases, by projecting yourself into possible outcomes, you elicit certain desires and let them play on you in ways that enable you to make the needed comparisons. In a sense you try to arrive at an evaluation of your desires by imagining what it would be like to fulfill them. This leads to a further point. These deliberative techniques are naturally extended to construct a conception of happiness, in which one's desires are ordered into a coherent system. By referring to an ideal of imagination, Kant implies that a conception of happiness can serve as a standard in terms of which individual desires may be assessed or rationally criticized. Both exercises of imagination and the construction of an ideal of happiness may lead to significant revisions of one's desires, and adjustments in their strengths. In this respect these deliberative techniques exercise some control over one's desires, so that one is not bound to the desires with which one began, or to any particular set of desires. Even so, this form of deliberation must take some desires for granted, and at certain points will rely on how one is, or will be, affected by various possibilities. This procedure for assessing desires stops when you arrive at those preferences judged to be strongest, to express what you want most. These are given priority, and may become the standard for further criticism. What this shows is that the reasons for action that this model of deliberation yields will depend at some point on the desires and dispositions that one already has, and their relative intensity, as a result of one's personal history. Thus we can still hold that it places practical reasoning at the service of inclinations, and will lead to results whose validity is conditional on having certain desires.

The claim that the principle of happiness ties reasons for action to one's existing desires and dispositions, and their relative strengths, needs clarification on two points. First, it should be clear that deliberation according to the principle of happiness can take you very far from your initial assessment of a prospective outcome or range of alternatives. It could get you to look at the outcome itself in a different light; that is, it could lead you to revise your initial assessment by taking into account different aspects of the outcome, or consequences you had not considered, while your preferences remain basically unchanged. It could also greatly alter your conception of what you desire, and indeed many of your desires—say, through a clearer ordering of your priorities, or by leading you to reconceive how you would react to a prospective outcome. Still it seems that some desires of the agent produced by the normal psychological processes of desire formation must serve as an evaluative reference point. Which desires play this role may be affected by one's deliberations; indeed, they may be desires either uncovered or brought into existence by the process of deliberation. In the latter case, we may assume that the altered or new desires result from existing dispositions in the agent that are a function of the agent's personal history, and that their formation within the context of deliberation will be governed by the same psychological processes that operate outside of deliberation. Such possibilities should be understood as included in the claim that the reasons for action yielded by the principle of happiness depend on desires and dispositions that one already has.

Second, the claim that reasons may depend on the relative strength or intensity of one's desires does not limit this to their strength in the present, or at the time of decision. Judgments about the strength, and in general the shape, that your desires will have at some point in the future can provide reasons for acting at a time when your desires have not yet taken that shape. To take a simple example, you are tired when you return home from work on Friday evening, and given the traffic you expect and the need to pack, you 'have no desire' to leave for the weekend in the country that you had planned. It would be nice not to go anywhere, and you consider calling it off. But you reflect that once you get there you will feel regenerated and will be glad that you went; or that if you don't go, you will find the prospect of a weekend in your steamy apartment depressing when Saturday arrives. So you go. (Or, since you arrive home late on Thursday night, you have no desire to pack your camping gear in order to leave easily on Friday after work. What gets you to do it is the thought that you will no more want to do it after work tomorrow, that if you don't do it now you may not get off, and that by Saturday afternoon you will regret the fact that you are at home.) In these instances, you are moved to act by a judgment about the strength of future preferences. Judging that you will regret it if you are still at home on Saturday gauges the strength of your desires (or amounts of satisfaction you can expect), by telling you that the desire you will have on Saturday to be away is stronger than the desire you now have not to go anywhere. The essential point is that in assessing actions or ends by the principle of happiness, you refer to the relative strengths that your desires will have at some point in time.[26] While these claims go beyond Kant's texts, his view that a conception of happiness (as an ideal of the satisfaction of desires over time) can serve as a standard for assessing individual desires allows for an extension of this sort.

To return to the main issue, Kant's 'Theorem II' is not arguing that the choices that he identifies as non-moral are alike in having the common aim of satisfaction or pleasurable feeling. Its point, rather, is the following: given the way in which material practical principles provide reasons for acting, the choices to which they lead will have a common structure or underlying form. This is expressed by the principle of happiness, as the general principle of choice and deliberation that underlies maxims of this sort. There are several structural features that the principle of happiness includes. First, it is the general principle of action, or a principle of choice, that Kant takes any material practical principle to exemplify—as I have said, the principle of acting so as to increase individual satisfactions, or of acting from the strongest desire on balance. This describes at the most general level what the agent is doing, and indicates what the agent counts as good reasons for acting. If you make the principle of happiness the 'supreme determining ground of choice', or your 'highest maxim', you will count particular maxims as reasons in so far as acting on them will contribute to the overall satisfaction of your desires. Thus its practical significance is that it provides a method of deciding how to act. This leads to the second point: the principle of happiness is a criterion of evaluation. It values proposed actions and ends, and assigns them priority, in so far as they are consistent with one's other desires and aims, and will contribute to one's overall satisfaction. Third, this principle of choice will be associated with specific deliberative procedures. To do what you will find most satisfying, you need a way to determine what that is. Thus, I have suggested that it will lead to a model of deliberation that relies on existing desires and dispositions, estimates and comparisons of expected satisfactions, and imaginative projections into various possible outcomes. In sum, it is a principle of choice that commits you to a certain kind of procedure for evaluating desires and ends, and deliberating about courses of action.

IV. THE PRINCIPLE OF HAPPINESS AS A MODEL OF CHOICE

Understanding the principle of happiness as a principle of choice clarifies the contrast that Kant intends between it and the moral law. The somewhat unexpected conclusion to which we are led is that the principle of happiness is a kind of decision procedure, and is a 'formal principle' in much the same way as the moral law.[27] Each is a general principle that states the underlying form of a kind of reason that we recognize, which leads to a procedure of deliberation that can be applied to individual cases. To see this we should bear in mind that the principle of acting so as to maximize satisfaction of one's desires does not direct an agent toward any specific end, or give the notion of happiness any definite content. What will bring happiness to an individual depends on facts about one's desires and dispositions. But then what distinguishes acting from the principle of happiness is not the object of choice, but the way in which one goes about assigning value to ends and choosing. As we have seen, it directs one to set priorities and decide how to act in a specific situation by surveying one's preferences, weighing prospective amounts of satisfaction, and so on. In this sense, the principle of happiness captures a set of formal features shared by a large class of choices. The moral law, on the other hand, states the general form of an unconditional requirement on action, or of a principle of conduct that is unconditionally valid. It yields an alternative procedure of deliberation in which one evaluates an action by asking whether one's reasons for performing it are sufficient to justify the action fully to anyone (are universally valid, consistent with the absolute value of humanity, and so on). Thus Kant's dichotomy between the principles of morality and happiness is a contrast between two models of choice, each of which is associated with its own procedures of deliberation and criteria of value.

This interpretation shows that a hedonistic psychology is not the rationale for treating material practical principles as a recognizable class. The argument of Kant's 'Theorem II' turns out not to contain any particular claims about the direction of human desires, and does not imply any limitations on the objects of choice. As we have seen, the principle of happiness refers not to what one chooses, but to how one goes about choosing. For this reason it seems somewhat misleading to term it the 'principle of self-love', as Kant does. A principle that directs an agent to act by determining what is desired most need not be egoistic, much less hedonistic. That depends on the nature of one's desires, and as we have seen, Kant recognizes that we can have inclinations that are straightforwardly other-regarding.[28] It is also clear that a hedonistic psychology is not used to explain why actions that fall under the principle of happiness are heteronomous. Choices are heteronomous when the reasons by which they are guided can be traced to sources external to the will—that is, when you decide how to act by assessing the strength of the desires you will have at some time, where their strength is a function of law-governed psychological processes. Kant characterizes 'heteronomy of choice' as 'dependence upon the natural law of following some impulse or inclination, [in which case] the will does not give itself the law, but only the precept for rationally following pathological law' (*KpV* 5: 33). The account of the principle of happiness given so far locates the sources of heteronomy both in what are recognized as reasons and in the procedures of evaluation and deliberation by which reasons are assessed. In acting from the principle of happiness, some desires must be taken for granted at some point during deliberation. Thus, what one counts as reasons is a function of the psychological mechanisms that govern the processes of desire formation. In addition, one relies on these same mechanisms in assessing and ordering one's desires. This can be seen in the way in which exercises of imagination are used to resolve a practical problem, such as deciding which of two alternatives is preferred. One attempts to project oneself into the outcomes under consideration and to elicit the responses one will have in order to determine how it will feel to attain them. This is heteronomy because practical deliberation uses the psychological mechanisms by which desires are formed to determine the value of an action or end; in a sense, you let your desires and feelings make the final determination.

In order to close this account of Kant's 'Theorem II' and the principle of happiness, an important qualification must be introduced. The interpretation proposed treats references to 'anticipated feelings of satisfaction or agreeableness' as functionally equivalent to what one desires, or what one desires most, and so on. This seems acceptable since what yields most overall satisfaction is best seen as a function of what one desires most strongly, or will desire most strongly at some point in time. In explaining how choices are made, there is no need to refer to a single feeling of satisfaction that an agent seeks to maximize. Yet Kant refers consistently to feelings of pleasure and expected agreeableness, and assumes that there is a definite feeling of satisfaction, experienced to greater degrees, that serves as a standard of comparison between any desired ends.[29] Here two comments are in order.

First, the emphasis that Kant places on feelings of satisfaction may be explainable by citing certain features of the deliberative process associated with the principle of happiness. As we have seen, it gives scope to the strength of certain preferences, and uses imaginative projection to stimulate one's desires and feelings. In addition, what an individual finds satisfying is a function of desires and dispositions particular to that individual. Thus his references to feelings of satisfaction can be viewed as a way of bringing out the subjective character of the deliberative processes involved.

Second, by assuming a common feeling of satisfaction experienced in relation to all desired ends, Kant does adopt one form of hedonism, though not a hedonistic theory of motivation. He treats this feeling as a 'common currency' that is used to compare the value of ends otherwise incommensurable. This supposes that one can compare amounts of this feeling along various magnitudes; he mentions intensity, duration, and repeatability.[30] While this aspect of Kant's view gives some support to a hedonistic interpretation of the principle of happiness, we need to look at the rationale behind these assumptions. Kant is asking how one orders preferences between desired alternatives that offer incommensurable kinds of satisfaction. (Recall that his examples stake the pleasures of sensibility against those of the understanding: it's a question of finishing an instructive book versus attending the hunt, intellectual conversation versus gambling, helping a poor man versus a ticket to the theater, and so on.) Kant argues that such comparisons are only possible if there is a common standard by which we can assess our desire for each. Since we make such comparisons all the time, there must be some such standard—a common feeling of satisfaction experienced in relation to each. However, most people would now reject the view that the ability to rank ends of this sort requires an identifiable feeling of satisfaction to serve as a common currency. Without wishing to defend Kant on this point, I would point out that the hedonism involved is not a theory of motivation, but what Rawls has called 'hedonism as a method of choice'.[31] In other words, Kant appeals to a homogeneous feeling of pleasure to serve as the criterion by which the value of different desired ends is determined. He thinks that it is required to explain our evident ability to make rational choices between certain kinds of desired alternatives.

To the extent that references to feelings of satisfaction lead to this common currency assumption, Kant's principle of happiness, as stated, embodies a certain form of hedonism. Though the assumption of a homogeneous feeling of pleasure seems mistaken, this point needs to be kept in perspective. Kant does not think that this feeling is the aim or motive of such conduct, but that it must be cited to explain how certain kinds of choices are possible. But everything that he says about choosing in terms of expected satisfactions and feelings of agreeableness could be cast in terms of deciding what one desires most, as explained above. The satisfaction to which he refers can be viewed as the overall satisfaction of one's preferences. On the issue of rankings, all that Kant needs to hold is that we do make comparisons in which the strength of one's present or future preferences plays a central role in the ways discussed above. This is a part of a recognizable method of evaluation that is distinct from moral evaluation. Thus, the recognition of the principle of happiness as a distinct model of choice and deliberation does not depend on there being a single feeling of pleasure that is experienced in relation to all desired ends. While this qualification needs to be noted, it does not affect the principal conclusions of this essay. A hedonistic psychology does not supply the rationale for treating non-moral motives as a recognizable class, nor does the principle of happiness express a hedonistic theory of motivation. Moreover, nothing that Kant wants to establish—in particular, his distinction between morality and happiness, or autonomy and heteronomy—presupposes any hedonistic assumptions.

V. ARE KANT'S GENERAL DISTINCTIONS REDUCTIVE?

We have been led to interpret the distinction between morality and happiness as a distinction between two models of choice, each associated with a specific procedure for deliberating about actions and ends. In acting from the principle of happiness, one decides how to act by determining what offers most satisfaction, given one's desires and dispositions. Moreover, one takes the fact that one will derive satisfaction from a course of action as a reason for performing it. For now let us understand moral conduct to be guided by a conception of objectively good reasons. In moral deliberation one assesses actions by asking whether one's reasons for performing them are universally valid, or sufficient to lead any rational agent to accept the action as justified, or as good. The plausibility of this distinction does not require that we be able to tell in every case which model best applies to a particular action. Its poles might be difficult to keep apart, since an agent's motives might draw on both principles. But one can still see autonomy as a coherent ideal. The more one is motivated by the recognition of the universal validity of one's reasons, the more autonomously one acts. Similarly, we can see why actions fall under heteronomy when what they count as reasons, or as conferring value, is a function of desires that arise according to law-governed psychological processes.

In this final section, I return to the broader issue of whether Kant's general and comprehensive distinctions are reductive in a way that undermines them. I want to suggest that the distinction that Kant is drawing, as understood above, is plausible; that it is significant and provides insight; and that it is not reductive. I will support these claims by reviewing some of the earlier conclusions which indicate that the classifications at the center of Kant's theory do not distort the phenomena they are intended to encompass, or obscure finer distinctions among them. Whether or not a general distinction is reductive depends on how it is made. In this case, showing why the classification of non-moral conduct under the principle of happiness does not rest on the adoption of a problematic hedonistic psychology also shows why it is not reductive.

One theme so far has been to stress the flexibility of Kant's principle of happiness, and to argue that it allows for complexity within the classifications established. The idea that feelings of pleasure and pain figure in the causal history of inclinations does not significantly limit either the processes of desire formation, or the objects that desires can have. In addition, Kant does not rely on any claims about the objects of desires to bring non-moral conduct under the principle of happiness, and this principle does not direct an agent toward the single aim of pleasure. Happiness must be understood as an inclusive end, whose scope is as extensive as that of our desires.[32]

We can explain why Kant's very general distinctions are not reductive by looking at certain unusual features about the way in which they are drawn, or the somewhat unusual property that they are intended to capture. I have argued that both the principle of happiness and the principle of morality state the common form underlying a kind of substantive reason. The principle of happiness expresses a model of choice that is distinguished by what one counts as reasons and criteria of value, and by a way of deciding how to act.[33] But commonality of form is compatible with diversity of substance, so to speak, and a principle that states a shared form leaves more particular distinctions intact. This point becomes clear when one considers the contrast between claiming that two apparently heterogeneous actions or motives share a common form and claiming that they have a common aim, or are really determinations of the same fundamental motive. The latter claims are reductive, and if Kant's was a view of this sort, there would be grounds for thinking that he was committed to holding, implausibly, that the friend of humanity and the prudent merchant are, in the end, pursuing the same ultimate aim—their own satisfaction; or that they are acting from the same fundamental motive, which, due to the peculiarities of their temperaments and differences in their circumstances, happens to be directed at different external ends. Or it might commit him to holding that my interest in intellectual conversation and my interest in gambling (or that my natural sympathy for the poor and my taste for theater) are really 'nothing but' different determinations of the desire for pleasure, and that in weighing these two alternatives, all that I need do is decide which is the most effective means to the uniform end of the sum of agreeable feeling in me.

But the claim that there is a common form underlying motives of this sort has none of these implications.

A view would be reductive in yet another way by holding that the substantive reasons being grouped together derive their normative force from the same general principle—that they become reasons through the application of a single general principle to an agent's circumstances, and that the normative force which they have for the agent flows from this principle.[34] Such an analysis might claim that whenever I take a set of considerations to give me a reason for acting ('The movie only runs for a week, and Thursday night is the only evening we are free—though that is when the benefit for Free South Africa is being held'), their normative force must be traced back to a practical syllogism, or perhaps through a series of syllogisms, in which the major premise is 'I am to act so as to maximize my own happiness'. These considerations would be reasons only because they instantiate this general or ultimate principle under the circumstances. But again, this is not how Kant analyzes the structure of non-moral reasons. Saying that a set of reasons shares a common form is compatible with saying that the members of this set stand on their own as reasons; there is no need to see reason-giving force as flowing exclusively from the top down, or to think that a consideration acquires normative force only through the application of a more general principle. To act from the principle of happiness is just to take substantive considerations as reasons on the basis of desires one has, and to deliberate and choose accordingly. To have happiness as a final aim (or to adopt the principle of happiness as one's 'highest maxim') is simply to give priority to actions and ends that you will find satisfying, and to use that as the criterion of what is of importance to you. (In the above example, you act from the principle of happiness if you choose between the film and the benefit by deciding which you will find most satisfying.)

I shall conclude by returning to some of the problems referred to at the beginning of this essay. Initially we were concerned that the distinction between autonomy and heteronomy would be undermined if it were shown to rest on a hedonistic psychology. The resulting dichotomy would not be plausible as an exhaustive classification, and would force many actions into a mold that does not fit them. The concept of heteronomy, in particular, would appear to involve a kind of leveling. In addition, it is not clear why autonomy should be a significant evaluative category when so many actions of importance to the individual fall under heteronomy, as at first appears. These are general problems that could be raised independently of whether Kant's distinctions rely on a hedonistic psychology. However, the interpretation that shows why they do not also shows how Kant may escape these general problems. I will close with two further observations. The first is that the principle of happiness, as interpreted, allows for ample complexity in conduct that falls under heteronomy; second, I want to outline a way in which autonomy can include the kinds of ends and activities that it initially appears to leave out.

Regarding the first, it is clear that Kant did not view conduct falling under heteronomy as mechanistically determined by the desire for pleasure, or indeed by the strength of one's existing desires, as some interpretations suggest. In addition to seeing that natural desires may have both complex ends and complex histories, we have seen that action which falls under the principle of happiness is not narrowly determined by the desires from which deliberation begins. The principle of happiness allows for rational criticism of desires, as well as the formulation of ends and ideals that go beyond one's existing desires. Though this form of deliberation must at some points accept certain desires and dispositions as given, the deliberative process affects which desires are taken as given. But the more general point is that heteronomous choice is still reasoned choice. The agent is motivated by the recognition of reasons and by taking ends or states of affairs to be of value. Such conduct may be structured around a set of priorities, in that certain ends or activities may be given an overriding weight relative to others, through which they may both initiate actions and limit those which there is reason to take. I would argue, in addition, that there is room for an agent to act out of a sense that an activity is of great importance. What distinguishes heteronomous conduct is not the absence of these general features of choice, but what it is that is taken to confer value or importance, and how it is that priorities are set. Value must be tied to one's desires and the processes of desire formation in the ways we have discussed.

If choice falling under heteronomy can encompass a wide range of ends, and leaves room for some notion of value and importance, then one might ask what is wrong with it. But Kant need not say that anything is wrong with it, where the desires on which one acts satisfy appropriate moral constraints. He is committed to holding only that autonomous conduct most fully manifests certain ideals and powers of the person, and thus has a value that other forms of conduct lack. He must show that acting from a conception of objective value that fully satisfies the criteria of objective value represents the most complete expression of our agency.

The other question concerns the range of activities that may be regarded as expressions of one's autonomy. Again we should consider ends of personal importance to the agent: long-term goals and interests, personal relationships, and characteristic desires. Certainly ends and activities which represent important forms of self-expression have a claim to being expressions of one's autonomy in the ordinary sense of the word; and it may be that an acceptable conception of autonomy must be able to include such activities. But it appears at first that something like Green's 'problem of the excluded middle' remains, since these activities still appear to fall on the wrong side of the fence when the conception of heteronomy is strictly applied.[35] Though such activities and goals may be consciously chosen, an interest in any particular end of this sort will presuppose some desires specific to the agent, which will exist due to contingent facts about that agent's history. These desires are not chosen by the agent, but are created by past experiences according to psychological laws that operate independently of the will. Moreover, actually experienced satisfactions play an important role in the formation of these desires; that is, feelings of pleasure and pain will figure in their causal history.

Because of these facts about the desires that underlie them, interests and activities of this sort would appear to fall under heteronomy.

To give an example, my interest in philosophy would appear to be an activity in which I express my autonomy. It is a long-term goal that gives structure to my life, and provides an avenue for realizing many important capacities; I also view it as a worthy activity to which to devote one's energy. But this interest rests on desires that are the result of my having found certain activities to be stimulating and fulfilling. I may have chosen philosophy as an end, but in doing so I was responding to dispositions that had developed in me in conjunction with many factors into which I had little input. I did not choose the desires that make philosophy a reasonable thing for me to have chosen. In this sense, my particular interest in philosophy is a function of my past history, and would appear to fall under heteronomy according to the account developed so far. This point is quite general, in that most personal ends presuppose desires specific to an individual, generated by causal processes in this way.

A response to this objection is suggested by noting a further element of flexibility in the application of Kant's framework. We have seen that the principle of happiness commits the agent to a model of evaluating ends, not to any substantive end, and that it imposes few restrictions on the objects of choice. Thus, the distinction between autonomy and heteronomy does not imply that all ends and activities fall into two categories, but only that the grounds for the adoption of ends do. Accordingly, many ends could be adopted on either moral grounds or those presented by the principle of happiness; the same action could instantiate either principle when performed by different people, or by the same person at different times. This fact allows an end to be an expression of autonomy when we can find reasons supporting its adoption based on a conception of objective value. Roughly, though an interest in a given end might initially fall under heteronomy, it can express autonomy when the agent values that end out of a recognition of its universal validity—for example, when the agent values the end as a realization of the power of humanity, or ties it to the development of one's natural perfection. Briefly, many personal ends can become expressions of autonomy when valued in the right way.

To develop this point: the processes of desire formation required for one's initial interest in an end might instantiate heteronomy. But there is a difference between desiring something and setting it as one's end, and we can distinguish the processes by which a desire is formed from the grounds that an agent has for acting on it. The initial reason for pursuing an end might be that it satisfies various preferences. When this is the source of one's reasons, it will determine how individual decisions are made in relation to that end, and how it is integrated with one's other ends. But, for example, if the end affords an opportunity to develop the power of humanity, a different kind of reason for pursuing the end is available. By viewing it in that light one would value it on different grounds, and this change would be reflected in one's deliberations and choices. In this way the Kantian can see it as an expression of the agent's autonomy, despite the fact that the initial interest depends on desires that develop independently of the agent's will.

This is no more than a sketch of an answer to a problem in Kant's moral theory that may be more difficult to resolve than it should be. But it does suggest a broader interpretation of Kant's conception of autonomy that allows it to include a wider range of ends. To pursue this suggestion, one would need an account of what it is to exercise the power of humanity and to set ends for oneself, and how the exercise of the power of humanity is an expression of an agent's rational autonomy. Offhand there is no reason to think that Kant must limit the power of humanity to the setting of moral goals, and see as fully autonomous only those uses of it that are directed at obligatory conduct and narrowly moral ends, such as justice, benevolence, and respect for others. It may be that personal ends can be viewed as expressions of autonomy when valued in the right way.[36]

APPENDIX[37]

My aim in this essay is to argue that Kant did not accept a simple and what many people will regard as a mistaken hedonistic psychology of non-moral choice, according to which inclinations are desires for pleasure and pleasure is the common end or motive of choice that falls under what Kant terms the principle of happiness or self-love. If Kant did not accept a simple hedonistic psychology, then none of his fundamental dichotomies, such as that between morality and happiness, depend on such a conception. I have not tried to show that Kant's views about non-moral motivation are correct—though I do not find the views that I ascribe to him implausible—but only that they are unexceptional and not at odds with either common or good philosophical sense. There are different interpretive stances that one might take here. One might deny that Kant accepts any form of hedonistic psychology. Or one could deny that he accepted a simple and obviously mistaken hedonistic psychology of non-moral choice. My position in this essay is sometimes ambiguous, but it should be the latter. It can allow (though it does not affirm) that Kant's views amount to a sophisticated form of hedonism about non-moral choice. One may conclude that the best reading of the texts attributes to Kant a sophisticated hedonism that, even if not ultimately correct or satisfactory, is not implausible, in that it permits him to say what good sense wants to say about non-moral motives and ends and to draw the distinctions that good sense wants to make.[38] That outcome would not undercut my aims of arguing that Kant's psychology of non-moral choice is unexceptional and that his fundamental dichotomies do not presuppose a conception of motivation that should be rejected out of hand.

A hedonistic reading of the passages from the second *Critique* discussed above is hard to avoid altogether. But often there is methodological value in seeing how far a text can be pushed in a certain direction. In this case, the attempt to move the texts away from a hedonistic (or simple hedonistic) psychology leads to a more philosophically satisfying understanding of Kant's principle of happiness and conception of non-moral choice. If we settle for the hedonistic reading too easily, we are likely to miss the deeper import of the principle of happiness. I have argued above that what the principle of happiness identifies is not the common aim or motive, but the shared structure of non-moral choice. It states the underlying form of a certain kind of choice—choice based on reasons with subjective conditions—that contrasts with the form of moral choice.

In Section III above I interpret Kant's remark at *MdS* 6: 212, that in 'interests of inclination' pleasure precedes the determination of the faculty of desire as its cause, as a thesis about the causal history of inclinations; in Section IV I claim that this thesis figures in Theorems I and II and elsewhere in the second *Critique*. This interpretation has been criticized and I now see that it is a misreading.[39] I believe that Kant did, or would have, accepted this thesis, and it is consistent with what he says in these passages (*KpV* 5: 21–3, *MdS* 6: 212 ff.); but it is not what he means when he says that pleasure precedes certain motivational states as their cause. What I say in Section III tries to move the feeling of pleasure both too far back and then too far forward in the causal process. I claim that in interests of inclination, past experiences of pleasure figure in desire formation and that pleasure reappears as a result of successful action on a motive, whether the motive is based on inclination or on reason. It is plausible to think that experiences of pleasure play this role in desire formation, that pleasure normally results from acting on inclination when all goes well, and that some form of satisfaction follows successful action on any interest. But I now see that the passages in question assign a different functional role to feelings of pleasure and satisfaction that locates them directly in the motivational state. I would like to offer a different interpretation here, though I do not think that these revisions require abandoning my main interpretive claims.

Kant thought that desire in the broad sense of a motivational state has a necessary connection with pleasure and displeasure. He says that '*pleasure* or *displeasure*, susceptibility to which is called *feeling*, is always connected with desire [*Begehren*] or aversion', and he defines 'practical pleasure' as 'that pleasure which is necessarily connected with desire (for an object whose representation affects feeling in this way) . . . whether it is the cause or effect of the desire' (*MdS* 6: 211, 212. Cf. also *KU* 204, 207). I take the connection that Kant draws between pleasure and motivation to be the following: it is by taking pleasure in the thought of an object that we experience interest quite generally—that is, it is how we experience both interests of inclination and interests of reason—and in some cases of interests of inclination, pleasure taken in the thought of an object is the cause of one's active interest. When feelings of pleasure are understood as the way in which we experience interest, taking pleasure in the thought of an object will be functionally equivalent to actively desiring or taking an interest in it. Further, finding the thought of an object agreeable can be seen as a way of coming to have an interest in that object that is immediate, though conditional on the receptivity and dispositions of the subject—a way of taking an interest that contrasts with interests produced by judgments of reason. But there is no implication that pleasure is the object of non-moral interest or the fundamental motive of choice that falls under the principle of happiness.

Let's begin with the definition of pleasure that Kant gives in a note in the second *Critique*:

Life is the faculty of a being to act in accordance with the laws of the faculty of desire. The *faculty of desire* is a being's *faculty to be by means of its representations the cause of the reality of the objects of these representations. Pleasure is the representation of the agreement of an object or of an action with the subjective conditions of life*, i.e., with the faculty of the *causality of a representation with respect to the reality of its object* (or with respect to the determination of the powers of the subject to action in order to produce the object). (*KpV* 5: 9 n)

Since this definition of pleasure applies to all practical pleasure (both those that cause and those that are the effect of a motivational state), the 'subjective conditions of life' here encompass the full range of a subject's desires and motivational states. They include susceptibilities and dispositions to take pleasure in certain objects ('propensities'), desires, and inclinations that arise from prior experience of various objects or activities, ongoing interests in various ends, but also motivational states produced by various practical judgments, including judgments about objective goodness. Pleasure is the feeling that results from the representation of an object that 'agrees with' or answers to (i.e., would satisfy) some prior disposition or motivational state in the subject. It is the way in which a subject is affected by the representation of an object or action that answers to or fits the subject's existing dispositions and motivational states, including those based on judgments of objective goodness. (A feeling of pleasure is a 'representation' of this agreement only in a subjective sense. It does not represent a feature that goes into cognition of the object, but only, as Kant says, 'a relation to the subject' (*KpV* 5: 21 f., *MdS* 6: 212; cf. *KU* 5: 206). It is a *feeling* because it is the effect of the representation of an object on a subject's sensibility, given the subject's existing dispositions and motivational states.) The connection that Kant draws between pleasure and desire or motivation, I'll now suggest, is that it is by taking pleasure in the representation of an object or an action that we experience or become conscious of an interest in it.

Where pleasure precedes the determination of the faculty of desire, Kant appears to have the following model in mind: the representation of an object (or action) is accompanied by feelings of pleasure—more specifically, by feelings of agreeableness—and thereby elicits active interest on the part of the subject in bringing it about. (That interest is the active 'desire' (*Begehren*) or 'determination of the faculty of desire', i.e. the motivational state of being interested in the existence of the object.) The representation of the object could lead to an expectation of pleasure or agreeable feeling, or perhaps the representation itself is agreeable. Either way, the pleasure taken in the representation of the object indicates that the object answers to existing susceptibilities and dispositions, or to existing inclinations in the subject. We might say that the resulting interest in the object is mediated by the feeling of agreeableness that represents the fit between the object and the dispositions and desires of the subject. Kant usually says that the feeling of pleasure causes the interest in the object.[40] Here the idea might be that the representation of the object causes or is accompanied by a feeling of agreeableness, given the subject's susceptibilities and dispositions, and that this feeling then causes or activates an interest in the object. But he can also allow that the pleasure makes one conscious of an existing desire or interest, as well as one's degree of interest. Since the feeling of pleasure is a subjective 'representation' of the 'agreement' of an object with 'the subjective conditions of life', it can, through the effect of the representation of the object on the subject, indicate that the object answers to a subject's existing dispositions and desires, thereby eliciting, in the sense of making one conscious of, an interest. I think that the idea that a feeling of pleasure elicits an active interest should include either pleasure causing interest or pleasure making one conscious of interest; both may be natural descriptions of the phenomena in many cases. If so, finding the representation of an object or end agreeable is functionally identical to actively desiring or taking an interest in it. It is a way of taking an immediate interest in an object that depends on the dispositions and desires to which the object answers, without which there would be no feeling of pleasure and no basis for interest. To take pleasure in the representation of an object in the sense of finding it agreeable is to have an active desire for or interest in that object, which is conditional on various subjective facts about oneself ('based on the receptivity of the subject' (*KpV* 5: 22)). The tight connection between taking pleasure in the thought of an object and having an active interest in it is confirmed by Kant's occasional identification of the pleasure and the interest: 'if a pleasure necessarily precedes a desire, *the practical pleasure must be called an interest of inclination*' (*MdS* 6: 212; emphasis added).[41]

This reading of the connection between pleasure and desire should be borne out by Kant's conception of interests of reason, and it is. Since Kant finds a necessary connection between practical pleasure and desire or motivation generally, we should expect the role of pleasure in interests of inclination and in interests of reason to be similar, despite the obvious differences. In the latter case, where pleasure follows from a prior determination of the faculty of desire, we have this model: an agent judges that there are objective reasons to perform a certain action and this judgment has motivational force; it interests the agent in that action. The agent now takes pleasure in the thought of the object or action, since this representation 'agrees with' or answers to this motivational state. The pleasure follows from the determination of the faculty of desire, since it is the effect of the representation of the object or action on the subject, given the motivational state produced by the judgment; given this interest, one takes satisfaction in the thought of the existence of the object or action (cf. *KU* 5: 207). Here, as with interests of inclination, the feeling of pleasure is the way in which we experience interest.

Let's return to Theorems I and II. How does this view of the functional role of pleasure bear on Kant's assertion that when one acts on a material practical principle, the feeling of agreeableness taken in the thought of an object is the determining ground of choice? He writes: 'For the determining ground of choice [*Willkür*] is then the representation of an object and that relation of the representation to the subject by which the faculty of desire is determined to realize the object. Such a relation to the subject is called pleasure in the reality of an object' (*KpV* 5: 21). Pleasure, as we have seen, is here that relation of an object to the subject—the fact that the object answers to the subject's susceptibilities, dispositions, and desires—that determines the faculty of desire in the sense of eliciting the motivational state of active interest in the object. When pleasure is the determining ground of *choice*, an agent's choice is determined by the fact that the object answers to the subject's dispositions and desires. I take that to mean that one's reason for choosing is the fact that one finds the object agreeable, that is to say, the fact that it answers to one's desires and dispositions. One might go further and say that the pleasure that one takes in certain features of the object brings to one's attention the specific ways in which it answers to one's desires; that is, it brings out those features of the object that are (or that one takes to be) reasons to realize it. If one did not find it agreeable—that is, if one did not desire it or find that it answers to one's desires—one would have no interest and see no reason to pursue it. This is the shared structure of action on material practical principles that is captured by the principle of happiness: it is a form of choice that takes reasons for action from the fact that an object or action satisfies one's existing desires and dispositions and evaluates actions or ends on these terms.

NOTES

1. This appears to be the standard interpretation. See Beck's *A Commentary on Kant's Critique of Practical Reason*, 92–102. See also the contributions to *Self and Nature in Kant's Philosophy*, ed. Allen W. Wood, by Terence Irwin (pp. 39 f.), Ralf Meerbote

(pp. 66–7), and Wood (p. 83). Cf. also Stephen L. Darwall, *Impartial Reason*, 174, and Irwin's more recent 'Kant's Criticisms of Eudaemonism'.

2. T. H. Green, *Collected Works*, ii, 139. I learned of Green's views from Irwin's essay, 'Morality and Personality: Kant and Green', in Wood, ed., *Self and Nature in Kant's Philosophy*.

3. Kant's distinction between autonomy and heteronomy is primarily a distinction between two kinds of moral theories. As I discuss in Chapter 5 below, the autonomy of the will is best understood, negatively, as the independence of the rational will from external sources of authority and externally imposed normative principles and, positively, as its capacity to give law. A moral theory bases morality on autonomy when it understands the basic principles of morality as laws that the will gives to itself. By contrast a theory of heteronomy bases morality on naturally desired ends (substantive ends in which agents have a contingent interest), and is thereby forced to understand moral principles as hypothetical imperatives. At *KpV* 5: 33, for example, Kant says that 'heteronomy of choice' results when a desire-based interest in some object is presupposed as a condition of the possibility of the moral law—that is, when the authority or normative force of moral principles is tied to a desire-based or contingent interest. Strictly speaking, the phrases 'acting autonomously' and 'acting heteronomously' are not Kant's, but their connection with his conception of autonomy is clear enough. We may say that conduct is autonomous when it fully expresses or realizes the autonomy of the will (when an agent acts from the will's own principles); it is heteronomous when, by taking desires or contingent interests to provide reasons for action, an agent follows an external source of reasons or authority.

4. Cf. Philippa Foot, 'Morality as a System of Hypothetical Imperatives', in *Virtues and Vices*, 158–9, and 165, where she writes that Kant 'was a psychological hedonist in respect of all actions except those done for the sake of the moral law, and this faulty theory of human nature was one of the things preventing him from seeing that moral virtues might be compatible with the rejection of the categorical imperative'. Bernard Williams writes: 'Kant . . . believed that all actions except those of moral principle were to be explained not only deterministically but in terms of egoistic hedonism. Only in acting from moral principle could we escape from being causally determined by the drive for pleasure, like animals; and sometimes he marked this by saying that only actions of principle counted as exercises of the will . . . and hence were truly free' (*Ethics and the Limits of Philosophy*, 64. Cf. also 15). See also A. Phillips Griffith, 'Kant's Psychological Hedonism'; Griffiths ascribes to Kant the view that, as phenomenal beings, pleasure is the only thing that we care about for its own sake and finds this view to be 'repugnant, derogatory and degrading' (pp. 210, 212).

5. Cf. Green, *Collected Works*, ii, §§ 119–20. To give this problem a name, I'll call it the 'problem of the excluded middle': the 'middle' is excluded since many actions that are neither hedonistically motivated nor morally motivated appear to be left out by Kant's classification, when interpreted in this way.

6. For a brief account see William K. Frankena, *Ethics*, 21–2, 85–7. This argument dates back to Butler, and is also endorsed by Green, *Collected Works*, ii, 140.

7. On this see also *Rel* 6: 29 n., where Kant mentions both the habitual character of inclinations and the fact that they presuppose previously experienced pleasure. Inclination is here distinguished from 'instinct', which is 'a felt need to do or enjoy something of which we still do not have a concept (such as the drive in animals to build

or the drive to sex)'. Since instincts are with us from birth, they are not caused by prior experiences of pleasure; they motivate toward certain activities, some (though not all) of which are immediately pleasurable.

8. See also *KpV* 5: 62 ff. Cf. also *KpV* 5: 9 n, 38 and *KU* 5: 178–9, 204, 209.

9. I now think that the interpretive claim that I make about this passage (that it is asserting that pleasure plays a causal role in generating inclinations) is mistaken, and in the appendix I revisit this and related passages. However the interpretation that I now favor still does not make pleasure the object of inclination or of action on inclination.

10. Kant refers to the satisfaction that results when one acts from the moral law as 'self-contentment' (*Selbstzufriedenheit*), which he understands as a satisfaction with oneself in having fulfilled the requirements of a standard of rationality. Cf. *KpV* 5: 115 f., 117–18.

11. I owe this phrase to Christine Korsgaard. I am indebted to her both for discussion of this issue, as well as for several comments about how to clarify this section of the chapter (including the second example in this paragraph).

12. That Kant actually held such a view can be seen in his essay 'Conjectural Beginning of Human History'.

13. Samuel Kerstein finds that I hold that 'once an agent has developed a Kantian inclination, it is *not* the case that he acts from it only on the condition that he expect pleasure from his action' (*Kant's Search for the Supreme Principle of Morality*, 26). I do not think that what I say has this implication. In any case, I agree that inclinations are connected with expected satisfaction (pleasure or agreeableness) and that feelings of satisfaction always attend the satisfaction of inclinations, as Kant understands them, though I do not think that these claims imply that pleasure is always the object of inclination (i.e., that inclinations are desires for pleasure) or that pleasure is the aim or the motive of action on inclination. I agree that Kant believes that an agent who desires some object, X, in the sense of having an inclination for X, finds the thought of X agreeable—but that is because to have an inclination for an object just is to find the thought of the object agreeable. An agent who did not find the thought of some object, X, agreeable (or did not feel satisfaction in the prospect of having or doing X) would not have an inclination for X. (Note that at *MdS* 6: 212 Kant says that 'if a pleasure necessarily precedes a desire, the practical pleasure must be called an interest of inclination'. Here he identifies the pleasure and the resulting interest or 'determination of the faculty of desire', suggesting that he thinks that to desire, i.e., have an inclination for, an object just is to find the prospect of that object agreeable.)

As an example, take someone who finds the thought of attending a certain concert 'agreeable', makes plans to attend the concert, and enjoys it. I take it that Kant would say that finding the thought of the concert agreeable interests one in the concert. But the object of one's interest (or desire) is attending the concert, and the motive of the resulting behavior is one's interest in the concert. Or perhaps one should say that the motive is one's interest in the concert as agreeable, or as something that one desires, in order to signal the particular way in which one comes to have the interest in this end. We might want to say here that one finds the thought of the concert agreeable because attending the concert answers to an existing desire, or elicits a desire due to an existing disposition. In many instances, finding the thought of the concert agreeable tells you that, and how much, you desire to attend it. Kant can say this as well.

14. Inclinations that constitute our 'animal nature' (*Tierheit*) generally include desires for food, sex, simple comforts, and self-preservation. At one point Kant terms them 'inclinations of enjoyment' (*Neigungen des Genußes*), which may imply (correctly or incorrectly) that they have pleasure as their object (*KU* 5: 433). However, elsewhere Kant simply refers to 'our natural drives for food, sex, rest, and movement' (*MdS* 6: 215) or to 'impulses of nature having to do with man's animality' through which 'nature aims at (a) his self-preservation, (b) the preservation of the species, and (c) the preservation of his capacity to enjoy life, though still on the animal level only' (*MdS* 6: 420. Cf. also *Rel* 6: 26). In any case, some of these activities (though not all) are immediately pleasurable—rendered thus by Nature in her wisdom, so that we will take them up on a regular basis.

15. See the discussion of the 'aptitude for culture', both as 'skill' and as 'discipline of inclinations' in § 83 of the *Critique of Judgment*, which becomes the 'predisposition to humanity' in *Religion*, I. Though Kant emphasizes the vices which grow out of these natural dispositions (including both the 'vices of culture', such as jealousy, rivalry, and ambition, and the taste for luxuries), it is clear that they comprise desires for things that are good (the development of talents, skills, knowledge, etc.), and presuppose developed cognitive capacities and a background of social practices.

16. Also worth noting is a reference to being just out of a 'love of order'; see *KpV* 5: 82. For discussions of sympathy and benevolence, see *KpV* 5: 34, 82, 118; *MdS* 6: 450–2, 456–7, some of which mention the duty to cultivate natural sympathy as an aid to the moral disposition. Paton collates several passages on inclinations in *The Categorical Imperative*, 55–7.

17. Kerstein rejects my claim that Kant understands the friend of humanity to be moved by an immediate concern for the happiness of others, without any motive of self-interest (*Kant's Search for the Supreme Principle of Morality*, 26–7). As he reads Kant, in acting from inclination one seeks to realize an end only if (on the condition that) one expects pleasure from the end. Therefore, in all such action, the expectation of pleasure is *a* motive (though not necessarily the only motive), and moreover, Kerstein implies, a motive of self-interest. Applying this point to the friend of humanity, this agent must have a motive of self-interest, namely the expectation of the pleasure that he or she expects to gain from helping. Kerstein takes Kant's remark that such people are 'so sympathetically attuned that, without any other motive of vanity or self-interest they find an inner satisfaction in spreading joy around them and can take delight in the satisfaction of others so far as it is their own work' (*G* 4: 398) to mean that they have no further motive of self-interest beyond the pleasure that they expect from spreading joy in others. Although this reading of 'without any further motive' is possible, I do not find it ultimately persuasive. The friend of humanity has an immediate inclination toward beneficence; that is to say that he has an immediate desire to do well for others. I find it more natural to read Kant's remark that he finds inner satisfaction in spreading joy 'without any other motive of vanity or self-interest' as ruling out *all* motives of self-interest. Compare here the description of the 'friend of humanity' in the *Doctrine of Virtue* as 'someone who finds satisfaction in the well-being (*salus*) of human beings considered simply as human beings for whom it is well when things go well for every other' (*MdS* 6: 450). These are people who take pleasure in spreading happiness and sparing others pain—that is, they have an immediate desire to make others happy. Their motive is their (amiable) concern that things go

well for others. Kant says that natural sympathy is 'one of the impulses that nature has implanted in us to do what the representation of duty alone might not accomplish' (*MdS* 6: 457). Since this motive attaches us to the same end as the duty of beneficence, there is no reason to think that it is either self-interested or hedonistic; the difference between natural sympathy and dutiful beneficence lies elsewhere. (For further discussion, see Christine Korsgaard, *Creating the Kingdom of Ends*, 56–8, and 'From Duty and for the Sake of the Noble: Kant and Aristotle on Morally Good Action', 206–10.) One should accept Kerstein's reading of 'no other motive'—as meaning no further motive of self-interest beyond the pleasure that they expect from spreading joy in others—only if one already has grounds for thinking that the expectation of one's own pleasure is a motive in all action from inclination. But the example of natural sympathy seems to be a clear counter-example to this general claim. (Or perhaps I should say: I regard Kant's discussions of natural sympathy in both the *Groundwork* and the *Doctrine of Virtue* as clear evidence that Kant did not believe that the expectation of one's own pleasure is a motive in all action from inclination.)

I agree with Kerstein that inclination-based interests in an object are conditional on the agent finding the object 'agreeable' or expecting satisfaction from it. He points to the footnote at *G* 4: 413 n. where Kant says that in acting from inclination ('from a pathological interest in the object of an action'), the object interests me 'insofar as it is agreeable to me'. Kant means to say, it seems, that should one no longer find the object agreeable (or what amounts to the same thing, should one lose one's desire for the object), one would lose one's interest in it. The friend of humanity's interest in the well-being of others, though immediate, is indeed conditional on his finding satisfaction in the well-being of others, or on his 'sensible feelings of pleasure or displeasure . . . at another's state of joy or pain . . .' (*MdS* 6: 456). But I don't think that this means that his own pleasure is either his aim or one of his motives. Rather, the references to the agent's feelings of satisfaction indicate the way in which he comes to take an interest in the well-being of others, or the basis of his concern. This agent comes to care about the well-being of others through feeling satisfaction in their well-being, or as one might also put it, because he desires to spread happiness and relieve suffering. Interests based in this way on an agent's receptivities are conditional on an agent's subjective responses. But they are nonetheless immediate interests in the well-being of others. In general, finding an end agreeable is (or can be) a way of coming to have an interest in that end for its own sake, where the interest is conditional on one being affected in a certain way by (having certain feelings in response to) that end.

18. Some people find evidence for the hedonistic interpretation in a passage where Kant says that the naturally sympathetic person acts out of a 'need' or 'want' (*Bedurfnis*). Here Kant argues that the duty to help others cannot have an empirical basis because 'one would have to presuppose that we find not only a natural satisfaction in the well-being of others but also a need, such as a sympathetic sensibility brings with it in human beings' (*KpV* 5: 34). This need can be understood as an exceptional sensitivity that leads the individual to feel pain at the thought of others suffering. But again, the point is that this trait creates a responsiveness in her to the welfare of others, and leads her to act on their behalf. By itself, the reference to an affective disposition of this kind does not imply that its object, or the agent's motive, must be her own feelings of satisfaction.

19. See n. 9 above.

20. *KpV* 5: 26, 58 ff., 62.
21. Cf. also *G* 4: 413 ff., and *KpV* 59 ff. This conception of choice eventually leads to the view that rational conduct is always motivated by reasons which can be cited to justify one's actions to others. That actions occur in this way is a part of their being free. These aspects of Kant's conception of rational choice are discussed in greater detail in Section IV of Chapter 1 and in Section IV of Chapter 3.
22. Cf. *G* 4: 412. General principles must be introduced to account for the generality pre-supposed by reasons and judgments of value. For a consideration to be a reason for an agent under certain circumstances (construed broadly to include desires that an agent may have), it must be possible for it to serve as a reason for other agents in those circumstances; moreover, it must be possible for others not in those circumstances to understand why it is a reason for someone in those circumstances. For this to be so, reasons must be derived from general principles that provide standards for how any-one ought to act in such circumstances (including standards whose applicability depends on an agent's having certain desires). In this way, general principles determine what substantive considerations count as reasons, or make an action good. (This is ambiguous: objectively valid principles determine what considerations are actually reasons, while those that agents accept determine what they take to be reasons. But the formal relationships are the same in each case.)
23. For discussion see Rawls, *A Theory of Justice*, 358–72, 480–91. Cf. also Williams, 'Internal and External Reasons', in *Moral Luck*.
24. *G* 4: 399, 418–19.
25. For discussion of the problem of the 'best specification' of an end desired under a vague description, see David Wiggins, 'Deliberation and Practical Reason', in *Needs, Values, Truth*, 219 ff., 225 ff.
26. Note that it is not even correct to say that you are motivated by the desire that is strongest after deliberation. Even the recognition that a future experience will be frus-trating need not lead you to 'feel' the motivation to avoid it in the present. Even after you resolve to leave on Friday, you may still have no desire to do so. On a Kantian view, it is not the felt strength of a desire that motivates, but a judgment about its strength.
27. The Categorical Imperative is a 'formal principle' for Kant because it gives sufficient and overriding reasons for choice simply in virtue of expressing the form of a practical law. I presume that particular (i.e., substantive) categorical imperatives are 'formal' in the same sense because they are reason-giving in virtue of having the form of law. The principle of happiness is not a formal principle in this technical sense. My point here, as I think the rest of this paragraph makes clear, is that both the moral law and the principle of happiness are principles that represent the form, or formal structure, of different kinds of choice.
28. Kant's inclusion of moral sense theories under the principle of happiness deserves comment, and may indicate that Kant viewed the principle of happiness in a more narrowly egoistic vein than he should have. Kant apparently interprets moral sense theories (rightly or wrongly) as positing a natural desire or feeling which provides both the standard of moral judgment and a direct motivation toward moral conduct, and which leads an agent to experience satisfaction at the contemplation of good conduct. Kant's reason for including the motive posited by such a theory under the principle of happiness is that it is an empirically given desire, the existence of which leads

'consciousness of virtue [to be] immediately associated with satisfaction and pleasure, and consciousness of vice with mental unease and pain, so that everything is still reduced to the desire for one's own happiness' (*KpV* 5: 38). In addition, as with any other empirically given desire, acting on this motive can contribute to an agent's happiness, in virtue of the existence of this motive. Thus Kant says that he counts 'the principle of moral feeling under that of happiness, because every empirical interest promises to contribute to our well-being by the agreeableness that something affords, whether this happens immediately and without a view to advantage or with regard to it' (*G* 4: 442 n.). Kant is correct to say that such a theory places moral motivation under the principle of happiness, given the interpretation of that principle developed here. It makes the moral motive a natural desire, and expected satisfaction serves as the criterion by which one determines the value of such actions. Furthermore, it would seem that when this desire is in competition with others, one would choose between alternative actions by ranking amounts of expected satisfaction. However, this move on Kant's part is innocuous enough. The arguments of the previous sections of this essay show that these facts are not sufficient to make action so motivated either hedonistic or egoistic, and there is no indication that Kant takes the moral sense theorist to be holding that the pleasure resulting from the operation of the moral sense is the aim of moral conduct. Thus one may blunt the force of including moral sense theories under the principle of happiness by showing that the latter is broader in intent than one might initially suppose. (Indeed in the passage from the *Groundwork*, that the satisfaction of an empirical interest can contribute to the agent's well-being 'immediately and without a view to advantage' shows that Kant does not construe the moral sense as a self-interested motive, and does not identify acting from the principle of happiness with self-interested conduct.)

29. Cf. *KpV* 5: 23 (quoted in Section III above).
30. The currency metaphor is explicit in the text. Cf. *KpV* 5: 23.
31. Cf. *A Theory of Justice*, 486–91. Rawls argues that what has tended to motivate the adoption of various forms of ethical and psychological hedonism is the desire to 'carry through the dominant end conception of deliberation' so as to show how a rational choice among desirable alternatives is always possible. As he says, 'the thesis that the pursuit of pleasure provides the only rational method of deliberation seems to be the fundamental idea of hedonism' (p. 488). For his critique of the common currency assumption see pp. 488–90. See also Williams, 'Conflicts of Values', in *Moral Luck*, 76–9.
32. A broader notion of happiness leads to a richer understanding of the contrast between morality and happiness, and an overly narrow interpretation of the principle of happiness may lead one to misconstrue certain features of Kant's moral conception. Since the principle of happiness is neither hedonistic or egoistic, it is a mistake to think that Kant's theory takes self-interest to be the polar opposite of moral conduct; this contrast is much more complex. Not all conduct that treats people improperly is self-interested; certain forms of paternalism or conduct motivated by flawed ideals show that actions can harm, offend, or show disrespect without being selfish. Similarly, if one accepts the idea of duties to oneself, not all moral conduct is other-regarding.
33. Though I have not argued the point here, I take similar things to be true of the moral law. Roughly, moral evaluation proceeds by applying a set of substantive considerations

or principles to actions and intentions (e.g. considerations of fairness and equal treatment, whether actions involve advantage-taking or manipulation, various forms of respect and concern for the interests of others, etc.). The moral law states the underlying form of such reasoning by expressing the form of a practical law, or of an unconditional requirement on action. That is, it states the criteria of necessity and universality that a principle must have to be a practical law.

34. This would be an example of a view in which particular reasons are regarded as applications of more general reasons and principles which provide their normative force. For a critique of theories that impose this structure on ethical reasons, see Williams, *Ethics and the Limits of Philosophy*, 111–19, especially 116–17.

35. See n. 5 above.

36. I would like to thank several people for comments and helpful discussion at various stages of writing this chapter: John Connolly, Stephen Engstrom, Jay Garfield, Murray Kiteley, Sally Sedgwick, and Thomas Wartenberg. A version of this essay was presented to the Department of Philosophy at North Carolina State University, and I am grateful for their response. In addition, I am particularly indebted to Christine Korsgaard, for written comments that led to changes in Section II; and to Barbara Herman, whose editorial comments prompted me to reconceive some of the aims of the essay, as well as to make extensive revisions in Sections III–V.

37. Added in 2005.

38. Barbara Herman argues for this interpretation in 'Rethinking Kant's Hedonism'. She suggests that Kant accepted a sophisticated form of hedonism that is worth taking seriously and that his larger aim is to show that absent the objective value grounded in morality, 'hedonism is the true theory of motivation and choice' (p. 130). I believe that I can accept many of her claims in this essay.

39. See Barbara Herman, 'Rethinking Kant's Hedonism', p. 132, and Samuel Kerstein, *Kant's Search for the Supreme Principle of Morality*, pp. 28–9.

40. Cf. *KU* 5: 207: 'Now that my judgment about an object by which I declare it agreeable expresses an interest in it is already clear from the fact that through sensation it excites a desire for objects of the same sort, hence the satisfaction presupposes not the mere judgment about it but the relation of its existence to my state insofar as it is affected by such an object. Hence one says of the agreeable not merely that it pleases but that it gratifies. It is not mere approval that I give it, rather inclination is thereby aroused . . .'.

41. Kant also identifies satisfaction taken in the thought of an object and interest when he discusses interest in what is good. See *KU* 5: 207, 209: Both what is good in itself and what is good as a means 'involve the concept of an end, hence the relation of reason to (at least) possible willing, and consequently a satisfaction in the existence of an object or of an action, i.e., some sort of interest'. 'But to will something and to have satisfaction in its existence, i.e., to take an interest in it, are identical.'

3

The Categorical Imperative and Kant's Conception of Practical Rationality

I. INTRODUCTION

The primary concern of this essay is to outline an explanation of how Kant grounds morality in reason. We all know that Kant thought that morality comprises a set of demands that are unconditionally and universally valid (valid for all rational beings). In addition, he thought that to support this understanding of moral principles, one must show that they originate in reason a priori, rather than in contingent facts about human psychology, or the circumstances of human life.[1] But it is difficult to articulate exactly how Kant tries to establish that moral principles originate in reason. In at least two passages in the second section of the *Groundwork*, Kant insists upon the importance of grounding the moral law in practical reason a priori, and subsequently states a conception of practical reason from which he appears to extract a formulation of the Categorical Imperative.[2] The reasoning employed in these passages is of central importance to the overall argument of the *Groundwork*, but in each case the route traveled from the definition of practical reason to the ensuing formulation of the moral law is obscure. My goal is to work out a plausible reconstruction of this portion of Kant's argument. At the very least, I hope that my interpretation will illuminate the distinctive structure of Kant's approach to questions of justification in ethics. What I understand of Kant's view leads me to believe that its aims and overall shape are different in important respects from what is often assumed. It also represents an approach to foundational issues in ethics that provides an alternative to many contemporary attempts to ground morality in reason.

I will be limiting myself to a small part of this very large question. Theories of this sort, Kant's included, tend to address two separate questions of justification. The first is that of justifying one substantive moral conception as opposed to another. This is primarily a concern with *content*: which moral principles should we adopt, given the fact that we are going to adopt some? The second is that of giving some account of why moral reasons make legitimate claims on agents, or why we should adhere to them (whatever they may involve). This is a concern with the reasons that one has for acting morally, or with the justification of the moral life. In part this is a question of identifying, or producing, the motivation for adhering to moral principles, but I shall refer to it as a concern with their *authority*. I will be examining Kant's approach to the first issue—how he derives the outline of a substantive moral conception from a concept of practical reason.[3] Here I shall be particularly concerned to identify the conception of practical rationality that Kant draws on, and to explain how it functions in his derivation of morality.

Contemporary attempts to derive morality from reason often seek an independent foundation for morality in a more basic conception of rationality. As David Wiggins has put it, such a theory supposes that one can 'construct an a priori theory of rationality or prudence such that . . . rationality is definable both independently of morality and ideals of agency and in such a way as to have independent leverage in these ancient disputes'.[4] In other words, it seeks a comprehensive and morally neutral definition of practical rationality that is universally valid, from which a set of moral principles can be derived. In this way, one would have provided a justification for a set of moral principles, and shown that adherence to them is a basic requirement of rationality on conduct, which has authority for any agent regardless of professed desires and motives.

It is often assumed that Kant's theory fits this pattern, by attempting to provide a foundation for morality that is morally neutral, and thus, in Bernard Williams's phrase, to construct morality 'from the ground up'.[5] I will argue that this is not the case. While the conception of practical rationality that Kant assumes is a priori and has a claim to universal validity, it is not empty of substantive ideals. Indeed a distinguishing feature of a Kantian view is that it does not attempt to derive morality from a morally neutral starting point. Its general structure is that it ties the content of a moral conception to a more general set of ideals—of the person, of agency, or of rationality—which, while applying widely, and providing some kind of independent perspective on morality, need not be empty of moral content. The authority of the moral conception for us is established by the fundamental character of these ideals and the reasonableness of applying them to ourselves, and the motivation to act from it comes ultimately from an understanding of the ideals in question, and of how they are expressed in the actions which it singles out.

If this is the case, Kant's account is not aimed at showing that bad conduct is irrational, or inconsistent with principles to which one is committed qua rational, as that is often understood, where the sense of irrationality is explained solely in terms of prudential or instrumental rationality plus logical consistency. More generally, Kant clearly did not think that any form of instrumental rationality (rationality as the effective pursuit of one's ends, or as consistency among desires, beliefs, and actions) is sufficient by itself to yield a moral conception. For it is fundamental to his moral view that we recognize different forms of practical reasoning, that moral evaluation is distinct from prudential and involves a set of concerns not reducible to something more primitive.[6] The Hypothetical

Imperative and the Categorical Imperative, which represent empirically practical reason and pure practical reason, are different kinds of normative standards and patterns of evaluation. It is a major aim of the *Critique of Practical Reason* to show that the 'empirically conditioned use of reason' does not exhaust the use of reason in the practical sphere, and that there is such a thing as pure practical reason (*KpV* 5: 15).

We may distinguish these two forms of practical reason provisionally as follows. The Hypothetical Imperative is the principle underlying the empirically conditioned use of reason. It states that if one wills an end, then one ought to will the means needed to achieve it in so far as they are in one's power (or else give up the end). It assesses the rationality of actions relative to the ends which one desires or has adopted, and thus yields specific judgments about what an individual ought to do only in conjunction with information about her ends.[7] What makes this use of reason 'empirically conditioned' is that it assesses actions relative to given desires or ends, and yields judgments whose application is conditional on one's desires or ends. The Hypothetical Imperative is often thought to apply primarily to the pursuit of one's own happiness, but in fact it applies to the pursuit of any end that an agent can adopt, including moral ends. In contrast, pure practical reason will address questions of evaluation that are beyond the scope of empirical practical reason. It will introduce standards for evaluating actions and ends that are non-instrumental, and apply independently of given desires and ends— principles which ground judgments of intrinsic goodness or acceptability to anyone, which for Kant are the basis of justification to others. There are grounds for thinking, in addition, that pure practical reason will be concerned with the evaluation and choice of ends for their own sake (in contrast to the choice of actions as means to ends). This will include the capacity to elect aims and goals viewed as intrinsically good or worthy of choice, which can initiate actions and structure larger practical pursuits.[8]

Any account of how Kant derives the content of the moral law from reason must be consistent with the existence of these distinct forms of rationality. But then the question arises of how a derivation of the moral law from reason can actually be carried out. The moral law cannot be derived from any notion of empirical practical reason, and a derivation from pure practical reason would seem to lack independent force, since it already contains the concerns essential to morality. In a sense this is right. On the interpretation that I develop, something like moral ideals are embedded in the conception of choice and the ordinary use of practical reason from the start. But the way to explain Kant's view is to show how moral choice builds on features present in any form of choice, and thus to trace morality to features of practical rationality found in all forms of conduct. The fact that moral rationality cannot be derived from a more primitive (non-moral) basis need not imply that it is not found in less developed forms.

The key here is that Kant thought that *both* forms of reasoning inform *all* rational choice, including choice of actions that we might not think of as morally motivated. Even in the pursuit of purely personal ends, the rational agent is not concerned solely to make her actions rational relative to her desires. She will also view at least some of her ends as good in themselves, and as providing reasons for her actions whose justifying force extends to the point of view of others. Thus the concern with justifying reasons and with the goodness of ends that define pure practical reason are found, in some form, in all choice; indeed, they comprise the essential element in choice.

If moral reasoning represents a distinct form of rationality found in all forms of choice, then Kant's derivation of the moral law from reason should be understood along the following lines: moral choice represents the most complete realization of an ideal of rationality found in all forms of choice. All choice meets certain conditions, which, in moral choice, are extended to their limit, or completed—so that the conditions that define moral choice are built into the ordinary notion of rational choice.

To explain: we think of choice as guided by reasons, or normative considerations that the agent takes to provide some justification for an action. The reasons that guide agents' choices lead them to view their actions as good in some respect (and this is the source of their motivating force). They also have normative force from the point of view of others. They may be cited to explain or justify an action to others; and even if such explanations do not get others to accept or approve, they may provide a partial justification by enabling others to see why the agent took the action to be a good thing to do. In addition, Kant assumes, not implausibly, that as rational agents we take some of our reasons to be final or ultimate. The particular reasons for action that we may cite are in turn supported by more general reasons or principles which give the particular reasons their normative force. Thus it would appear to be a structural feature of practical reason that some reasons function as final or ultimate reasons: they are viewed (by an agent) as good per se, and as conferring support on more specific concerns from which we act. What different agents take to provide final reasons may be quite varied. They could include specific ends or activities, such as a successful career, a personal relationship, or involvement in a social cause; or more general aims such as happiness, or leading an honorable life. They might also be values such as honesty, fairness, or protecting one's own interests. Furthermore, an agent's final reasons may be more or less admirable. Some, properly cited, may be sufficient to get others to accept or approve of the resulting actions; others may fall short of this, rendering an action intelligible without fully justifying it.

This characterization of rational choice allows us to see the way in which moral choice might be viewed as the most complete realization of an ideal of practical rationality found in all forms of choice. Morally good choices are those that are fully justified in that the agent acts from reasons that are final and universally valid. What happens in moral choice is that the normative force characteristic of any reason has been extended along certain dimensions, as it were. In particular the justifying force that they have for the agent is universal and extends to the point of view of any agent—so that it is sufficient to lead anyone to accept the action as good. In short, all rational choice is guided by normative considerations (reasons with normative force for the agent). In moral choice, the reasons from which the agent acts are in fact sufficient to justify the action to anyone.

I will now argue that such a view underlies Kant's derivation of the Categorical Imperative, and offers the best understanding of the connection that he draws between moral principles and the nature of practical reason. To do so I will offer a reconstruction of the derivation of the Formula of Universal Law in the first two sections of the *Groundwork*. Section II provides an overview of the argument of *Groundwork*, I, which explains how Kant thinks that the concept of morality implicit in ordinary thought leads to the FUL. Sections III through V explain, respectively, what leads Kant to undertake another derivation of the FUL in *Groundwork*, II—this time one that traces it to the nature of practical reason; his conception of practical reason; and how it is most fully expressed by the Categorical Imperative.

II. THE AIMS OF *GROUNDWORK*, I

The *Groundwork* offers a foundational account of a concept of morality that Kant takes to be well established in ordinary thought and practice; indeed he takes it to be *the* concept of morality. His concern is to provide an account that preserves and grounds its essential features. The aim of the First Section is to articulate the defining features of this concept of morality through an examination of ordinary moral consciousness—specifically, through a set of examples that brings out common beliefs about the special value of a good will and through an analysis of our concept of a 'duty'. Kant's theses about moral worth—that an action has moral worth when done from the motive of duty, and that its moral worth is determined by its underlying principle, rather than its results or intended consequences—have tended to dominate discussion of the First Section. But while they are important Kantian doctrines, they should be viewed as intermediate conclusions on the way to the larger objective of formulating the Categorical Imperative. Kant uses his discussion of when an action displays a good will (has moral worth) to get at the principle of right conduct that a good will uses in assessing possible maxims of action and deciding how to act.[9]

Kant's examination of ordinary moral consciousness in *Groundwork*, I produces two principal results. First, it reveals the special authority that (it is part of our concept of morality that) moral reasons and value have in practical deliberation. In more general terms, it reveals the formal features of moral reasons that define our concept of morality—the necessity and universality with which they are thought to apply. Second, from this concept of morality Kant derives the moral principle implicit in ordinary thought. He attempts to move from the formal features of moral reasons to the principle that allows us to determine what moral reasons there are in a given situation. This principle will turn out to be a representation of the general form of reasoning implicit in actual instances of moral deliberation.[10] The movement of the argument here is from form toward content, or more accurately, from formal considerations to a principle that, with suitable input, may be used to construct a substantive moral conception. Argumentation of this sort is characteristic of Kant's moral theory, and this same move is repeated in *Groundwork*, II. Here Kant argues that the very concept of a categorical imperative provides the only principle that can be a categorical imperative. An imperative that commands categorically (whatever its content) specifies an action as unconditionally and absolutely good, and thus applies with the necessity of a practical law.[11] Kant thinks that these concepts lead to the FUL, as a principle that expresses the concept of a practical law, or states the form of an unconditional requirement on action. Ultimately Kant will argue that the '*form* of *volition* as such' yields a principle by which one may guide one's particular volitions and choices (cf. *G* 4: 444). Here we see an important aspect of his claim that morality must rest on the principle of autonomy: the very nature of the will yields the basic principle from which moral standards are derived.

In the text, the notion of respect for the moral law provides the bridge between the claims about moral worth and the statement of the moral law, by focusing our attention on the overriding authority that moral concerns have in practical thought.[12] Kant's examples have shown that the agent who exhibits the exemplary moral attitude that we recognize as a good will is motivated simply by the recognition that his action is right—that is, by respect for the moral law. Respect is a response to a kind of intrinsic value or source of reasons that is not mediated by an agent's desires. But more importantly, it is the recognition of a value that limits the force of and overrides other forms of value—'an estimation of a worth that far outweighs any worth that is recommended by inclination' (*G* 4: 403; cf. 401 n.). The moral law, as the object of respect, 'outweighs [inclination] or at least excludes it altogether from calculations in making a choice' (*G* 4: 400). To show respect for the moral law is to give the reasons that it yields an absolute weight in practical deliberation. In this way, the attitude of respect for the law shows us that we take moral reasons to apply with *necessity* (do not presuppose any particular desires or contingent interests on the part of the agent) and to have *deliberative priority* over other kinds of reasons (limit the force of and are overriding relative to the reasons given by an agent's desires). Their application must also be *universally valid*, since it is independent of contingent features of the self and motives that an agent could lack.[13] They represent reasons that would hold for anyone in the relevant situation, and reasons that anyone can recognize as valid and authoritative. Necessity, deliberative priority, and universal validity are formal features in that they can be attributed to moral reasons without specifying the particular actions which such reasons pick out, and they may be taken as definitive of morality.[14] It is part of our concept of morality that, whatever moral reasons there are, they apply to us in this way.

Otherwise put, reflection on the attitude of respect shows that we take moral principles and reasons to have the status of *law*. As the recognition of an order of value that limits the normative force of other forms of value, respect is the proper attitude towards a law as such. Thus it shows that the idea of a practical law is central to our concept of morality. Here it is important to note that a practical law is not just a principle which makes claims about how anyone should act in a kind of situation, or one whose validity anyone can recognize—that is, one which is universal in form. A practical law, in addition, provides reasons of special weight. Its application to an agent's circumstances yields determinate reasons for acting that apply with necessity; they take priority over and limit the influence of other kinds of reasons.[15] By noting how the conditions of necessity and universality function together, we can see that a practical law also grounds a kind of justification that will be equally central to our concept of morality. The absolute weight that moral reasons possess must itself be one of the features that applies universally. Thus, the application of a practical law yields reasons for acting that *anyone* can recognize as having *deliberative priority* in that situation. That would seem to be the strongest kind of reason that there is, and one that justifies completely.

This suggests a way of understanding Kant's final move to the statement of the FUL in *Groundwork*, I. When moved by respect for the law, one is concerned with the 'conformity of [one's] actions to universal law as such' (*G* 4: 402). That is, one wants one's action to be supported by reasons that are necessary and universally valid (unconditionally valid), and thus sufficient to justify the action fully to anyone. The following would seem to be a principle that expresses the practical implications of these concepts, and as such a candidate for the 'supreme principle of morality':

> P: Let your reasons for performing an action at the same time suffice to justify your action fully to anyone no matter how situated (give anyone reason to accept what you do).

It is a plausible expression of the requirement that the agent's maxim have the 'form of a practical law' (meet the formal criteria of necessity and universality implied by the concept of a practical law), and one who acts from this principle would be realizing the ideals central to the concept of morality. The principle that Kant in fact states is:

> FUL: Act only on a maxim that you can also will to hold as a universal law.

Thus, Kant must take the idea of acting from maxims that you could act on while willing that everyone act on them to be equivalent to, or to express, the idea of acting from reasons that are necessary and universally valid. The argument needs supplementation to see why the idea of necessity and universal validity gets cashed out in terms of universalizability. If these principles are equivalent, it is because the FUL provides a procedure for determining whether one's reasons are unconditionally valid. As I interpret it, the key idea is that of reasons sufficient to justify one's action fully to anyone. Since this ideal is quite abstract, we need a way to determine when a maxim satisfies it. This must be the intent of the FUL: asking whether your maxim is one you can at the same time will as a universal law should be construed as the way of determining whether you are acting from reasons that anyone can accept.

III. WHY MORAL PRINCIPLES MUST ORIGINATE IN REASON

Early in *Groundwork*, II Kant stresses at several points that moral principles must originate in reason a priori, and at least two of these passages prepare for another derivation of the FUL.[16] It is evident that Kant now seeks a deeper grounding for the concept of morality articulated thus far, by connecting it directly with the nature of practical reason. Why? His primary motivation must be that a grounding of this sort is needed to explain and to preserve the necessity and universality which have emerged as definitive of moral reasons in ordinary thought. If substantive moral reasons do have the unconditional validity that we take them to have, they must come from a principle that originates in reason a priori, since only reason yields principles that apply in this way. A theory that seeks the origin of moral principles elsewhere, such as an empiricist theory, cannot account for their standing as practical laws. Thus, Kant's insistence on the importance of deriving moral principles from reason is in part a rejection of alternative accounts as inadequate, in being unable to ground what he has identified as the features essential to our concept of morality.

To get clear about the problem that Kant is addressing, we might note that the First Section of the *Groundwork* simply assumes the ordinary concept of morality, and that Kant thinks that mere clarification of what this concept implies leaves open the possibility that it involves a kind of delusion, or is an empty idea.[17] Perhaps the considerations that we recognize as moral do not really have the authority that we accord them. We may take certain substantive principles such as truth-telling, refraining from manipulation and coercion of others, helping others, and so on, when properly applied, to yield unconditional reasons for acting. But our taking them in this way may reflect nothing more than a process of social conditioning for which no further justification can be given. Or the validity of these principles may depend on desires and interests that one could lack, so that an agent without them could claim exemption from the principle. Perhaps there are no unconditional reasons for acting, and the concept of morality, defined as the set of such reasons (or the set of practical laws), while perfectly coherent, is empty and contains nothing. At issue here for Kant is whether there is such a thing as 'morality' in the sense of that term implicit in ordinary practice. If morality is what it claims to be, it consists of practical laws; but principles with the character of law must originate in reason.

Kant's account is not directed toward individuals who claim that the authority of moral concerns is illusory, but rather toward those whose understanding of morality threatens to make it an illusion, or to undermine its central features.[18] These include both agents whose moral practice implicitly fails to acknowledge that moral principles have the status of law, and theorists whose account of morality is unable to explain how moral conclusions can have this status. Regarding the first, one of the major obstacles to good conduct in Kant's eyes is not the explicit denial of moral claims, but the tendency to exempt oneself from moral requirements through various forms of rationalization.[19] We often weaken principles we otherwise accept by making exceptions for ourselves, or by interpreting them so as not to apply to the situation in which one is acting. This is to act as though the claims of self-interest are on a par with, or even limit, moral claims, and is equivalent in practice to denying that moral requirements have the status of law. What is needed to counter this tendency is an unambiguous recognition of the authority of moral claims and a story that explains where it comes from. In this respect, moral theory plays a particular practical role for Kant: a proper understanding of the nature and status of moral claims is integral to producing the moral disposition.

Second, Kant's insistence on deriving morality from reason is a rejection of influential empiricist theories that ground moral obligation in empirical facts about human beings, including both psychological facts and facts about the needs of human society and the structure of social interaction. The empiricist may assume some principles of prudential rationality; but he will avoid a priori principles or normative standards whose motivation cannot be supplied by desires and behavioral tendencies that people are generally observed to have. Kant's general criticism is that by deriving moral principles from empirically given desires, such theories are unable to ground the notion of a practical law. If the validity of a principle depends on the presence of a desire or interest that one may lack, then there may be agents without that motive, to whom the principle would not apply. Such an agent could only be subject to criticism for lacking the motive presupposed by the principle. But that is to depart from the empiricist viewpoint, by introducing an a priori normative standard to which an individual's desires and motives ought to conform.

Kant wishes to provide an understanding of moral requirements that supports their unconditional validity, and his alternative to empiricism is to derive the moral law from a conception of practical reason that is given a priori. Since Kant is concerned with both content and validity, he must first give a characterization of rational agency that yields this principle and, in addition, guides its application.[20] The best way to understand the connection is to say that the principle as stated expresses the conception of rational agency. This is to say that it is a principle of choice that an agent defined by that conception of rational agency would choose as his fundamental maxim, in which his practical rationality is most fully realized. Second, Kant must establish the authority of the principle for us by showing that we are rational beings in the required sense, or have reason to view ourselves in that way.[21] Though this involves a separate and further step, which is not without its complications, it must to some extent depend on how the first step is carried out. Much of the issue of validity hinges on showing that the principle does express the conception of rational agency, or is the appropriate principle for a being with this nature to act on.

IV. KANT'S CONCEPTION OF PRACTICAL RATIONALITY

At the core of Kant's conception of rational agency is the idea that rational action is guided by considerations that the agent takes to provide justifications for acting in a certain way. We find this view in the following well known and very important passage:

Everything in nature works in accordance with laws. Only a rational being has the power to act *in accordance with the representation* of laws, that is, in accordance with principles, or has a will [*Wille*]. Since *reason* is required for the derivation of actions from laws, the will is nothing other than practical reason . . . the will is a capacity to choose *only that* which reason independently of inclination cognizes as practically necessary, that is, as good. (*G* 4: 412)

The features of rationality cited are quite general, in that in addition to action, they apply to the formation of belief, the carrying out of a proof, and so on. Rational agency is defined here as the capacity to guide one's actions by normative standards that are generally applicable, such that one's understanding, acceptance, and application of these standards to one's circumstances of action figure in the origination of actions. This section will take up the most significant assertions made in the passage, which amount to an ideal of practical rationality. (1) First, it makes claims about the way in which rational conduct originates in the conscious activity of the agent. (2) In addition, it proposes a distinctive view about the nature of practical reasoning and the structure of justification, in which general normative principles play a central role. (3) What emerges is that for Kant, practical reason is in the business of evaluation and justification, and that its essential role is to produce judgments about the goodness of actions. Rational conduct is motivated by the recognition of an action as good in some respect, where the goodness of the action consists in the fact that it follows from a general normative principle, or is justified by reasons whose force can be recognized by others. This will be a property of anything we can recognize as a choice.

First, regarding the origin of actions, Thomas Nagel interprets the passage as pointing out that rational action requires a certain form of explanation. He writes: 'Kant observed that rational motivation is unique among systems of causation because any explanation of action in terms of the theory refers essentially to the application of its principles by individuals to themselves in the determination of their actions'.[22]

An agent's understanding of principles and reasons, and the resulting evaluative judgments, are the determining features of the causal process by which an action originates, and this must be reflected in any appropriate explanation of why the action occurred.[23]

To see how Kant understands the structure of practical reasoning, we should unpack his remarks that rational agency involves the ability to act 'in accordance with the representation of laws, that is, in accordance with principles'. Kant is viewing practical rationality as the capacity to act from 'objective practical principles'.[24] These are normative principles, general in form, which state how an agent ought to act in a specified kind of situation.[25] As normative, they correct against distortions in one's judgment about how to act that come from inclinations, or other subjective factors such as lack of information, limited foresight, and so on. Their objectivity consists in the fact that they yield results valid for anyone, and this will have two sides. When properly applied to a situation, they will yield a conclusion about action that will have motivating force for anyone in that situation. In addition, the force that these conclusions have for the agent (in the relevant situation) can be understood by anyone, including by agents not in the relevant situation, for whom they are not reasons to act.[26] It is import-ant to note that under objective practical principles Kant includes both principles that are conditionally valid as well as those that are unconditionally valid—in other words hypothetical as well as categorical imperatives.[27] A principle may make claims about how one ought to act given the fact that one desires certain ends. It would be objective because it states how anyone with certain desires has (some kind of) reason to act in the kind of situation covered. Properly applied, it will yield conclusions about action that have force for anyone in that situation with the relevant desires; and the force of these conclusions can be understood by anyone, including those for whom they are not reasons to act (because they are not in that situation, because they lack or perhaps disapprove of the assumed desires, and so on). In short, an objective practical principle translates facts about one's situation and one's ends and desires into conclusions about how to act whose force can be understood by anyone.

By conceiving of practical reason, or will, as the ability to derive actions from principles, Kant suggests a model in which one arrives at a maxim or course of action by determining whether it is the correct instantiation of a normative principle judged to cover the situation in question. Deliberation proceeds by finding a principle covering the circumstances, and then determining what it requires in that situation. This process is open-ended in that the more general principles themselves may be evaluated by the same pattern of reasoning until one reaches an ultimate principle, which neither needs nor is susceptible to further evaluation. Though somewhat awkward as a picture of decision-making, this conception does establish a plausible pattern for evaluating proposed actions: an intention already formulated can be assessed by seeing if it is the correct application of a general principle with justifying force for that kind of situation. Moreover, this is the pattern of reasoning that an agent might engage in when explaining why he did a certain action (either to others, or to himself viewing his action from a detached perspective).[28]

There are several points to note here. The first is that this conception locates choice within a thoroughly normative context, since it conceives of choice as motivated by what the agent takes to be a reason for acting. In this regard, practical reasoning should not be reduced to a kind of calculation or deduction (as might be suggested by one reading of 'deriving actions from principles'). It does not simply select actions by deducing them from habitually followed rules, but is rather the ability to choose an action by seeing that it instantiates a normative principle taken to have justifying force. Practical reason evaluates according to normative principles. Second, since this pattern of reasoning may be carried out at higher and higher levels, the structure of practical reasoning leaves room for and creates a push toward ultimate principles that are a source of final reasons. This provides one ground for reading into the text the assumption that rational conduct is guided by some high level principles or ends. A rational agent will have a set of priorities and final ends that provide reasons for action in specific situations, as well as setting limits on the actions there are reasons to perform.

Third, because of their objectivity, the principles that figure in practical reasoning can ground justifications to others; indeed that is the primary impetus of objectivity in the practical sphere. To provide a justification for an action is just to support it with reasons whose force extends beyond the point of view of the agent for whom they are reasons to act. This one does by connecting an action (or maxim) with a general principle stating how anyone ought to act in a certain kind of situation. This provides support for the action that may potentially lead others to accept it (or may lead the agent to accept his own action when viewing it impartially, or from a later point in time). Kant expresses this by saying that objective practical principles issue in judgments of goodness of one sort or another (conditional or unconditional). To call an action or an end good in some respect is just to support it with reasons whose force can be understood by anyone—in other words to provide a justification, by bringing it under an appropriate principle. The goodness of a particular action is a function of the objectivity of the grounding normative principles.[29]

Fourth, these points make it plain that one pattern of reasoning serves the dual role of guiding decision and of justifying to others. It is distinctive of the Kantian view of practical rationality that there is a deep connection between motivation and justification: the same considerations by which an agent is motivated also provide some justification of the action to others. The rationality of choice lies in the fact that it is motivated by considerations with justifying force that can be understood by anyone. In this respect it is built into the concept of a rational choice that it proceeds from the recognition of justifying reasons that can be stated in general form, or from judgments of goodness, and that these supply its motivation. It is in this sense that practical reason, as conceived by Kant, is essentially in the business of evaluation and justification.

To make this discussion less schematic and abstract, it may help to give some examples of principles from which an agent might act which might figure in practical reasoning. Such principles might be formal, such as Kant's Hypothetical Imperative, or the standard principles of rational choice. But of greater interest are agents' substantive principles, which they take to state good ways of acting (to be objectively valid). These are principles accepted by an agent which are sources of reasons for the agent in particular situations, and which they might cite to others to justify their actions. Here some categories are needed, though their boundaries must remain approximate and inexact. One might first distinguish principles taken to represent objective, desire-independent values, for example:

(a) One should always be truthful, except when dishonesty is needed to resist manipulation, or to prevent harm to another.
(b) When someone on the street asks you for money, give what you can if they appear truly destitute, but not otherwise.
(c) Never respond to those Publisher's Clearing House mass mailings (since that plays into a deplorable commercialism).

Some desire-dependent principles state generally reliable ways of satisfying desires that most people have, or might come to have at some point. These fit what Kant terms 'counsels of prudence':

(d) Honesty is the best policy.
(e) Always respond to those Publisher's Clearing House mass mailings; it does not take much time and you never know when you might win.
(f) Never give a sucker a break. (Since a sucker is an easy target, that is an effective way of furthering your ends.)

Other desire-dependent principles depend more openly on desires peculiar to specific individuals:

(g) When you see someone who is about to ask you for money, cross the street right away (so that you won't feel pressure to give, can avoid a repulsive sight).
(h) Leading a life of luxury and ease is important above all else.

A principle that an agent accepts as objectively valid may or may not have the status that he or she takes it to have. A principle such as (c) might be viewed by the agent as unconditionally valid; but it might turn out to be no more than an expression of a value or a desire peculiar to the agent that is not universally supportable, and is thus only conditionally valid. A principle such as (d) might simply be false if, in the circumstances intended by the agent, honesty is not the best way of furthering one's interests. (In that case, as stated, it would only be a subjective principle—a principle from which the agent acts, though not objectively valid.)

Principles in the last group do not appear to have much normative force; they seem more like characteristic principles of specific individuals, rather than principles that make claims about how people in general ought to act. But they may be viewed as (elliptical) hypothetical imperatives directed to individuals with certain desires (those undone by the sight of destitute people, or those who dislike hard work, uncertainty, and anxiety, etc.). If they in fact stated effective means of satisfying certain desires, and thus conformed to the Hypothetical Imperative, they would be objective practical principles. And they might have derivative normative force if they were instantiations for an individual of a higher level principle taken to have final justifying force, which (following Kant) could be termed the Principle of Happiness:

> (PH) Act so as to maximize over time the satisfaction of your own desires, whatever they may be.

I include these latter examples to show that some conditional principles may have only minimal justifying force. The reasons derived from a principle may at most render an action intelligible, and fall far short of giving others reason to accept or approve of the actions that fall under it. In cases of this sort, objectivity may amount to nothing more than an appropriate connection between an action and the given desires and aims of an individual in a particular situation, that anyone can discern. For example, if your guiding aim is to lead a life of luxury and ease, that will be a source of reasons for you in specific circumstances, even if not good reasons. I, favoring penury and struggle (or perhaps as someone in great need), can appreciate that you have a reason not to be generous in some situation given this general aim, even though I may reject the aim from which these reasons get their force, and thus the actions to which they lead.

This passage stresses the ability to act from normative principles, but that does not exhaust Kant's understanding of practical rationality. Elsewhere in the *Groundwork* Kant articulates other aspects of his conception of rational agency, which appear to be implicit in the fundamental notion.[30] In a second important passage preceding the introduction of the Formula of Humanity (FH), Kant writes: 'The will is thought of as a capacity to determine itself to acting in conformity with the *representation of certain laws*. And such a capacity can be found only in rational beings. Now what serves the will as the objective ground of its self-determination is an end . . .' (*G* 4: 427). This passage and the ensuing discussion add the idea that rational agency also involves the ability to set and pursue ends. In light of the preceding account of practical reason, this capacity must be understood as a responsiveness to objective value. The rational agent does not simply act so as to satisfy given preferences, but adopts ends (including objects of its preferences) for reasons that have force from the point of view of others. Thus, it involves the capacity to select ends viewed as good or worthy of choice, or to recognize or place a value on a state of affairs. To say that in adopting an end one regards it as good or of value implies several things. An agent adopts an end because it instantiates a higher level end or value taken to be good per se (in which case the value of the end is derivative), or because it is taken to be good in itself. Once adopted, the end becomes a source of reasons for the agent that give it some degree of priority relative to one's other desires and ends. These reasons are desire independent to the extent that their force can remain constant despite fluctuations in the strengths of one's desires, and can override desires that may interfere with the pursuit of the end. They are sufficient both to initiate courses of action, as well as restrict other actions and pursuits that are inconsistent with the end. In addition, the agent's reasons for adopting an end should allow other agents to see why he takes it to be worthy of choice. Presumably its value to the agent can be recognized by others, and gives them a reason to respect the agent's pursuit of the end (though one that can be overridden in various ways).[31]

V. PRACTICAL REASON AND COMPLETE JUSTIFICATION

To understand how Kant locates the origin of moral principles in reason, we must consider how the above conception of practical rationality leads to a statement of the moral law. The view that I want to attribute to Kant is that the idea of a practical law is implicit in the nature of practical reason as a faculty that evaluates according to normative principles and constructs justifications. If so, the arguments of *Groundwork*, I and II discussed earlier would give Kant what he needs. Recall his view that the idea of a practical law, or equivalently, the concept of a categorical imperative, yields a formulation of the only principle that can be a categorical imperative—that is, the idea of a practical law yields the Categorical Imperative.[32] If this argument holds, and if the idea of a practical law may be derived from the nature of practical reason (as understood by Kant), then the Categorical Imperative would have been traced to the nature of practical reason. What we want to see here is how the Categorical Imperative can be viewed as the principle in which this conception of practical rationality is most fully expressed—say, as the principle by which the business of practical reason is most fully carried out or completed. Roughly, it is because movement toward the unconditional is built into the process of evaluation and justification, and it is by finding justifications that are unconditionally valid that the process is completed. But justifications of this sort require grounding in a practical law. Since the Categorical Imperative states the form that any practical law will have, it is the principle by which the business of practical reason is completed. In this way, the characteristics of moral evaluation are tied to the nature of practical reason, and shown to be expressed in the Categorical Imperative.

To develop this point, let us consider what is needed to arrive at justifications that are complete. The discussion of the last section shows that objective practical principles, and the justifications that they ground, need only be conditionally valid. The objectivity of a practical principle requires only that its application yield conclusions about action that have force for anyone in the relevant situation, and that their force can be understood by anyone. This allows that an objective principle may show that an action is a good thing to do, or that there are reasons to perform it, given certain further conditions (the agent desires certain ends, accepts certain values, and so on). Justifications of this sort are partial or incomplete, and the ways in which they are conditioned lay out directions in which development toward completion is possible. Complete justification is achieved by extending the normative force of reasons as far as possible in these directions.

We may distinguish two different dimensions along which justification must move toward completion. The first is the direction of finality. You may judge that an action is good as a means to an end, or relative to certain desires. In that case, there is reason to perform the action only if there is reason to pursue the end, or if the desires in question are good ones to act on. Or, you might judge that an action or an end is good in itself, but that there is reason to pursue it only if certain limiting conditions are satisfied. It is good 'other things being equal'—that is, if it is consistent with your other priorities, violates no prior obligations, and so on. Such judgments lead one to look for further reasons beyond those initially advanced in support of the action—either to seek reasons for the end, in the first case, or to determine whether the limiting conditions are satisfied, as in the second case. In both cases a search is initiated for final reasons not in need of further support, which either provide positive support for the action, or show that it is fully consistent with other considerations that have priority.

The other direction is toward universal validity. What you take to be a sufficient reason for acting may fall short of giving others reason to accept what you do. You intend to do X because it promotes a life of luxury and ease, which is for you a final aim of overriding importance. (It will give you happiness, and after all, what else is there?) I can see why X is a good thing for you given your aims, but since I do not place the same value on the aim as you, I am not moved by your explanation. (Besides, X shows a disregard for my person.) Here your justification is shown to be conditional on an assumption that is not universally acceptable; specifically, I have no reason to accept it. Justification is complete in this direction when the objectivity of reasons has been pushed toward universal validity. That is, in addition to leading others to see why you take the action to be a good thing to do, your reasons lead them to see it as good and to accept it. In this case, an agent's reasons for acting are at the same time sufficient to give anyone reason to accept what he does.

One has traveled as far as one can in each direction when one arrives at reasons whose finality is universally valid. Such reasons are necessary, universal, and take deliberative priority over others; that is, they have the status of a practical law. They complete the process of justification in that they are sufficient to justify an action fully to anyone. This represents the most complete exercise of practical rationality, in that the normative features present in any reason are found in their most complete form, and the normal function of practical reason is carried out to a maximal degree.

I hope to have shown how, in Kant's view, moral choice builds on and extends a concern for justification and evaluation present in all forms of reasoning and choice. A strength of this interpretation is that it reveals a continuity between moral and non-moral choice that we tend to overlook due to various of Kant's dichotomies. It suggests, for example, that the psychology needed to explain how we can care about and act from the moral law is provided by the capacities constitutive of rational agency. Moral conduct requires no fundamentally different abilities or motives beyond those that go into the reasoned choice of actions and ends in ordinary contexts. What makes this possible, of course, is that Kant's conception of practical rationality already incorporates substantive ideals with a recognizably moral component. But that should not trouble us as long as the ideals are sufficiently fundamental to our way of viewing ourselves. Kant's project, as I have said, is not to derive the moral law from a morally neutral starting point, but to connect it with basic features of reasoning and choice, and to show how deeply embedded the elements of morality are in all forms of deliberation.

This essay has focused on the FUL. Since Kant derives three principal formulations of what he thinks is a single imperative, to complete this account would require showing that the framework that it develops may be extended to the other formulas and their equivalence. I will conclude with a suggestion about how this may be done which I can only sketch here. It is that the alternate formulations of the Categorical Imperative express different aspects of a single conception of rational agency, and that we look to the relationships between these aspects of practical rationality to throw light on the equivalence of the formulas. We have seen that the core notion of practical rationality is the capacity to act from general normative principles that may be used to justify one's actions to others. The FUL may be regarded as the principle by which this capacity is most completely expressed, in that it embodies the ideal of acting from reasons that are unconditionally valid. In representing the general form of a practical law, it states the ideal of complete justification. Rational agency also involves the ability to set and pursue ends, which in this context should be understood as the capacity to adopt ends viewed as good or of value. This aspect of practical rationality is most fully expressed in the FH, which states the requirement of guiding one's conduct by the recognition of an end of absolute value which conditions the value of any end. Finally, the ideas of freedom and self-determination are built into this conception of practical rationality. The actions of a rational agent are self-determined in that they result from the agent's understanding and application to herself of reasons and principles that she accepts. The capacity to be guided by normative considerations makes one free by giving one the capacity to choose actions other than those that would result from the balance of existing desires and the capacity to determine oneself to act by one's judgment of what one has most reason to do; you can do what you ought to do, regardless of what you desire. This aspect of practical rationality is part of what underlies the Formula of Autonomy (FA).

That the FA follows directly from the FUL (G 4: 431–3) shows that autonomy is the foundation of morality—that moral principles are such that we can regard ourselves as their authors and subject to them for that reason, and that when we act from the moral law we most fully realize our free capacities. The latter point in particular must rest on the idea that in acting from reasons that are unconditionally valid, one's actions are most completely guided by one's capacity to act from reasons, and thus most completely self-determined. Thus the powers of freedom and self-determination implicit in all rational choice are most fully realized in morally good conduct. Kant thinks that the form of a practical law is identical with the form of volition in general, or the general structure of what it is to act from will.

Here is a way of relating the different formulas by showing that each is the full expression of a different aspect of a single ideal of rational agency. It offers support for the contention that they are just different versions of the same Idea. One of the more remarkable features of Kant's theory is its attempt to demonstrate the deep connections between these ideals, and to weld them together into a single moral conception.[33]

NOTES

1. Cf. e.g. *G* 4: 389.
2. Cf. *G* 4: 412 ff. and 426 ff., which precede, respectively, the statements of the first two formulations of the Categorical Imperative. In the first Kant writes that 'just because moral laws are to hold for every rational being as such', one 'must derive them from the universal concept of a rational being as such'. He then says that to carry this out, he will 'present distinctly the practical faculty of reason, from its general rules of determination to the point where the concept of duty arises from it'. In the second, Kant says that the moral law 'must already be connected (completely a priori) with the concept of the will of a rational being as such'. The discovery of this connection requires that 'one step forth, namely into metaphysics' and investigate the possibility of reason determining conduct a priori.
3. In the Preface, Kant writes that 'the present groundwork . . . is nothing more than the search for and establishment of the *supreme principle of morality* . . .' (*G* 4: 392). The 'search for' the supreme principle occupies the first two sections of the *Groundwork*; their concern is the proper formulation of the moral law (the content) and they leave open the question of its authority. For Kant, the latter is the question of whether the demands contained in our ordinary concept of morality are indeed valid and real: do they really bind us and do we have authoritative reasons for acting from them? (For different statements of the question of authority see *G* 4: 426, 445, and especially 449 ff.: 'But why, then, ought I to subject myself to this principle and do so simply as a rational being, thus subjecting to it all other beings endowed with reason?' '[F]or if someone asked us why the universal validity of our maxim as a law must be the limiting condition of our action . . . we could give him no satisfactory answer'.) The moral law is not 'established' until the Third Section, when this issue is addressed. My discussion in this essay is limited to the arguments of the first two sections of the *Groundwork*.

Commentators concerned with Kant's derivation of morality from reason have tended to take the authority of the moral law to be the main issue, and have thus focused on the Third Section, and related arguments in the *Critique of Practical Reason*. See e.g. Thomas E. Hill, 'Kant's Argument for the Rationality of Moral Conduct', in *Dignity and Practical Reason*; Henry E. Allison, *Kant's Theory of Freedom*, chs. 11–12; and Christine M. Korsgaard, 'Morality as Freedom', in *Creating the Kingdom of Ends*. But it is also important to see how Kant derives the content of the moral law from a conception of practical reason.

4. 'Truth, Invention, and the Meaning of Life', in *Needs, Values, Truth*, 122 n. For discussion and response to Wiggins's critique of this project see David Gauthier, 'The Unity of Reason: A Subversive Reinterpretation of Kant', in *Moral Dealing: Contract, Ethics, and Reason*, 120–3.

5. See *Ethics and the Limits of Philosophy*, 28. Williams's discussion of Kant (see Chapter 4) by and large assumes that Kant's conception of practical reason is morally neutral.

6. Here note Kant's distinction between the 'predisposition to *humanity* in the human being, as a living and at the same time a *rational* being' and the 'predisposition to *personality*, as a rational and a *responsible* being' (*Rel* 6: 26 ff.). The former is a conception of instrumental rationality in that it involves, among other things, the ability to set and pursue ends on the basis of their contribution to one's overall happiness, understood to involve the maximally harmonious satisfaction of given desires. The predisposition to personality is the basis of morality, and Kant stresses that it is a 'special predisposition' not included in the first. I am indebted to Stephen Engstrom for discussion of this passage and related issues.

7. This point is made by Thomas E. Hill, Jr., 'The Hypothetical Imperative', in *Dignity and Practical Reason*, 28–31, whose account I follow in this paragraph.

8. For textual evidence of this interpretation see *MdS* 6: 395; while in the Introduction to *The Metaphysics of Morals* pure practical reason is described as a 'faculty of principles' (*MdS* 6: 214), here it is called 'a faculty of ends generally'. See also the 'Conjectural Beginning of Human History', where reason is viewed as the power to set ends beyond those given by instinct and inclination (and which can create new desires), as well as the power to make provision for future ends one may have (8: 111–15). Though the uses of reason referred to here are not 'pure', it is worth noting its independence from inclination, as well as the continuity between these uses of reason and the form of moral reasoning referred to at the end of the passage.

9. By a principle of right conduct, I mean a principle that a deliberating agent can use to determine the normative status of an action as done for certain reasons. Since the Categorical Imperative assesses maxims, it is not concerned with the external features of action (actions viewed as 'outward performances'), but with actions as done for certain reasons. Alternatively one may say that the Categorical Imperative assesses actions if the agent's reasons for action are part of the action description (in which case an agent who acts honestly out of a concern for reputation and one who acts honestly out of duty have performed different actions).

There is some ambiguity in the *Groundwork* as to whether Kant's primary focus is moral worth or moral rightness. I take it to be the latter, as just qualified, despite Kant's constant attention to acting from the motive of duty. Thus, I view the discussion of moral worth in the First Section as a step on the way to a statement of the principle of right conduct, understood as a principle to be used by deliberating agents to determine the normative status of an action as done for certain reasons. It is important to recognize that the examples in the middle of the First Section (*G* 4: 397–400) ask us to make *retrospective* judgments of moral worth that we are not generally in a position to make, either about others or ourselves. Since these judgments turn on whether an agent in some situation (normally an agent who acted in conformity to duty) was motivated by respect for morality, they require that we determine the operative motive or incentive (or the actual maxim) on which the agent acted—after the fact, as it were. Kant cannot think that such retrospective judgments of moral worth are the main focus of moral thought, because he does not think that experience enables us to determine the motives (or the actual maxims) on which an agent has acted. As Kant says, 'when moral worth is at issue, what counts is not actions, which one sees, but those inner principles of action that one does not see' (*G* 4: 407). We can make judgments of moral worth about the actions in these examples only because Kant's construction of the examples stipulates the operative incentives of these agents. But the main concern of moral thought, and the aim of the Categorical Imperative, is a different kind of judgment. The Categorical Imperative guides the deliberative task of an agent trying to determine the normative status of a prospective action as done for certain reasons. Because what is assessed here are actions as done for certain reasons rather than the outward features of actions, some theorists have said that Kant's ethics is concerned with moral worth (of actions or maxims), rather than with moral rightness. (Cf. Onora O'Neill, *Constructions of Reason*, 85–6.) But I believe that this is a matter of terminology. One can say that deliberative judgments about the normative status of a prospective action as done for certain reasons are judgments of 'moral worth', as long as one distinguishes these judgments from retrospective judgments of moral worth. Perhaps for clarity one might call the former 'deliberative' or 'prospective' judgments of moral worth as a way of noting that they are different in kind from the retrospective judgments of moral worth at issue in the middle of *Groundwork*, I.

One further point: the importance for Kant of acting from duty, thus striving to act with moral worth, emerges directly from certain features of the content or demands of morality. The necessity and deliberative priority of moral considerations are part of the content of morality, and are reflected in the statement of the Categorical Imperative. That is, the moral law among other things tells us to give deliberative priority to moral considerations and to take them as sufficient and overriding reasons for action. Thus, when we satisfy the demands of morality, not only will we act in certain ways—we will be motivated to act in these ways by respect for morality, and our actions will have moral worth.

10. In other words, moral deliberation will generally be about actions under descriptions, in which agents bring certain kinds of substantive considerations to bear on a situation (honesty, fairness, and so on). The Categorical Imperative is the schematic rendering of the reasoning implicitly used, which states its underlying form.

11. As he says, the 'mere concept of a categorical imperative . . . [may] also provide its formula containing the proposition which can alone be a categorical imperative'; and that 'when I think of a *categorical* imperative, I know at once what it contains' (*G* 4: 420). I comment on this argument in n. 32 below.

12. Here see Kant's 'third proposition' (*G* 4: 400): 'duty is the necessity of an action from respect for the law'. While much is packed into this statement, the main idea is that the special weight of moral considerations is central to the concept of duty. (A duty is

an action picked by respect for morality as unconditionally necessary—as supported by reasons that exclude the force of and take priority over other kinds of reasons. What morality demands of us is that we acknowledge the unconditional necessity of moral considerations.) The 'third proposition' articulates the special necessity of moral considerations, to which the attitude of respect is the appropriate response.

In this passage Kant focuses on the motivational state that fully recognizes the authority of moral reasons as a way of bringing out their defining features. But he could also have looked simply at what is implied by the concept of a duty, in so far as the necessity and universality of particular duties are a part of their content. This Kant does in the Preface (*G* 4: 389), when he says that 'the common idea of duty' must carry with it 'absolute necessity'. Kant's preference for the 'subjective route' (through attention to the characteristic motivational attitude) might be explained by the fact that much of the First Section works through an appeal to moral experience. The defining features of morality are not just described; Kant wishes to elicit through examples a recognition of them that has motivating force.

13. That is, 'conditions . . . only contingently connected to the will', or 'contingent, subjective conditions that distinguish one rational being from another'. See *KpV* 5: 20 f.

14. I am calling necessity and deliberative priority what I take to be slightly different features contained in Kant's usage of 'necessity' (*Notwendigkeit*). For brevity, I will generally refer (as he does) simply to the necessity and universality of moral reasons, or to their unconditional validity.

15. Any practical principle is going to be universal in that it applies to anyone who satisfies its conditions. Universality in this sense is, of course, not sufficient to make a practical principle a law. (In fact, this feature is better called its 'generality'.) Here it is worth noting that the distinction between principles and ends is not important in the derivation of a practical law. To show that there is an end with intrinsic and absolute value (i.e., one which takes priority over and limits other forms of value) is to have established the existence of a practical law. This, of course, is what Kant does in his derivation of the Formula of Humanity, and it explains in part why the first two formulas are equivalent. What is crucial to the concept of a practical law is the notion of reasons that have deliberative priority, and this can be expressed equally in a principle that yields determinate prescriptions with overriding weight, or in the idea of an end of absolute value.

16. Cf. *G* 4: 408–9, 411–12, 425–7; see also 389–90.

17. Kant raises the possibility that the concept of morality might lack objective reality, though not always in the same sense, at *G* 4: 402, 405, 407–8, 421, 425, and 445. He writes that 'mere conformity to law as such' must be the principle of the will 'if duty is not to be everywhere an empty delusion [*ein leerer Wahn*] and a chimerical idea [*chimärischer Begriff*]' (402); and that the aim of the step into practical philosophy in the Second Section is to 'obtain information and distinct instruction regarding the source of its own principle and the correct determination of this principle in comparison with maxims based on need and inclination, so that [common human reason] . . . may not run the risk of being deprived of all genuine moral principles through the ambiguity into which it easily falls' (405). Here his point is that our concept of duty requires that we treat moral considerations as unconditionally valid, which presupposes that they originate in reason a priori. (Somewhat optimistically he thinks that clarity about the origin of moral requirements in reason is enough to get us

to accept the practical impact of their having the status of law.) See in particular 408: '. . . unless we want to deny to the concept of morality any truth and any relation to some possible object, we cannot dispute that its law . . . [must hold] for all *rational beings as such*, not merely under contingent conditions and with exceptions but with *absolute necessity*'.

It seems that different questions about the 'reality' of the moral law are left open at different stages of the argument, and that both *Groundwork*, II and III address a question of whether the moral law might only be an empty idea. The First Section articulates some of the essential features of moral claims, as we understand them; but they would still be illusory unless they originate in reason. The Second Section is a more detailed analysis of the concept of morality that shows that duties must be expressed in categorical imperatives (G 4: 425) and that the autonomy of the will must be the foundation of morality (G 4: 445), and gives the proper formulation of the moral law. It addresses the issue left open by the First Section by tracing the Categorical Imperative to the nature of practical reason (G 4: 412–16, 420 ff.), but stops short of establishing the authority of its requirements for us (G 4: 425, 440–5). That requires a 'synthetic use' of reason, presumably one that shows that we have the rational nature presupposed by the moral law, and is the subject of the Third Section.

18. Here I am in agreement with Thomas Hill, who argues that Kant is not addressing the moral skeptic, but rather an audience with ordinary moral concerns 'whose moral commitment is liable to be called into question by philosophical accounts of practical reason which imply that morality could not be grounded in reason'. See 'Kant on the Rationality of Moral Conduct', in *Dignity and Practical Reason*, 99.

I might add that if Kant is not addressing an audience that is initially indifferent to moral concerns, then his conception of reason need not be devoid of substantive ideals (of the person, or of agency). Indeed a theory that does proceed from such a starting point is likely to obscure the way of viewing persons to which Kant thinks that moral thought provides access.

19. This is the 'natural dialectic' within practical reason which Kant describes as 'a propensity to rationalize against those strict laws of duty and to cast doubt upon their validity, or at least upon their purity and strictness, and, where possible, to make them better suited to our wishes and inclinations . . .' (G 4: 405; see also G 4: 424 f. and KpV 5: 16.).

20. Ideally the notion of rational agency will be a foundation that really supports and animates the structure. That is, it does not just yield the basic principle; it will also figure in the application of the principle to concrete situations, and thus hold a substantive role in the moral conception that it grounds. The conception of rational agency should be an ideal that we can plausibly apply to ourselves and others in normal social interactions, which will have implications for how individuals are appropriately treated. (Certain ways of treating others recognize their rationality in the relevant sense, and an understanding of the conception of rational agency should guide one's judgments, and make one better at applying the principle.)

21. In *Groundwork*, III, Kant grounds the *authority* of the moral law in reason with analytic arguments to the effect that any rational agent acts under the idea of freedom (must regard itself as free) and that an agent that acts under the idea of freedom is committed to acting from the moral law, and a synthetic argument to the effect that we human beings are rational agents in the requisite sense. For discussion, see the literature cited in n. 3 above. I discuss the argument in Section VIII of Chapter 5.

22. *The Possibility of Altruism*, 22. See also Thomas E. Hill, Jr.'s discussion in *Dignity and Practical Reason*, 106. Hill notes that a rational agent is able

to make things happen in such a way that the appropriate explanation is reference to the principles, laws, or reasons on which the person acted. Principles, even laws, enter into the explanation of why a rational agent did something . . . as the agent's guiding 'ideas' or rationale, not as empirically observable regularities among types of events.

Cf. also H. J. Paton, in *The Categorical Imperative*, 81–2.

23. Of course, other forms of explanation are possible, but they no longer view the causality as rational. Many people would agree that such explanations are incomplete because they ignore aspects of an agent's perspective on his or her conduct, which are central to the agent's self-conception. For a discussion of this point in a different context, see H. L. A. Hart on the 'internal aspect of rules', and his argument that certain positivist accounts of law fail by ignoring it: *The Concept of Law*, 55–7, 88–91, 102–3. See also Nagel's discussion in *The View from Nowhere*, 141–3, 150–2.

24. The text is made somewhat unclear by a terminological slide from 'objective laws' to 'objective principles' or 'imperatives'. Kant may appear to define rational agency as the capacity to act from practical laws (i.e., categorical imperatives), but the context makes it clear that he intends the weaker definition as the capacity to act from objective practical principles, which, as I explain, include both hypothetical and categorical imperatives. (The first interpretation would make rational agency a moral capacity by definition.) A similar ambiguity is seen in the definition of practical principles early in the second *Critique* (*KpV* 5: 19 ff.). Here Kant begins by distinguishing practical laws from maxims, or subjective principles of action—that is, those actually adopted by an agent. But it becomes clear that his interest is in the distinction between subjective principles of action and objective practical principles valid for any rational being, including both practical laws and valid prudential precepts.

25. Thus, a practical principle does not simply state a characteristic way of acting, or a rule to which an agent's behavior conforms. That would assimilate practical laws to the model of laws of nature. Rational conduct presupposes not just that behavior conform to a principle, but that it be guided by an awareness or acceptance of that principle. It provides a description of the behavior that the agent would apply to himself, which could be used to state his intentions, or would be accepted as relevant to evaluation of the action.

26. Here I draw on Nagel's discussions of objectivity in *The View from Nowhere*, 152–4.

27. Hypothetical imperatives are objectively valid, in that they embody claims about the means needed to achieve a given end that are true for anyone. However they give reasons conditionally, in that they lead to determinate prescriptions only in conjunction with facts about an individual's desires. Thus, hypothetical imperatives are practical principles that are objectively, but conditionally valid, stated in imperative form for finite rational beings. For discussion, see Thomas E. Hill Jr., 'The Hypothetical Imperative', in *Dignity and Practical Reason*.

28. It is implausible to think that an agent must consciously go through such a process in deciding how to act, but that need not be Kant's view. Rather, a structure of this sort may be implicit in practical reasoning, and presupposed by what agents offer as justifications for their actions. Thus I would argue that Kant views a maxim (first personal principle stating an agent's underlying intention) as providing a prima facie

justification for an action. But since it must instantiate a general principle stating how anyone ought to act in order to function in this way, some such principle is presupposed in the background. It is enough for Kant's purposes that this structure is brought into play in assessing proposed alternatives; it need not describe how an agent arrives at these alternatives.

29. Thus Kant writes: 'Practical good, however, is that which determines the will by means of representations of reason, hence not by subjective causes but objectively, that is, from grounds that are valid for every rational being as such' (*G* 4: 413). What is good is also 'practically necessary'—an action supported by an ought judgment of some kind. Cf. *G* 4: 412. See also *KpV* 5: 58 ff., especially 61: 'What we are to call good must be an object of the faculty of desire in the judgment of every reasonable human being . . .'; and *KU* § 4.

30. See also *G* 4: 448:

> Now, one cannot possibly think of a reason that would consciously receive direction from any other quarter with respect to its judgments, since the subject would then attribute the determination of his judgment not to his reason but to an impulse. Reason must regard itself as the author of its principles independently of alien influences.

Here Kant views rationality as a power of self-determination.

31. In support of this interpretation of the attitude of rational agents toward their ends, note that when Kant discusses the adoption of ends he standardly refers to their value or worth (*Wert*). He asks whether it is conditional, relative, or absolute (*G* 4: 428 ff.); he also refers to the question of whether an end is 'reasonable and good' and comments on the importance of 'judgments about the worth of the things that they might make their ends' (*G* 4: 415).

32. This argument begins from an understanding of categorical imperatives as practical laws, or unconditional requirements on choice and action. Kant writes:

> For, since the imperative contains, beyond the law, only the necessity that the maxim be in conformity with this law, while the law contains no condition to which it would be limited, nothing is left with which the maxim of action is to conform but the universality of law as such; and this conformity alone is what the imperative properly represents as necessary. (*G* 4: 421)

> I gloss this passage as follows. We know, first, that a (particular) categorical imperative will contain some law—that is, some substantive requirement on choice and action. Further, the imperative will represent this requirement as applying universally—as applying to any rational agent, qua rational agent, regardless of the agent's desires and subjective ends. (The 'law contains no condition to which it would be limited . . .'.) Beyond the substantive law represented to apply universally, the imperative will contain 'only the necessity that the maxim be in conformity with this law . . .'. It will state that conforming one's maxims to this substantive requirement is necessary, in the sense that the requirement provides reasons for action that exclude the force of and take priority over competing reasons for action based on desire and subjective ends. Thus we know that the Categorical Imperative—as the principle underlying all particular categorical imperatives, which states their general form—can only contain the necessity of conformity to universal law as such. It states the requirement of acting from

reasons that satisfy the criteria of necessity and universality, or are sufficient to justify one's actions fully to anyone. So the supreme practical law says: act from maxims that have the form of universal law.

33. I received support for this essay from a National Endowment for the Humanities Summer Stipend (No. FT-29143-87). I am also indebted to Stephen Engstrom, Hannah Ginsberg, and Christine Korsgaard for discussion of various issues while I was writing this essay that no doubt influenced its present form.

4

Legislating the Moral Law

I. INTRODUCTION

Kant believed that the moral law is a law that the rational will in some sense legislates. He regarded this thesis as an important philosophical discovery, and it first appears with the introduction of the Formula of Autonomy, whose central idea is that of 'the will of every rational being as a will giving universal law' (*G* 4: 431).[1] Thereafter he refers to the rational will as legislating or giving law to itself, as the 'author' (*Urheber*) of the laws to which it is subject, and as bound only to its own legislation, or will. The will is 'subject to [the law] in such a way that it must be viewed as also giving law to itself [*als selbstgesetzgebend*] and just because of this as first subject to the law (of which it can regard itself as the author)' (*G* 4: 431). 'The human being . . . is subject *only to laws given by himself but still universal* and . . . is bound only to act in conformity with his own will, which, however, in accordance with nature's end is a will giving universal law' (*G* 4: 432). The 'ground of the dignity' of rational nature is that a rational being 'obeys no law other than that which he himself at the same time gives', 'obeys only those [laws] which he himself gives' (*G* 4: 434, 435. Cf. 440). The moral law 'interests because it is valid for us as human beings, since it arose from our will as intelligence and so from our proper self' (*G* 4: 461). Finally, Kant defines the autonomy of the will as 'the property of the will by which it is a law to itself (independently of any property of the objects of volition)' (*G* 4: 440. Cf. 447). Here the law that the autonomous will gives to itself is the moral law. As one might say, the rational will is a law to itself, and the moral law is that law.[2]

Several distinct claims are embedded in these remarks. First, there is the claim that the moral law, and the requirements to which it leads, are laws that the rational will legislates.[3] One also finds the claim that rational agents are bound only to laws which they have given, or laws of which they can regard themselves as legislators. My primary concern is with the first claim, which I shall refer to as the Legislation Thesis, and I want to raise two general questions about it. (1) What does Kant mean when he says that we are the legislators of the moral law, or of the moral requirements to which we are bound? In what sense is the moral law, or are moral principles, legislated by the rational will? (2) What role does this thesis play in Kant's theory? My hesitation over the framing of the first question suggests alternative readings of the Legislation Thesis. Is it that 'we legislate the moral law', or that 'the rational will legislates the moral law'? The first reading suggests that we as individuals arrive at and will moral principles through rational deliberation. The second suggests that the willing is done 'impersonally' by the rational will—for instance, that moral principles are principles that every rational agent necessarily wills in virtue of being rational, or which in some way derive from the nature of rational willing.

The central issue raised by the first question is how to combine Kant's pronouncements about the autonomy of the will and the will's own legislation of the moral law with the necessity and universal validity of moral requirements. The presence of these two strains in Kant's moral theory is both a defining characteristic and a deep source of tension. Given the necessity and universality of moral principles, one is not free to decide for oneself upon the content of morality; nor is it a matter of voluntary choice whether one is bound by moral considerations (though one must choose whether to comply). But if the concept of legislation is to have any connection to its ordinary meaning, one must preserve the idea that laws get their authority from the acts of a legislative agent. If the notion of 'legislating' or 'giving law' is to apply, the legislator must have some authority to decide what to enact as law (i.e., to decide upon its content). Even when a legislator only has authority to enact laws meeting certain conditions, what is law is undetermined prior to the legislator's enactment. In addition, the legislator's enactment must create law, in the sense that it creates binding reasons for subjects to act in certain ways, which they did not have prior to that act. A law may require the performance of actions that there are independent reasons to perform; but once the law is enacted, subjects have a reason for performing those actions that they did not have before—reasons that result from an authoritative deliberative process. Simply put, the fact that it has been enacted as law is now a reason for them to act in the required way, whatever that may be. Where significant external constraints determine the content of legislation, and where the reasons to comply with a body of principles exist prior to the legislative enactment, the agent in question does not exercise sovereignty in any interesting sense.

Many people think that this tension can only be resolved by weakening one of these two strains. Some hold that Kant ought to have given up his views about the objective validity of moral principles.[4] Others assume that, in the end, Kant's remarks about self-legislation should be understood metaphorically. However, I believe that a satisfactory account of Kant's theory should aim to combine these two strains in an uncompromising way, and thus would like to find a fairly literal reading of the 'legislation' of moral principles that is consistent with moral objectivity. Where we are forced to settle for a looser interpretation, the selection of this metaphor should have a point: the resulting picture of moral deliberation should preserve some of the main features of legislation.

As far as the second question is concerned, there are different roles that one might ascribe to the Legislation Thesis. One might think that it is a thesis about the source of the content of morality—for example, that the content of morality originates in our legislation rather than in God's, or in a prior order of intrinsic values. Or it may play an essential role in saying why we are bound and ought to give authority to the moral law. Many of Kant's remarks suggest the latter, and most people assume that the Legislation Thesis is used to establish the authority of moral requirements. Showing that a principle of conduct is a law that one has given to oneself, or which represents 'one's own will', would seem to settle any questions as to why one should obey. However, in the final section I will argue that, while the Legislation Thesis may function as a supporting lemma in a longer argument, it does not directly establish the authority of the moral law and is not introduced for that purpose.

Before turning to the interpretive options in Kant, it may be useful to consider briefly how these questions apply to Rousseau, since both his views and language influenced Kant. Rousseau's primary concern in *On the Social Contract* (hereafter referred to as *SC*) is to set out conditions of legitimacy for coercive social and political arrangements. Laws are legitimate only when they represent the general will, and to do that they must, among other things, be self-imposed. 'The people subject to the laws ought to be their author. . .'[5] Rousseau understands self-legislation in the political sphere quite literally as involving active participation in the legislative process. The sovereign, or final legislative authority, is the collective body of all citizens,[6] and public deliberation must be structured so that all citizens have equal access to and input into the legislative process.[7] Moreover a law cannot be put forward as representing the general will unless the legislative process has actually been carried out.[8] In sum, the concept of the general will establishes the conditions that a system of laws and coercive arrangements must satisfy, and one is the complex requirement that laws be enacted by an open legislative process in which there is full participation by those subject to them. Presumably the fact that a norm has been enacted by this legitimizing process, and thereby has title to express the general will, is what makes it a law.

Why, according to Rousseau, must laws be enacted by the collective body of all citizens (express the general will) to be legitimate? His intention to 'combine what right permits with what interest prescribes' (*SC* I, §1) indicates that his conception of legitimacy comprises different elements. First, a system of law must protect certain natural and privately formed interests of individuals, and thus be in their rational self-interest. But legitimacy also requires more directly moral conditions. For example, his concern to show how freedom and subjection to law can be combined indicates that laws must preserve the freedom and independence of each citizen.[9] Self-legislation plays an importantly different role in relation to each aspect of legitimacy. In regard to the first, the requirement that laws be self-legislated has only instrumental value; that is, it is a way of ensuring that a further and independently definable constraint is met. The concern here is that a system of laws protect certain natural, private interests of individuals (e.g., their interest in self-preservation). Since individuals are good judges of their interests and strongly motivated to further them, placing legislative authority in the hands of those subject to the laws may be the most reliable way of satisfying this condition. Considerations of both information and authorization are involved here. Active citizen legislators will frame laws with their own interests in mind. Moreover, they will not approve laws that fail to protect them. But if the protection of these natural interests were the sole requirement of legitimacy, and if this could be achieved without citizen participation in the legislative process, then laws enacted by a non-democratic process could be legitimate. The same point holds for the bearing of self-legislation on certain conditions of equity and fairness—for example, that laws benefit and restrict all citizens equally, or that they do not impose restrictions without good reason. Public deliberation in which all citizens participate equally would uncover inequities in proposed laws, and would prevent their acceptance. Thus the requirement that laws be self-legislated could be a means to seeing that other, independently definable conditions (e.g., equal benefit, etc.) are satisfied. But if one's sole concern were to fulfill such substantive requirements, and if one could do so in a legislative process without citizen participation, the results of this process would be legitimate and give no one cause to complain.

By contrast, there is a direct connection between self-legislation and the preservation of freedom and independence. Since laws are coercive, they will only be consistent with individual freedom and independence if they somehow combine freedom and subjection. For Rousseau one is not free if one is subject to the will of another, or bound to the dictates of an external authority; one must obey only one's own (true) will.[10] It follows that a system of laws must be self-imposed in order to have legitimacy. When this is achieved, freedom and subjection to law have been combined, one obeys only one's own will, and, in being bound only to a system of law that meets these conditions, each citizen has a 'guarantee against all personal dependence' on the arbitrary will of another.[11] Since the second element of legitimacy is more central to Rousseau's political view, the principal implication of being bound only to one's own legislation is that one is free: 'the impulse of appetite alone is slavery, and freedom is obedience to the law one has prescribed for oneself'.[12]

The fact that a system of laws is self-legislated, and thus preserves freedom and independence, is a necessary condition of its legitimacy. But it plays no singular role in explaining why one ought to comply with it. For Rousseau, once one has shown that a system of legislation is legitimate, no further question remains as to why one should comply. One can hold that the reason to obey any given law is the fact that it is a properly enacted law, and is a proper expression of the general will. Thus, whatever shows that it is legitimate (i.e., that it expresses the general will) exhausts what there is to say about the reasons for compliance.[13]

The point I wish to make is this. For Rousseau, the fact that you had a role in enacting a system of laws is not a further reason why it binds you, and has no special bearing on why you ought to obey, over and above the contribution made by this fact to its legitimacy. What binds you, and gives you reason to comply with the law, is the fact that it is a properly enacted law. A necessary condition of its being properly enacted is that you had an active role in the legislative process. But the fact that a system of laws is self-legislated is one of several conditions that work together to determine what makes them legitimate expressions of the general will. If, for example, a serious question arises as to why you should comply with a particular law, it will not be answered merely by citing your legislative role. You will want to know what made it a good law to have enacted. It would seem that the proximate reasons for complying with particular laws will be the reasons that guided the sovereign body (of which you are a part) in the process of their enactment. The reasoning that led you to enact the law should now give you reason to comply. The authority of a law comes from the fact that it is properly enacted, but its enactment is a structured deliberative process that gives weight to various reasons; it is not an arbitrary act of volition.

II. SOME APPROACHES TO THE LEGISLATION THESIS

This section considers some possible interpretations of the Legislation Thesis. All have textual support and contain ideas that belong in an account of the Legislation Thesis, but as they stand they are incomplete.[14] The sections that follow develop how this thesis should be explicated.

The idea that we legislate the moral law for ourselves may grow out of Kant's views about rational agency. A central component of Kant's conception of free choice is what Henry Allison has called the 'Incorporation Thesis'.[15] Kant held that an incentive never determines the will except through a choice made by the individual, which is to be understood as the spontaneous adoption of a maxim. The root idea is that choice is guided by normative considerations, and that nothing can become an effective motivating reason for an agent except by his or her taking it to be one. We get a picture of choice as guided by general principles that agents adopt (incorporate or take up into their wills), and take to have some kind of normative force both for themselves and for others. Since normative considerations may be experienced as constraints by imperfectly rational agents, this conception may include the idea that in choosing, I lay down principles for myself. When maxims are viewed as 'self-imposed rules', all rational choice may be thought to involve some kind of self-legislation.[16]

From this conception of rational choice one might extract different versions of the Legislation Thesis. The first would bear on the content of the moral law, while the second and third would offer accounts of its authority.[17]

A. Moral legislation as *Wille* as legislating for *Willkür*

Kant's distinction between *Wille* and *Willkür*, as a distinction between the legislative and executive functions of the will, leads explicitly to a view about the structure of the self within which reason plays a legislative role.[18] Kant assigns *Wille* the function of laying down principles to regulate the adoption of maxims by *Willkür*. He writes that 'laws proceed from the will [*von dem Wille*], maxims from choice [*Willkür*]; the will [*Wille*], which is directed to nothing beyond the law itself, cannot be called either free or unfree, since it is not directed to actions but immediately to giving laws for the maxims of actions (and is, therefore, practical reason itself)' (*MdS* 6: 226). The view may be that every individual's practical reason contains a legislative component, by which one wills a body of normative principles. (Here there are evident parallels with Rousseau, who appears to hold that each individual has a general will, in addition to one's private will, that wills a body of principles aimed at the common good). The Legislation Thesis would then trace the content of morality to the activity of *Wille* by the claim that *Wille* legislates the moral law for *Willkür*.

Until more is said about what guides the legislative activity of *Wille*, this interpretation of the Legislation Thesis simply raises further questions. On what grounds does *Wille* will its laws? What discretion does *Wille* have in its lawgiving? Here the tension between autonomy and objectivity becomes apparent. If *Wille* is unguided and 'just wills' certain laws, then almost anything could be willed as a moral principle. But that is incompatible with the objectivity of morality and would make its content arbitrary. On the other hand, if *Wille* must will a fixed set of principles, or if the content of its legislation is determined by prior considerations of rationality, then it will not be a sovereign legislator.

B. The Legislation Thesis as grounding the authority of moral requirements

One might hold that, given the motivational structure of a free will, the Legislation Thesis is needed to explain how moral principles can have authority for individuals. According to Kant's Incorporation Thesis, an incentive or motive can only determine a free will through a choice by the agent. One might think that this implies that a principle or requirement can bind a rational agent only through an act of the agent's will (choice, commitment, acceptance, and so on)—that is, that rational agents are bound to self-given laws *because* they legislate them, and that some act of the individual's will is a necessary condition of that individual having an obligation.[19] We might call this the 'Principle of Individual Sovereignty'.

Let me note two general problems with this line of thought. First, if one recognizes a distinction between justifying reasons and motivating reasons, it is not clear that Kant's Incorporation Thesis implies the Principle of Individual Sovereignty. Grant that a consideration can only motivate me by my taking it to be a reason. Still, this does not rule out the possibility of considerations that do justify, whose authority I ought to, but fail to acknowledge. The fact that I can only be motivated to act through my taking some consideration to be a good reason does not imply that no consideration can provide a justification except through an act of choice or recognition on my part.[20] Conversely, one can 'take up into one's will' a principle given by an external authority, by regarding it as a good reason for action. Thus, if the claim that a rational agent acts only from self-given laws is read as a motivational thesis, it need not entail that the agent is the ultimate source of their authority.

Second, and independently, it is not clear how the Principle of Individual Sovereignty can be squared with the universal validity of moral requirements. To maintain this principle, while holding that moral requirements are valid for all rational beings, Kant must show that every rational agent performs the relevant act of will (necessarily wills moral principles). Can that be done? Since I do not wish to defend this interpretation, I will not pursue the question. But once one allows that not everyone engages in the relevant act of will, one is led to the 'anarchist conception' which would make the validity of moral requirements a matter of voluntary commitment.[21] This is certainly not what Kant intended by the Legislation Thesis.

C. Moral legislation as willing acceptance of and identification with moral principles

A third possible approach, while conceding the difficulties of reconciling autonomy of the will with the universal validity of moral requirements, might focus on Kant's assertion that moral requirements bind agents in such a way that they must be viewed as legislating them. (Cf. *G* 4: 431, discussed below.) The idea might be that if one sees oneself as bound to moral requirements in the way that Kant thinks we are, one must view them as originating in one's own will.[22] Moral requirements are rationally grounded requirements that bind unconditionally. Someone bound in this way must understand their basis, and as a result be strongly disposed to acknowledge their authority over the entire range of sentiment and action. Such an agent views moral requirements as a set of commitments that cannot be given up without a sense of loss. That I am so bound is a conclusion about what I have reason to do, to which I am led by my own conscientious reasoning. As an imperfectly rational agent who does not automatically follow the conclusions of reason, I experience moral principles as constraints. Nevertheless I fully acknowledge their authority, and as a result, find that in my clearer moments I am willing to accept the obligations to which they lead. Moreover, since I see my ability to act from moral reasons as representing my higher self, I do not experience morality as a body of external constraints.

According to this approach, the Legislation Thesis is a metaphorical rendition of the fact that one's grasp of the rational basis of moral requirements leads one to acknowledge their authority and impose them on oneself, and to identify with them, with the result that they are not experienced as externally legislated. However, if our 'legislation' of moral requirements amounts to no more than the above process of rationally based acceptance and identification, it is not clear why it should be thought of as a process of legislating. Moreover, this account does not rule out the possibility that moral principles originate in some authority or set of values external to the will. A rational intuitionist or a natural law theorist might argue that our understanding of the rational basis of moral requirements has the same motivational effect. But such a theorist would certainly reject Kant's Legislation Thesis.

One might attempt to strengthen this account by asking what could explain the fact that I feel bound in the above way. One could argue that neither the will of God, an order of intrinsic values, nor objective relations between objects grasped by intuition (etc.) can explain the authority of moral requirements in the proper way. I can always ask why I should be bound to any of these, but in reflective moments, I find that it makes no sense to ask why I should fulfill my moral obligations. The only remaining explanation of these obligations is that moral principles in some sense originate in my reason and are self-imposed. However, mightn't the intuitionist or natural law theorist also hold that grasping the external basis of moral requirements leads to a comparable process of acceptance and identification, and that agents who fully grasp this basis will see no sense in asking why it is a ground of obligation?[23] These considerations aside, this interpretation says only *that* moral requirements must be (viewed as) self-legislated, without saying what that means, or without providing detail about the way in which we legislate the moral law. But rather than pursue these questions further, I will now outline an interpretation of the Legislation Thesis that attempts to fill this gap.

III. SUBJECT IN SUCH A WAY THAT ONE MUST BE REGARDED AS LEGISLATING

There are two distinct senses in which we may be said to legislate the moral law, that, taken together, preserve the objectivity of moral requirements and the autonomy of agents. The reason that there are these two senses is that there are two levels of principle that are candidates for being legislated, and that a different sense of legislation is appropriate to each. First, there is Kant's general formal principle—the Categorical Imperative. Second, there are the substantive moral principles and requirements that are arrived at (or as we might say, 'enacted') by deliberation guided by the Categorical Imperative. Rational agents legislate substantive moral requirements in this sense: one is bound to these requirements in such a way that one models the legislator from whom they receive their authority (the source of their authority). This is because one is bound to such requirements by the process of reasoning that makes them laws. The sense in which the rational will 'legislates' the Categorical Imperative is seen in the idea that the rational will is a law to itself, as it is understood by Kant: the Categorical Imperative is the law that emerges from the very nature of rational volition. In the next three sections I develop these ideas, and use them to interpret the Legislation Thesis.

To explain the first element of the Legislation Thesis, let me return to the important transitional point in *Groundwork*, II, where Kant writes:

According to this principle, all maxims are rejected which are not consistent with the will's own giving of universal law. Hence the will is not merely subject to the law, but *subject to it in such a way that it must be regarded as also giving law to itself* and just because of this as first subject to the law (of which it can regard itself as author). (*G* 4: 431; emphasis added)

Among other things, this remark expresses Kant's belief that the Formula of Universal Law may be restated as the Formula of Autonomy. Argument for this claim is offered in the three paragraphs following, and is generally thought to run as follows: A categorical imperative lays down unconditional requirements whose authority is not based on any contingent interests in the agents to whom they apply. But if the authority of a principle is not based in any contingent interest or desire, it could only come from the fact that the principle is self-legislated. Thus, we must view categorical imperatives as legislated by those whom they bind. The problem with this rendition of the argument is that it does not make evident *why* a principle whose authority is desire-independent must be legislated by those to whom it applies. For example, it is not clear how anything that Kant has said so far rules out a form of rational intuitionism that accepts objective obligations that apply unconditionally, but which originate externally to the will, and thus cannot be viewed as self-imposed.[24]

Kant's point is a deep one which can be defended, but to do so, we must be clear about exactly what it asserts. First the claim is that one is bound to an unconditionally valid principle *in such a way* that one must regard oneself as its legislator. It follows from the way in which one is bound to an unconditional principle that one must regard oneself as legislating it. Kant means exactly what he says here, and it is by taking this claim quite literally that one sees how to support it. One might think that the reason that one must *regard* oneself as legislator is that one *is* its legislator; but that is the conclusion to be demonstrated. What I shall argue is that someone bound to an unconditionally valid principle bears the same relation to that principle as its legislator would, so that, for all practical purposes, the distinction between subject and legislator collapses. Second, it is worth bearing in mind that this remark occurs within the context of the limited analytical task of saying what the moral law contains if there is such a thing. Just as Kant earlier argues that the concept of a moral requirement is sufficient to yield a statement of the supreme principle of morality (*G* 4: 420), here he asserts that it leads to an important fact about the relationship of moral principles to the agents to whom they apply (if there are such agents). The assertion is conditional, and does not yet claim that any moral principles are valid for us, or that they are valid for us because we legislate them. In sum, the claim at issue could be restated as follows:

> If an agent is subject to an unconditionally valid principle, that agent is bound to the principle in such a way that he or she must be viewed as its legislator.

How may this assertion be supported? The general idea is this: an agent subject to a principle that applies unconditionally will bear the same relation to this principle that its legislator would, in that the reasoning that would lead a legislator to enact it also explains why an agent ought to comply with it. The process of reasoning that justifies and establishes the principle as valid is also the source of its authority for an agent. The agent is bound to this principle and is motivated to comply by going through the deliberative process that confers validity on the principle and makes it a moral requirement—in other words, by carrying out the deliberative process through which a legislator would enact it as law. Such an agent models the source of the principle's authority, and in this way, an unconditionally valid principle collapses the distinction between subject and legislator.[25]

To bring out the intuitive basis of the argument, let us consider a situation in which the distinction between subject and legislator might collapse. Take the example of a (wise) professor setting policies for her course, which include procedures for selecting paper topics, submitting drafts, grading standards, and so on. Her policies and standards are demanding, but since she has taken care to explain their rationale, the students recognize that they are good: they are fair, they serve educational purposes which they accept, and her decisions have been guided by pedagogical concerns. The students are motivated to meet the requirements in different ways: some naively believe that high grades eventually bring great wealth, some wish to avoid the shame of submitting their work late or to maintain favor with their professor, and some rather unthinkingly have the habit of doing whatever their teachers say. But there is a select group whose reasons are more complex. Their primary motive for complying with the professor's policy is that it serves educational purposes that they accept, in a fair way. For them, the policy receives its authority from the same considerations that make it a good policy and led the professor to adopt it. This presupposes that they have gone through some version of the deliberative process that the professor used to evaluate different options in light of their pedagogical value, and these facts indicate certain parallels between students and professor. Their motivation to comply with her policy comes from their going through the process of reasoning that justifies the policy, and led her to enact it. Since they are motivated by their understanding of why it is a good policy, the students use the same rational capacities in complying that the professor used in framing and adopting the policy. This, of course, presupposes that they possess the same rational capacities as the professor. These students do not see the policy as externally imposed, and one might think that their relation to the policy is no different in any important respect from that of their professor.

However this story has to be more complex. What if the students differed with the professor over the merits of the policy; or what if it were not pedagogically best? Though they might question her policies, as long as the policies recognizably served pedagogical ends, they would feel bound to accept them, as they ought to. What explains that?

The students recognize (and are prepared to articulate) reasons for teachers to occupy positions of authority, where that implies that a teacher's announcing a policy, or set of requirements, creates an obligation for the class and is a reason for the students to fulfill it. They also realize that the justification for giving teachers this authority implies that its exercise should be guided by pedagogical concerns. The concern with educational aims should orient and structure the deliberative process by which policy decisions are approached, rendering certain features of prospective policies salient, and relevant to the decision of whether to adopt them; in short, it determines criteria for evaluating prospective policies. In light of these beliefs, they recognize a policy as (in their terminology) 'valid' for a class when it satisfies this condition: it is announced by someone in a position of authority, who adopts it as a result of a deliberative process guided by a concern for pedagogical value. Once they have ascertained that a policy is valid for their class, they need nothing further to conclude that they ought to accept it. For these students, the policy receives its authority from their understanding of why it is valid—that is, from the fact that it has been adopted by someone in a position of authority through a deliberative process guided by a concern for pedagogical value. There are two things to note here. To determine that the policy is 'valid' in this sense, the students must go through this deliberative process. Thus their assessment of the reasons they have for accepting the policy leads them to go through the deliberative process that the professor used, and which renders it a valid policy. Second, since going through this deliberative process will lead them to look at the substantive considerations for and against the policy, their understanding of its validity will include an understanding of its substantive merits (what makes it a good policy).

These points might be made as follows. If we were to spell out the considerations that motivate these students to comply with their professor's policy, we would end up giving the complete account of what makes it valid for the class. This would include the justification for putting teachers in a position of authority and giving them the right to set policies, as well as the values that guide, and sometimes limit, the exercise of this right. For the students to determine that this right has been properly exercised, they must also carry out this deliberative process, and thus go through the deliberations that led the professor to adopt it. Their motivational state will be given by this rather complex process of reasoning, which gives the full explanation of the validity of the policy. These students enjoy a status comparable to that of their professor, in that they are led to comply with the policy by the reasoning that justifies and confers validity on it.

It is worth noting that the professor best expresses her authority when she adopts a policy that the students can regard as supported by good reasons. Their understanding of its justification will lead them to respect it for its validity (rather than for contingent reasons). By contrast, a policy that was arbitrary could not carry authority in itself; to gain compliance, it would have to rely on external factors such as sanctions, reward, habits of obedience, and so on. Someone in power who enacts a policy that could only gain obedience through such external factors would have compromised her authority, in that her subjects would not be moved by her adoption of the policy, but by the sanctions attached to it. Thus the principle of adopting only policies that can be justified to all of her students, far from restricting the professor's authority, seems essential to preserving it. Someone in power exercises authority when the obedience of her subjects is based on their ability to recognize the soundness of her enactments.

This example points to the argument that Kant needs to support his claim that an agent bound to an unconditionally valid principle must be regarded as its legislator. A principle that applies unconditionally must receive its authority from the reasoning that explains why it is a valid moral principle. Accordingly, the argument on which Kant relies must work like this: if moral requirements apply unconditionally, they must carry an immediate authority that does not depend on an agent's desires. In that case, their authority must derive from the reasoning that explains why it is a valid moral requirement which a legislator would use to enact it as law. Thus the agent is bound to the requirement by the deliberative process that makes it a law (gives it the status of law). Now, an agent who can be bound in this way must be able to understand and be motivated by the justification of the law, and thus must possess the same rational capacities as would be required of its legislator. Moreover, the agent who is moved by an understanding of why it is a law goes through the same deliberative process as a legislator does in enacting it. In acting from the principle, the agent displays the same volitional state as the legislator. But if the legislator's volitional state is law-creating, the subject's volitional state is law-creating, and the subject may be regarded as legislating. Or as Kant says, one is bound to the law in such a way that one must be regarded as legislating. In this way one can claim that a principle that is unconditionally valid collapses the distinction between subject and legislator (or source of its authority).

As an example, assume a situation in which I am bound by a requirement of honesty. The reasons for me to acknowledge this requirement are given by the reasoning that explains why honesty is a duty in this situation. For Kant, the application of the Categorical Imperative gives a principle its moral status; in this case, the fact that the relevant maxims of dishonesty cannot be willed as universal law renders dishonesty impermissible. Thus the reasons to comply with this duty are given by the reasoning that shows why dishonesty cannot be willed as a universal law. In addition to showing *that* the maxim cannot be willed as universal law, the application of the Categorical Imperative will also reveal *why* it fails of universality. Asking whether a maxim can hold as universal law should bring to light substantive features of the action that can be used to explain what is wrong with an impermissible maxim. For example, attempting to universalize a maxim of dishonesty shows that it relies on the expectations produced by a general background of honesty to induce false beliefs in other agents for the purpose of controlling the outcome of their choices and actions. It is thus a maxim to intervene in the decision-making process of another and to manipulate others by their rational capacities, and fails to respect the sovereignty of other agents over their own decisions and choices.[26] Accordingly, an agent who carries out the universalization procedure is led to an understanding of the moral reasons for and against performing a certain kind of action. My point is that when I am led to act honestly by my application of the justificatory process that explains why it is a duty, I carry out the deliberative procedure by which a legislator would enact the principle of honesty as a law, and display the same volitional state. In carrying out the deliberative procedure that makes honesty a duty, I model the source of its authority.

One might object to this argument that moral requirements are not 'enacted' in the same way that political laws and other kinds of policies are, and that it makes no sense to introduce a legislator for moral requirements whom the agent is then to model. Since what is at stake is the propriety of talking about legislating moral requirements in the first place, one cannot assume any legislator of moral principles in advance of the argument we are trying to establish. The response to this worry is to show that the argument can be carried through in all its essentials without reference to any legislator whom the agent models. All that is required is that there be a deliberative procedure that explains what makes a principle a valid moral requirement, or confers validity on a principle, and is in that sense 'law-creating'. As long as moral requirements admit of a justification of this sort, there will be a legislative role that the moral agent is suited to step into by virtue of his or her rational capacities.

To recast the argument in those terms: The authority for an agent of an unconditionally valid principle comes from the reasoning that justifies and confers validity on it. In acting from this principle, the agent goes through the deliberative procedure that explains its validity, and makes it a valid principle; one is thus moved by considerations that create law. Since the agent is moved by considerations that anyone can regard as valid, his or her volitional state also carries authority for others. In short, the agent is moved by a process of reasoning that is law-creating, and this renders the agent's volitional state law-creating. Such an agent gives law through his or her willing.

However, there is a further worry. This argument relies on the idea of a deliberative procedure that has been termed 'law-creating'. This process provides the final justification of the principle, confers authority on the act of will, and, by extension, on the agent. But this appears to introduce an external source of authority that binds the rational will. Rational agents can only 'give law' when they guide their willing by this process of reasoning, and this process, rather than the agent's will, gives authority to any principles so chosen. Since a legislator bound to an externally given standard is not fully sovereign, one might ask: in what sense does the will legislate? The response must be that the process of reasoning by which law is created is not an external source of authority, but originates in the nature of rational volition per se. For Kant, the final justification of any principle is a formal condition of universal validity—that it can be willed to hold as universal law (has the form of law). What one must now show is that this is not an externally imposed standard, but is the law that emerges from the will's own nature, thus the law which the rational will gives to itself. To do so, I turn to the second element of the Legislation Thesis.

IV. THE RATIONAL WILL AS A LAW TO ITSELF

In a number of passages, Kant asserts that the rational will is a law to itself.[27] Late in *Groundwork*, II, he makes it clear that the law that the rational will gives to itself is the Categorical Imperative (specifically here the Formula of Universal Law): '. . . the fitness of the maxims of every good will to make themselves into universal law is itself the sole law that the will of every rational being imposes on itself, without having to put underneath it some incentive or interest as basis' (*G* 4: 444).[28] The idea that the will is a law to itself is arguably the principal theme of the second half of the *Groundwork* (from *G* 4: 431 on). I propose to explain it by connecting it to the principal theme of the first half, which is Kant's concern to ground the moral law in reason. Early on, Kant states that moral requirements must originate in reason if they are to have the necessity which ordinary moral thought attributes to them, and then, in two separate places, extracts a statement of the moral law from a conception of practical reason. One passage produces a statement of the Formula of Universal Law, and the other leads to the Formula of Humanity.[29] Each of these guiding themes tells us how the other is to be understood. The way in which the moral law is derived from practical reason reveals what it means to say that the rational will is a law to itself, and if we are to understand how Kant grounds the moral law in reason, we must see how it has this consequence. Kant does not announce in advance that moral requirements can carry necessity only if the moral law is a law of autonomy. He begins by stressing the importance of grounding moral requirements in practical reason, and only later claims to have shown that the moral law is the law that the rational will gives to itself. But it is clear that one extended argument is intended to accomplish both tasks.

These themes are connected by Kant's unusual method of deriving statements of the Categorical Imperative from practical reason, which might be termed a movement from form towards content. Kant arrives at two versions of the Categorical Imperative in this way, and we understand the sense in which the rational will is a law to itself when we see, in each case, how Kant moves from the stated conception of practical reason to the formula of the Categorical Imperative. Rather than provide a complete account of these arguments here, I will settle for an analysis of their general structure that clarifies this basic idea. I focus first on the derivation of the Formula of Universal Law (FUL), in which the movement from form toward content is most evident, and then touch briefly on the Formula of Humanity (FH).

Here is the territory covered by the first argument. Kant holds that an account of moral principles requires a 'metaphysics of morals', by which he means the inquiry into what can be derived from the concept of a pure rational will, setting aside empirical information about the conditions of human life. In order to advance to a metaphysics of morals, one must 'follow and present distinctly the practical faculty of reason, from its general rules of determination to the point where the concept of duty arises from it' (*G* 4: 412). Shortly after characterizing rational agency as 'the capacity to act in accordance with the representation of laws, that is, in accordance with principles', and the will as 'a capacity to choose *only that* which reason independently of inclination cognizes as practically necessary, that is, as good' (*G* 4: 412), Kant is noting the differences between hypothetical and categorical imperatives. Presumably they are the two kinds of objective principle through which practical reason judges the goodness of actions (its *allgemeinen Bestimmungsregeln*). Kant now asks 'whether the mere concept of a categorical imperative may not also provide its formula containing the proposition which can alone be a categorical imperative'. And indeed it does: 'when I think of a categorical imperative I know at once what it contains' (*G* 4: 420). Once Kant has in hand the *concept* of a categorical imperative, or practical law, he believes he is in a position to state *the* Categorical Imperative.

The key to understanding how the will is a law to itself is this last move—Kant's view that the concept of a practical law is sufficient to yield the only principle that can serve as one. By a 'practical law' Kant means a principle that can ground normative judgments that everyone can regard as authoritative, to the effect that an action is fully justified (e.g., that an action is good, permitted, required, etc., in an unqualified way). Thus his claim is that from the *concept* of a principle that can ground evaluative judgments that hold unconditionally, one can derive the *principle* by which such judgments can be made in particular instances. The concept of this kind of evaluation is taken to be sufficient to yield a principle by which this evaluative activity may be carried out. Now Kant appears to think that the idea of a practical law is implicit in the nature of practical reason, and since practical laws are principles that apply unconditionally, they should regulate all uses of practical reason. Thus, if Kant's argument is successful, it shows that the very nature of practical reason is sufficient to yield the regulative principle that is to govern its own proper exercise. Since the ability to guide one's actions by normative standards of some kind is central to the notion of willing, practical reason and rational volition are intimately tied for Kant. Accordingly, the argument would show that the nature of rational volition is sufficient to yield the highest normative principle that is to govern individual acts of volition. That is, the nature of rational volition is sufficient to yield the principle that authoritatively governs its own exercise. But that is to say that the rational will is a law to itself.

There are at least two points in this argument where serious questions arise. How is the idea of a practical law implicit in the nature of practical reason, or derived from an analysis of the structure of practical reasoning? Second, how does the concept of a practical law lead to a statement of the Categorical Imperative? We can make some progress here by looking at the connection between rational choice and justification implied by Kant's conception of rational agency. (See *G* 4: 412.) Kant defines rational agency as the capacity to guide one's actions by the application to oneself of general normative standards; simply put, it is the capacity to act from reasons.[30] This makes practical reason, as the cognitive faculty underlying choice or volition, an evaluative capacity. It is the capacity to construct justifications and to make judgments about the goodness of actions, and rational choice is conceived to be motivated by the justifying reasons at which this faculty arrives. Once one takes practical reason to be concerned with justification, and choice to be motivated by normative considerations, it is natural to introduce the idea of principles whose role in practical reasoning is to ground justifications that are unconditional. Such a principle would determine when an action is fully justified, or good without qualification, and could ground ought-judgments that hold unconditionally. Kant thinks that from the concept of a practical law one can extract the formal conditions that a principle must satisfy in order to serve as a practical law, and that a statement of these conditions should lead to a procedure for determining when they are satisfied by a principle or maxim. If a principle is to play the role of a practical law in practical reasoning it must be universally valid; it must be one that anyone can accept (thus one whose normative force is desire-independent). It must also be fully authoritative: its normative force must take priority over and exclude the force of the reasons given by one's desires; and it cannot get its authority from any higher or external principle, but must contain the ground of its own authority in itself.[31] (This implies that its normative force must reside in its form, rather than in its matter.) The FUL should be understood as a procedure for determining whether a principle satisfies these formal conditions, or has the form of a practical law. Roughly one determines whether a maxim has the form of law (and is thus fully justified) by asking whether it is a principle that anyone can regard as fully authoritative—more precisely, by asking whether you can regard the maxim as stating a sufficient reason for action while willing that everyone regard it as stating a sufficient reason for action, without inconsistency.

The path just traveled is something like this. A conception of practical reason as concerned with justification introduces the idea of a complete, or unconditionally valid justification and the correlative notion of a practical law. The concept of a practical law is sufficient to yield the supreme practical law, where that states the formal conditions that must be satisfied by any justifying principle or justified action, as well as the necessity of conforming to these conditions. In this way the nature of practical reason, or rational volition, yields a law that can guide its own proper exercise. I would not claim that what I have said so far makes complete sense of Kant's argument; but here is where we must look if we are to understand how the rational will is a law to itself.

Another route to this conclusion might be as follows. Practical rationality includes the capacity to evaluate actions by constructing justifications with normative force across agents. Though this process allows for creativity and invention, agents will normally have the experience of weighing normative considerations that are fixed independently of their choices. This conception of practical reason and rational choice suggests the highest-order principle of constructing and acting from substantive justifications which all other agents can regard as sufficient through the use of their evaluative capacities. This would be the principle that any individual's exercise of her practical reason must be such that all other agents, through the use of their practical reason, can arrive at and endorse the same evaluative conclusions. Moreover, one ascertains whether individual uses of practical reason meet this standard by asking whether all other rational agents can use their practical reason in the same way to arrive at and endorse the same conclusions. Since in this way individual uses of practical reason are assessed by testing them against the possibility of their universal exercise, the same process of reasoning that went into the initial normative conclusion is now transformed and redeployed to assess itself.[32]

I will now sketch briefly how the rational will is a law to itself in the Formula of Humanity. The introduction of this formula is preceded by a catalogue of different kinds of ends organized around their differing forms of value. Kant appears to be focusing on a different aspect of his conception of rational agency, now viewing it as the capacity to set ends for oneself taken to be of value or worthy of choice. As noted earlier, agents may experience the evaluation involved in the adoption of ends as a weighing of reasons and values fixed independently of their preferences and choices. However, the capacity to choose in this way is also a source of value; Kant believes that it possesses an absolute value which must be respected in all choices. In effect, the absolute value of rational nature constrains its own proper exercise by imposing limits on what ends can be of value, and what ways of pursuing them permissible. The way in which it does so can be expressed in a principle similar to that just given: individual uses of rational nature to place value on and adopt ends for oneself are to be limited by the ability of others to place value on and endorse one's pursuit of those ends through the use of their evaluative capacities. That is to say that one must limit one's exercise of one's rational powers by the condition that others can endorse and come to share one's conclusions through the exercise of their rational powers, and that one's choices can be justified to others in this way. Here is a fairly straightforward sense in which rational nature is a law to itself: rational nature yields a principle that can guide its own exercise.

Two final points. The first component of the Legislation Thesis applies to the substantive moral conclusions arrived at by the Categorical Imperative. In the last section we saw that it is established by further reflection on the concept of an unconditional principle, showing that the FUL can be restated as the Formula of Autonomy. In contrast, the argument that the will is a law to itself does not turn on the introduction of a new formula of the Categorical Imperative, but comes from reflecting on the shape of the arguments by which the FUL and the FH were earlier derived.

Second, if the gaps in the arguments can be filled in, it will be fair to say that the Categorical Imperative is a law that 'arose from our will as intelligence . . .' (*G*4: 461). Is it then a law that we give to ourselves? Since the elements of choice and discretion are absent, it is not a law that each of us gives to ourselves as individuals. Kant's typical phrasing is quite appropriate: it is the law given by *the* rational will—the law that springs from the nature of rational volition, or practical reason. (You and I have no say in this, but simply find that we have wills with this nature.) This is not a surprising result, for how else would one arrive at a principle that applies with the necessity Kant wants? Even so, this account provides a model that allows for objective necessity without presupposing an external source of reasons or value. It shows how there can be general principles that apply with necessity and create objective constraints on action that are not externally imposed. Moreover, as I will argue in the next section, a general formal principle of this sort is needed to make sense of the notion of 'legislating' at the level of substantive constraints, and the requirements set out by the FUL secure, rather than limit, the sovereign authority of the individual rational will.

V. LEGISLATING THE MORAL LAW

So far I have argued that the Legislation Thesis must be broken down into two separate ideas, one of which captures our relation to the substantive moral requirements established by the Categorical Imperative, and the other our relation to the Categorical Imperative itself. First, we are bound to substantive moral requirements in such a way that we must be regarded as their legislators. Since agents are bound to unconditional requirements by the reasoning that makes them laws, these agents model the source of their authority; in acting from them, they display a legislative will. Second, the way in which the Categorical Imperative is derived from the nature of practical reason shows that the will is a law to itself, and that the Categorical Imperative is that law. That is to say that the nature of rational volition is sufficient to yield a principle that authoritatively governs its own exercise.

It is time to see how these notions combine to yield an account of moral deliberation that preserves the necessity of moral requirements, while still allowing us to view them as autonomously legislated. We noted initially that for the notion of legislation to apply, law must be created by an act of a legislator. First, the (purported) legislator must have some discretion over the content of the law, so that what the law is remains open until the legislative process has been carried out. Second, the enactment of a law must create reasons for acting in certain ways which the subjects did not have before—reasons that result from an authoritative deliberative process. A sovereign legislator is not bound to any external standard or authority which fixes the content of law, or gives agents reason to conform to it, prior to the legislative process. I will maintain that one can make sense of the idea that rational agents legislate at the level of substantive moral principles and requirements by showing that there is an interesting analogy between moral deliberation and political legislation. The fit between the two is not perfect, but the parallels are rich enough to warrant Kant's talk of legislating the moral law. The proposal is that we regard the Formula of Universal Law as the 'constitution' of the rational will. It is the fundamental law that sets out the procedure that agents (citizen-legislators) must follow in order to enact substantive principles as law, just as a political constitution sets out the procedure that a sovereign body must follow in order to create law. Substantive moral requirements are the results of the proper application of this procedure, and receive their authority from this fact. When agents guide their deliberations and subsequent actions by the Categorical Imperative, they enact their maxims as law (enact law through their wills).

The plausibility of this analogy rests on certain features of the Categorical Imperative. First, the Categorical Imperative leads to a formal procedure for evaluating proposed reasons for action in the form of maxims. This means that it is up to individual agents to initiate deliberation by framing substantive maxims that they then bring to the procedure for assessment. Second, the aim of the procedure is to determine whether an agent's reasons for action provide a justification that anyone can view as sufficient. Since a principle that provides such justifications is a practical law, the Categorical Imperative asks whether the maxim stating the agent's proposed reasons is of the form to serve as a practical law (has the form of law). Since a maxim is always the subjective principle of some agent, it is not yet a practical law. But then, moral assessment, so understood, really is a question of determining whether a proposed maxim can be made into a practical law. Kant thinks that one settles the question by asking whether one can view one's maxim as stating a sufficient reason for action, while at the same time willing that everyone view it as a sufficient reason for action.[33] Finally, it is fair to say that by showing that your maxim *can* be willed as a universal law and adopting it on that basis, you have made universal law. You have used the Categorical Imperative to show that your subjective principle meets the conditions of universal validity, and thereby make it available for use as a practical law. In that way, the Categorical Imperative is a deliberative procedure that confers the status of law on those maxims (or their generalized versions) that it passes.

Now the FUL plays the same role in establishing and structuring the process of moral deliberation that a constitution plays in a legislative process. A constitution establishes a political process by which law may be enacted, and this process provides the final criterion of legal validity. Positive law is created when (and only when) the legislative process is properly carried out, and what makes something a law is that it has been duly enacted in accordance with this procedure. In addition, a constitution has an enabling function in relation to individuals.[34] In establishing a political process, it creates a sovereign body with which it invests the authority to make law (to confer the status of law on a proposal by taking it through the legislative process). Like a constitution, the FUL establishes a legislative process by which one gives a principle the status of law, and which serves as the final criterion of moral validity. It lays out what one must do to make one's subjective principles of action into valid justifying principles. In showing that a maxim of one's own can serve as a practical law, one frames a principle to which anyone may appeal in resolving matters of justification. Thus, one who acts on the basis of deliberation guided by the Categorical Imperative does give universal law. Finally, since the FUL is a procedure that creates the possibility of giving law through one's will, it confers legislative authority on the individual agent. When one acts from maxims with legislative form, one has framed a principle that anyone must regard as valid. One's taking the principle through the Categorical Imperative procedure gives it the status of law, and creates reasons for other agents to accept its normative implications. Moreover the FUL gives authority to enact law to any rational agent with the capacity to engage in this process of deliberation. (Every rational agent has a seat in Kant's assembly, with the right to bring proposals to the floor, simply in virtue of possessing the relevant rational capacities.)

Since the Categorical Imperative establishes substantive normative conclusions by showing that they meet the conditions of universal validity, it is clear how this picture of moral deliberation secures the objective necessity of moral requirements. But how does it leave room for the essential features of legislation?

The fact that the FUL leads to a formal procedure for evaluating substantive maxims allows for an element of discretion in determining the content of morality. Agents initiate deliberation by articulating maxims, which can be responses to many different kinds of deliberative problems. The question could be one of deciding whether a desirable action is permissible or finding a rationale under which it would be permissible, arriving at a course of action that strikes a reasonable balance between competing values, finding the best response to a problem of moral choice, and so on. Individuals must originate proposals of their own, and a good deal of creativity may go into their maxims. Since problems of choice and judgment need not have unique solutions, individuals have discretion over which maxims are taken through the evaluative procedure. The general point is that, while the FUL constrains the results of moral deliberation, its content will depend largely on the maxims that individuals bring to it. In addition, since one cannot say what can result from this procedure of deliberation in advance of carrying it out, the question of content is settled by the application of this procedure.

The second general element of legislation is that a legislator is thought to give other agents binding reasons for action through his will. The fact that he has properly enacted a law is a reason for agents in his domain to accept its normative force. If the principle establishes requirements or prohibitions, its enactment is a reason to fulfill any duties that it creates. If it establishes a permission, its enactment is a reason to regard the actions as ones to which agents have a right. In general, a legislative enactment is taken to settle the shape of the normative landscape for the issue in question. This feature is preserved by the account of moral deliberation, because carrying out the Categorical Imperative procedure resolves the question of what choices are justified in a given situation. When I reason and act from the Categorical Imperative, I have followed the deliberative procedure which makes a normative principle or conclusion valid, and my reasoning binds others to recognize its validity. Since my volitional state is given by the process of reasoning that confers validity on its conclusions, I give others reasons through my willing. Even if my deliberative conclusion is simply that a maxim is permissibly adopted, it makes available justifying reasons for action that cannot be specified independently of this process.

One may still ask why one is not following an external authority when one's deliberation is guided by the Categorical Imperative. Since the FUL is a principle constraining rational volition that we do not impose on ourselves as individuals, it is worth considering why it does not limit the autonomy, or sovereign authority, of individual agents. Since the FUL is derived from the nature of rational volition, it is not an externally imposed principle. It is the will's own principle, and as an ideal of universal validity or universal agreement, the FUL gives every rational agent rights of participation in the deliberative process. The fact that a deliberative conclusion may not be acceptable to some is a consideration that may have to be weighed by others. (While it may indicate a failure of rationality, it may also force one to conclude that the ideal of universal validity has not yet been achieved.) But the important point to stress is that the FUL invests individual rational agents with a kind of legislative authority. It is a deliberative procedure that enables any rational agent to give law, and to articulate practical principles that all must acknowledge. As such, it creates, rather than limits, the sovereign authority of the moral agent. Perhaps the point can be put as follows: a normative procedure which a legislative agent is bound to follow in order to give law also creates the possibility of exercising authority, because it binds other agents to accept the results of this procedure when properly carried out. Here it is instructive to bear the constitutional analogy in mind: the fundamental law establishes the procedure that must be followed in order to enact law, and sets limits to legislative authority. But it also creates legislative authority and confers it on a sovereign body. Without this law, there is no such thing as authority and no possibility of giving law.

A final question arises from the fact that individuals share a world with other rational agents who can also enact their maxims as laws and whose moral conclusions one may be bound to accept. Part of the problem is that I must often respect the judgments and choices of others, accept their justifications, and defer to their resolutions of moral problems, and so on. Aren't these situations in which I am bound to a principle that I cannot view myself as legislating? But the arguments of Section III provide a way to deal with this question. In arguing that 'the will is subject to the law in such a way that it must be viewed as also giving the law to itself . . .', Kant's intent is to show that I must be regarded as legislating any moral requirements that apply to my conduct. However, this argument can be generalized to show that the distinction between 'subject' and 'legislator' collapses in the case of the normative conclusions of others that are unconditionally valid. In such cases, I am bound to accept their normative principles, and their implications for conduct, by the reasoning that led them to adopt them, and which makes them valid. In seeing why I ought to acknowledge their conclusions as authoritative, I go through the same deliberative procedure, and recognize them as decisions I myself could have made.

To conclude, the substance of Kant's Legislation Thesis is found in the following complex of claims. (a) The fundamental law regulating moral deliberation is a principle derived from the nature of rational volition; it is thus the law that the rational will gives to itself. (b) This law leads to an evaluative procedure which assesses an individual use of practical reason by asking whether it is a use of practical reason that all can engage in and regard as valid, rather than by testing it against a given rule. Since the standard for evaluating individual uses of practical reason is the possibility of their universal exercise, this is a procedure in which practical reason need not refer to anything beyond the conditions of its continued exercise. (c) The fundamental law invests all rational agents with authority to enact substantive maxims of action as universal law (to enact law through their wills), and thereby enables them to adopt and act from principles that anyone must recognize as sufficient. (d) Substantive moral principles and normative conclusions are those that individual agents arrive at by the application of the fundamental law, and they apply to individuals in such a way that they may be regarded as their legislators: one is bound by the reasoning that explains why they are valid, one carries out the same deliberative process and exercises the same capacities in acting from a principle as would be exercised in enacting it as law, one's volitional state models the reasoning process that confers validity on the principle, and so on.

VI. SELF-LEGISLATION AND DIGNITY

In this final section, I touch briefly on some questions about the larger role of the Legislation Thesis in Kant's theory. It is commonly assumed that the Legislation Thesis establishes the authority of moral requirements. The thought is that we are bound to moral requirements because they are principles that we legislate. But this cannot be an adequate representation of Kant's view. The Legislation Thesis may be used to argue for the claim that we are bound *only* to requirements that we legislate; and it follows from the Sovereignty Thesis that a principle cannot bind a rational agent unless it is one which the agent legislates, or of which one can regard oneself as legislator. It would then be a condition on the validity of any moral principle that it be legislated by those to whom it applies. But it does not follow that we are bound to moral requirements simply *because* we legislate them. In this section I will argue that there is nothing extraordinary in this last assertion.

First, given the overall structure of Kant's argument, it cannot be his intention to argue directly from the Legislation Thesis to the authority of moral requirements. The elements of the Legislation Thesis are introduced in *Groundwork*, II, which is an extended analysis of the ordinary concept of duty. The general aim of this section is to state what morality contains if there is such a thing, and the authority of moral requirements is explicitly left unresolved, and deferred until *Groundwork*, III. The arguments for the authority of the moral law rely on earlier results, such as the equivalence of the Formulas of Universal Law and Autonomy. But nothing in *Groundwork*, II could lead directly to the authority of the moral law. In addition, since Kant's argument for the first element of the Legislation Thesis presupposes that moral requirements are authoritative, it cannot be used to argue for their authority.

Second, it is an open question how one can be bound to a principle by the simple fact that one has willed it. An obligation created by the fact that one has enacted a law is only as deeply grounded as the relevant act of will. If one can obligate oneself by one's own legislation, why couldn't one release oneself if one chooses? (Legislators can repeal, as well as enact laws.) If a mere act of will can create an obligation, it would seem that one could bind oneself to almost any principle whatsoever, regardless of content.[35] One might try to persuade an agent to acknowledge the authority of a law by noting the fact he or she has enacted it, but that might best be viewed as an invitation to reflect on what made it worth enacting, or why the agent initially made a commitment to the law. The reasoning that led one to enact a law should also give one reason to fulfill the duties that it creates.[36]

Instead of saying that you are bound to a law because you have legislated it, it is more accurate to say that you are bound to the law by the fact that it is a properly enacted law, and then add that your legislative role is part of what makes it properly enacted. Simply citing your legislative role is at best a partial explanation of its validity and authority. One must also say what makes your act of will an act of legislation, and cite the considerations that led you to exercise your powers in that way.

But then what does follow from the Legislation Thesis? Its principle role is to establish the 'ground of the dignity of human nature and of every rational nature' (*G* 4: 436). What gives the morally good disposition a claim to dignity is

the share it affords a rational being *in the giving of universal laws,* by which it makes him fit to be a member of a possible kingdom of ends, which he was already destined to be by his own nature as an end in itself and, for that very reason, as lawgiving in the kingdom of ends. (*G* 4: 435)

[T]he dignity of humanity consists just in this capacity to legislate universal law . . . (*G* 4: 440)

The connection between the Legislation Thesis and the dignity of humanity must be this. If we assume the absolute priority of moral considerations, the Legislation Thesis implies that rational agents legislate the highest regulative principles that apply to their conduct. Agents with this capacity are a kind of sovereign authority who ought to be accorded dignity. The Legislation Thesis thus explains why rational agents are worthy of moral consideration, as well as indicating what moral consideration requires. In virtue of their role in legislating moral requirements, they are entitled to the respect normally given to a sovereign authority, and should be treated in ways that acknowledge their sovereign status. They are to be treated only in ways that they can accept while at the same time regarding themselves as autonomous—that is, as free from subjection to any external authority, and as having the power to give law through their wills. A second implication of the Legislation Thesis is that moral requirements preserve human freedom and autonomy, along the lines of Rousseau's famous remark. In acting from duty, we do not submit to any external standard or authority. We act freely, because we act from principles that we legislate.

The authority of moral requirements raises large questions that I cannot resolve here. But having claimed that the Legislation Thesis does not explain why rational agents are bound to moral requirements, I should indicate in closing what does. What I have to say should hold no surprises. If one grants that we legislate moral requirements (as interpreted above), we are bound to them by the reasoning that leads us to legislate them—that is to say, by the reasoning that explains and confers their validity.

This thought must be spelled out in different ways, depending on the level of principle involved. A crucial step in Kant's arguments for the authority of the FUL is that it is the principle of a free will.[37] One way to develop this idea is to argue that an autonomous will would adopt the FUL as its fundamental principle. But one should then hold that it is bound to this principle by whatever would lead it to adopt it (rather than by the bare fact that it would or does choose it). And there are good reasons for it to choose this principle over alternatives, since only when it guides its volition by the FUL does it preserve its sovereign status. One can then omit the reference to its act of choice and argue that the FUL is the principle of an autonomous will because it is the principle that establishes and maintains its sovereign status. It is the principle that expresses the nature of sovereignty per se. The general authority of moral conduct would then be grounded in our interest in preserving the sovereign status that we have in virtue of our rationality.

We are bound to substantive moral requirements by the process of reasoning that shows that they are valid moral conclusions. This deliberative procedure has the guiding aim of determining whether the reasons offered for a proposed action are sufficient to justify it to anyone, and in carrying it out one uncovers substantive reasons that determine when an action is choiceworthy. These considerations have a role in explaining the moral status of the action, and thus in explaining why one should recognize the authority of the normative conclusion. One might think that this account binds moral agents to externally given reasons in a way that compromises their autonomy, but that would ignore several things. The guiding aim of moral deliberation is what renders certain features of actions morally salient and relevant as reasons for action, and we have seen that this aim is given by the will's own nature. And as I have tried to show in this essay, the process of reasoning that makes normative conclusions valid gives the rational agent a legislative capacity. Another route to the authority of substantive moral conclusions might also help allay this concern. I have suggested that the FUL is the fundamental principle of an autonomous will because it is the principle through which it establishes and maintains its sovereign status. But the FUL commits one to restricting one's substantive maxims to those that have legislative form (can serve as practical laws). Then it is only by acting from substantive maxims that have the form of law that a rational agent maintains its sovereign status, and enacts law through its will.[38]

NOTES

1. By Kant's count this is the third formula of the categorical imperative, though several paragraphs occur before he states it in imperative form. See, for example, *G* 4: 432: 'that everything be done from the maxim of one's will as a will that could at the same time have as its object only itself regarded as giving universal law'. It might be stated more clearly: act only from maxims which are such that, by adopting the maxim, one can at the same time enact it as a universally valid principle from which anyone may act.

2. Cf. also *KpV* 5: 31: 'Pure reason is practical of itself alone, and gives (to the human being) a universal law, which we call the *moral law*'. Through the fact of reason, reason 'announces itself as originally lawgiving' (*KpV* 5: 31).

3. Though I sometimes refer to the main idea behind the Legislation Thesis as 'self-legislation', I have not called it the 'Self-Legislation Thesis'. Though suggested by

some of Kant's phrasing, I believe that it distorts his moral view to say that one legislates 'for oneself'. As the remarks cited in the opening paragraph indicate, Kant believed that a rational agent is bound only to his or her own legislation—that is, to principles that one legislates in virtue of being a rational agent, however that is to be interpreted. However, the Legislation Thesis holds that one legislates, not 'for oneself', but for agents generally: one gives laws for a community of rational agents (a Realm of Ends). One is bound to these laws because they are properly enacted laws that hold for a community of which one is a member.

4. See, for example, Robert Paul Wolff, *The Autonomy of Reason*, and more recently, Rüdiger Bittner, *What Reason Demands*. Wolff holds that Kant was right to think that human beings are bound to moral principles only in so far as they legislate them, but wrong to think that such principles are necessarily willed by all rational agents. Thus he thinks that there are no universally valid moral principles, and that Kant's position on autonomy should have led him to conclude that valid moral requirements can only arise through freely chosen commitments (pp. 180–1, 219 ff.). Bittner's view is more subtle. He argues that Kant accepts a 'principle of autonomy' which imposes two conditions that must be conjointly satisfied by a valid moral principle: that the principle must *actually* be willed by the agent, and that it be *capable* of being universally legislated, or receiving assent from all rational beings. Principles that satisfy these two conditions would be valid moral principles. But it follows that one is not bound to any principle with which one is unwilling to comply: that one is unwilling to comply shows that the first component has not been satisfied. In this sense, Kant's principle of autonomy implies that there are no 'moral demands'; that is, moral demands have no authority for those unwilling to comply with them (pp. 104–10).

5. Jean-Jacques Rousseau, *Of the Social Contract*, II, vi, § 10 (hereafter referred to as *SC*).

6. *SC* I, vi–vii.

7. *SC* II, iii–iv, vi.

8. In other words, the conditions of generality that a law must satisfy contain certain requirements of procedural justice. For a law to express the general will it is not enough that it be directed at the common good, take the interests of all citizens into account, benefit and restrict all citizens equally, be limited to matters of common interest, and so on. Laws enacted by a ruling elite could satisfy these conditions, but could not claim the backing of the general will. In addition, they must be adopted by the right kind of political process (one to which all have equal access, equal input, in which there are no factions, and so on) and this process must actually take place. One might see the general will as the body of legislation that actually results from the operation of a properly structured democratic political process.

9. *SC* II, vi, § 7; IV, ii, §§ 7–8.

10. *SC* II, iv, § 8.

11. *SC* I, ix.

12. *SC* I, ix.

13. It is true that Rousseau's approach to the question of legitimacy is shaped by his recognition that private and public interests may conflict. He holds that a just and stable social order requires both the submission of all citizens to the general will (*SC* I, vi) and the transformation of each individual from a creature moved by private interests into a public-spirited citizen who thinks of him or herself as part of a social whole (*SC* I, viii; II, iv; and II, vi). Since this transformation is unlikely to be complete, conflicts between

private interests and the general will remain (*SC* I, vii) and citizens may fail to see their true interests (*SC* II, iii, § 1; II, vi, § 10). Thus Rousseau is concerned to show that the general will is, in some sense, one's true will, and that in submitting to it, citizens obey 'solely their own will' (*SC* II, iv, § 8) and act freely (*SC* I, vii, § 8; I, viii, § 4; IV, ii, § 8). But the implication is that one of the principal conditions of legitimacy is thereby met.

14. Thus, I do not mean to reject these interpretations in this section. My doubts about (b) are explained in Section VI, and I think that one can develop a more literal rendition of the Legislation Thesis than that suggested by (c).

15. See Henry E. Allison, *Kant's Theory of Freedom*, 39–41, 85–91. Kant states the Incorporation Thesis at *Rel* 6: 23–4.

16. Bittner develops such an interpretation of Kant's theory of action in his analysis of *G* 4: 412; see *What Reason Demands*, 96–9. See also Allison, *Kant's Theory of Freedom*, 88, 95–6. Both note that Kant at one point refers to maxims as 'self-imposed rules' (*G* 4: 438). Cf. also *MdS* 6: 225: 'A *maxim* is a *subjective* principle of action, a principle which the subject makes his rule (how he wills to act)'.

17. At issue here is the distinction between the 'search for' (*Aufsuchung*) the moral law (accomplished in the First and Second sections of the *Groundwork*) and its 'establishment' (*Feststellung*) (attempted in the Third Section) (*G* 4: 392). Though the latter is often described as establishing the 'validity' of the moral law, I use 'authority' for the sake of consistency with terms used elsewhere.

18. Here I draw on Allison's illuminating distinction between the executive and legislative functions of the will. See Allison, *Kant's Theory of Freedom*, 129–36.

19. Bittner endorses such a move, arguing that Kant's conception of action implies that a rational agent always acts from self-given laws, and that this in turn implies that only self-given laws are valid. See Bittner, *What Reason Demands*, 96–103, especially p. 96.

20. Some clarification is in order here, since I want to maintain a deep connection between justifying reasons and motivating reasons. I grant that nothing could count as a justifying reason that would not gain acceptance by, and motivate, a fully rational agent. Kant also held the view that nothing could count as a justifying reason, or valid requirement, which is inconsistent with the autonomy of the will, understood as the will's sovereignty over itself. That is, authoritative reasons must be such that a rational agent can acknowledge their normative force and continue to regard its will as autonomous. But the gap between ideal and actual rational agents warrants a distinction between justifying and motivating reasons.

21. Versions of this view are seen in Wolff, *The Autonomy of Reason*, and in Bittner, *What Reason Demands*.

22. Many of the ideas in this section were suggested to me by Thomas E. Hill, Jr. in conversation. For some of his discussions of self-legislation, see, *inter alia*, 'Kant's Conception of Autonomy' and 'Kant's Conception of Practical Reason', in *Dignity and Practical Reason*, 76–91 and 139–46.

23. For example, consider a natural law or divine command theory that regards moral requirements as God's will, and grounds the obligation to obey on the fact that he is our creator, to whom we are indebted for our existence. Such a theorist might hold that when we reflect on God's nature and our dependence on him, we see sufficient reason to conform to his will; indeed that it would be absurd to seek any further reason for why we ought to. He might also hold that we identify with our capacity to submit to the governance of an acknowledged superior. Similarly, a rational intuitionist might

hold that one's grasp of the necessary truths underlying moral obligation have a similar motivational effect, leading one to accept these obligations and impose them on oneself, and that one identifies with one's capacity to govern one's conduct in this way. Neither theorist would accept the idea that moral requirements are self-legislated.

24. This objection has been raised by several people. See, for example, Gerald Dworkin, *The Theory and Practice of Autonomy*, 39–40, and Bittner, *What Reason Demands*, 94–6.

25. The idea of being 'subject to an unconditionally valid principle', or what amounts to the same thing, 'bound by a practical law', is most naturally applied to moral requirements and prohibitions. However I understand 'unconditionally valid principles' and 'practical laws' more broadly to include principles of permissibility, and assume that what I say about requirements and prohibitions can be extended to permissions. By an unconditionally valid principle I mean a normative principle stating a requirement, prohibition, or permission, where that principle (a) is a valid conclusion of moral reasoning or derivable from moral principles; and (b) its normative force is not conditional on any desires or contingent interests, and takes priority over and excludes the force of reasons given by an agent's desires when they conflict with the principle. Its being unconditional means that its normative claims (e.g., that certain actions in specified situations are required, permitted, good or fully justified, etc.) ought to be accepted by anyone. Such a principle should guide the thinking of reasoners in general. If it holds that an action is morally permissible for an agent, then anyone ought to view that action as fully justified. Of course it also states desire-independent reasons for action that apply to agents in the situations covered by the principle. Requirements and prohibitions bind agents straightforwardly, by giving reasons for performing or refraining from an action that override reasons given by contrary desires. By contrast, permissions hold that an agent is fully justified in performing an action, and bind other agents not to complain or interfere. Unconditionally valid principles bind agents and reasoners in essentially the same way, though of course their action-guiding implications can differ, depending on an agent's circumstances.

It may seem odd to talk about 'legislating' principles of permissibility. But clearly legal systems do create permissions (liberty rights), and permissibility is a status that presupposes and is conferred on actions by a system of norms.

26. I want to hold both that the Categorical Imperative procedure (CI procedure) is the final criterion of right which determines the moral status of any maxim, and that the application of the CI procedure reveals substantive wrong-making characteristics of impermissible maxims. However, the latter may appear to suggest that there are substantive wrong-making characteristics that exist independently of the Categorical Imperative, and that these features of a maxim, rather than the fact that it fails the universalization procedure, are in the end what make it impermissible. Though I cannot give a full treatment here, some comment is in order. This problem will not arise if the right connection exists between the CI procedure and such wrong-making characteristics (for instance, that a maxim manipulates and attempts to control the decision-making processes of others). First, one would want the existence of these wrong-making characteristics in a maxim to be revealed by the application of the CI procedure. Second, they should be established as *wrong-making* features by certain aspects of the CI procedure, or by the guiding deliberative aim that underlies and leads to the CI procedure. In other words, the account of why they are wrong-making features

should not be independent of this deliberative procedure. For instance, the guiding aim of acting from principles that justify one's actions to any rational agent should render certain features of maxims morally salient and relevant to their assessment. If the guiding deliberative aim establishes what count as reasons for or against alternatives, then the proper application of the procedure shows that there is sufficient reason for choosing a given alternative—that is, it determines whether it is rationally willed. The fact that it is, or is not, rationally willed by this procedure determines the moral status of the action, but at the same time there is something to say about the considerations that guide this willing. One might decide that one can say either that a maxim of dishonesty is impermissible because it cannot be willed as universal law, or equivalently, that it is impermissible because it aims to manipulate others through their rational capacities and therefore fails to respect their sovereignty over their own choices. But there would be nothing wrong with showing that the Formula of Universal Law and the Formula of Humanity really are getting at the same thing.

For further discussion of the interpretation of the Categorical Imperative procedure see Onora O'Neil, *Constructions of Reason*, chs. 5–7; Christine M. Korsgaard, *Creating the Kingdom of Ends*, chs. 3–5; and, especially, Barbara Herman, *The Practice of Moral Judgment*, chs. 6–7 and 10. I take up some of these issues in Chapter 7 below.

27. Herein lies its autonomy. Kant writes: 'Autonomy of the will is the property of the will by which it is a law to itself (independently of any property of the objects of volition)' (*G* 4: 440. Cf. *G* 4: 447).

28. Cf. also *G* 4: 447: 'But the proposition, the will is in all its actions a law to itself, indicates only the principle, to act on no other maxim than that which can also have as its object itself as a universal law'. Kant writes:

If the will seeks the law that is to determine it *anywhere else* than in the fitness of its maxims for its own giving of universal laws—consequently if in going beyond itself, it seeks this law in a property of any of its objects—*heteronomy* always results. The will in that case does not give itself the law; instead the object, by means of its relation to the will, gives the law to it. (*G* 4: 441)

In other words, when the will takes as its fundamental principle something other than the FUL (the Categorical Imperative), 'it goes outside of itself'—it accepts a law other than the one that emerges from its own nature. In that case, it 'does not give itself the law', because it gives authority to a law taken from an external source.

29. At *G* 4: 412, Kant states that one must 'derive [moral principles] from the universal concept of a rational being as such', and then gives a conception of practical reason. This leads subsequently to the FUL at *G* 4: 421. Beginning at *G* 4: 426 we appear to find the same process in somewhat different form. Kant says that if a principle is to serve as a law for all rational beings, it 'must already be connected . . . with the concept of the will of a rational being as such', and proceeds to state a different aspect of his conception of practical reason, from which the FH appears. The appearance of the Categorical Imperative is somewhat miraculous in each case, and I do not go into these details here.

30. The normative standards involved include both hypothetical and categorical imperatives. For further discussion, see Chapter 3, Section IV.

31. For discussion of the idea that a law cannot get its justification from any external principle, see Korsgaard, *Creating the Kingdom of Ends*, 61–7.

32. This form of assessment, in which a use of reason is tested against the possibility of its own universalization, should be contrasted with one in which one asks whether

an agent's normative conclusion conforms with an independently given rule. In a rule-based model of evaluation, a further use of reason is required to test the result of the initial process of reasoning against a given rule, while in the model suggested by Kant's FUL, the reasoning that goes into a maxim is used to assess itself.

33. This interpretation of the CI procedure is a variant of the Scanlon–Pogge interpretation. See T. M. Scanlon, 'Kant's Groundwork: From Freedom to Moral Community' and Thomas Pogge, 'The Categorical Imperative'.

34. Compare H. L. A. Hart's discussion of 'power-conferring rules' as rules by which duties are created or altered in Hart, *The Concept of Law*, 26–41, 77–9.

35. For such reasons, acts of will (acts of consent, rational choice, agreement, and so on) are taken to create obligations only when they occur in the proper context. Both the background conditions of a choice and the reasoning guiding it can be as important as choice itself in explaining what creates an obligation. Contractarian theories try to derive obligations by asking what rational agents would choose under certain idealized conditions. The choice situation is set up so that the agents are free from certain restrictions (i.e., coercion of various kinds), but also so that the agents are properly responsive to various normative considerations. The contract seems designed to insure that the agents give these considerations due weight, and is a device for seeing what principles they lead to. But then the reasons for setting up the choice situation in this way, as well as the reasons that guide the choice of principles, figure in the justification of the principles. I find this point suggested by Thomas Nagel in 'Rawls on Justice', 5.

36. Imagine someone who on a whim commits himself to an arduous task. Is he in any way bound to carry it out? Years later you encounter him struggling with his 'self-imposed' burden. Do you admire his perseverance and urge him to continue? In urging someone to persevere in a self-imposed project, one often appeals to the reasons that led the other to undertake it in the first place, but no such rationale is available in this case.

37. See *G* 4: 447: 'a free will and a will under moral laws are one and the same'; and *KpV* 5: 29: the FUL is 'the law that alone is competent to determine a free will necessarily' and 'freedom and unconditional practical law reciprocally imply each other'.

38. This essay was first presented to a Workshop on Kantian Ethics held in Chapel Hill, North Carolina, in November of 1991. I am indebted to several of the participants, including Stephen Engstrom, Thomas E. Hill, Jr., Christine Korsgaard, Gerald Postema, Geoff Sayre-McCord, Nancy Sherman, and Michael Zimmerman, for their responses. I also would like to thank Thomas Pogge for written comments on the essay. Finally, I am especially grateful to Tom Hill whose comments on an earlier paper of mine helped shape the thinking that went into this one, and for continuing discussion of this paper and these issues. This essay was written with support from an NEH Grant to spend a year at the National Humanities Center.

5

Autonomy of the Will as the Foundation of Morality

I. INTRODUCTION

Kant concludes the analytical arguments of the Second Section of the *Groundwork* by claiming to have shown that autonomy of the will is the foundation of morality:

We simply showed by developing the generally received concept of morality that an autonomy of the will is unavoidably bound up with it, or rather is its very foundation [*zum Grunde liege*]. Thus whoever holds morality to be something and not a chimerical idea without any truth must also admit the principle of morality brought forward here. (*G* 4: 445; II, ¶ 90)[1]

In the preceding pages, Kant has advanced a battery of assertions about moral autonomy that to many represent a deeply appealing facet of his moral theory. We find a set of claims about the moral agent—for instance, that rational agents are in some sense the authors of the moral law, are subject only to laws that they give to themselves, and that such facts are the ground of human dignity. We also find various claims, implicit or explicit, about the content of moral principles, about conditions on the justification of moral principles, and about the proper understanding of morality. Taken together, they constitute Kant's general thesis that autonomy of the will is the foundation of morality.

Autonomy first appears in the *Groundwork* at a key transition in the Second Section that is arguably a critical moment in the history of ethics. Kant writes that from the first two formulas of the Categorical Imperative (the Formula of Universal Law and the Formula of Humanity) 'there now follows the third practical principle of the will . . .' here stated as 'the idea *of the will of every rational being as a will that legislates universal law*' (*G* 4: 431; II, ¶ 55). This formula, along with its variants, may be referred to as the Formula of Autonomy. Following the introduction of the FA, Kant's presentation of his moral theory undergoes a fundamental shift. He articulates an amended self-conception of the moral agent—that moral agents are not just subject to moral requirements, but are in some sense their legislators. With this conception of the agent comes a particular understanding of morality. The fundamental principle of morality is now referred to as 'the principle of autonomy',[2] and it is made clear that genuine moral requirements originate in the activity of rational volition, and cannot be based on values, principles, or ends that are externally imposed on the will. The warrant for this shift is found in a rather obscure stretch of text:

... all maxims are rejected which are not consistent with the will's own legislation of universal law. Hence the will is not merely subject to the law, but subject to it in such a way that it must be regarded as also giving law to itself and just because of this as first subject to the law (of which it can regard itself as author). (*G* 4: 431; II, ¶ 56)

This passage asserts a key component of Kant's doctrine of autonomy that I shall call 'The Sovereignty Thesis':

> *Sovereignty Thesis*: An agent who is subject to an unconditionally valid principle (i.e., a practical law) must be (regarded as) the legislator from whom it receives its authority.

My aim in this essay is to distinguish the various claims that make up the thesis that autonomy of the will is the foundation of morality and to offer a reconstruction of the arguments on which they depend. To do so I shall argue that autonomy should be interpreted as a kind of sovereignty. The model for the autonomous agent is the political sovereign not subject to any outside authority, who has the power to enact law. I elucidate the basic ideas and explicate various turns in Kant's arguments by developing the parallels between autonomy in agents and political sovereignty. Though the parallels give out at a certain point, developing them as far as they permit enables us to explain central features of Kant's doctrine of autonomy that otherwise remain obscure.

Several factors make this a fruitful approach to Kant's general thesis. Prior to Kant, autonomy was primarily a political concept applied to sovereign states with powers of self-rule.[3] Kant provides (in his view) key insights into the nature of morality and moral obligation by extending this concept into the moral domain. Moreover, it is noteworthy that the underlying framework of much of Kant's moral theory is established by his use of political and juridical concepts, such as 'law', 'legislation', 'autonomy', the 'realm of ends', 'subject' versus 'sovereign', and so on. We might expect that focusing on the inner logic of these concepts will yield important insights into various components of his moral theory.

Furthermore, understanding the autonomy of the moral agent on the model of political sovereignty naturally raises, and, I shall take on the burden of showing, permits a satisfactory resolution of, certain ongoing questions about the relation between autonomy and obligation in Kant's moral theory. Kant held that there are objective moral requirements that have unconditional authority. He also attributes autonomy to the moral agent by arguing that moral requirements are in some sense self-legislated—'every human will [is] *a will giving universal law through all its maxims*' (*G* 4: 432; II, ¶ 59). Autonomy is often taken to imply that one is subject only to self-imposed requirements and is free to place oneself under any requirements that one wishes. Clearly Kant does not intend the autonomy of the moral agent to have these implications. But many philosophers who recognize this fact have difficulty seeing how he can avoid them. How are objective and unconditionally binding obligations consistent with ascribing a meaningful conception of autonomy to the moral agent?

Exploring the parallels between moral autonomy and sovereignty raises these issues in a well-defined form. Viewing the moral agent as a kind of sovereign who is subject only to autonomously legislated requirements prompts two sets of questions. If the moral agent is not bound to any external authority, are there any limits on the principles or requirements that one can impose on oneself? Does sovereignty imply the absence of constraints on the use of one's legislative powers, so that one could, as it were, give any principle the status of law? If so, moral autonomy undermines moral objectivity. Second, if moral principles are self-imposed principles given the status of law through our own volitional activity, does that mean that we can change these laws at will? If we give ourselves these laws, can we also 'repeal' them, or release ourselves at will?[4] A related question is whether an agent's obligations depend on his actually performing certain volitional acts. In other words, if an agent fails to engage in the act of willing a principle that is generally viewed as morally required, is the agent then not bound by that requirement? If so, autonomy does not sit well with the unconditional character of moral obligation. These questions lead to a third and converse question: if there are significant constraints on the use of an agent's legislative powers and the agent is not free to repeal self-legislated laws, in what sense does that agent have autonomy? Modeling moral autonomy on political sovereignty gives us a better understanding of how these issues should be treated in Kant's moral theory.

We will see that the general thesis that autonomy of the will is the foundation of morality depends on two principal ideas. One is the Sovereignty Thesis—that agents subject to moral requirements must be regarded as their legislators and the source of their authority. Sections IV and V of this essay develop a reconstruction of the arguments for the Sovereignty Thesis that tells us how to understand this central but elusive notion. I shall develop two claims that give the sense in which moral agents are a kind of legislator. First, (a) an agent is bound to a moral requirement by the reasoning that makes it a law, and so must have the capacity to carry out the reasoning that makes a principle a law. Accordingly, such agents have a legislative capacity—the capacity to carry out the reasoning that makes a principle a law—that confers a legislative status on the agent. Second, (b) an agent who complies with duty out of respect for the moral law actually carries out the reasoning that makes a principle a law. This agent exercises her legislative powers, and in a sense to be explained, 'gives law through her will'. This rendition of the Sovereignty Thesis locates the autonomy of the moral agent in her capacity to employ a legislative process—a deliberative process that gives a practical principle its normative status. Possession of these capacities gives the moral agent a role in the rational process that gives certain substantive principles the status of (moral) law. In this respect it confers a legislative power on the agent.

The second principal idea, taken up in Section VII, is that the FUL is the basic principle of a will with autonomy. That is: (c) the FUL is the principle that is constitutive of the rational agent's legislative power (autonomy) in the sense that it is by following this principle that one gives law though one's will. By guiding one's will by the FUL one preserves and realizes one's sovereign status, and, as it is often put, one exercises one's autonomy. Establishing that the FUL is constitutive of our lawgiving capacities shows why the ascription of moral autonomy does not undermine the objective and unconditional character of moral obligation. By laying out the procedure that one must follow in order to give law, the FUL constrains what can be willed as universal law. Furthermore, it is only by guiding one's will by the FUL that one gives law through one's will. Thus, not just any act of volition can establish a law.

In order to forestall possible misunderstandings, let me clarify at the outset what I think one can and cannot establish on Kant's behalf. One could take Kant's doctrine of autonomy, including the Sovereignty Thesis, to apply either to 'the rational will'—that is, as indicated in the next section, to our idealized rational capacities—or to individual rational agents. The Sovereignty Thesis does straightforwardly apply to 'the rational will', in which case it is the less tendentious thesis that practical reason is an autonomous legislative power that generates authoritative moral standards, and that individual rational agents are subject only to requirements that issue from this power. But one of my concerns is to explore ways in which the Sovereignty Thesis and associated claims about autonomy and 'self-legislation' apply to individual agents. To this end, I will argue, first, that the Kantian moral agent possesses a kind of legislative power. Agents who are subject to duty, as Kant understands duty, possess rational capacities that give them a role in establishing moral principles and these capacities are the source of their dignity. Second, there is a recognizable (though limited) sense in which such agents exercise their legislative powers and give law through their will when they are moved by respect for the moral law. Finally, the FUL is the principle that is constitutive of these powers in that an agent (successfully) exercises these powers by deliberating from the FUL.

However, the Sovereignty Thesis does not imply that one is subject to a duty only if one has performed a specific volitional act (e.g., the act of willing the relevant moral principle, or of carrying out the reasoning that establishes a moral requirement). Kant's views about 'self-legislation' do not lead to a kind of voluntarism that ties moral obligation to actual (and specific) volitions—so as to imply that a duty or moral requirement would not apply to an agent who fails to perform the relevant volitional act (however it is understood). The unconditional character of obligation is undermined if the applicability of a moral requirement depends on an act of will that an agent can fail to engage in. I shall argue that Kant's understanding of autonomy implies that an agent is subject to a duty if there is a process of reasoning available to the agent that establishes that the action is required, whether or not the agent actually carries this reasoning out.

The structure of this chapter is as follows. Section II distinguishes some of the claims that go into Kant's doctrine of autonomy. Since, as we shall see, the Sovereignty Thesis follows analytically from the concept of an unconditional moral requirement, Section III takes up Kant's concept of a practical law, to provide supporting material for later arguments. Sections IV to VII are organized around showing that the FUL and the FA are equivalent in content. The equivalence of the FUL and FA, as I understand it, is established by the two ideas just cited (the Sovereignty Thesis and the claim that the FUL is the constitutive principle of a will with autonomy). It serves as a capsule statement of Kant's thesis that autonomy of the will is the foundation of morality. Finally, in Section VIII I show how the normative conception of autonomy developed in this chapter bears on the analytical arguments of *Groundwork*, III, where Kant identifies freedom with autonomy on the way to arguing that a free will is subject to moral principles.

II. SENSES OF AUTONOMY

Autonomy appears in the second half of the *Groundwork* in varying forms. For example, Kant refers to a principle of autonomy, but also views autonomy as a property of the rational will with implications for the nature of morality.[5] In this section I look first at the principle and its purpose within the overall argument. I then comment on autonomy as a property of the will and distinguish a set of related claims about morality and moral agency that follow from the attribution of autonomy to the moral agent.

A. The Formula of Autonomy

The Formula of Autonomy is another version of the Categorical Imperative, the more complete renderings of which include the following:

...all maxims are rejected which are not consistent with the will's own giving of universal law. (*G* 4: 431; II, ¶ 56)

...the principle of every human will as a will giving universal law through all its maxims...(*G* 4: 432; II, ¶ 59)

...that everything be done from the maxim of one's will as a will that could at the same time have as its object itself as giving universal law .... (*G* 4: 432; II, ¶ 59)

...to act on no other maxim than one such that it would be consistent with it to be a universal law, and hence to act only so that the will could regard itself as at the same time giving universal law through its maxim. (*G* 4: 434; II, ¶ 66)

The principle of autonomy is, therefore: to choose only in such a way that the maxims of your choice are also included as universal law in the same volition. (*G* 4: 440; II, ¶ 80)[6]

The FA holds that one's maxim of action must be such that, in adopting it, one can at the same time view oneself as legislating universal law (for a community of rational agents) in this sense: one is to proceed as though one's adoption of a maxim makes it a universally valid principle from which anyone may act and to which anyone may appeal in resolving questions of justification. In this way the FA demands that one act in such a way that one can regard oneself as giving universal law through one's willing. The principle might be stated as follows:

> *FA*: act only from maxims which are such that both of the following are simultaneously possible: (a) one acts from that maxim; and (b) by adopting the maxim, one enacts it as a universally valid principle of justification.

What does the FA add and what is its relation to the FUL? The FA does not lead to a new procedure of moral judgment that amplifies the FUL or the FH.[7] But neither is it a simple rewording of the FUL. Though Kant thinks that the two formulae are equivalent, he does not think that their equivalence is self-evident, since he argues for it in the ensuing paragraphs (*G* 4: 431–3; II, ¶¶ 57–9). Moreover, the FA introduces a substantially new idea into the overall argument of the *Groundwork*, by making explicit a feature of our relation to moral requirements that is not evident from the FUL.

Up to this point, Kant stresses the unconditional nature of moral requirements. Beginning from an analysis of the ordinary concept of duty, Kant claims that duties must be represented as categorical imperatives, or unconditional requirements. Furthermore, he argues that the very concept of a categorical imperative yields the principle that can be used to determine whether a maxim conforms to duty: we ask whether the maxim can without inconsistency be willed as universal law for agents with autonomy.[8] The FUL is thus the principle presupposed by the common idea that we are subject to duties.

The FA, on the other hand, expresses an idea that initially seems inconsistent with subjection to duty—that we are the legislators from whom moral requirements get their authority. The introduction of the FA is accompanied by the Sovereignty Thesis, that the will is 'subject [to the law] in such a way that it must be regarded as giving law to itself [... *so unterworfen das er auch als selbstgesetzgeben ... angesehen werden muß*] and just because of this as first subject to the law (of which it can regard itself as author)' (*G* 4: 431; II, ¶ 56). The phrases 'must be *regarded as* giving law for itself' and 'can *regard itself as* author' (emphasis added) raise questions that will be addressed later in this chapter. Setting them aside for now, the claim that emerges from this stretch of text is that rational agents are subject only to their own legislation, or bound only to their own will, which 'in accordance with nature's end is a will giving universal law' (*G* 4: 433; II, ¶ 60). That is to say that in introducing the FA, Kant asserts that moral agents are a kind of lawgiver and that moral requirements originate in their legislative capacities rather than being externally imposed.

Kant says that the FA follows from the previous formulas of the Categorical Imperative. But as we shall see, close attention to his arguments reveals that the FA and the Sovereignty Thesis follow simply from the unconditional character of moral requirements—the fact that categorical imperatives 'exclude from their commanding authority any admixture of interest as incentive . . .' (*G* 4: 431; II, ¶ 57). The Sovereignty Thesis claims that from the way in which the will is subject to law, it follows that the will must be regarded as its legislator. The support for this thesis is that it best explains how a practical law gets its authority. Kant seems to argue, roughly, that since a practical law applies unconditionally, its authority cannot be based on an agent's desires, or any contingent or empirically given interests. Instead, it comes from the fact that the agent is its legislator: only if the agent subject to the law is its legislator will its authority be independent of any empirically given interest, and so unconditional. Thus, both the FA and the FUL are derived from the concept of a practical law. Though the two formulae express what appear to be very different ideas, they turn out to be different aspects of our relation to the moral law, if Kant's arguments go through.

The function of the FA, then, is to signal a change in the self-understanding of the moral agent, and this in turn leads to a new understanding of what the Categorical Imperative says. It may now be stated as the requirement to act from maxims through which one can regard oneself as a sovereign legislator creating law through one's will—in effect that one should act in such a way as to express and maintain one's sovereign status. This is why Kant can say that 'Morality is thus the relation of actions to the autonomy of the will . . . An action that can coexist with the autonomy of the will is permitted; one that does not accord with it is forbidden' (*G* 4: 439; II, ¶ 78), and that 'the above principle of autonomy is the sole principle of morals . . .[which] commands neither more nor less than just this autonomy' (*G* 4: 440; II, 79). The quoted phrases turn out to be different ways of saying what morality demands. As we shall see in Section VIII, this understanding of what morality demands advances the overall argument of the *Groundwork* by setting up the argument in the Third Section that a free will is subject to moral laws: the equivalence of the FUL and the FA is one of the key components of this argument.

B. Autonomy as a Property of the Will

Kant defines autonomy of the will as 'the property of the will by which it is a law to itself (independently of any property of the objects of volition)' (*G* 4: 440; II, ¶ 80). Contemporary theory tends to regard autonomy as a psychological or motivational capacity—for instance, the capacity to govern one's actions, preferences, and values through rational, critical reflection.[9] But it is clear from Kant's characterizations of the autonomy of rational agents that he employs it as a normative concept: 'man is subject only to laws given by himself but still universal and he is bound only to act in conformity with his own will, which, however, in accordance with nature's end is a will giving universal law' (*G* 4: 432; II, ¶ 60), or is 'free with respect to all laws of nature, obeying only those which he himself gives and in accordance with which his maxims can belong to a giving of universal law (to which he at the same time subjects himself)'[10] (*G* 4: 435; II, ¶ 71). Such passages make claims about the sorts of authority to which the will is subject. When Kant attributes autonomy to the will he is asserting that the rational will is not subject to any higher or external authority, or bound by any principles that originate outside of its own activity, and that it is the source of the laws to which it is subject. The political metaphors framing his discussion indicate that the model for the autonomous will is the sovereign legislator answering to no higher authority, and that autonomy should be understood as a normative power, along the lines of a legal power, possession of which gives an agent a certain normative status. So understood, autonomy has both a negative and a positive aspect. Negatively, a will with autonomy is not bound to any external authority. As a lawgiver it is not bound to follow any external authority, and as a subject of action it is bound only to its own lawgiving. The positive dimension of autonomy is the lawgiving power of the will—its authority to generate normative standards through its willing. It is a law to itself in that it is sovereign over itself, and its own nature provides the final standards to which it is bound.[11]

For this reason we should reject psychological interpretations of Kant's notion of autonomy, and more generally, of the autonomy/heteronomy dichotomy. Kantian autonomy is commonly interpreted as a capacity to be motivated by reasons that make no reference to one's sensible inclinations and needs.[12] Kant certainly thinks that we have (and autonomy certainly presupposes) this motivational capacity. But his deeper point is that autonomy is the independence of the rational will from externally imposed principles and its capacity to generate authoritative norms. As some commentators have pointed out, Kant's primary use of the autonomy/heteronomy dichotomy is to distinguish two kinds of moral theories.[13] The first, exemplified by Kant's theory, takes the fundamental principle of morality to be a formal principle derived from the nature of rational volition in which we have a necessary interest, that, accordingly, grounds categorical imperatives. The other wrongly bases morality on a 'material principle'—a substantive value or end that is given independently of the nature of rational volition, on which any given agent's interest is therefore contingent. Such principles yield only hypothetical imperatives, because they are not principles to which an agent is committed simply in virtue of having reason, but rather have authority only for those with interests that a rational agent could have or lack; in short, they can be rationally rejected. What distinguishes these theories is whether they take the rational will to be the source of its own norms or to be subject to norms presented to it from outside.

Psychological interpretations lead to a similarly thin notion of heteronomy. Kant writes that when the will '. . . in going beyond itself, seeks the law that is to determine it in a property of any of its objects, *heteronomy* always results' (*G* 4: 441; II, ¶ 81). There is a tendency to think that 'heteronomy results' because the motive to act from such a principle must be supplied by a desire, understood narrowly as a 'sensible inclination'. But his point is that theories that ground morality in an end or value given independently of the will subject it to heteronomy because they bind it to an external source of reasons or authority. Desire-based principles produce heteronomy, not simply because they base motivation in desire, but because in taking desires to be sources of sufficient reasons, they accept a source of reasons or authority external to the rational will. But practical principles that are not obviously desire-based also lead to heteronomy—for example, theories that demand deference to social, political, or religious authority, as well as rational intuitionism, perfectionism, or divine command theories. Under moral theories of heteronomy, Kant includes both empiricist theories that base principles on feeling and sensibility and rationalist principles, such as the principle of perfection, based on ends grasped by understanding or reason (cf. *G* 4: 442 ff.). It is implausible to think that the motivational attachment to the latter is 'desire-based' in the narrow sense. The motivation presupposed by theories that base morality in heteronomy is desire-based only in a very broad sense in which 'desire' refers to any contingent interest or motivation that a rational agent could have or lack.[14]

Two further comments about autonomy as a property of the will are in order. First, viewing the will as sovereign over itself does not imply that an autonomous will is free from all norms. Certainly an autonomous will is subject to any principles that it imposes on itself, just as a political sovereign is obligated by any of its laws that apply to its own conduct. The larger question is whether there are any constraints on the principles that it can impose—that is, constraints on its lawgiving. Can it select its norms arbitrarily, or change them at will? Here it is instructive to note that familiar conceptions of political sovereignty found in the social contract tradition allow for constraints on a sovereign's legislative powers. A political sovereign is normally bound by the original agreement that, in creating its legislative authority, sets its limits. This agreement may be expressed in a constitution that constrains the exercise of legislative power by setting out the political process that must be followed to enact or to change law. It may also impose some substantive restrictions on what can be enacted as law. The sovereign can only enact valid laws by carrying out this constitutionally defined process. Put another way, its actions do not count as sovereign acts unless they follow this procedure. While constitutional limits may appear to restrict sovereignty, one must bear in mind that a constitution establishes sovereignty by defining the legislative process and conferring legislative power on some body or individual. Limits on legislative power that are built into this process are an aspect of the provisions that create it, and for that reason are not 'externally imposed'. What matters is not whether the constitution limits legislative authority, but whether it confers substantial and valuable powers.[15]

This conception of political sovereignty suggests an understanding of autonomy that makes it consistent with certain kinds of constraints. Autonomy is the will's sovereignty over itself, where that includes the power to establish particular normative standards. If so, the legislative activity of the will would be constrained by any principles whose role is analogous to that of a political constitution in defining its legislative powers. I will argue that the FUL should be understood as such a principle. It is the principle that is constitutive of autonomy, that sets out the deliberative process that the rational will must follow in order to exercise its legislative powers. So understood it is not an external constraint on the will since it is what enables a rational agent to give law through his or her will. This understanding of Kant's conception of autonomy, if it can be made to work, shows why it is consistent with the objectivity and unconditional character of moral obligation.[16]

Second, one might ask to whom—or to what—do Kant's claims about autonomy apply. Many (though not all) of Kant's remarks in these pages attribute autonomy to 'the will'. For example, the Sovereignty Thesis claims that 'the will [*Der Wille*] is . . . subject to [the law] in such a way that it must be viewed as also giving the law to itself . . .' Such remarks suggest that what for Kant has autonomy and legislates moral laws is the rational will. What, then, is the relationship between 'the rational will' and my individual will, or the will of a living and breathing finite rational agent?

References to 'the will' suggest the idealized capacity of human rational agents to reason and deliberate according to certain normative standards. Kant certainly thinks that the rational will, so understood, has autonomy (is sovereign over itself) in the ways just described: it is a lawgiving power that does not answer to any external authority, whose constitutive principle is the FUL.[17] The principles 'legislated' by the rational will are the idealized product of what human rational agents would will and include various principles to which agents are rationally committed. That is to say that they are principles that I would will if I exercised my rational capacities so as to satisfy the relevant standards. Idealized rational volition provides a normative standard for assessing the actual volition of individuals, but it should not be understood in a way that isolates it from the actual willing of individuals. For example, it should not imply a level of factual knowledge, vision and sensitivity, or impartiality that is beyond the reach of real human agents. It is what we would will if we follow all the relevant standards of practical reason, and when we engage in rational deliberation we presume that we *can* follow these standards. Moreover, we determine for ourselves what it is fully rational to will through the actual conscientious exercise of our individual rational capacities, sometimes on our own, but normally by hashing things out with other fallible agents like ourselves.

While it is the 'rational will' that in the first instance has autonomy, one important remark ascribes this autonomy straightforwardly to individual agents. In explaining what gives the rational agent a dignity that is beyond all price, Kant writes:

It is nothing less than the share [*Anteil*] it [the morally good disposition] affords the rational being in the giving of universal laws, by which it makes him fit to be a member of a possible kingdom of ends, which he was already destined to be by his own nature as an end in itself and, for that very reason, as lawgiving in the kingdom of ends . . .(*G* 4: 435; II, ¶ 71)

The autonomy of individual agents is their 'share' in legislating universal laws—the role that their rational capacities enable them to play in establishing moral principles through their individual use of these capacities. Their rational capacities give them the power to participate in this legislative process, and therefore confer the status of 'legislator in a kingdom of ends'.

We may say that an autonomous will is subject to two kinds of principles—principles that are constitutive of its legislative powers and principles that it legislates for itself through their exercise. This conception of autonomy as a property of the will leads to two further claims that I take Kant to accept:

> *Autonomy Condition on Valid Requirements*: A law or principle that binds a rational agent must be such that the agent can view himself as the legislator from whom it receives its authority. That is to say, the agent must be able to accept that requirement while at the same time regarding himself as autonomous (i.e., bound to no external authority and having authority to create normative standards through his will).

The Autonomy Condition is not a constraint on actions, but on the kinds of principles that apply to agents with autonomy. It holds that a requirement does not apply to an agent with autonomy unless it is supported with reasons that address the agent as autonomous.[18] The Autonomy Condition leads, as a special case, to a condition on moral theory: that a sound moral theory must represent moral requirements as legislated by (originating in the will of) the agents to whom they apply. As we have noted, Kant holds that common-sense morality understands duties as unconditional requirements on action, and he argues that it follows from the concept of an unconditional requirement that the agents subject to them must be regarded as their legislators. This leads to the surprising conclusion that a theory cannot capture the necessary and overriding character of duty unless it represents moral requirements as self-legislated. That is, the unconditional character of moral obligation *requires* that duties be represented as self-legislated. The implication that a moral theory *must* be able to express the supreme principle of morality as the FA is the basis of Kant's rejection of all moral theories of heteronomy, under which he includes all theories whose grounding of duty differs from his own (cf. *G* 4: 441–4). To summarize:

> *The Adequacy Condition on Moral Theory*: A moral theory that is adequate to the ordinary conception of duty must represent moral requirements as legislated by those agents to whom they apply.

III. THE CONCEPT OF A PRACTICAL LAW

This section explores the concept of a practical law that I believe underlies Kant's moral thought. A practical law should not be viewed as a 'command' to act in certain ways, but rather as a principle that plays a certain role in practical reasoning and justification for agents with autonomy. When correctly applied to an agent's circumstances it yields reasons for acting that are unconditionally valid. It is thus a principle to which one may appeal to resolve questions of justification in ways that anyone can regard as authoritative. Kant is led to the concept of a practical law through the need to ground conclusions about duty. The claim that an agent has a duty to act in a certain way holds that there are reasons for an action that apply with necessity (that apply independently of and limit the reasons given by the agent's desires) and universality (that anyone can regard as valid). Since conclusions about how one ought to act are derived from practical principles, claims about duty must be traced to a kind of practical principle that can ground their normative force.[19]

I want to suggest that a principle must satisfy two sorts of conditions in order to play this role in practical reasoning. First, a practical law must provide sufficient justification for an action. It must provide the final reason why the action is required or right in that it, or the pattern of reasoning which it initiates, brings the search for reasons to an end. A practical law could not do this if it were grounded in any higher principle, since that principle would then be the final source of justification.[20] In addition, a practical law must have immediate authority for an agent by providing a sufficient reason to perform the action. Thus, the normative force of a claim of duty must be grounded in a practical law whose application is not governed by any higher principle from which it gets authority.

The second condition is that a practical law must have some kind of justification or rational support. This is a strong requirement since it means that rational principles must be supported 'all the way down', or that a chain of reasoning, to be complete, cannot terminate in anything other than a reason. One can argue for this conclusion by appealing to the fact that we are dealing with principles of practical (as opposed to theoretical) reason which address rational agents. Kant's view of rational agency is that maxims and principles are adopted by agents through an act of choice, and that choice is always guided by reasons which provide both justification and motivation. Thus, a principle that binds rational agents must admit of some kind of rational support which explains why it is valid and which is available to move an agent to adhere. Without some reason available to the agent that could motivate its adoption, a principle could not get a motivational hold that is rationally based.

Accepting both of these features creates an obvious problem. A practical law must confer authority on lower level principles and conclusions about duty, without receiving its authority from any higher principle. Yet, it must have some rational support that gives it authority and motivating force. How can these conditions be combined? My hypothesis is that both conditions are operative in Kant's conception of a practical law and that they may be combined by saying that a practical law must contain the reasons for its validity and the source of its own authority in itself. The explanation of its validity must be found in some feature of the principle, and cannot take one outside the principle (say, by citing its conformity to some further principle). We may think of this quite abstractly and in purely formal terms as the requirement that a practical law *contain the ground of its own validity in itself*.[21] This requirement would be part of the concept of a practical law, since it is arrived at by analyzing what must be true of a principle that is to play the role of a practical law.[22]

Offhand it is not clear what it could mean for a principle to 'contain the ground of its own validity in itself'. However, we can find a sense for this idea in Kant's view that it is the 'form' of a practical principle rather than its 'matter' that gives it the status of law.[23] The form of a principle would be some internal structural feature. Then if the validity of a morally good maxim or principle comes from its having the right form (the 'form of law'), it will contain the ground of its validity in itself. Furthermore, a deliberative procedure that shows whether a principle has the right form aims at determining whether it can contain the ground of its own validity in itself, and thus whether it satisfies the conditions for being a practical law.

To pursue this idea we need to say more about how the Formula of Universal Law assesses the form of a maxim. Christine Korsgaard has observed that the form of a thing is its 'functional arrangement', or that 'arrangement of the matter or of the parts which enables the thing to serve its purpose, to do whatever it does'.[24] The form of a maxim would be the arrangement of its parts, which, to take the simplest case, are the action to be performed and its purpose. She explains Kant's view that the moral status of a maxim is determined by its form as the view that its moral status is not determined simply by the action or by its purpose—in a word, by its matter—but by the relations between them. The point of the universalizability test is to determine whether the components of a maxim are related in a way that allows the maxim to play the role of a practical law.[25]

This suggestion might be elaborated along the following lines. The maxim of an action may be understood as a principle that gives an agent's underlying reasons for performing an action.[26] It need not be limited to a statement of the proposed action and its end, but can include any information relevant to showing why the agent regards the action as choiceworthy. If so, the structural relationship that unifies the components of the maxim is a *grounding* relation between reasons and actions. When maxims are viewed as stating the reasons that the agent takes to justify an action, it is natural to understand the aim of moral evaluation as determining whether the agent's reasons for an action provide a justification that anyone can regard as sufficient—in other words, whether the agent's maxim is suited to play the role of a practical law in practical reasoning for agents with autonomy. The FUL addresses this question by asking whether one can take the maxim to state a sufficient justification for an action, while at the same time willing that anyone take it to provide sufficient justification, without inconsistency.[27] That a maxim cannot be willed as universal law in accordance with this procedure shows that it cannot play the role (does not have the form) of a practical law and that there are authoritative reasons not to adopt it. Here the FUL establishes a law, in the form of a prohibition or requirement. If a maxim can be willed in accordance with this procedure, it can serve as a practical law—that is, as a universally valid principle of permissibility that fully justifies an action.

This approach to moral evaluation does make it a question of a maxim's form. First, in asking whether the reasons stated by an agent's maxim provide sufficient justification for the action, one is asking whether the relation between reasons and action proposed by a maxim is the grounding relation required in a practical law. Are the components of the maxim related in such a way that it can play the role of (has the form of) a practical law? Second, the deliberative procedure provided by the FUL is plausibly understood as concerned with internal features of the maxim, because it focuses on the reasoning going into the maxim, rather than assessing a maxim in terms of its conformity to a further substantive principle, or conduciveness to an end. In looking for inconsistency between the simultaneous willing of the maxim and its universalization, the procedure in essence asks whether a maxim represents a use of practical reason that anyone can engage in and endorse. In that sense, the focus is on the normative claims implicit in the maxim.[28]

The legislative form of a practical law is the reason why it is valid and the basis of its authority. Since the test of legislative form is whether the principle can be willed as a universal law in accordance with the FUL, what makes a principle valid is that it can be willed as a universal law. Furthermore, since the FUL assesses whether a maxim has the form of a practical law, it shows whether a maxim has that internal feature which is the ultimate source of validity. Thus, a maxim certified by the FUL will contain the ground of its own validity in itself.

Further support for the hypothesis that this concept of practical law is operative in Kant's theory comes from various puzzling versions of the FUL which state that a maxim must be able to have its own universal validity as its object. Two examples are:

Act in accordance with maxims that can at the same time have as their object themselves as universal laws of nature. (*G* 4: 437; II, ¶ 76)

Act on a maxim that at the same time contains in itself its own universal validity for every rational being. (*G* 4: 438; II, ¶ 77)[29]

These formulas appear to state that valid maxims must have a kind of self-referential character, in that it is possible for them to contain their own universal validity in themselves, or to have it as part of what they will. To explain: any maxim has as its object some substantive content—that is, that one act in a certain way, for a certain end, for a certain reason, and so on. These formulas hold that a permissible maxim must also be able to contain as part of its object the universal validity of acting in this way, for this reason, and so on. In other words, it must be possible to add the universal validity of the maxim to the object (or content) that it already has. If universal validity is assessed by converting a maxim into a universal law— that is, a practical principle that everyone adopts and regards as having justifying force—these formulas lead to the evaluative procedure standardly associated with the FUL. But what is noteworthy about these self-referential versions is that they appear to express the requirement that a practical law be able to contain the ground of its validity in itself. The peculiar way in which they state the Categorical Imperative can then be explained as an expression of this feature of a practical law.[30]

In this section I have tried to show, first, that reflection on the concept of a practical law leads to the conclusion that such a principle must contain the grounds of its validity and authority in itself. Second, this abstract requirement is made intelligible by Kant's view that the form of a principle ultimately determines its moral validity. Third, since the FUL determines whether a maxim has the form that enables it to serve as a practical law, it shows whether a maxim has the form that renders it morally valid, and thus whether it contains the ground of its own validity in itself. This analysis tries to connect the concept of a practical law with the categorical imperative procedure. Since Kant thinks that the fundamental principle of moral evaluation can be derived from the concept of a practical law, we ought to be able to see how the features of that concept are reflected in the aims and operation of the categorical imperative procedure.

IV. THE EQUIVALENCE OF THE FUL AND THE FA

In the following sections I reconstruct the argumentative support for Kant's doctrine of autonomy, by focusing on the equivalence that Kant takes to hold between the FUL and the FA. After introducing the Sovereignty Thesis, Kant gives arguments for it in the three paragraphs that follow (*G* II, ¶¶ 57–9). The third paragraph, in stating the conclusion of the argument, comes close to laying out a bi-conditional asserting the equivalence of the FUL and the FA:

Thus the principle of every human will as *a will giving universal law through all its maxims* . . . would be very *well suited* to be the categorical imperative by this: that just because of the idea of giving universal law it is based on no interest, and therefore, among all possible imperatives, can alone be unconditional; or still better by converting the proposition, if there is a categorical imperative . . . it can only command that everything be done from the maxim of one's will as a will that could at the same time have as its object itself as giving universal law; for only then is the practical principle and the imperative that the will obeys unconditional, since it can have no interest as its basis. (*G* 4: 432; II, ¶ 59)

The first half of the paragraph says that, since the authority of the FA is not based on any interest, it holds unconditionally and is therefore suited to be the categorical imperative. Since the FUL follows from and expresses the concept of a categorical imperative (and since, moreover, 'there is only a single categorical imperative' (*G* 4: 421; II, ¶ 31)), the implication is that the FA is equivalent to the FUL (FA → FUL). The underlying idea (as we see in Section VI) is that a rational agent acts as a sovereign legislator and creates law through its willing by guiding its will by the FUL. The balance of the paragraph says that if there is a categorical imperative, it is the demand to act from maxims through which one can regard oneself as giving universal law (and thus through which one can regard oneself as a sovereign legislator). Again, we know that if there is a categorical imperative, it can be stated as the FUL. So the claim implied here is that the FUL may be re-stated as the FA (FUL → FA).

I begin with the argument moving from the FUL to the FA, which depends on the Sovereignty Thesis. Kant says that the FA (and with it the Sovereignty Thesis) follows from the two previous formulas of the Categorical Imperative, the FUL and the FH (*G* 4: 431; II, ¶ 55). But the arguments that he actually gives rely only on the formal feature of a categorical imperative which, of course, holds of both formulas, but is the explicit basis of the FUL—that categorical imperatives have unconditional authority. Kant writes that imperatives 'as represented above . . . exclude from their authority any admixture of interest as incentive, just by their having been represented as categorical . . .' (*G* 4: 431; II, ¶ 57). He is not yet in a position to establish that there really are any categorical imperatives, but one thing can still be done:

> . . . namely to indicate in the imperative itself, by means of some determination that it contains, the renunciation of all interest [*die Lossagung von allem Interesse*] in volition from duty, as the specific mark distinguishing categorical from hypothetical imperatives; and this is done in the present third formula of the principle, namely the idea of the will of every rational being as will giving universal law. (*G* 4: 431–2; II, ¶ 57)

In other words, Kant can advance the overall argument through a new formula of the Categorical Imperative that makes explicit through some feature of the formula ('by means of some determination' that the imperative contains) the distinguishing mark of a categorical imperative, that being the 'renunciation of all interest'. He appears to argue for the Sovereignty Thesis in the following way. Since a categorical imperative lays down requirements that are unconditionally valid, their authority cannot be based on appeals to empirically given or contingent interests.[31] How then are we to understand the relation between an agent and a principle that binds unconditionally? Kant seems to think that if one is not bound to a principle by a contingent interest, the only possible explanation of its authority is that one is (or can be viewed as) its legislator.[32]

A few points are worth noting here. First, the claim is made conditionally. Since at this point in the *Groundwork*, Kant is still engaged in the analytical task of saying what the moral law must contain if there is such a thing, the assertion is that if any agents are bound by categorical imperatives, they must be viewed as their legislators. But whether we are really subject to the moral law, and thus have this sovereign status, is left open until the Third Section. Second, the Sovereignty Thesis leads naturally to Kant's claim that 'the human being . . . is bound only to act in conformity with his own will' (*G* 4: 433; II, ¶ 60) and 'obey[s] only [those laws] which he himself gives . . .' (*G* 4: 435; II, ¶ 71). Agents who must be regarded as legislating those principles that take priority over any other principles and reasons that apply to their conduct are presumably bound only to their own legislation. Finally, the Sovereignty Thesis supports the Adequacy Condition on moral theory. If the agents subject to moral laws must be regarded as their leg-islators, then a theory that does not represent moral agents as legislating cannot ground the common notion of duty. That is, theories that locate the source of obligation externally to the will cannot capture the necessity of duty.[33]

However an immediate problem with this conclusion is that it seems to ignore the possibility of moral principles that apply unconditionally, but whose origin is external to the rational will. In particular, it is not clear that Kant has offered any reason to reject a version of rational intuitionism which holds that: (a) the first principles of morals state truths about right action that obtain in virtue of intrinsic values or relationships between objects that exist independently of the will; (b) these principles lay down unconditionally valid obligations, whose authority is independent of any contingent interests; and (c) our grasp of the validity of these principles has motivating force.[34] Furthermore, this argument does nothing to clarify the sense in which moral agents must be regarded as legislators. The argument as just presented, then, neither establishes nor explains the Sovereignty Thesis. Is there an argument that does?

V. THE SOVEREIGN STATUS OF THE MORAL AGENT

In this section I support and explicate Kant's Sovereignty Thesis by arguing that it is the nature of a practical law to collapse the distinction between subject and legislator. The main thrust of Kant's thesis that an agent who is subject to a prac-tical law must be regarded as its legislator is that no significant distinction can be drawn between 'subject' (the agent bound to a practical law) and 'sovereign' (the agent from whom such laws get their authority) for the kind of requirement that Kant takes moral requirements to be. The idea that we are subject to moral laws and the idea that we legislate them capture different aspects of our complex relationship to moral requirements. Put another way, the thesis that an agent who is subject to a practical law must be regarded as its legislator means that the agent bears the same relationship to the law as its legislator.

The aspect of this relationship signaled by our subjection to moral require-ments is straightforward: moral requirements provide reasons for action that apply unconditionally, limiting and taking priority over competing reasons for action. It is harder to see how our legislative role follows from, or is just another aspect of, the unconditional character of moral requirements. I will identify two respects in which agents subject to a practical law 'must be regarded as legislating', and in doing so explain how the Sovereignty Thesis should be understood. First, since a practical law applies unconditionally, an agent is bound to such a law by the reasoning that makes it a law. That is to say that the reasons for the agent to comply with the law are given by the deliberative process that makes it a law, which is the reasoning by which a legislator would enact it as law. An agent who is bound to law in this way must have the same rational capacities as its legislator and must be able to occupy the role of legislator—that is, must be able to carry out the deliberative process that gives it the status of law. Second, an agent who complies with a practical law—that is, complies out of respect for that law—has stepped into the legislator's position. This agent acknowledges the authority of the law by going through the deliberative process that a legislator would use in enacting it, the process of reasoning that makes it a law. I will argue that one can plausibly hold that this agent uses this deliberative process to give law through his willing, and thus can be viewed as legislating. Furthermore, it is because of the requirement that a practical law contain the ground of its validity and the source of its authority that the distinction between subject and legislator collapses in these ways. The authority of such a law must come from what makes it valid—the reasoning that makes it a law. Thus the reasoning that makes it a law binds an agent and is sufficient reason to comply. And an agent who complies with this law carries out and is moved by the reasoning that makes it a law; in other words, this agent does what a legislator would do to enact it as law.

I should caution that the parallels between practical laws and civil laws give out at a certain point. It is not my contention that the moral agent legislates in the same way that a civil sovereign enacts law, or that moral autonomy has all the same features as political sovereignty. Rather, there are substantial parallels that give Kant's use of juridical terms a point, and they can be used to unpack Kant's view that agents subject to a practical law must be regarded as legislating.

In order to develop these points, let us first see how the distinction between subject and legislator might begin to collapse in the case of ordinary civil laws, by considering different reasons that citizens might have for obeying them. (1) A citizen could be motivated to obey a law by the sanctions attached to it. In this case, the law does not have immediate authority for the citizen, since he complies in order to avoid punishment. He acts out of self-interest, not respect for the law. (2) A citizen could take the existence of a law as sufficient reason to obey it without, for example, considering why it was enacted, or why there is reason for individuals in certain offices to have legislative power. Such a citizen has a settled habit of obedience to law, but it is not based on an understanding of why the law is valid. Arguably this citizen does not act on a principle of respect for the law.[35] (3) A citizen might be moved to obey a law by the reasons that led the legislator to think it worth enacting.[36] This citizen, in contrast to the first two cases, takes on certain features of the legislator. He is led to give authority to the law by going through a deliberative process which parallels that employed by the legislator, and uses the same rational capacities in complying with the law which the legislator uses in enacting it. In this sense, citizen and legislator share the same motivational state. This relationship to a law is possible only among citizens who possess the same rational faculties as the legislator, and are able to comprehend the reasons for enacting a law and take them as reasons to comply. Since he goes through the deliberative process employed by the legislator in enacting the law, such a citizen is one who could occupy the role of legislator.

The third case presents a model of an enlightened citizen who is less likely to see the law as externally imposed. In addition, there is a kind of fundamental equality between citizen and legislator. Though they occupy different social positions, this fact does not mark any inherent differences in the agents involved. This citizen shares with the legislator the same capacity to evaluate reasons for and against a law, and could also occupy the legislator's role. However, as many theorists would point out, this case cannot serve as a general model of legal authority. What makes a positive law valid is not its content or its substantive merits, but the fact that it has been duly enacted by an agent in a position of authority in accordance with an established legislative procedure. And the formal fact that it has been properly enacted is generally viewed as giving citizens an authoritative reason for complying with and supporting the law.[37]

With this in mind, let us consider (4) a citizen who is moved to obey a law by a comprehensive understanding of why it is valid. The complete explanation of the validity of a law will be fairly complex. It is the sovereign's legislative act that determines what is law and gives citizens a reason to obey it, but only against the background of a general duty to take the will of a legitimate sovereign as a reason. Thus, the explanation of the validity of a law will include an explanation of the legislative procedure whose application gives citizens binding reasons for acting which they did not have before. It must also address the justification of legislative authority. It will say why there is reason to have individuals in positions of authority and what puts someone in that social position. In turn, the justification of legislative authority may bear on how it is constituted by specifying the ends, as well as various substantive (and procedural) constraints, that are to guide its exercise. This citizen's reasons for complying with the law are given by the complete explanation of its validity, and she is moved to acknowledge the law by her understanding of this explanation.

To elaborate: if one were to detail the considerations that lead this citizen to give authority to a law, one would give the complete account of what makes it valid. This would include an explanation of the origin of legislative authority, a specification of any values that either guide or limit its exercise, and an account of how the resulting legislative procedure creates law. Since this citizen is motivated by her understanding of why the law is valid, she thinks through the legislative procedure, asking whether the law is one that could have been enacted by a proper application of this procedure. By going through the deliberative process employed by the legislator, she is led to consider the substantive reasons that support the law and will see why the legislator thought it worth enacting. This citizen models the source of the law's authority in the sense that the reasoning that leads her to comply with the law is the process of reasoning that determines that it is valid. For her the authority of the law comes from what makes it a valid law. Since her understanding of its validity will take her through the deliberative process employed by the legislator, the parity between citizen and legislator seen in the third case also exists here. That is, in acknowledging the authority of the law, she exercises the same rational capacities that the legislator uses in enacting it; thus she must possess the same capacities of reason and judgment, and be the kind of agent who could occupy the role of legislator.[38]

With civil laws it is clear that the distinction between sovereign and subject never disappears. Although the citizen just described goes through the same deliberative process as the legislator, she is not for that reason its legislator. And only the deliberations of an authorized sovereign create law. To see why a practical law does fully collapse this distinction, let me note some obvious differences between civil laws and what Kant regards as practical laws that indicate why the distinction between lawgiver and subject remains significant for one but not the other.

First, the obligation of a civil law, though genuine, is derivative, since the explanation of its validity must say what puts its legislator in a position of authority. Ultimately, the authority of a civil law is grounded not just in its enactment, but in the legitimation of the political system. Second, even theorists who regard the positive enactment of a law as a sufficient reason for obeying it do not hesitate to include sanctions in their definition of law. The regulatory function of civil laws does not require citizens to comply out of an understanding of what makes something a law; any cluster of motives (including sanctions or habits of obedience) that leads them to give the laws their proper deliberative weight will do. But since a practical law must contain the source of its own validity and authority, its authority cannot be derivative, or based on appeals to contingent interests. Because of these features, a practical law collapses the distinction between sovereign and subject in a way that civil laws do not.

I shall now turn to the two sets of claims that explicate the Sovereignty Thesis, both of which can be supported by argument that begins from the nature of a practical law. First, since the authority of such a principle is unconditional and is not based on appeals to an agent's desires or contingent interests, it must stem from whatever it is that makes the principle valid. In Section III we saw that the validity of a practical law comes from its having the form of law—that form that enables it to resolve questions of justification. We also found a connection between legislative form and a specific deliberative procedure, since what determines whether a principle has that form is its universalizability according to the FUL. Thus the authority of a practical law comes from its having the form of law, or, what amounts to the same thing, from the reasoning that determines that the relevant maxim can or cannot be willed as universal law without inconsistency. That is to say that an agent subject to a practical law is bound to the law, and given sufficient reason to comply, by the reasoning that makes it a law. Now one could not be bound by a chain of practical reasoning unless one's carrying that reasoning out could motivate one to act. Accordingly an agent who is bound in this way must be able to carry out and be motivated by the reasoning that makes the principle a law. But a legislator (or legislative body) enacts law by carrying out an established legislative procedure that is acknowledged to create law. (A legislator wills a principle as law, as it were, by taking it through an established legislative procedure.) Thus, an agent who can carry out and be motivated by the reasoning that makes a principle a law has the capacity to carry out the process that a legislator employs in enacting it as law. Such an agent has the same rational capacities as the legislator and is the kind of agent who could occupy the legislative role.

Here is a more formal statement of this argument:

(a1) A practical law is a principle that is unconditionally valid, and has the ground of its validity and the source of its authority in itself. The ground of its validity (the reason why it is valid) is the fact that it has the form of law, as determined by the FUL.

(a2) Its authority cannot depend on appeal to contingent interests in the agents to whom it applies, but must be based on whatever makes it a law (the ground of its validity). That is, its authority comes from the fact that the relevant principle can or cannot be willed as universal law through the FUL.

(a3) Thus an agent subject to a practical law is bound by the reasoning that determines that the relevant principle can or cannot be willed as universal law, that is, by the reasoning that makes it a law.

(a4) An agent who is bound in this way has the capacity to carry out the deliberative procedure that makes the principle a law. That is to say that the agent has the capacity to carry out the procedure that a legislator employs in enacting the principle as law and has the same rational capacities required of its legislator.

The second dimension of the Sovereignty Thesis is this: an agent who accepts a practical law as a law actually carries out the reasoning that makes the principle a law. This agent must be regarded as legislating because he or she does, in a sense to be explored, give law through his or her willing. An agent who accepts a practical law as a law—in other words, an agent who acts *out of respect* for the law—regards it as a principle that is unconditionally required and complies for this reason. This agent acknowledges the authority of the law by carrying out the reasoning that makes it a law. That is to say that this agent carries out the deliberative procedure through which its legislator enacts it as law and displays the same volitional state as its legislator. We have noted that a legislator has the power to 'create law through his will' by carrying out an established legislative procedure. But if the legislator creates law through his will (i.e., by taking a principle through an established legislative procedure), so does the subject, since their volitional state is the same. Thus, an agent who complies with a practical law out of respect for that law gives law through his or her will. Here the distinction between subject and sovereign of a practical law has collapsed. To summarize:

(b1) Since the authority of a practical law comes from the reasoning that makes it a law, an agent who accepts the law as unconditionally required carries out the deliberative procedure that makes it a law (i.e., carries out the reasoning that determines whether it can or cannot be willed as universal law).

(b2) This agent carries out the deliberative procedure through which the legislator enacts, or wills the principle as law. Since the agent is motivated to act by this reasoning, the agent displays the same volitional state as the legislator.

(b3) Since a legislator creates law through his will and this agent displays the volitional state of the legislator, the agent creates law through his or her will.

(b4) Thus, an agent who acknowledges a principle as a law and who acts on that law, that is, acts out of respect for a practical law, must be (regarded as) the legislator from whom it receives its authority.

To sum up the argument to this point, we have identified two respects in which the agent who is subject to a practical law bears the same relationship to the law as its legislator. Because of the way in which a practical law gets its authority, an agent subject to a practical law is bound by the reasoning that makes it a law, and must have the same rational capacities as its legislator (a3–4). Furthermore an agent who complies with a practical law out of respect for that law carries out the process that makes it a law and thus gives law through her will (b1–4). The first argument shows only that the moral agent has the rational capacities required of a legislator. Is that agent actually a legislator? If the agent who acts from respect legislates in any interesting sense, then the arguments together establish that any moral agent is a legislator with the capacity to give law, whether or not the capacity is actually exercised. Since any agent who is subject to a practical law can in principle do exactly what is done by the agent who acts out of respect for a practical law, there is no relevant difference that justifies regarding one but not the other as a legislator. As I interpret it, then, the Sovereignty Thesis is that any moral agent is a legislator (whether or not she exercises her legislative capacities) and that the agent moved by respect does give law through her will.

Let me interject several comments needed both to fill out the above arguments and to qualify the analogies between moral autonomy and political sovereignty. In the next section I will consider some objections to the assertion that the moral agent acting from respect for the moral law gives law through her will in any meaningful sense.

First, most theorists would maintain that citizens are obligated to comply with a civil law by the fact that it has been properly enacted. But they would not assume that the validity of a law suffices to motivate compliance, or that the standard route by which citizens acknowledge its authority will take them through the reasoning that makes it a law. In these respects practical and civil laws differ. An agent is bound to and acknowledges the authority of a practical law only through the reasoning that makes it a law. One who complies with a practical law out of something other than an understanding of its validity does not act on that law, but on an altogether different principle. For example, if my reason for keeping my agreements is to avoid embarrassment to myself, then the fundamental principle that determines what I regard as a reason will be a principle of self-interest. An agent who keeps agreements because that is what is done, without understanding why it is done, acts on the underlying principle of doing what is approved (or something comparable). In neither case does one act from a principle that treats keeping agreements as unconditionally required, though one may act on a shadow principle that picks out the same actions while valuing them in a different way. Likewise, prudence or the avoidance of shame may provide good reasons for keeping agreements. But they do not ground any law of keeping agreements since they make fidelity conditional on interests that fidelity only contingently advances. There are two points here. One is that since the content of a practical principle is partly a function of the reasons that support it, the reasons to adhere to a practical law come only from the reasoning that makes it a law. A different set of reasons would be reasons for acting on a different principle, and moreover, one that is not a practical law. The other is that one acts on a practical law (rather than a shadow principle that resembles the law) only when one's compliance is motivated by one's understanding of the deliberative process that makes it a law.[39]

Second, both of the above arguments depend on viewing the FUL as a deliberative process that gives a principle its moral status; in other words, they suppose that the FUL is a kind of legislative process that confers the status of law on a principle.[40] The validity of a civil law comes from the formal fact that it has been properly enacted by an agent in a position of authority. The validity of a practical law derives from a comparable (though not the same) formal fact—the fact that the relevant principle can or cannot be willed as universal law without inconsistency. The important point is that the FUL is not a way of determining whether a maxim satisfies some further substantive principle, but rather is the procedure that makes a principle a law; it lays out the reasoning that gives a principle its moral status. The fact that a maxim cannot be willed as universal law makes it impermissible and establishes a law against its adoption. What makes a maxim permissibly adopted is that it can be willed as universal law.[41] Support for regarding moral agents as legislators comes in part from their having the capacity to employ this legislative process.

Third, one salient difference between civil and moral legislation that needs to be acknowledged is that a civil law is only in force when it has actually been enacted by a legislature. But a moral requirement applies as long there is a process of reasoning available to agents in that situation that establishes that it is required. We have seen that one dimension of the Sovereignty Thesis is that agents subject to a practical law are bound by the reasoning that makes it a law. For example, the fact that the maxim of deception for self-interest cannot be willed as universal law for agents with autonomy is sufficient reason for an agent in the relevant circumstances to refrain from deception. The Sovereignty Thesis does not suppose that one is subject to this requirement only if one has actually carried out this reasoning. It holds rather that a chain of reasoning that establishes the requirement must be available to the agent, and accordingly that the agent have the capacity to understand and be moved by this reasoning, whether or not the agent actually carries this reasoning out.[42]

This rendition of the Sovereignty Thesis is desirable, since agents can have duties that they fail to recognize. Moreover, if moral requirements applied only to agents who actually performed certain volitional acts, the unconditional character of duty that is central to Kant's view would be lost. On the other hand, one might object that once one takes the Sovereignty Thesis in this direction, one can no longer maintain that an agent who acts from respect for the moral law 'gives law'. However, I contend that there is a recognizable, though limited sense in which an agent moved by respect for the moral law gives law through his or her will, and thereby exercises autonomy: this agent employs a legislative procedure to give a maxim or subjective principle of action the status of law.

One essential component of legislation is that an agent in a position of authority uses a legislative procedure to give a proposed principle the status of law, and in doing so gives other agents a reason to acknowledge its authority. We have noted that the FUL is the basis of a deliberative process that gives a principle its moral status, or makes a principle a law. Moreover, it is a procedure that agents apply to maxims—subjective principles framed by an individual that express the reasons taken to support a proposed action. Given these features of moral deliberation in Kant's theory, the FUL is a procedure that an individual can employ to establish practical laws. If you determine that your maxim of action cannot be willed as universal law, you establish a law against its adoption by conferring the status of 'impermissible' on the proposed maxim. If you can universalize the maxim, you establish its permissibility and make it available as a justifying principle. In both cases, you establish a principle that resolves questions of justification and you give others authoritative reason to accept it. Furthermore, when you act from respect for the moral law, you are moved by the reasoning that gives your principle its normative status, whatever it is. Here I maintain that you are in the volitional state of a legislator, that is to say, of an agent who gives law through his will by carrying out a lawgiving procedure. In acting from respect for the moral law, you are moved to refrain from adopting an impermissible maxim (i.e., moved to comply with the prohibition) by the reasoning that shows the maxim to be non-universalizable. Your motivational state is given by the reasoning that makes it a law not to adopt this maxim. In the case of a permissible maxim, you adopt it on the condition of its universalizability, and your motivational state includes the reasoning that makes it a justifying principle. In each instance, you are in the volitional state that gives the principle on which you act its normative status. Your volitional state is in this way that of a legislator and you give law through your will.

The parallels between civil and moral legislation are imperfect. By showing that your maxim *can* be willed as universal law, you establish it as a justifying principle that other agents must acknowledge; but this 'practical law' is a principle of permission. Furthermore, other agents could 'establish' the same law (either permissions or prohibitions) at different times by determining the universalizability of the same maxim. But the important parallel with civil legislation is that an agent can use the FUL to confer normative status on a subjective principle.

The capacity to employ this principle gives the agent a role in generating moral principles (a 'share . . . in the giving of universal laws').

VI. OBJECTIONS AND REPLIES

In this section, I'll consider some objections that might be leveled at my reconstruction of the Sovereignty Thesis, both philosophical and textual. To begin, one might object on different grounds that moral agents lack legislative authority in any meaningful sense. First, the agent has no discretion over what laws to enact and thus does not determine the content of morality in any meaningful way. Second, the fact that one can only give law by following the FUL seems like an external constraint that undermines the agent's sovereignty. The textual objection is prompted by a passage in the *Metaphysics of Morals*. I'll begin with the latter, since the distinction that it draws between two different roles that a lawgiver can fill clarifies the intent of the Sovereignty Thesis.

The passage in question draws a distinction between the 'author of the law' (*Urheber des Gesetz*) and the 'author of the obligation in accordance with the law' (*Urheber der Verbindlichkeit nach dem Gesetze*). Kant writes:

One who commands (*imperans*) through a law is the *lawgiver* (*legislator*). He is the author (*autor*) of the obligation in accordance with the law, but not always the author of the law. In the latter case the law would be a positive (contingent) and chosen law. A law that binds us a priori and unconditionally through our own reason can also be expressed as proceeding from the will of a supreme lawgiver, that is, one who has only rights and no duties (hence from the divine will); but this signifies only the idea of a moral being whose will is a law for everyone, without his being thought as the author of the law. (*MdS* 6: 227)

Kant here asserts that a lawgiver can be the author of the obligation attached to a law without being the author of the law.[43] The author of a law is presumably the agent who 'writes' the law, or determines its content at his discretion. Only 'positive (contingent) and chosen [*willkürlich*]' or discretionary laws are authored in this sense. The author of the obligation, by contrast, is the agent whose will confers authority on the law and makes it a binding law. The author of the obligation in some sense addresses the law to some group of agents, and this volitional act is an authoritative reason to comply with the law that is independent of its content (or additional to any reasons for complying that may be found in the content of the law). The passage makes it clear that the moral law has no author in the first sense. Only laws whose content is contingent and discretionary are authored in this sense, and since the moral law is an unconditional law of reason, its content (including the particular categorical imperatives that give the content of morality) is not discretionary. But unconditional laws of reason can be expressed as proceeding from the will of a supreme lawgiver—here the divine will—in which case the divine will would be represented as author of the obligation attached to moral laws, though not author of these laws. By addressing a law whose content is given by reason to a group of agents, a supreme lawgiver with authority over those agents can make the law binding for them; his volition is a sufficient reason for them to comply with the law (i.e., a reason for compliance over and above any reasons based on the content of the law). In light of this passage, the intent of the Sovereignty Thesis, in asserting that the will subject to a practical law must be regarded as its author, must be to claim that such a will is the author of the obligation but not the discretionary author of the content of the law. More generally, when the *Groundwork* describes the rational will as giving universal moral law, we should take the will to be a lawgiver only in the sense of being the author of the obligation and not author of the law in the discretionary sense.

One might think that my reconstruction of Kant's conception of autonomy runs afoul of the distinctions drawn in this passage. According to my account, the agents subject to a practical law are bound by and have the capacity to carry out the reasoning that makes it a law. But the 'reasoning that makes a principle a law', as I have understood it, is the reasoning that generates particular categorical imperatives, and thus the content of the moral law. It may then seem that I am committed to holding that moral subjects are (in some extended sense) authors of moral laws, or that they legislate the content of the moral law, in contradiction to this passage.

However, my focus throughout has been on the authority of moral requirements. I take the Sovereignty Thesis to claim that the agents subject to practical laws are the legislators from whom these laws get their authority—in other words, the 'authors of the obligation' attached to these laws. One element of my account of the Sovereignty Thesis is that the FUL is the basis of a deliberative procedure that generates particular practical laws. But it is not thereby committed to holding that moral agents are *discretionary* authors of the content of the moral law. The claim that moral agents are bound by the reasoning that makes a principle a law is the claim that the reasoning that generates a practical law provides sufficient reason to adopt and to comply with this law (or: the fact that a principle results from this deliberative process is sufficient reason to comply with it); and it supposes that moral agents have the capacity to carry this reasoning out. That means that moral agents have the capacity to carry out the deliberative procedure that confers authority on these principles. An agent who is motivated to act by this deliberative procedure displays the volitional state that confers authority on that principle. Since that agent has followed a law-creating procedure, he may be regarded as the legislator who is the 'author of the obligation' attached to the law. In short, what makes moral agents the lawgivers from whom moral principles get their authority is their capacity to carry out the reasoning that generates the content of morality— since the fact that a principle results from this deliberative process is sufficient reason to comply with it. (Compare: the fact that a law is the result of an authoritative legislative procedure confers authority on and is sufficient reason to comply with that law.)

What the passage from the *Metaphysics of Morals* insists is that the moral law is not authored in a discretionary sense, presumably because its content is fixed by reason. But it is consistent with this claim to hold that objectively valid principles are generated by reason or a process of reasoning. Moreover, by factoring in a conception of reasoning as a norm-guided activity, we can use the idea of a deliberative procedure that generates the content of the moral law to make sense of the otherwise obscure idea that this content is 'fixed by reason'.

Furthermore, we need some deliberative procedure to make sense of the idea that obligation has an author—an idea which Kant accepts in both the *Groundwork* and in the *Metaphysics of Morals*. The author of an obligation creates authoritative reasons for action through his willing. I contend that to make sense of the idea of creating reasons for action through one's will, we need to refer to a structured act of volition, or a volitional act guided by a normative procedure. Civil legislation gives us a model here: a legislative body creates reasons for action and makes a principle obligatory by carrying out a recognized legislative procedure. My suggestion is that the deliberative procedure that generates the content of the moral law—a process of reasoning that individual agents can employ to arrive at conclusions about duty—enables us to make sense of the idea of moral lawgiving (creating obligation through one's will).

Regarding the objections that moral agents lack legislative authority, first, I grant that moral agents do not have discretion over the content of the moral law since there is no discretion over whether a maxim is universalizable. But, as I have just tried to make clear, the Sovereignty Thesis does not require such discretion, since its claim is that moral agents are 'authors of the obligation' and not the discretionary 'authors of the laws'. That point aside, it is worth noting that the FUL does leave agents discretion over which maxim to consider as laws. For Kant moral assessment begins from subjective principles that represents agents' responses to their contexts of action and that they take to provide good reasons for action. Maxims may be viewed as agents' proposals for possible laws that are to be assessed by the FUL. To put the point another way, since the FUL places formal constraints on willing, it leaves agents free to formulate substantive principles for consideration as laws, and moreover, yields substantive results only in application to such principles. (The parallel in the political realm is that a constitution creates a legislative process, rather than a complete body of law; positive laws result when proposals are taken through the legislative process. The limit of this parallel is that once a maxim is proposed, its universalizability is determined.)

Second, we have seen that there is no general inconsistency between legislative authority and constitutionally imposed constraints. Sovereign authority must be constituted by some set of rules that specify the legislator's powers and lay out the procedures through which they are exercised. The constitutive rules that create legislative authority also define its limits. But to the extent that they make it possible for an agent in a position of authority to give law, they are power-conferring rules, and should not be viewed as constraints. The FUL is not an external constraint if it is the general principle that is constitutive of legislative authority and that confers it on an agent.

A related objection is that the kinds of principles that Kant regards as practical laws are not originally enacted by a sovereign in the way that positive civil laws are. If so, one might think that little is gained by setting up parallels between civil laws and moral principles and then pointing to ways in which the moral agent models a political sovereign. However, the argument does not require an original moral sovereign who 'enacts' moral principles as laws; all that is needed is a deliberative procedure that gives its results the status of law, with a role that individual agents can step into. The view of the FUL as a kind of legislative process supplies this component of the argument. An individual who establishes whether his or her maxim can be willed as universal law has carried out the procedure that makes that principle a law and has effectively filled the legislative role.[44]

A final objection to consider is that what prevents the distinction between sovereign and subject from collapsing in the case of a civil law keeps it intact here: an agent with the *capacity* to carry out a legislative process, or who simulates a legislator's reasoning, does not thereby have the *authority* to give law. Law can only be created by an agent with legislative authority. What, then, gives the moral agent the authority to legislate? I believe that Kant's considered view is that an agent with the capacity to carry out the deliberative process that makes a principle a practical law has the authority to do so. Possession of the relevant rational capacity confers legislative authority (gives one a 'share . . . of legislating universal laws') just because it is the capacity to carry out the procedure that makes a principle a law. While this supposition is another point at which civil and moral legislation diverge, it also indicates a deep-seated feature of Kant's attribution of autonomy to the moral agent. A civil legislator (or legislature) occupies a privileged social position that confers powers not given to agents who are merely subject to law. But the role of 'moral legislator' is not a socially established position that some individuals occupy to the exclusion of others. The sole qualification for occupying this role with respect to a practical law is that one have a certain kind of rational nature, and any agent with these capacities is in a position to use the legislative procedure to give a maxim the status of law.

An instructive parallel that remains in each case is that legislative authority is constrained by the way in which it is constituted. The position of civil legislator is established by a set of social arrangements, in particular the constitutional provisions that confer legislative authority on certain individuals and define its exercise. As I shall argue in the next section, the FUL plays an analogous role. It is constitutive of moral autonomy by laying out the procedure that one must employ to give law through one's will. By defining this procedure, it confers lawgiving power on the moral agent. But at the same time it constrains an agent's legislative authority since one only gives law when one guides one's will by the FUL.

In the last two sections, I have tried to explicate and to support Kant's Sovereignty Thesis by detailing different ways in which a practical law collapses the distinction between sovereign and subject. First, since an agent subject to a practical law is bound by the reasoning that makes it a law, the agent must have the same rational capacities that are required of a legislator. Second, an agent who acts from a practical law carries out the reasoning that makes a principle a law. Since this agent uses the FUL to give his maxim the status of law and is in the volitional state that makes a principle a law, he gives law through his will. The Sovereignty Thesis, as I have interpreted it, does not imply that one is bound to a requirement only if one has actually carried out the reasoning that makes it a requirement. Rather, it holds that an agent who is subject to a practical law is a legislator, whether or not he or she has carried out the reasoning that makes the principle a law, and that agents who act from the FUL exercise their share in giving universal law. These arguments show that for the kinds of principles that Kant thinks of as practical laws, 'subject' and 'sovereign' are ultimately the same role.

VII. THE PRINCIPLE OF A SOVEREIGN WILL

An argument that establishes the equivalence of the FUL and the FA in the other direction (FA → FUL) is suggested by the following paragraph:

> When such a will is thought of, then even though a will which is subject to law may be bound to this law by means of some interest, nevertheless a will that is itself supremely lawgiving [*ein Wille, der selbst zuoberst gesetzgebend ist*] cannot possibly, as such, depend upon some interest; for a will that is dependent in this way would itself need yet another law that would limit the interest of its self-love to the condition of a validity for universal law. (*G* 4: 432; II, ¶ 58)

This passage is best read as making the following conceptual claim about a sovereign legislator:

> A supreme lawgiver is not guided by any contingent interest in the exercise of its legislative power—that is, the reasons for enacting any of its laws are not given by any contingent interest.

(A non-contingent interest in this case would be one that the legislator has qua legislator—for example, the interest in expressing and maintaining one's status as a legislator.)

This claim may be supported by showing how it follows from the logic of the juridical concepts of sovereignty, legislative validity, and authority. Political sovereignty (understood as resting either in an individual or in a body of individuals) can be specified along these lines. (i) Defined negatively, a sovereign legislator is not bound to any higher political authority, but is subject only to laws of its own making. (ii) Defined positively, a sovereign legislator has authority to enact law, in that its enactment of a law is normally sufficient reason for anyone subject to the law to comply (even apart from sanctions attached to the law).

What I will call (following Kant) a 'supreme sovereign authority' further idealizes this concept of political sovereignty. Condition (i) does not rule out obligations to an independent moral order that constrain lawmaking. But a supreme sovereign authority would not be bound by any authority external to its own will. Understood positively, a supreme sovereign authority has the capacity to create law through its will in the sense that its legislative act is sufficient by itself to create law. That is to say that the complete explanation of the authority of a law will not refer to anything beyond the sovereign's legislative act. Even a supreme sovereign authority, so understood, must guide its legislative activity by any principles that are constitutive of its authority. But that is not a restriction, since these are the rules that define what counts as lawgiving and thus make it possible to give law. This amounts to no more than the condition that it use its legislative powers in ways that can be regarded as fully authoritative, and it is reasonable to attribute to a sovereign authority a higher-order interest in expressing and maintaining its sovereign status.

One may interpret the above paragraph of *Groundwork*, II as stating the conditions that must be satisfied for legislative activity to count as that of a supreme sovereign authority. It claims that when a legislator takes its reason to enact a law from a contingent interest, it does not act as a supreme sovereign authority. To do so, a legislator must guide its lawgiving activity by reasoning that anyone can recognize as valid. To explain: a legislator whose activity is guided by a contingent interest satisfies neither of the two conditions of supreme sovereign authority. First, in basing a law on a contingent interest that it counts as a reason for the law, the legislator ties itself to an external principle. Since in effect it cedes its authority to an external principle, it does not satisfy the negative condition. Second, when a legislator takes its reasons for enacting a law from a contingent interest, nothing in its willing per se provides any reason to adhere to the law. The law will have authority only if there is a further principle which gives the subjects reason to accept that particular law, or which requires them to take the sovereign's will as a reason, whatever its content. Since the authority of the law depends on 'yet another law', the legislative activity is no longer sufficient by itself to create law.

The second part of this argument can be elaborated by noting how the requirement that law originate in the legislator's willing rules out certain bases of authority. Other agents could have reasons to acknowledge a law through sanctions attached to it, or from their having an interest in some good provided by the law, or a desire to do what the legislator wills. But in all of these cases, it is some interest in these agents, rather than the legislator's willing, that is the ultimate source of reasons to acknowledge the law. Its normative force is then conditional on their having such interests, or in some contingent alignment of the interests of legislator and subject. Alternatively, the authority of the law could derive from a higher-order principle that obligates these agents to take the willing of the legislator as an authoritative reason for acting, whatever the legislator wills. In this case, the normative force of specific laws willed by the legislator derives from this higher principle, which explains why they are binding. Either way, the laws get their authority from a source external to the legislator's will, and the legislator's willing is not sufficient by itself to create law.

This account of legislative authority raises at least two further questions: How could a volitional act be law-creating in itself? And since ruling out motivation by 'contingent interests' eliminates almost every motive attributable to a rational agent, what interests could guide the activity of a sovereign authority? The arguments to this point indicate that a legislative act is law-creating when it is guided by reasoning that anyone can regard as authoritative. A sovereign whose will is guided by reasoning that anyone can accept will produce principles that anyone can regard as authoritative— that is, principles whose form suits them to serve as practical laws. Thus, if a sovereign is to create law through its willing and to qualify as a sovereign authority, it must have the fundamental principle of willing principles with the form of law. The FUL would then be the deliberative procedure that a sovereign must follow in order to create law through its will, and, in that sense, is the principle constitutive of sovereign authority.

This account shows that the sovereign's willing is a source of law since the properties of an agent's volitional state are determined by the principles willed and the agent's reasons for willing them. Since the sovereign who guides his willing by the FUL adopts principles with the form of law because they have the form of law, his volitional state will, so to speak, have the form of law. It is a volitional state that anyone must regard as authoritative, that gives other agents sufficient reasons to acknowledge the principles adopted. One might say that the sovereign's will has 'the form of lawgiving'.

We now have the material needed to argue from FA to FUL. If we assume that a sovereign authority has a highest-order interest in expressing and maintaining its sovereign status, then it has the principle of acting so as to satisfy the conditions of sovereignty—that is, of exercising its legislative powers so as to preserve its independence from external authority and to create law through its will. This principle is the Formula of Autonomy. But in order to exercise its will in ways that are fully law-creating, it must guide its legislative activity by reasoning that everyone can regard as valid, and enact principles with the form of law. Its fundamental legislative principle will then be the FUL. If we take a supreme sovereign authority to be the model for an autonomous will, we have here an argument for the conclusion that a will with autonomy must have the FUL as its principle, which can be summarized as follows:

(c1) A will with autonomy is not bound to any external authority and has the power to create law through its will.

(c2) The principle of an autonomous will is the FA: the principle of acting only from maxims through whose adoption one can regard oneself as giving law through one's will.

(c3) If an autonomous will is to create law through its willing, it cannot take its reasons for enacting law from any contingent interests, or enact laws whose authority comes from contingent interests in those whom they address. It must guide its legislative activity by reasoning that anyone can regard as valid, and thus will enact principles that can serve as practical laws (have the form of law).

(c4) Thus the fundamental legislative principle of a will with autonomy, through which it exercises its sovereignty, is to will only principles with the form of law (principles that can be willed to serve as practical laws in accordance with the FUL) (c1–3).

(c5) Since a legislator is bound to its own laws, a will with autonomy has the principle of acting only from maxims that can be willed to serve as practical laws (c4).

As a final point, this argument provides a way to make sense of Kant's claim that a will with autonomy 'is a law to itself (independently of any property of the objects of volition)', as well as showing why the FUL is that law. The argument begins from the concept of an autonomous will, understood as a sovereign will, and shows through an analysis of this concept that the FUL is the principle internal to or constitutive of its legislative power. The authority of the FUL for a will with autonomy rests on this fact; a will that rejects this principle cannot think of itself as autonomous. Since the FUL is the principle derivable from the concept of a will with autonomy and is its own internal principle, it is the law that the autonomous will is to itself.

VIII. AUTONOMY AND FREEDOM

I have argued for a normative interpretation of Kant's conception of autonomy as the sovereignty or legislative power of the rational will. In its lawgiving, the will is not subject to any laws beyond the enabling principle constitutive of its legislative power. Since this principle constitutes and defines its legislative power, and is derivable from the idea of sovereign lawgiving, it is not externally imposed but is the law that the rational will gives to itself. As a subject of action, the rational will is bound only to its own lawgiving (i.e., to substantive principles arrived at through its own constitutive principle), and it has the capacity to act from its own laws. Up to this point I have employed this reading of autonomy to gain insight into the analytical claims of *Groundwork*, II through which Kant argues that autonomy of the will is the foundation of 'the generally received concept of morality' (*G* 4: 445; II, ¶ 90). But Kant's analytical arguments extend into the opening paragraphs of *Groundwork*, III, where he argues that 'a free will and a will under moral laws are one and the same'—by which I take him to mean that the moral law is the basic principle that is constitutive of free volition (*G* 4: 447; III, ¶ 2). In the course of this argument, Kant claims that the freedom of the will is its autonomy. In this section I will carry my reading of autonomy through to the arguments of *Groundwork*, III.

It may seem at first that autonomy, as I interpret it, and freedom are different kinds of properties and that the differences complicate the straightforward identification that Kant asserts in *Groundwork*, III, ¶ 2. Autonomy is a normative property of the will—the sovereign independence of its legislative power—while freedom is the form of causality characteristic of rational agency. Here it will help to note again that autonomy is primarily a feature of the will in its legislative function. Freedom, on the other hand, is a property of the will in its executive function as a subject of action—specifically the capacity to determine oneself to act on one's own laws, that is to say, on the laws that the will issues in its legislative function in accordance with its own constitutive principle.[45] Autonomy then is a necessary condition of freedom. It is in virtue of possessing autonomy that a rational will has a causal capacity that satisfies the concept of freedom. Simply put, a free will has the capacity to initiate its own actions, independently of external influence; it is in some fashion a self-originating cause of action. Any rational will is the source of its actions in the weaker and generic sense that its actions originate in its own judgments of what it has reason to do. To satisfy the definition of freedom (i.e., to initiate its own actions), a will must in addition be the source of the principles that guide its judgments of what it has reason to do. It must have the power to give itself laws, where its lawgiving is guided by its own internal principle and not by any external influence or source of authority. And that power is what Kant means by autonomy.[46]

Kant's well-known argument that 'a free will and a will under moral laws are one and the same' begins with this definition of freedom: Will is a kind of causality of living beings in so far as they are rational, and freedom would be the property of such causality that it can be efficient independently of alien causes determining it . . . (*G* 4: 446; III, ¶ 1).

This definition of freedom of the will is 'negative', since it indicates the kinds of determination that such a will is free from without specifying the principle of its operation or what a free will is the capacity to do. The main steps of the argument are as follows:

(1) A free will is free in a negative sense (by definition).
(2) A will that is free in this sense has autonomy.
(3) The basic principle of a will with autonomy is the FUL.
(4) Thus the basic principle of a free will is the FUL: a free will is subject to the moral law in the sense that the moral law is the basic principle of free volition.

The argument unfolds out of an analysis of the 'mere concept' of freedom of the will (*G* 4: 447; III, ¶ 3) and does not show that any such wills exist or that we have them. The linchpin of this argument is autonomy. The new move made in *Groundwork*, III, ¶ 2 is Kant's assertion that the freedom of the will is its autonomy. Step (3) then relies on the arguments of the Second Section, discussed in Section VII above, to connect autonomy and the principle of morality.[47] At this point we see how the turn to autonomy at *Groundwork*, 4: 431 is intended to advance the overall argument of the book: its contribution is to set up this argument connecting freedom and morality. Here I will consider the move from freedom to autonomy (Steps (1) and (2)).

Will is the capacity to act from the representation of laws and principles (*G* 4: 412 (II, ¶ 12), 427 (II, ¶ 46)), or the capacity to initiate actions through normative judgments about what one has reason to do. Freedom of will negatively defined is the independence of this capacity from determination by 'alien causes' or external influences. This independence certainly includes freedom from causal determination. In free volition, desires and incentives do not cause action directly, but only lead to action through the judgment that the incentive is a good reason for action (through the incorporation of the incentive into a maxim). The spontaneity of such judgments consists in the fact that they are normatively guided; they are directed by an agent's grasp and weighing of the relevant normative considerations and not by anything external to the agent's grasp of reasons. Presumably the negative concept of freedom also includes 'motivational independence'. The presence of a desire or empirically given incentive is not per se a reason for action. A free will has the capacity to reflect critically on its desires and the capacity to be moved by reasons whose normative force does not depend on empirically given incentives.[48] To that should be added the capacity to act from reasons that are not presented to the will from any external source (e.g., by an external source of authority). A will that took all its reasons from externally given incentives would simply be a conduit for the influences that give rise to these incentives—even if they lead to action in the manner characteristic of rational volition, through a normative judgment on the part of the agent.[49] Simply stated, a free will can act without being told what to do by something outside of itself, be that an empirically given incentive or some outside authority. If it always required outside direction, it would not satisfy the definition of freedom as independence from determination by external influence.

At the same time, a free will is not lawless. As a form of volition (rational causality), it must act on some law or principle that connects the actions to the agent. At this point Kant asks: 'what, then, can freedom be other than autonomy, that is the will's property of being a law to itself?' (*G* 4: 447; III, ¶ 2). What else, indeed? Free will is the capacity to determine oneself to act independently of externally given reasons, but action must be guided by some principle or reason. So it must be the capacity to act on principles that one gives to oneself. That means that, in addition to the capacity to act from principles and reasons, free will involves the capacity to give oneself principles; moreover, the latter capacity must be autonomous and function independently of determination by external influence. A form of agency that could give itself principles, but which invariably took its principles from some external source—that is, whose lawgiving was subject to or dependent upon external guidance—would not satisfy the concept of freedom. Thus, freedom of the will requires not only a capacity for choice that is motivationally independent, but a lawgiving capacity that is independent of determination by external influence and is guided by its own internal principle—in other words, by a principle that is constitutive of lawgiving. That is to say that a free will must have autonomy (the capacity to give itself laws through its own internal principle) and its basic principle—the principle that positively constitutes the capacity for free volition—will be Kant's FA, the principle of acting from principles through whose adoption one can regard oneself as giving law.[50] To put the point another way, the FA is the law that a free will gives to itself.[51]

Much of what follows in *Groundwork*, III considers the warrant for ascribing freedom to ourselves that would complete a deduction of the authority of the moral law that is sufficient for practical purposes. The arguments are notoriously obscure and Kant appears to abandon them in the second *Critique*. I will not consider them in detail, but will indicate schematically how the balance of the argument might be understood. As background, recall that common moral thought takes moral principles and requirements to apply with an unconditional necessity that is expressed in categorical imperatives, and the project of the *Groundwork* is to establish that this normative necessity is the authority of reason. Early in *Groundwork*, II Kant characterizes this aim as that of showing how categorical imperatives are possible: How could there be requirements and reasons for action that have necessary authority without presupposing any empirically given incentives or prior act of volition (*G* 4: 417; II, ¶ 24)? The question reappears as a subheading in the Third Section (*G* 4: 453), and I take the answer given there, greatly simplified, to be that the necessity of moral requirements is grounded in the fact that the Categorical Imperative is the principle that is internal to or constitutive of a necessary identity or self-conception. As rational agents we necessarily think of ourselves as free and we identify with our free rational capacities. And the Categorical Imperative is the principle that is constitutive of free volition. So it is constitutive of, thus necessary to, a necessary identity or self-conception. The extended argument that supports these claims is Kant's attempt to ground morality in reason.

In *Groundwork*, III Kant famously claims that rational agents necessarily act under the idea of freedom and that 'all human beings think of themselves as having free will' (*G* 4: 455; III, ¶ 20) The issue that he must address (raised by the issue of the 'circle' (*G* 4: 450; III, ¶9)) is whether the fact that we think of ourselves as free provides any warrant for ascribing freedom to ourselves that is independent of moral consciousness. He takes our capacities for theoretical reason to provide such warrant. Theoretical reason displays a spontaneity that is independent of sensibility by constructing regulative ideas that go beyond anything that is given in sensible experience. It prescribes the limits to the understanding, and it issues regulative norms that guide empirical inquiry and systematize empirical knowledge (*G* 4: 452; III, ¶ 13). Theoretical reason is thus, like pure practical reason, an autonomous lawgiver, and it would appear to satisfy the definition of a free capacity: it is a capacity to guide empirical judgment through norms that it gives to itself independently of what is presented in sensibility. Finding this power of reason in ourselves we are warranted in thinking of ourselves as members of an intelligible world governed by norms of reason that we have the capacity to follow and apply to ourselves. Kant writes that 'as a rational being, and thus as a being belonging to the intelligible world, the human being can never think of the causality of his own will otherwise than under the idea of freedom . . .' (*G* 4: 452; III, ¶ 15). Presumably his thought is that our possession of theoretical reason, as an autonomous and free capacity, warrants our ascribing freedom to our wills. If reason is free, then the will of a being who can guide his volition by reason is free. Or perhaps the claim is that since we possess an autonomous and free capacity in theoretical reason, the necessity of acting under the idea of freedom does indeed provide a warrant for ascribing freedom to our wills that is sufficient for practical purposes. If it were only in the practical sphere that we think of ourselves as free (and thus as members of the intelligible world), and if our doing so there were tacitly supported by various features of moral consciousness, then the fact that we find this way of regarding ourselves to be inescapable would provide no independent support for an argument aimed at establishing the authority of the moral law. But we adopt the same self-conception when we engage in theoretical activity, and certain specific features of theoretical reason support a conception of reason as free. The fact that we engage in other forms of reasoning under the idea of freedom supports this self-conception when applied to rational volition.

I speculate that it is certain inescapable features of the deliberative perspective, both in practical experience and in the theoretical sphere, that provide the needed synthetic element of the argument and 'transfer us into the intelligible world'. In taking up the deliberative perspective we necessarily take ourselves to be free, and, since it is through our capacities for practical reason that we are agents properly speaking, we identify with our rational capacities and think of them as our 'proper self'[52] (*G* 4: 457–8, 460–1). Identification with our rational capacities transfers us into the intelligible world because it entails that we necessarily think of ourselves in terms of the concepts and norms of the intelligible world and of the normative capacities that they presuppose.

The fact that we necessarily act under the idea of freedom and identify with our rational capacities establishes freedom as a necessary identity or self-conception. The earlier analytic arguments have shown that the Categorical Imperative is the principle that is constitutive of free agency. That makes it the internal principle of a necessary self-conception. Here perhaps we can get a clearer idea of how Kant might argue for the initially surprising claim that only a moral theory that grounds morality in autonomy can capture the unconditional character of moral obligation—that categorically necessary principles must be represented as self-legislated. (See the 'Adequacy Condition', Section II above.) Grant for the sake of argument a normative principle that is constitutive of what it is to be an agent, in so far as the capacity to follow this principle is what makes you an agent. As a principle that is internal to or constitutive of rational volition, it would 'arise from one's will' or would be given to the will by itself. This principle would also be categorically necessary for any rational agent: you could not reject its authority and continue to think of yourself as an agent. Moreover, it seems that only a principle that is in this way self-legislated could be categorically necessary, since a rational agent could reject the authority of any other principle and still think of himself or herself as an agent. In the *Groundwork* Kant tries to establish the authority of the Categorical Imperative by showing that it has this relationship to free agency. The capacity to follow the moral law is what makes you a free agent. It is the principle that the free will gives to itself, since it is constitutive of free volition. As such, it has necessary authority for any agent committed to thinking of himself or herself as free. And we necessarily think of ourselves as free. Kant's view (in the *Groundwork*) is that only a moral theory that grounds morality in the nature of free volition in this way can account for its unconditional character.

IX. CONCLUSION

This essay has explored Kant's general thesis that autonomy of the will is the foundation of morality by exploiting the juridical origins of the concepts that provide much of the framework of Kant's moral theory—for example, by showing that moral autonomy is best understood on the model of political sovereignty as a kind of legislative power, and by interpreting the Categorical Imperative as a kind of legislative process. Autonomy is the capacity of the rational will to legislate universal moral principles and the capacity of individuals to participate in universal lawgiving through their use of their rational powers. Subjection to unconditional law (as represented by the FUL) and autonomy (as represented by the FA) are two of the modalities of Kant's moral theory. To see how *autonomy* is the foundation of *moral* laws we need to understand how the theory connects these modalities. I have approached this task by developing Kant's arguments for thinking that the FUL and the FA are equivalent—or as I like to put it, are different versions of the same Idea. One element of this equivalence is the Sovereignty Thesis: that an agent subject to moral laws is an autonomous legislator with the capacity to give law through his or her will, and that this capacity is exercised when one acts from respect for the moral law. From the Sovereignty Thesis it follows that the fundamental requirement of acting only from maxims that have the form of law is just the demand to act so as to give law through one's will, that is, to act as a sovereign legislator. The other element of this equivalence is the claim that the FUL is constitutive of autonomy, understood as a legislative power. One gives law through one's will, and thus expresses and maintains one's sovereign status, by guiding one's deliberation by the FUL.

Construing autonomy on the model of sovereignty gives us a handle on various interrelated strands of Kant's general thesis. It gives a clear sense to the idea that autonomy of the will is the fundamental source of moral requirements. Moral requirements are established by a deliberative process that is constitutive of the will's legislative powers, that is, its autonomy. Since the reason for an individual to comply with a moral requirement is given by the reasoning that makes it a law, such requirements presuppose autonomous subjects with legislative capacities (agents with a share of giving universal law). Likewise, agents subject to moral requirements must be represented as legislating. If a requirement applies unconditionally, it follows that agents are bound to that requirement by the reasoning that makes it a law. (A different set of reasons would be reasons for complying with a different principle.) Furthermore, autonomous agents are bound only to requirements that they can view as self-legislated—that is to say, to requirements that are supported by reasoning definitive of their legislative capacities. Finally, since the equivalence of the FUL and the FA tells us that the principle presupposed by the ordinary concept of duty demands only that one act as a sovereign legislator, autonomy is the basic demand that reason puts to the will.

One virtue of this approach is that it addresses common worries that Kant's views about autonomy undermine his views about the objective and unconditional character of moral requirements. Modeling autonomy of the will on sovereignty shows how there can be constraints on the exercise of autonomy and why the autonomy of the will does not imply that the content of morality is a matter of individual decision. Since the FUL is the principle that defines the will's legislative powers, only volition guided by the FUL gives law and counts as an exercise of autonomy. Furthermore, Kant's views about autonomy do not imply that moral requirements are self-imposed in a discretionary sense, by implying that an obligation exists only through an actual act of volition on the part of the agent. The Sovereignty Thesis implies that a moral requirement applies to an agent as long as the process of reasoning that establishes it is available to the agent, whether or not the agent carries this reasoning out. And if moral requirements are established by potential or available reasoning, rather than actual reasoning, the worry that agents can 'repeal' moral laws at will is taken off the table. The converse concern of how such constraints as these are consistent with autonomy is addressed by noting that these constraints are the enabling conditions of autonomy understood as a legislative capacity.

These arguments explain in addition why the autonomy of the will is the ground of the dignity of rational nature. Kant thinks that we ascribe dignity to those who (have the capacity to) act from duty, even though duty, on its face, implies subjection:

For there is indeed no sublimity in him insofar as he is subject to the moral law, but there certainly is insofar as he is at the same time lawgiving with respect to it and only for that reason subject to it . . . [T]he dignity of humanity consists just in this capacity to give universal law . . .' (*G* 4: 440; II, ¶ 79)

Somewhat paradoxically, Kant can claim that the consciousness of subjection to an unconditional law reveals that rational agents are sovereign agents not bound by any authority higher than their own practical reason, with the power to give law through their willing, and are thereby entitled to the respect accorded a supreme sovereign authority.[53] It is worth noting that Kant has the resources to establish that human beings have autonomy in the recognition that we are bound by requirements of a certain kind. A supreme practical law binds its subject in ways that presuppose that they must be viewed as the final source of its authority. Thus, the argument establishing that we are bound by the moral law shows that we possess autonomous wills. Our subjection to the law then serves as the *ratio cognoscendi* of our sovereign status, and of the moral privileges to which that entitles us.[54]

NOTES

1. In this essay, citations to the *Groundwork* will include the paragraph number as well as the Academy paging.
2. See *G* 4: 433; II, ¶ 60: 'I will therefore call this basic principle the principle of the autonomy of the will, in contrast with every other, which I accordingly count as heteronomy'.
3. Cf. J. B. Schneewind, *The Invention of Autonomy*, 3 n. 2, and 483. Schneewind refers to Joachim Ritter's discussion of autonomy in *Historisches Wörterbuch der Philosophie*.
4. That Kant's view of the moral agent as legislator is inconsistent with the binding character of moral requirements is a standard worry. For a recent discussion see G. A. Cohen's comments on Christine M. Korsgaard ('Reason, Humanity and the Moral Law') and her 'Reply' in Korsgaard's *The Sources of Normativity*, 167–74, 234–8. I comment on this exchange in n. 16 below. Kant himself raises this worry in discussing the concept of a duty to oneself in the *Metaphysics of Morals*, 6: 417–18. I discuss this issue in Chapter 8.
5. Henry Allison has noted that Kant's use of 'autonomy' is ambiguous in that it refers both to a property of the will and to a principle. See *Kant's Theory of Freedom*, 94–9, 105–6. I agree with him that these ambiguities are not problems for Kant's views. However, in *What Reason Demands*, Rüdiger Bittner argues that Kant is led by an ambiguity in the notion of 'one's own universal legislation' to confuse the Categorical Imperative with what he terms the 'principle of autonomy'—the principle that a rational agent is bound only to his own universal legislation. The first is a 'criterion for actions' (one is 'to do only those actions through whose maxims the will can regard itself as making universal law'), while the second is 'a criterion for laws of action' (one is 'subject only to laws deriving from [one's] own and yet universal legislation') (pp. 76–7). Bittner claims that Kant slides without argument from the first sense of autonomy to the second. For instance, it is not obvious that the Categorical Imperative satisfies the condition set out by the Principle of Autonomy (see pp. 75–80). I agree that Kant fails to distinguish separate uses of 'autonomy', and Bittner makes the right challenge: Kant must show that the Categorical Imperative meets the conditions set out by the Principle of Autonomy. I believe that the arguments developed in Sections V–VII below show that Bittner's Principle of Autonomy is true of any agent bound by the Categorical Imperative.
6. Cf. also: '. . . the concept of every rational being as one who must regard himself as giving universal law through all the maxims of his will, so as to appraise himself and his actions from this point of view . . .' (*G* 4: 433; II, ¶ 61); '. . . the proposition, the will is in all its actions a law to itself . . .' (*G* 4: 447; III, ¶ 2). Other statements of autonomy are found at *G* II, ¶¶ 55, 57, 71, 78, 81, and 89. Note that most formulations say that rational agents ('every rational being') must regard themselves as giving universal law (II, ¶¶ 55, 57, 59, 61, 66, 71, 78, 89), but some say that the rational will legislates universal law (II, ¶¶ 56, 80, 81; III, ¶ 2).

7. One might object at this point that differences in the phrasing of FUL and FA indicate that they are not equivalent and that the FA leads to a different procedure of moral judgment. Allen Wood, for example, argues that the two formulas are quite distinct. The FUL is a test of permissibility whose criterion is whether a maxim is a possible universal law. His view is that it is negative in character, rejecting maxims that are not possible as universal law without requiring the adoption of any specific maxims or normative principles. The FA, in contrast 'positively commands us to act on certain maxims: either those that contain the volition that they themselves should be universal laws or those that are 'universally valid' for the rational will. The positive command corresponds to a very different test from those involved in FUL and FLN' (*Kant's Ethical Thought*, 164; cf. also 100 ff., 188–9.)

In reply, linking the FA with the idea of a realm of ends certainly does suggest a more expansive procedure than the test of permissibility associated with the FUL and FLN— for example, that one is to act from principles that autonomous legislators would will as law for a community of ends in themselves. Thomas E. Hill, Jr. has proposed such a framework in a number of essays (though not as a strict reading of the texts); see, for example, 'Kantian Constructivism in Ethics', in *Dignity and Practical Reason*, or 'A Kantian Perspective on Moral Rules', in *Respect, Pluralism and Justice*. However, I see nothing in the wording of the FUL and FA to indicate that Kant thought that they lead to different deliberative procedures and many reasons to think that he assumed that they lead to the same procedure. First, a footnote dispenses with illustrating the application of the FA, because the examples 'that have already illustrated the categorical imperative and its formula can all serve for the same end here' (*G* 4: 432 n.). This note suggests that Kant does not intend the FA to introduce a significantly different deliberative procedure or one that leads to different results (from either the FUL or the FH). Second (as explained in Section IV), Kant derives both the FUL and the FA from the concept of a practical law and takes them to express different features of this concept. But if the two formulas have the same basis, it is implausible to think that they lead to different deliberative procedures (or that Kant thought that they did). Third, I find the wording of variants of both formulas to be systematically ambiguous between the negative (reject maxims that cannot be universalized) and the positive (adopt maxims that are universally valid). Statements of FUL tend toward the negative and those of the FA toward the positive, but there are contrary examples of each. (See, e.g., *G* 4: 437; II, ¶¶ 75–7 for several instances of the FUL that take the latter form.) The real question here is whether the FUL leads to any positive requirements beyond the rejection of non-universalizable maxims. Though most naturally read as a test of permissibility, I believe that it does; I say more about this in Chapter 7. In general I do not see an unbridgeable gap between 'Reject maxims that are not universally valid' and 'Choose maxims that are universally valid'.

One final comment on Wood's reading. Certain formulations of the Categorical Imperative that I discuss in the next section have a curious self-referential character in that they say that a maxim must be able to 'contain' its own universal validity or 'have as its object itself as universal law'. See, for example, *G* 4: 437; II, ¶ 76: 'act in accordance with maxims that can at the same time have as their object themselves as universal laws of nature'. Other examples appear at *G* 4: 432 (II, ¶ 59), 437–8 (II, ¶ 77), 4: 440 (II, ¶ 80) and 4: 447 (III, ¶ 2). Wood claims that this phrasing is a mark of the FA and is never seen in variants of the FUL (*Kant's Ethical Thought*, 164, 188–9). But I find this unpersuasive.

First, the context makes it clear that, contra Wood, three of these formulations are variants of the FUL (those in II, ¶¶ 76, 77 and III, ¶ 2). The first two occur in the recapitulation of the argument of the Second Section where Kant reprises the claim that the FUL is the principle of a good will and tries to show why FUL and FH are equivalent. The third occurs in an argument to the effect that the FUL is the principle of a will with autonomy. Second, I suggest at the end of the next section that this self-referential phrasing leads to the test of simultaneous volition associated with FUL. Finally, the principles at II, ¶ 59 and ¶ 80 clearly are instances of the FA. But if Kant uses this phrasing in *both* the FUL and the FA, that further supports the conclusion that he intends them to be equivalent.

8. I support this reading of the FUL in Chapter 7.

9. For some contemporary discussions of autonomy see Gerald Dworkin, *The Theory and Practice of Autonomy*, chs. 1–4; the essays in John Christman, ed., *The Inner Citadel*; and Thomas M. Scanlon, 'The Significance of Choice', and *What We Owe to Each Other*, ch. 6. See also Scanlon's 'A Theory of Freedom of Expression', sect. III–V. The latter bases a principle of free expression on a conception of citizens as equal, autonomous, rational agents, where to 'regard himself as autonomous . . . a person must see himself as sovereign in deciding what to believe and in weighing competing reasons for action' (p. 215). Someone who avoids the psychological interpretation of Kant is Thomas E. Hill, Jr. See *Dignity and Practical Reason*, chs. 5 and 7, as well as chs. 3 and 4 in his *Autonomy and Self-Respect*. See also Onora O'Neill, 'Agency and Autonomy', in her *Bounds of Justice*. Another important statement of Kant's view is John Rawls, 'Themes in Kant's Moral Philosophy', 95–102; and *Lectures on the History of Moral Philosophy*, lectures V–VI. See also Korsgaard, *The Sources of Normativity*, chs. 3–4.

10. See also *G* 4: 434; II, ¶ 67, where Kant refers to 'the dignity of a rational being who obeys no law other than that which he himself at the same time gives'.

11. A note about the term 'will': In the *Groundwork*, Kant has not yet drawn the distinction between *Wille* and *Willkür* seen, for example, at *MdS* 6: 213 f. and 226 f. Indeed, he seems unaware of the distinction in the *Groundwork*, since, in one paragraph (*G* 4: 412; II, ¶ 12) he identifies the will (*der Wille*) both with practical reason (which corresponds to *Wille* in his later usage) and with 'a capacity to choose only that which reason independently of inclination cognizes as practically necessary, that is, as good' (which corresponds to *Willkür* in his later usage). Henry Allison has written that 'Kant uses the terms *Wille* and *Willkür* to characterize respectively the legislative and executive functions of a unified faculty of volition, which he likewise refers to as *Wille*. Accordingly, *Wille* has both a broad sense in which it connotes the faculty of volition or will as a whole and a narrow sense in which it connotes one function of that faculty' (*Kant's Theory of Freedom*, 129). In the *Groundwork*, 'will' is best understood in the broad sense, nicely described by Allison, and I use the term that way in this chapter.

The normative conception of autonomy that I develop has slightly different connotations in relation to the different functions of the will, and it is useful to spell them out in the interests of precision. Will in its legislative function (*Wille* in the narrower sense) has autonomy in both the positive and negative senses outlined in this paragraph: it is a lawgiving power that does not answer to any external authority. (As we shall see, it is the power to generate specific moral norms through the FUL.) My understanding of autonomy applies in the first instance to the will in its legislative function. *Willkür* has both causal and motivational independence (discussed below in Section VIII), and, if it makes sense to say that *Willkür* (rather than will in the broad sense) is subject to norms, it is bound only to the laws given by the will in its legislative function; thus it is autonomous in a negative sense. In its positive specification, *Willkür* is not a law-giving capacity. Rather it is the capacity to act from the laws generated by *Wille*, which is Kant's positive conception of freedom of the will. All of these features belong to the will in the broad sense: it is an autonomous lawgiving power, is bound only to its own legislation, and includes the capacity to act from its own norms independently of motivation by desire and empirically given interests. In addition, as Allison points out, will in the broad sense is a law to itself, since *Wille* gives laws for *Willkür* (*Kant's Theory of Freedom*, 130–1).

12. See e.g., Allison, *Kant's Theory of Freedom*, 97–8.

13. See, e.g., Hill, *Dignity and Practical Reason*, 84–5, 110 ff., 110 n., 128–31, 141–2; and Rawls, *Lectures on the History of Moral Philosophy*, 226–30.

14. For this understanding of 'desire' see Hill, *Dignity and Practical Reason*, 114. Much of Kant's language supports the claim that the defining feature of heteronomy is the recognition of sources of reasons or authority that are external to the rational will; for example, according to principles[s] of heteronomy, practical reason 'administer[s] an interest not belonging to it', and 'nature' or a 'foreign impulse' gives the will a law (by which Kant should mean a normative practical principle rather than a natural law) (*G* 4: 441, 444; II, ¶¶ 81, 88). I contrast this reading with one that locates heteronomy in motivation that is desire-based in the narrow sense of resting on sensible inclination. The problem with heteronomous accounts of morality, of course, is that they cannot account for its necessary authority. Such theories try to ground moral principles in an object or value given independently of the will in which rational agents are assumed to have an interest. In this case, the will 'does not give itself the law; instead the object, by means of its relation to the will, gives the law to it' (*G* 4: 441; II, ¶ 81). But unless rational agents necessarily have an interest in the object—if the interest is due to contingent features of the subject's nature or psychology—the resulting principles are hypothetical, rather than categorical imperatives. Kant says that 'the relation [of the object] to the will' through which the object 'gives the law' can rest 'either on inclination or on representations of reason' (*G* 4: 441; II, ¶ 81). In the latter, rationalist case, the object provides a ground of choice through a feeling of pleasure or delight; but Kant distinguishes this case from motivation that presupposes sensible inclination. Kant writes: '. . . because the impulse that the representation of an object possible through our powers is to exert on the will of the subject in accordance with his natural constitution belongs to the nature of the subject—whether to his sensibility (inclination and taste) or to his understanding and reason, which by the special constitution of their nature employ themselves with delight upon the object—it would, strictly speaking, be nature that gives the law' (*G* 4: 444; II, ¶ 88). The picture in the rationalist case is this: due to contingent psychological facts, the rational representation of certain objects (say, of the perfection achievable through an action) causes a feeling of 'delight' that exerts a motivational impulse (where the delight either gives rise to, or just is the motivational impulse). To this we should add that in order to act on this representation, the subject takes this feeling of delight to be a reason to pursue the object; or perhaps the delight just is the subject taking himself to have a reason that is due to a contingent psychological feature. When Kant says that 'nature gives the law' or that 'a foreign impulse gives the law by means of the subject's nature, which is

attuned to be receptive to it', I take him to mean that the object gives the law through, or on the condition of, a contingent psychological interest or response that a subject takes to be reason-giving. In acting to produce the object, the subject is moved by a source of reasons external to the will, and it is there that the heteronomous theory locates the authority of morality.

What is the alternative to heteronomy and determination through contingent interests or reasons with subjective conditions? Imagine that we can identify a practical principle that is constitutive of or internal to rational volition—so that following this principle defines what counts as rational volition. Or imagine that there is some object that is implicated in any act of rational volition, an object that one wills in so far as one wills at all. Rational agents would have a necessary interest in this principle or object, since an agent who rejected it would no longer count as willing. Furthermore the principle or object would be given to the will by itself in the sense that it is internal to or constitutive of rational volition. Here we see the connection between autonomy and categorical necessity that Kant is after: a principle that is internal to or constitutive of rational volition (an activity or self-conception in which rational agents have a necessary interest) will have categorical necessity. But, as internal to rational volition, it is a principle that the will gives to itself. Moreover only principles that are internal to the will in this sense have categorical necessity.

15. One may object that my discussion of sovereignty ignores important differences between the position of representative legislatures in a constitutional regime and 'the people', who (in theory) are sovereign. Restrictions on the powers of the legislature (such as constitutionally protected rights enforced by judicial review) appear to indicate that they are not ultimately sovereign, but must answer to the people. Two points in reply. First, a legislative body, as the people's representative, does have lawmaking power that it exercises on its own through a political process set out by the constitution. Restrictions on the kinds of laws that it may enact are an aspect of the complex law that creates its powers in the first place. Indeed, one can argue that the provisions that appear restrictive are a condition of its legislation having authority, and are thus constitutive of its legislative power. Alternatively, one may argue that sovereignty resides in the people as a body, rather than in the legislature. Still, the people must constitute themselves in some way and establish some process in order to exercise sovereignty. Here a constitutional regime with separation of powers that assigns roles to different branches of government is the complex political process through which law is enacted. The people as a body exercise their sovereignty through this (representative) process. This process is autonomous. It is established through the people's enactment of their constitution and is a genuine lawmaking process that answers to no external authority. And again, what may appear to be constraints on actors within the system (including limits on what the people may do to themselves) are part of the complex law that creates sovereign power.

16. To explain why Kant's agent is not free to repeal the moral laws that she legislates, G. A. Cohen cites Kant's remark at *G* 4: 432; II, ¶ 60 that the rational will is 'designed by nature to be a will giving universal law'. On Cohen's understanding of Kant, the criterion of universal validity is a standard imposed on the will's legislative capacities by reason. As he says, 'reason is sovereign over us' and gives stability to the laws that we legislate, and 'although you legislate the law, the content of the law comes from reason' ('Reason, Humanity and the Moral Law', 172, 173–4). Cohen is right to hold that

Kant's standard of universal validity closes off the possibility of repealing self-legislated moral laws. But his account makes reason an external constraint that seems inconsistent with autonomy and makes it unclear in what sense the moral agent is a legislator. In Sections V–VII, I try to show that the standard of universal validity is not an external constraint, but an enabling condition that makes it possible to give law. Thus I agree with Korsgaard's response to Cohen that universal validity is constitutive of our legislative powers (ibid. 235).

However, I use 'law' in a much narrower sense than Korsgaard. As I understand her view, a law is a fundamental principle of choice associated with a practical identity that determines what counts as reasons for an agent. For her, laws are universal in the sense of being normative principles that apply with generality over a range of situations. But a law could be a norm that applies to and has normative force for just one person, and in that case would not be universally valid (as normally understood) (ibid. 98–9, 220, 225 ff.). For Kant, practical laws, properly speaking, are universally valid moral principles that have normative force for all rational beings (as Korsgaard says, range over the domain of all rational beings). Here I am only concerned with the sense in which we legislate moral laws.

17. A constructivist account of Kant's moral theory offers one way to spell out what it is for 'the rational will' to have autonomy as understood in this section. One main feature of constructivism is the idea that moral requirements are in some sense generated by a process of rational deliberation. Constructivists hold that moral requirements can be represented as the outcome of an idealized process of deliberation—a 'procedure of construction'—that incorporates the relevant standards of practical reason. (See Rawls, *Lectures on the History of Moral Philosophy*, 'Kant VI'.) A constructivist theory captures the positive dimension of autonomy (the capacity of the rational will to give law) by representing basic moral principles as the result of this deliberative procedure. The fact that this deliberative procedure is not constrained by any external normative standards or sources of authority captures the negative dimension of autonomy. This does not mean that the process is unconstrained by any standards. Rather the standards that structure the process are internal to practical reason or constitutive of rational volition, rather than external standards to which reason must answer. I discuss constructivism further in Section II of Chapter 7. (N. 40 below indicates other ways in which my account of autonomy relies on a constructivist understanding of the Categorical Imperative.)

18. One can understand the Formula of Humanity as stating an 'autonomy condition' on actions: that one's treatment of others should be guided by principles which they can view as self-legislated, or which they could accept while continuing to view themselves as autonomous. My suggestion is that the Autonomy Condition applies the same condition to principles and requirements that the FH applies to actions. If the FUL and the FH are equivalent, then it is also the principle which the former applies to actions. The Autonomy Condition then applies the same underlying idea as the Categorical Imperative, but at a higher level of generality.

19. To determine just what sorts of principles should count as 'practical laws', one would have to address many issues about the application of the first formula of the Categorical Imperative that are beyond the scope of this chapter. This chapter assumes that the FUL yields substantive results of some kind when applied to maxims at some level of generality. Writers who have persuasively defended this conclusion include

Onora O'Neill, *Constructions of Reason*, chs. 5–8; Barbara Herman, *The Practice of Moral Judgment*, chs. 6–7, 10; and Christine M. Korsgaard, *Creating the Kingdom of Ends*, ch. 3. Practical laws are best thought of as general substantive principles arrived at through moral deliberation (such as the principle that lying for certain kinds of reasons is wrong). But one might equally view them as particular conclusions that hold 'with the force of law'—for example, that it would be wrong for me to lie in this situation. One might argue that the Categorical Imperative is the sole practical law, but I prefer to see it as an abstract principle stating the form that any substantive principle must have to serve as a practical law. Aside from the question of whether the FUL yields substantive results, my claims in this essay are compatible with different ways of working out the details of the Categorical Imperative.

Since I assume an oversimplified picture of the FUL in order to focus on other issues, a few brief comments are in order. The most straightforward kind of 'law' established by the FUL is the impermissibility of adopting certain maxims. Showing that a maxim cannot be universalized establishes a prohibition against its adoption. I am inclined to think that requirements to adopt certain maxims can be accommodated within a framework aimed at establishing impermissibility. (The judgment that a specific action is required might be more complex. For example, one might have to consider all the maxims reasonably judged to apply to the situation that support not performing the action, and show that all are impermissible.) Another question is whether 'practical laws' should include principles of permissibility that anyone can endorse, in addition to requirements and prohibitions. A 'law of permission' is an awkward notion, but if practical laws have the role of resolving questions of justification, it seems to me that they should include universally valid principles of permissibility, and I adopt this assumption. I must also set aside the vexing question whether prohibitions or requirements and permissibly adopted maxims have the 'form of law' in the same sense. One might want to say that the former are laws (and have the form of law), while the latter are simply consistent with (the form of) law. But what both share is that they authoritatively settle questions of justification.

Finally, I am inclined to follow Barbara Herman in thinking that the most satisfactory account of the Categorical Imperative has it establishing 'deliberative presumptions' when applied to 'generic maxims' (rather than yielding a set of rules or duties, or supplying a test for agents' actual, and quite detailed, maxims), where such a presumption is 'a principle that contains the moral knowledge necessary for routine moral judgment and moral deliberation' (Herman, *The Practice of Moral Judgment*, 147 ff.). If so, the 'practical laws' established by the Categorical Imperative would be deliberative presumptions about the deontic status of various generic maxims. On such a view, the moral assessment of specific courses of action would require further judgment and deliberation from the relevant deliberative presumptions.

20. Here I draw on Christine M. Korsgaard's analysis in 'Kant's Analysis of Obligation: The Argument of *Foundations I*', in *Creating the Kingdom of Ends*, 60–5.

21. In saying that a practical law 'contains the ground of its own validity in itself' I do not mean to imply that it needs no justification. Rather, one must look for its justification (both of a particular law and of the higher order law stated by the Categorical Imperative) in a certain place, namely in some internal feature of the principle. I thank Henry Allison for pointing out the need to clarify this point.

22. Rational intuitionism might offer a simpler solution by assigning the function of practical laws to self-evident principles. But Kant might claim that intuitionism cannot give an adequate account of the authority of such principles. Or at least, in order to establish the authority of such principles, one must go outside such principles and attach some further interest to them, in which case they will no longer satisfy the first of the above conditions (that they have immediate authority). As standardly understood, if a principle is self-evident, any rational being on reflection can grasp its validity and authority, but no further justification for the principle can be given. But then its normative force is unexplained and it will appear to be rationally rejectable; one can coherently ask why one should follow it. In that case, its authority will depend upon some external motive or sanction. Or to put the point another way, since there is nothing within the principle to motivate its adoption, a further interest will be needed to give it motivational force. But if some such interest is the source of the authority of a principle, it does not qualify as a practical law.

23. Cf. *KpV*, 5: 27 'Theorem III'.

24. Korsgaard, *The Sources of Normativity*, 107.

25. Ibid. 108. See also her *Creating the Kingdom of Ends*, 75, n. 59.

26. For further discussion of the nature of maxims see O'Neill, *Constructions of Reason*, 83–9 and 128–31 (including the references given at 129 n.); Allison, *Kant's Theory of Freedom*, 85–94; and Herman, *The Practice of Moral Judgment*, esp. 143–6, 217–24.

27. For this interpretation of the Categorical Imperative procedure see Thomas Pogge, 'The Categorical Imperative'. It is also suggested by T. M. Scanlon, 'Kant's *Groundwork*: From Freedom to Moral Community'.

28. Note also that the moral validity of a maxim depends on a kind of formal fact. Maxims are assessed not by looking directly at the substance of the maxim, but by determining whether they can be willed in accordance with the procedure set out by the FUL.

    Kant's notion of 'the form of law' remains regrettably obscure, and what I say here certainly needs elaboration. We can begin to get a handle on this notion by focusing on the fact that the FUL does not assess a maxim by determining whether it satisfies a substantive principle or promotes an end. Moreover, the FUL employs a formal notion of universalizability that, as I understand it, is geared toward determining whether a principle can play the functional role of a practical law in the reasoning of agents with autonomy. (Universalizability is, as it were, an operation performed on the reasoning that goes into a maxim.) A formal test is a test of form, where form is linked to the functional role of a practical law. Is the FUL a *purely* formal procedure? I suggest not in Chapter 7, where I argue that a conception of 'agents with autonomy' plays a role in generating the contradictions that result from the universalization of certain maxims.

29. I count five 'self-referential' versions of the Categorical Imperative in the *Groundwork*. Three are variants of the FUL, and two are variants of FA. (See the last paragraph of n. 7 above.) The variants of FUL are the two just cited and the version at *G* 4: 447; (III, ¶ 2): '. . . to act on no other maxim than that which can also have as object itself as a universal law'. The variants of the FA occur at *G* 4: 432 (II, ¶ 59) and *G* 4: 440; (II, ¶ 80), and are cited above in Section II.A.

30. The self-referential versions of the FUL say only that a maxim must be able to contain its own validity in itself. But the universal validity of a maxim is determined by its universal adoptability, which in turn is a question of its form (whether the arrangements of its

part suit it for the role of practical law). Thus a maxim that can 'contain its own universal validity' contains the ground of (i.e., reason for) its own validity.

31. Kant consistently says that a categorical imperative can have 'no interest as its basis'. But I assume that he means that the authority of a categorical imperative cannot be based on any empirically given or contingent interest—that is, one that is not essential to or constitutive of an agent's rationality, and thus one that a rational agent could have or lack. To establish the authority of the Categorical Imperative Kant could appeal to interests that we necessarily have as rational agents or that are constitutive of our self-conception as rational agents—for example, an interest in being free rational agents who are the source of their actions. (In saying that the authority of a categorical imperative cannot depend upon 'empirically given or contingent interest', I intend to rule out the interest in happiness, that Kant says that we have necessarily as finite agents.)

32. Kant appears to assume that there are only two possible explanations of the authority of a principle. Either (a) a principle applies conditionally, in which case its authority is based on certain contingent interests of the agent; or (b) it applies unconditionally, in which case its authority comes from the fact that it is valid. The only possible explanation of (b) (i.e., how authority could be based on validity per se) is that it is valid in virtue of being a legislative enactment of the agent in question. Thus, if its authority is not based on any interests, it must be a principle enacted by the agent, and authoritative for that reason.

Kant gives an argument in II, ¶ 58 (*G* 4: 432) that is both obscure and unsatisfying. He writes: 'although a will that *stands under law* may be bound to this law by means of some interest, a will that is itself supremely lawgiving [*ein Wille, der selbst zuoberst gesetzgebend ist*] cannot possibly, as such, depend upon some interest; for a will that is dependent in this way would itself need yet another law that would limit the interest of its self-love to the condition of a validity for universal law'. The first clause appears to claim that if a will is only subject to a law, then it is bound by a (contingent) interest—in which case the principle to which it is bound is conditional. The contra-positive of this argument seems close to the Sovereignty Thesis: (i) if a principle is unconditional, it does not bind through any (contingent) interest; (ii) if an agent is not bound to a principle by some (contingent) interest, then the agent is not just subject to the principle (but must also be its legislator). However for the reasons given at the end of this section, a rational intuitionist might object to the second step.

What about the claim that '. . . a will that is itself supremely lawgiving cannot possibly, as such, depend upon some interest . . .'? We should probably assume that a 'supremely lawgiving' will gives unconditionally valid laws and that it is bound by its own laws. But the claim is ambiguous. Does Kant mean 'depend upon some interest' in its lawgiving—that is, that a supreme lawgiver is not guided by any contingent interests in exercising its legislative powers? Or does he mean that the authority of its own laws for itself does not depend upon any contingent interest? The first is the more interesting claim, and I consider it in Section VII. If we take it the second way (as the claim that a supreme lawgiver is not bound to its own laws by any contingent interest), the argument seems to be the following:

    (1) Assume a supremely lawgiving will that is bound to one of its own laws by some (contingent) interest.

(2) The law or principle to which this will is bound would be necessary only if the interest from which it gets its authority is necessary—that is, only if there is some further law requiring that one have the interest on which the authority of the first law depends. (Let this step interpret the need for 'yet another law that would limit the interest of its self-love to the condition of a validity of a universal law . . .')

(3) If there is a need for a further law, then the first law is not unconditional.

(4) If the first law is not unconditional, then the giver of that law is not 'supremely lawgiving' (since a 'supremely lawgiving will' gives unconditional laws).

(5) Therefore, a supremely lawgiving will is not bound to its own laws by any (contingent) interest.

33. Among other things, this condition implies that no rational intuitionist theory can truly represent moral duties as categorical imperatives. The contra-positive of the Sovereignty Thesis is that if the agent subject to a requirement is not its legislator, the requirement is not unconditional—not a categorical imperative. Because intuitionism locates moral principles externally to the will, it does not represent moral agents as legislators. But then it does not represent moral principles as categorical imperatives.

34. In laying out this position I draw on Rawls's discussion in 'Themes in Kant's Moral Philosophy', 95–8. See also *Lectures on the History of Moral Philosophy*, 70–6, 235–7. A view of this sort was adopted by Samuel Clarke; see 'A Discourse of Natural Religion', 193–225. Clause (b) is seen in Clarke's view that there are objective moral truths that are intrinsically binding on rational creatures, independently of any interest. He writes:

> these eternal and necessary differences of things make it fit and reasonable for creatures so to act; they cause it to be their duty, or lay down an obligation upon them, so to do; even separate from the consideration of these rules being the positive will or command of God; and also antecedent to any . . . particular private and personal advantage or disadvantage, reward or punishment, either present or future . . . (p. 192)

For a discussion of Clarke and other intuitionists tying them to Kant, and of the problem of intrinsic normativity in general, see Korsgaard, 'Kant's Analysis of Obligation', in *Creating the Kingdom of Ends*, and *The Sources of Normativity*, 28–32.

35. This citizen does not act from respect for the law since no thoughts about why one ought to obey the law contribute to his motivation. I am inclined to think that respect for a law requires some understanding of its justification, and that you cannot respect someone in a position of authority without some evaluation of how that authority is exercised. Though many people take (2) as the model of authority, a Kantian theory, as I see it, cannot accept a model of authority that leaves no room for evaluating the merits of particular exercises of legislative power.

36. A simple illustration: if speed limits are enacted because they will enhance public safety and conserve fuel, these facts will figure in the enlightened citizen's reasons for complying.

37. Taking (3) as the primary model of authority would imply that one could only be bound to good laws, or laws made for good reasons. But bad or second-best laws can still create obligations, and a legislator's reasons for enacting a law would appear to have no bearing on whether it is binding. I am grateful to many people for help thinking through this issue.

38. This example, in addition to depicting an idealized citizen who has internalized the source of the law's authority, also idealizes the legislative process in obvious ways. For example, it assumes that one can identify the substantive considerations that favor a law and the weight actually given them in the legislative process. This may be unfeasible in most actual legislation, where one must assess the intentions of several legislators, whose reasons for supporting a law may be opaque. The point of the example is to show how the distinction between subject and legislator, as I say, 'might begin to collapse' in the case of a civil law. In this example, the distinction comes as close to collapsing as it can; but it never completely collapses in the case of a civil law.

39. My interpretation of the Sovereignty Thesis supposes that one acts on a moral requirement only when one is motivated by an understanding of why it is morally required, since an agent's principle of action is partly determined by her underlying reasons for viewing an action as choiceworthy. Here it may not be enough to regard an action as required; one may need a certain understanding of why it is required.

This rendition of the Sovereignty Thesis may appear to have the unwelcome consequence of putting action on moral principles out of reach. Taken to extremes, it may imply that acting on a moral principle requires a grasp of why the moral law is a requirement of reason—something that even devoted scholars are often reluctant to claim! Let me offer a brief response. First, it is consistent with Kant's general views about reason and autonomy that an agent with no understanding of why an action is morally required fails to act on a moral principle. Second, the condition that one understand why an action is morally required is implicitly satisfied by ordinary actors who can give reasonably good explanations of why certain ways of acting are wrong, and others required, using concepts found in Kant's theory; or by agents who recognize the basic outlines of a Kantian theory as the proper articulation of the sorts of considerations by which they are implicitly moved. After all, Kant does claim to be setting out the theory present to ordinary human reason (*G* 4: 403–5), and he consistently traces out the implications of ideas that are arguably present in ordinary thought. For these reasons, I do not think that the unwelcome consequence looms on the horizon. But if one insisted that it does, it would be consistent with Kant's reluctance to admit the occurrence of actions with true moral worth, though by raising the bar to moral worth in a different way. Kant emphasizes 'covert impulses of self-love' as the obstacle to acting from respect for morality (*G* 4: 407; II, ¶ 2); what this account adds is that respect for a moral principle requires an understanding of why it is required.

40. Here is another way in which my reconstruction of Kant's Sovereignty Thesis requires a constructivist reading of the FUL. (See also n. 17 above.) A constructivist account takes the FUL to be the basis of a procedure of moral deliberation (a 'procedure of construction') that is the final criterion of right in the sense that the outcome of applying the FUL, whatever it is, defines the moral status of a maxim.

41. Note that the 'legislative process' laid out by the FUL contains a modal element: the deliberative procedure that determines the moral status of a maxim asks whether a maxim *can* rationally be willed as universal law. One establishes a practical law by determining whether a maxim *can* or *cannot* be willed as universal law. (Showing that a maxim *can* be willed as universal law establishes its permissibility. Showing that it *cannot* be willed as universal law establishes a prohibition against adopting it. A requirement is established by showing that the maxims that would permit omission

of the action are impermissible.) I mention this to forestall the objection that determining that a principle *can be willed* as universal law is not the same as *willing* it as universal law and therefore does not establish any practical laws. Here think of a civil legislature that wants to know whether a law that they are considering is constitutional. Ascertaining that it is constitutionally permitted, that is, that it *can be* enacted, does not make it a law since assessing the constitutionality of a potential law is not the established legislative process. The 'legislative process' defined by the FUL, however, does proceed by determining whether a maxim *can* be willed as universal law. My contention is that the FUL can be understood as a legislative process that rational agents are authorized to employ and that when one acts on a universalizable maxim because of its universalizability, or refrains from adopting a maxim because of its non-universalizability, one can be said to give law through one's will.

42. I am indebted to various readers of the essay for prompting me to clarify this point.

43. The same point can be found in Kant's *Lectures on Ethics*. See the Collins *Moral Philosophy*, where Kant claims: 'The lawgiver is not always simultaneously an originator of the law; he is that only if the laws are contingent. But if the laws are practically necessary, and he merely declares that they conform to his will, then he is a lawgiver' (*MP-C* 27: 282–3). Since the Collins lectures date from 1784–5, we may presume that they reflect Kant's views in the *Groundwork*.

44. Bear in mind that one aim of this section is to interpret the Sovereignty Thesis by showing how a practical law collapses the distinction between subject and sovereign, or implies that no significant distinction can be drawn between subject and sovereign. There are at least two ways of understanding this claim. One is that practical laws create roles for both sovereign and subject, and that in virtue of occupying the latter one occupies the former as well. Alternatively, the two roles might be ways of capturing different aspects of the complex relation in which we stand to moral requirements. As far as I can see, both ways of understanding the argument require only that there be a legislative role that individuals can occupy, not that there be some original moral sovereign whom agents model.

45. Using Kant's later terminology, autonomy is a property of *Wille* in the narrow sense; freedom is a property of *Willkür*, specifically the capacity (of *Willkür*) to act from the normative principles that *Wille* legislates as pure practical reason. The latter claim fits the explanations of the positive concept of freedom that Kant gives in his published works; see *KpV* 5: 33, *MdS* 6: 213–14 and 226–7. Autonomy and freedom are both properties of the will in the broad sense (following Allison, *Kant's Theory of Freedom*, 129) of a unified faculty of volition that includes both functions. I depart from Kant in one respect. He appears to identify freedom and autonomy, both at *G* 4: 446; (III, ¶ 2) and at *G* 4: 450; (III, ¶ 9): 'freedom and the will's own lawgiving are both autonomy'. As I read it, they are not strictly speaking the same property. But it seems clear that freedom presupposes autonomy, and that autonomy is what needs to be added to the spontaneity of rational volition to get transcendental freedom as Kant understands it. Likewise an autonomous will is free since it has the capacity to act from self-given laws.

46. Part of the idea here is that the argument exploits structural parallels between transcendental freedom and sovereign authority. A sovereign authority is a kind of self-originating cause of a set of practical principles, in that he has the capacity to create law, and thus reasons for action, through his will without being bound to any external source of authority. An agent who autonomously legislates the fundamental

norms applying to his conduct and acts from those norms would be the self-originating cause of his actions. In this way transcendental freedom presupposes autonomy, and autonomous conduct provides a normative modeling of free agency.

47. This claim is seen in the following: 'But the proposition, the will is in all its actions a law to itself, indicates only the principle, to act on no other maxim than that which can also have as object itself as a universal law. This, however, is precisely the formula of the categorical imperative and is the principle of morality . . .' (*G* 4: 447; III, ¶ 2). I read 'the will is in all its actions a law to itself' as an incomplete rendering of the FA, which Kant then claims to be equivalent to the FUL ('the principle, to act on no other maxim . . .'). Many commentators on this argument do not put much weight on the difference between steps (2) and (3), but I think that it is important to recognize that they are distinct components of the argument.

48. Several commentators read motivational independence in some form into Kant's negative definition of freedom. See, for example, Hill, *Dignity and Practical Reason*, 108–11, 136–8; Allison, *Kant's Theory of Freedom*, 97–8, 207–8; and Korsgaard, *Creating the Kingdom of Ends*, 163–6. I take the term 'motivational independence' from Allison, *Kant's Theory of Freedom*, 97.

49. Cf. Korsgaard, *Creating the Kingdom of Ends*, 168–9.

50. The FA constitutes the capacity for freedom of volition because it is the positive specification of the capacity that satisfies the definition of freedom as the capacity to act independently of determination by external influences. Freedom has to be understood as the capacity to act from the moral law. Of course an agent who has this capacity can fail to exercise it; actions are free for the purposes of imputation if performed by an agent with this capacity. At *MdS* 6: 226–7 Kant makes the point that freedom of choice cannot be defined as liberty of indifference, 'the ability to make a choice for or against the [moral] law', even though an agent with this ability can choose to act against the law: 'Only freedom in relation to the internal lawgiving of reason is really an ability; the possibility of deviating from it is an inability. How can the former be defined as the latter?'

51. Korsgaard's reconstruction and defense of this argument begins by defining 'the moment of spontaneity' as the (hypothetical) point at which a free will must choose a fundamental principle that determines what considerations count as reasons for it. She then argues that a free will has a reason to choose the FUL as its basic principle of operation (or that it already is its basic principle) since the FUL simply describes the task faced by a free will. That task is to choose some law or principle on which to act. Since the will is free, nothing outside of its choice determines what that law or principle will be. As she says (of the task of a free will), 'Nothing provides any content for that law. All that it has to be is a law.' But the FUL merely tells us to choose some law (or principle) subject only to the constraint that it have the form of a law. As she says (here characterizing the import of the FUL), 'Nothing provides any content for that law. All that it has to be is a law' ('Morality as Freedom', in *Creating the Kingdom of Ends*, 166). Since the FUL simply describes the task of a free will, it is its fundamental norm. As she says in *The Sources of Normativity*, the FUL 'describes what a free will must do to be what it is' (*Sources*, 98, which summarizes the argument given in 'Morality as Freedom').

I would like to think that a version of this argument can be defended, and have tried to present a defensible version above. But there are two problems with the way in which Korsgaard presents it. First, there is some equivocation in the sense of 'law' over the two occurrences of 'All that it has to be is a law'. Where this phrase describes the task of a free will, 'law' most naturally refers to some general principle, including subjective principles of action. But in the second occurrence, where this phrase characterizes the FUL, 'law' must refer to a necessary and universally valid principle. If so, the FUL does not describe the task of a free will. A free will must choose some general principle for itself in order to operate as a will, but that is not to say that the principle must have the 'form of law' as Kant understands it. In the *Sources of Normativity* she tacitly acknowledges this problem by distinguishing 'the categorical imperative', which she identifies with the FUL, and 'the moral law' (identified with a version of the FRE), and by claiming that the argument as she reconstructs it only establishes that the categorical imperative (i.e., FUL) is the law of a free will, and not that the moral law is (*Sources*, 98–9). (Here see n. 16 above.) The second problem that I see with her argument—as a strict reading of Kant—is that it makes no real use of the concept of autonomy to connect a free will and the moral law. As I understand it, the claim that a free will has autonomy and the claim that the FUL is the basic principle of a will with autonomy are distinct components in Kant's argument that a free will is subject to moral laws.

52. The idea that we necessarily identify with our rational capacities is suggested by several references in these pages to the 'proper self' (*das eigentliche Selbst*): 'The causality of such actions [actions that can be done only by disregarding all desires and sensible incitements] lies in him as intelligence and in the laws of effects and actions in accordance with principles of an intelligible world... and, in addition, since it is there, as intelligence only, that he is his proper self..., those laws apply to him immediately and categorically...' (*G* 4: 457; III, ¶ 26). (Note here that the laws of the intelligible world apply *immediately* and *categorically*, since it is there that he is his *proper self*). '...He does not hold himself accountable for [inclinations and impulses] or ascribe them to his proper self, that is, to his will, though he does ascribe to it the indulgence he would show them if he allowed them to influence his maxims...' (*G* 4: 458; III, ¶ 26). 'The law interests us because it is valid for us as human beings, since it arose from our will as intelligence and so from our proper self...' (*G* 4: 460; III, ¶ 31).

53. This is why Kant holds in the second *Critique* that consciousness of subjection to a law which humiliates by checking self-love and striking down self-conceit at the same time 'awaken[s] respect by setting before our eyes the sublimity of our own nature (in its vocation)' (*KpV* 5: 87). The elevating dimension of moral consciousness is that recognition of our subjection reveals the autonomy, or sovereign status, of the will.

54. Versions of this essay were presented to the Triangle Ethics Circle of Chapel Hill, NC; to the Departments of Philosophy at the University of California at San Diego, and the University of California at Los Angeles. A presentation to the Philosophy and Legal Theory Workshop at the University of Chicago in the fall of 1998 led to a further round of revisions. I would like to thank many people for their comments, questions, and suggestions—in particular, Henry Allison, Barbara Herman, Thomas Hill, Jr., Christine Korsgaard, Charles Larmore, Martha Nussbaum, Robert Pippin, Jay Rosenberg, Geoff Sayre-McCord, Carol Voeller, and Candace Vogler.

The initial draft of this essay was written with support from an NEH grant to spend 1991–2 at the National Humanities Center.

6

Legislating for a Realm of Ends: The Social Dimension of Autonomy

I. INTRODUCTION: A PUZZLE ABOUT AUTONOMY

Shortly after Kant claims autonomy for the moral agent, the argument of the *Groundwork* takes a turn that leads one to question what this autonomy amounts to. In attributing autonomy to rational agents, Kant regards them as a kind of sovereign legislator with authority over the use of their rational capacities. He holds that they have (in some sense) the power to enact law through their wills, without being bound to any external authority, and are subject only to their own legislation. Kant also says that this conception of the moral agent leads to the concept of a 'realm of ends': 'The concept of every rational being as one who must regard himself as giving universal law through all the maxims of his will, so as to appraise himself and all his actions from this point of view, leads to a very fruitful concept dependent on it, namely that *of a realm of ends*' (*G* 4: 433). The subsequent discussion makes it clear that Kant believes that autonomy is exercised by enacting principles that could serve as law for a community of agents, each of whom possesses the same legislative capacities as oneself (*G* 4: 433–40). It would then seem that the laws enacted by such an agent must be able to gain the agreement of all members of this community of ends. But how is one autonomous if the laws that one wills are subject to the constraint that they can be accepted by, or justified to, all members of a realm of ends? This question is an instance of the general problem of how Kant can combine the universal validity of moral requirements with the autonomy of moral agents. Kant ties moral autonomy to the capacity to guide volition by reasons or practical principles that are universally valid. But why isn't the condition that one's willing be universally valid a limitation on an agent's sovereign authority, and a restriction of autonomy?

This essay uses the connection between Kant's conception of autonomy and his concept of a realm of ends as the occasion to explore a number of issues about the nature of autonomy. The core of Kant's conception of autonomy is that rational agents are sovereign over the employment of their rational capacities. One's exercise of one's reason is not subject to the governance of any external authority, or to any standards other than those generated by one's reason. Kant explicitly views moral agents as a kind of sovereign legislator who are autonomous in both a negative and a positive sense: they are not bound to any higher external authority, and have the power to give law through their wills. He believes that moral agents exercise or fully express their autonomy by guiding their willing by certain kinds of principles and norms. We can see why this is a conception of autonomy if agents choose these principles themselves, and if governance by these principles creates the control over external and subjective influences that is needed for self-determination. But Kant also holds that one's adoption of particular norms is constrained by a higher-order norm of universal validity, which agents do not choose. So it is natural to ask how Kant can attribute autonomy to the moral agent while holding that its exercise must meet this condition of universal validity.

The idea that one exercises moral autonomy by legislating for a realm of ends leads to further complications. Kant defines a realm of ends as a 'systematic union of various rational beings through common laws', and it is his ideal of a social order in which relations between agents are governed by moral principles (*G*4: 433). Situating the autonomous agent in a community of agents who share the same legislative capacities appears to introduce a dependence on the judgments of other agents, whose potential responses may constrain what one can will. One does not decide in isolation whether one's willing is universally valid, since that is a question of whether one's principles can gain the acceptance of other rational agents. Either one is bound to exercise one's autonomy by willing principles acceptable to the members of a realm of ends, or the measure of whether this capacity is fully exercised is that one's volition has this general acceptability. Either way, the willing of an autonomous agent appears subject to socially applied norms not chosen by the agent, including the general norm that one's willing be acceptable to the members of a realm of ends. Again, one may wonder why that does not limit autonomy.

A standard approach to these issues is to note that Kant's thought contains conflicting strains. While roughly the first half of the *Groundwork* stresses the necessity and universality of moral requirements, Kant introduces the notion of autonomy at a crucial transition in the text and thereafter views moral agents as a kind of sovereign legislator bound only to self-given laws. The interpretive question is how to fit these strains together. The approach that takes these concepts to need reconciliation sees them as separate and self-standing ideas, whose consistency is problematic. Clearly there are difficulties here, but they are more easily resolved if, instead of initially assuming an inherent opposition between autonomy and universal validity, we look for ways in which they are mutually dependent. Accordingly, I want to explore ways in which the exercise of autonomy is made possible by the capacity to think, act, and judge in ways that can make claims to universal validity, or as Kant might put it, in ways that can gain 'the agreement of free citizens, each of whom must be able to express his reservations, indeed even his *veto*, without holding back' (*KrV* B766–7). Kant calls such agreement the 'claim' or 'verdict' (*Ausspruch*) of reason, and it has an obvious tie to the ideal of consensus implicit in the idea of a Realm of Ends. I will approach this issue by asking how Kant's conception of autonomy leads to the notion of a realm of ends. Reflection about the connection between these concepts reveals that the autonomous agent is neither unbound by rules, nor free from all socially applied constraints. Autonomy (in individuals) is made possible by certain kinds of laws, norms, and standards that guide an agent's willing, and it presupposes, and is only exercised among, a community of rational agents with equal capacity to give law. In sum, the introduction of the concept of a realm of ends makes explicit the social dimension to Kant's conception of autonomy.

This puzzle—how could one have autonomy if one's willing must be acceptable to all members of a realm of ends (i.e., meet a condition of universal validity)?— arises from our expectation that autonomy and constraint by socially applied rules and standards are incompatible. Why do we expect an inconsistency here? One answer is that, for Kant, autonomy involves (the capacity for) independence from certain kinds of external influence on the use of one's reason, specifiable in different ways. Autonomy requires the capacity to reason and act independently of inclinations—that is, to arrive at conclusions and to act from reasons and principles that are not based on inclination and private conditions in oneself. It also requires the capacity for independence from certain kinds of social influence (e.g., custom, tradition, social convention, or established political and religious authorities, etc.) in the formation of beliefs, desires, values, and general principles of conduct.[1] It may in addition require freedom from subjection to external authority in the use of one's reason—for instance in the judgment of what one has reason to do, or in the choice of ends, principles of action, or higher-order values. Since focusing on this aspect of autonomy leads one to detail the kinds of influence and authority from which the autonomous agent is free, it tempts one to think that autonomy insulates the agent from all unchosen constraints and social influence. One is led to view the autonomous agent as a sovereign lawgiver, unbound by tradition, convention, and authority, who legislates for himself (boldly and proudly!). But while agents with autonomy must be able to abstract from certain kinds of psychological and social influence, they do not for that reason think and act in isolation. Autonomy has a positive aspect, and without specifying the kind of meaningful activity that the agent is free to engage in, it remains an empty concept. The positive specification of autonomy is likely to do two things: it will introduce rules that structure and make possible the activity which the agent is free to engage in, and it will introduce interaction with other agents. The activities providing the positive specification of autonomy will be rule-governed activities that require the participation of others, and presuppose social practices sustained by a community of agents.

One element in my proposal for dissolving the tension between autonomy and subjection to rules and social constraint is to approach autonomy through the triadic analysis of liberty. We should begin by viewing autonomy schematically as the freedom of a rational agent from certain kinds of constraint and authority to engage in certain kinds of meaningful and creative activity.[2] While the negative component of the schema (the 'independence condition') removes the agent from certain kinds of social influence, its positive specification will make it clear that autonomy is only a possibility for agents located within sets of practices which structure their activity and interaction with other agents. This is not for the psychological reason that it is only under certain social conditions that one can develop the capacity for independent and critical thought. Rather it is because the kinds of activities that provide the positive specification of autonomy presuppose systems of constitutive rules and the participation of other rational agents. As the rules that define various kinds of rational activity, they are the rules that one must follow in order to exercise the capacity with which autonomy is identified. In addition, this capacity is exercised in relation to other agents, who can recognize that the constitutive rules have been followed and can respond in appropriate ways. Thus the exercise of autonomy presupposes a community of agents with the capacity to follow a system of rules, judge their correct application, and respond as called for.

I pursue these issues in different stages. Before going into the connection between Kant's substantive conception of autonomy and the notion of a realm of ends, I develop some general observations about how freedom and autonomy may be related to governance by rules and standards. We tend to think that rules restrict free activity, but there are also rules that make meaningful and creative activities possible. Attention to the different functions that rules serve, specifically to their constitutive role, supplies another key element in dissolving the conflict between autonomy and governance by rules. In the next section I look at instances where the freedom to engage in certain activities and governance by rules are not in tension. The point I will make requires the introduction of rules with a special (non-restrictive) function, but there is no thought that these rules are self-imposed or self-chosen. In Sections III and IV, I apply this framework to Kant's conception of the autonomy of the moral agent.

II. AUTONOMY AND GOVERNANCE BY NORMS

Are speakers 'bound' by linguistic rules in a way that limits their freedom? Do the rules of a language restrict my ability to express my thoughts and communicate them to others? Clearly not, since they make expression and communication possible in the first place. When I follow the rules of a language, I have accomplished something that is recognizable by others. I have said something, made sense, conveyed a thought. The possibilities are more elaborate when further rules and standards are in place. By conforming to the relevant rules, one can say something that is recognizable as an apology or a reproach, an act of encouragement or consolation. One can make a true statement, construct a valid argument, develop an analysis, or write a poem; and by meeting further standards covering that activity, one can do it well or insightfully, in a way that gains the appreciation or respect of others. Presumably the same rules and standards that the speaker follows are employed by others in the linguistic community to recognize, interpret, and evaluate his or her activity. Thus they must share, and the speaker must presuppose that they share, the same basic understanding of and ability to apply these rules. The responses of others can indicate the extent to which one has conformed to these rules, and can measure one's success in the intended activity. Others finding you unintelligible, or reflecting back a meaning that you did not intend, may be a sign that you failed to conform to the rules. To the extent that one can only communicate a thought by following the relevant rules, they limit what one can intelligibly do. But when one does conform to the rules, one has accomplished something and has the right to certain responses from others who share the system of norms—for instance, that they interpret one's act in a certain way, that they acknowledge one's achievement, or where appropriate, that they respond as prescribed by a further rule of the practice (accept the apology, either acknowledge the validity of a reproach or defend against it, show gratitude for the encouragement, and so on).

The general point that I wish to make draws on an important insight of H. L. A. Hart. One of Hart's concerns in *The Concept of Law* is to demonstrate the flaws in the 'imperative theory of law' whose model of law is that of 'general orders backed by threats given by one generally obeyed'.[3] The imperative theory attempts to fit all laws to the model of coercive rules requiring individuals to perform or omit certain types of action. Hart observes that, while this model may be adequate for criminal law and for certain features of tort law, it fails as a general theory because it ignores the variety of functions that laws can serve. Many laws are not coercive and do not play the role of social control. In particular, Hart points to what he calls 'power-conferring' laws, whose function is to enable individuals to enter into and create legal arrangements, to modify existing legal relations, or to introduce new legal rules. Hart writes:

But there are important classes of law where this analogy with orders backed by threats altogether fails, since they perform a quite different social function. Legal rules defining the ways in which valid contracts or wills or marriages are made do not require persons to act in certain ways whether they wish to or not. Such laws do not impose duties or obligations. Instead they provide individuals with facilities for realizing their wishes, by conferring legal powers upon them to create, by certain specified procedures and subject to certain conditions, structures of rights and duties within the coercive framework of law.[4]

Hart distinguishes laws conferring 'private powers', such as those governing the creation of contracts, trusts, or wills, from laws conferring 'public powers', which include laws that set out the procedure by which a legislature enacts or repeals laws or which determine the adjudication of laws in the courts. A common feature of each is that they are rules by which individuals (in either a private or a public capacity) can create rights and duties.[5]

The rules defining the practice of promising or the rules of a game are obvious examples of power-conferring rules found outside the law. Let us rehearse some of their principal structural features. First, power-conferring rules are *constitutive* of the activity that they govern. They define certain kinds of activities (such as promising, scoring, or making an exchange), as well as relationships, moves that one can make, or roles that one can occupy within a practice, none of which can exist apart from these rules.[6] Rather than restricting action, they *enable* individuals to engage in certain activities and arrangements by setting out the procedure to follow, broadly construed to include the actions that must be performed and qualifications or other conditions that one must satisfy, in order to make a promise, enact a law, score a goal, and so on. They determine what counts as performing any of these activities. But though power-conferring rules are not primarily restrictive, they limit the exercise of the powers that they define. As rules that can be applied correctly or incorrectly, they introduce the notion of *validity*. One can perform the act in question only when one properly follows the relevant procedure and meets its qualifications. But as Hart points out, the consequence of not following the rule is not that one is liable to a sanction, but simply that one has failed to perform the intended act.[7] In addition, a set of constitutive rules may contain substantive limitations on the exercise of a power, failure to conform to which nullifies an attempted use of the power. For example, a constitution may authorize a legislature to enact laws only on certain subjects, or may contain a bill of rights invalidating certain kinds of laws. A body of contract law may not allow individuals to enter into certain kinds of contracts—which is to say, that it will not view certain (purported) agreements as binding contracts.

Finally by conferring important powers and capacities on agents, power-conferring rules give one a social stature that one could not otherwise have. Restrictive rules also give agents a social status, since, in addition to imposing duties, they give individuals rights and entitle them to consideration from others. But power-conferring rules give one an active role in shaping the progress of social life, over and above the passive role of bearer of rights and duties.[8] They enable individuals to make moves, to create arrangements, relationships, and structures whose validity others must acknowledge. For example, the rules constitutive of promising and private legal powers give one a capacity to create rights and duties and, by enabling one to create reasons binding others, give one a kind of authority in relation to others. Other such rules create the framework within which one can perform meaningful activities that others can acknowledge and—if one's performance satisfies further standards—admire. Both confer a distinct kind of social status on an agent. They make one an active participant in a public life and open up possibilities for various kinds of recognition and respect from others.

In short, power-conferring rules make one a player in social life. And obviously one cannot play on one's own: anyone's ability to exercise these capacities is made possible by general understanding of and adherence to complex systems of rules and standards, and one's success on any particular occasion depends on other agents recognizing that one has properly exercised the capacity in question (properly followed the rules, met the standards, and so on).

This notion of a power-conferring rule is most readily applied to social practices with a fairly explicit (formalizable) structure—law, language, and logic come to mind. But it is applicable to many other areas of social life. Indeed, the real question is whether one can find an important range of human activities that are not structured by something like constitutive rules. Most intelligible and meaningful conduct is guided by rules that sort actions into socially significant categories. These norms and standards govern the production of meaningful actions, and are used by others to recognize and interpret what an agent has done. Systems of rules and practices of this sort are the framework within which individual agents form their aims and intentions, as well as their responses, evaluative and otherwise, to the actions of others. Without them, a human agent could do little that is meaningful and significant. Claiming that such rules render an action intelligible is not to claim that they render an action rational in the sense of cohering with an agent's beliefs and desires; they may not. The point is that there is a kind of conformity to rule that seems prior to this kind of rationality, which has to be established before one knows how to assess the coherence of an action with an agent's beliefs and desires, or even to know that it is a candidate for this kind of assessment.[9]

Though this topic is too complex for adequate treatment here, a few examples are in order. Consider the background of rules and practices that is presupposed for an action to count as a gift, insult, expression of gratitude, gesture of hospitality, act of religious devotion, assertion of authority, or piece of performance art. Actions with a communicative or expressive dimension provide another kind of example. Think about the role of social convention in determining what counts as the expression of certain attitudes and emotions such as deference, contempt, sympathy, humility, or indignation. Both sorts of action presuppose some shared constitutive rules that determine what counts as engaging in that activity or expressing that attitude. These rules are embedded in a larger complex that includes standards for the situations in which such actions are appropriate, who can (sensibly) perform them, appropriate responses from others, and so on. It is the existence of such systems of rules and of a community that can apply them which makes it possible to do any of these things.

The concept of a power-conferring rule suggests a strategy for dissolving the appearance of inconsistency between autonomy and governance by rules, by reminding us that not all governance by rules is restrictive. Certain kinds of rules are constitutive of the possibility of free, creative human activity. Their primary function is not to constrain, since there is no independently describable activity which they prevent one from doing. The alternative to conforming to these rules is not doing something else that one prefers, but random activity, failing to do anything at all. Most intelligible human activity presupposes governance by some kind of rule.[10]

In closing this section, let me note a further structural feature of power-conferring (constitutive) rules, which might be termed their *reciprocal* character. We have seen that they govern the exercise of the power or activity that they create by setting out standards of validity; but they also govern proper responses from members of the community that shares these rules. (This is part of what it is for such rules to confer powers.) When an agent properly follows a constitutive rule, other agents are bound to interpret the act, and to acknowledge its validity, as an instance of a particular category (as a promise, gift, expression of sympathy, argument, legislative act), and, in the case of communicative and expressive acts, to interpret it as carrying a particular meaning. Some acts will oblige others to perform further actions (keep an agreement, show gratitude for a gift, accept the conclusion of an argument, obey a law). And an agent who satisfies further evaluative standards may earn various kinds of admiration and respect. An agent who exercises a power is bound by its constitutive rules, and whether one has validly exercised the power may require confirmation by the judgments of others. But the rules that govern the agent and bind one to the community also bind the community to recognize the validity of one's activity and to respond accordingly. Rules of this sort play a mediating role in social interaction. They are the laws of interaction of a community of rational agents, the laws governing the mutual and reciprocal influence that we exert on each other, that make action and coexistence in a shared world possible.[11]

III. THE CATEGORICAL IMPERATIVE AS POWER-CONFERRING NORM

Can moral rules and principles that initially strike us as restrictive also be regarded as rules that enable rational agents to engage in certain kinds of meaningful and creative activities? I believe that this shift in perspective is possible, and that it offers a way to understand certain aspects of Kant's view that a will with autonomy is subject to the moral law, or to the principle of willing in ways that can gain the agreement of the members of a realm of ends. I will argue that the Categorical Imperative is, and is understood by Kant to be, a principle that is constitutive of a certain kind of rational activity and that creates and confers on rational agents certain powers. To put the point paradoxically, an 'imperative theory of imperatives' presents too narrow a view of moral imperatives, as Kant understands them. Moral imperatives are restrictive in their capacity of limiting permissible conduct through requirements and prohibitions, but that does not exhaust their practical role.

This point requires some attention to the distinction between particular categorical imperatives and the Categorical Imperative, and some clarification of the practical or social role of both. The distinction between particular categorical imperatives and the Categorical Imperative marks a difference between two levels of principle. Particular categorical imperatives are best understood as the substantive results of moral deliberation. They could include either substantive moral principles that determine duties, rights and permissions, or conclusions about how agents ought to, or may, act in a specific situation. Kant's tendency to depict moral principles as yielding 'commands' carrying absolute necessity, along with his choice of the term 'imperative', suggests that their social role is to control conduct.[12] Certainly that is one of their functions, but there are grounds for viewing their primary social role more broadly as that of justification. They are principles used to resolve normative questions in an authoritative way, by which agents can justify their conduct to each other and live on terms of mutual respect.[13] They are the principles underlying the things that we say to each other in our (conscientious) attempts to achieve reasoned consensus on normative questions.

The Categorical Imperative is the general moral principle by which one arrives at particular imperatives, and thus the principle that, at the highest level, guides and makes possible the activity of justification. As the general criterion of moral acceptability, its application establishes the norms that create duties, rights, and permissions. What determines the normative status of an action or principle is whether the relevant maxim can be willed as universal law in accordance with the procedure set out by the Categorical Imperative. Kant regards the Categorical Imperative as a principle to be applied by agents already in the business of acting from considerations that they take to be good reasons, and to have some kind of justificatory force for others as well as themselves. The primary question of moral evaluation is whether the reasons for action expressed in one's maxim are in fact reasons that anyone can regard as sufficient. In this respect moral deliberation aims at determining whether an agent's underlying principle of action is suited to play a certain social role: can it be made into a principle that yields authoritative justifications and can settle questions about the normative status of an action? That is to say, can it be made into a practical law? So understood, the Categorical Imperative is a 'norm for norms': it is the higher-order norm by which one can assess the substantive norms that underlie particular choices and that might be cited in their justification.

Since the Categorical Imperative is a higher-order requirement of acting only from reasons that anyone can regard as sufficient, it limits permissible conduct as do categorical imperatives. But because it sets out and structures the activity of justification, the Categorical Imperative also confers a capacity to engage in a meaningful and creative activity. It is the deliberative procedure that determines whether a maxim can serve as a practical law, and by properly employing this procedure, one makes one's maxim available as a principle that can resolve questions of justification. That is to say, one gives it the status of a practical law. It is thus a kind of legislative procedure which any rational agent can employ to arrive at first-order norms for conduct, whose authority others must acknowledge and which can settle questions of justification.

We have seen that autonomy may be understood schematically as the freedom of a rational agent from certain kinds of constraints to engage in certain kinds of rational activity. The power-conferring aspect of the Categorical Imperative can be clarified further by saying more about the kinds of activity that it enables a rational agent to engage in, and this will help show why autonomy is exercised by willing principles that can gain the agreement of other rational agents with the same legislative capacities as oneself. In Kant's conception of autonomy, the negative component, or independence condition, is that one is not bound to any standards or authority external to one's reason. Put another way, the autonomous agent's activity is guided by a process of reasoning in which what count as reasons is not settled by (is independent of) facts about one's desires or other private features of one's condition, or by what social convention, tradition, or any uncritically accepted external authority (civil, ecclesiastical, familial, and so on) regard as reasons.[14] The three main versions of the Categorical Imperative suggest the following positive specifications of autonomy:[15]

(1) the power to formulate and act from reasons and principles that can justify one's actions to other rational agents;
(2) the power to confer a value on objects, activities, and states of affairs which other agents must acknowledge, by adopting them as the ends of one's rational choice;
(3) the power to adopt principles that can serve as practical laws—for a community of moral agents—that is, principles to which one can appeal to resolve questions of justification, or questions about the normative status of an action.

To combine these with the independence condition, the agent with autonomy is free from constraint by any standards or authority external to one's reason to engage in the relevant rational activity. When the reasoning that guides his or her activity satisfies the independence condition, the validity of its results is not conditioned by private or subjective facts about the reasoner, or conditional upon taking social convention, tradition, or the will of an external authority by itself as a source of reasons. That is to say, one has not arrived at one's conclusions simply in virtue of factors such as beliefs, desires, or values peculiar to oneself; nor is the acceptability of one's conclusions contingent upon taking approval by social convention, tradition, or an external authority as a reason in its favor. The validity of the conclusions does not depend on accepting any source of authority external to reason, or that cannot be shared by all potential reasoners.[16] Kant thinks that a form of reasoning that satisfies the independence condition is unconditionally valid, and that its authority extends to all reasoners. Thus autonomy will be interpreted, roughly, as the capacity to construct and act from justifications, or the capacity to confer value, or the capacity to adopt justifying principles—in each case, whose validity and authority are unconditional and can be acknowledged by any rational agent.

A common feature of these activities is that they are deliberative procedures by which one can create reasons that bind other agents. They are procedures through which a deliberating agent can establish principles that determine the normative status of an action and affect normative relations between agents—that is, principles that create permissions, rights, and duties, or that confer value, which others must acknowledge. As such, they interpret autonomy as a capacity to create reasons and value. For example, through moral deliberation that establishes the permissibility of an action, one shows that one may rightfully perform the action, and gives others reasons to accept or endorse one's choice. One uses the deliberative procedure that is the final criterion of validity to confer a normative status on an action, and one's employment of this procedure gives others reasons to adopt various evaluative attitudes, and may lead to reasons for action (e.g., not to interfere, to give aid, and so on). One confers a value on an object when one adopts it as one's end through a rational process in which the value of humanity limits acceptable ends or choices. Rational deliberation that is constrained by respect for humanity leads one to regard the object as choiceworthy, and by making it one's end, one singles it out for a consideration that it would not have apart from one's choice. When one shows that a maxim can be willed as law for a realm of ends, one establishes it as a practical law (normative principle) that other agents must acknowledge. In each case, the Categorical Imperative may be viewed as the principle constitutive of this activity, which confers a power on the agent. By enabling one to create permissions, rights, and duties, or to confer value, or to establish authoritative practical principles, it enables one to create reasons that other agents must acknowledge. It thus renders that agent a kind of sovereign authority.

When autonomy is understood in any of these ways, it is a power exercised in relation to others, made possible by their responses and requiring their participation. The construction of justifications, the conferral of value, or the adoption of authoritative normative principles are not the kinds of activity that one can do on one's own, and would make no sense for an agent not engaged in ongoing social interaction. This dependence on the participation and responses of other agents can be elaborated in various ways.

First, when autonomy is specified as a capacity to engage in deliberation through which one creates reasons for others, it presupposes as the locus of its exercise a community of agents with the ability to guide their conduct by what they regard as good reasons. They must be able to recognize when one has carried out a reason-creating procedure, and to take one's doing so as giving them authoritative reasons for action.

Second, when one exercises a power in relation to others, those agents must be disposed to display the appropriate responses—in this case, to take one's employment of the deliberative procedure as giving them reasons. Since autonomy (as interpreted here) is a power to move other agents through their rationality by one's employment of one's own, the responses of others provide a partial measure of whether an agent has successfully exercised this capacity. For example, an aim of moral justification is to move other agents to share an evaluation of an action by presenting them with sufficient reasons. Since justification succeeds when it moves other agents through their own reason to take up the intended evaluative attitude, one who engages in this activity must advance normative claims with which others can be expected to concur. The failure to gain the agreement of others can be prima facie evidence that the force of a claim depends upon a private condition in the agent, or on accepting a source of authority that need not be generally shared. While it is not a decisive indication that one's normative claim cannot play the intended role in justification, it does give the agent a reason to reconsider the grounds of his claim and to continue his deliberations. Similar points may be made about conferring value on the end of one's rational choice. Value presupposes the possibility of shared evaluative attitudes. In viewing one's end as having value and as a source of reasons for others, one supposes that other agents can come to endorse one's evaluative attitude toward the end and regard one's pursuit of it as good. The capacity to confer value thus presupposes a community of agents with the same basic evaluative capacities as oneself, whose (potential) agreement with one's use of this capacity confirms its successful exercise. In each case, the failure of others to share one's evaluative conclusions can indicate that the capacity for autonomy has not been properly exercised, while their concurrence can confirm that it has.

Third, since one's capacity to construct justifications and to confer value depends on the dispositions of other agents to take one's deliberations as giving them reasons, its exercise is limited by the possibility of their sharing one's conclusions. But that is to say that the ability of others to accept one's conclusions is constitutive of autonomy, and that nothing could count as a proper exercise of this deliberative procedure which other agents could not regard as giving them reasons for action. (This point can be extended to any use of authority: since authority is only effectively exercised when other agents respond in a certain way, the limits of what they can regard as reasons for acting will set the limits to the exercise of authority.)

Such considerations show why the identification of autonomy with the capacity to create authoritative reasons for others makes its exercise subject to the condition that it can gain the agreement of other rational agents. The underlying regulative principle of the agent with autonomy will be that of exercising his or her reason in ways that other rational agents can freely agree with. As one might say, the possibility of such agreement is a condition of the possibility of exercising autonomy.

IV. LEGISLATING FOR A COMMUNITY OF ENDS

In this section I address in more detail the question of why the concept of the moral agent as autonomous legislator leads to '. . . a very fruitful concept, dependent upon it, namely that *of a realm of ends*' (*G*4: 433). I will explore the mutual dependence between these concepts by arguing that autonomy, as Kant understands it, presupposes and can only be exercised among a community of rational agents, each of whom possesses the same basic rational capacities and the same sovereign status. We have seen that there is no difficulty in understanding how autonomy is consistent with governance by socially applied rules once it is viewed in substantive terms as the ability to engage in certain kinds of activities. This framework can be used to explain why one exercises autonomy by using one's reason in ways that can gain the agreement of the members of a community of ends. Kant's conception of autonomy has been characterized as the freedom of a rational agent from constraint by external authority to engage in certain kinds of rational activities. The principle of willing in ways that can gain the agreement of the members of a realm of ends is the fundamental principle that is constitutive of these activities, and thus of the exercise of autonomy. I now wish to take these suggestions a step further by viewing autonomy more narrowly in terms of what Kant regards as its central feature—the capacity to give law through one's will.

The concept of autonomy first appears in the *Groundwork* with Kant's argument that the moral agent is not just subject to the moral law, but is also a lawgiver. His claim is that agents subject to moral principles are bound in such a way that they must be regarded as their legislators.[17] The basis of this claim is that the reasons for an agent to comply with such a principle are given by the reasoning that makes it a law—that is, the reasoning that confers validity on it, through which a sovereign legislator would enact it as law. Thus agents bound to such principles must possess the same rational capacities as would be required of a legislator, and go through the same deliberative process in complying with the principle (display the same volitional state) as a legislator would use in enacting it. This conception of the moral agent is supported by a corresponding view of the Categorical Imperative as a kind of legislative procedure that any rational agent can employ to confer on a practical principle the status of practical law.

When autonomy is viewed as a capacity to give law, questions about autonomy become questions about the nature of authority. In the political realm, the mark of legislative authority is the ability to create reasons for others through the exercise of one's will. The fact that a legislator wills, or duly enacts, a rule or principle makes it a law, and gives the subjects a reason to perform certain kinds of action that they did not have prior to the legislator's act. These reasons are generally viewed as final in the sense that the legislator's enactment precludes the need for further deliberation on the part of those subject to the law about how to act.[18] In the same way, an agent with autonomy has the capacity to will principles that have unconditional authority for others. That is to say, one has the capacity, through the (proper) exercise of one's will, to create reasons that are binding on other agents, which those agents did not have prior to the exercise of one's will.

How might this conception of the moral agent as autonomous lead to the concept of a realm of ends? In a rather uninteresting way, this concept results from generalization. Kant's arguments show that any agent bound to moral principle may be regarded as a sovereign legislator who should be accorded dignity, and one cannot apply this conception to oneself without also applying it to all other rational agents. But more to the point, some social notions are implicit in this conception of the moral agent. It makes no sense to conceive of the moral agent as legislator without bringing in a community to whom law is being given, as well as a conception of the social role of these laws within it. Laws are norms that regulate the interaction of rational agents with the ability to guide their conduct by the application of such norms. As I indicated earlier, in Kant's view moral principles are principles by which agents can justify their conduct to each other, and which make possible social relationships based on mutual respect. In addition, legislative authority is a power exercised in relation to other agents, and presupposes a certain kind of relationship between sovereign and subject. A sovereign has the power to move other rational agents to action through their rational capacities in specific ways. It thus presupposes a community of agents who can recognize exercises of authority and can take the fact that an agent in a position of authority has duly enacted a law as a reason to comply with it. Moreover, for the exercise of authority to be effective, the subjects must be disposed to do what the legislator wills for non-accidental reasons: because they regard the legislator's will as a source of sufficient reasons, and not, for example, out of self-interest or fear. Thus authority is exercised over agents who possess certain normative capacities, and who acknowledge and respond to uses of authority as a result of their exercise of these capacities.

At this point the original puzzle reappears, now cast as a problem about the nature of legislative authority. An agent with autonomy is not bound to any external authority and has the power to give law through her will. But such an agent must also be regarded as giving law to a community of agents, each of whom is as much a sovereign legislator as she. Since one is addressing agents with the same basic capacity to propose and evaluate normative principles, it would be unreasonable to will legislation that one knows could not withstand the critical scrutiny of other members of the community of ends. So it seems that one must guide one's legislative powers by the higher-order principle of willing principles that can gain the assent of all members of a community of ends. The question then is why that higher-order principle does not limit the agent's legislative authority. How is such an agent free from external authority to give law through her will? The answer must be that the principle of willing in ways that can gain the agreement of all members of a community of ends is constitutive of sovereign authority; it is the principle that confers authority on the agent, through which one gives law through one's will.

To develop this claim, let us take the central element of legislative authority to be the power of a legislator to create law through the exercise of his or her will, and ask how that is possible. How can a legislator's willing (enacting) a principle as law create reasons that bind other agents? One might approach this question through the following schematic model of legislative authority: law is created when an agent in a position of authority enacts a regulative principle addressed to some group of rational agents which that agent sees reason and is authorized to enact, and backs it with sanctions. One must then develop the elements of the model to explain how an authorized agent's carrying out a legislative procedure creates reasons for other agents to conform to its results.

If the legislator's *willing* of a principle is to create reasons, it must carry immediate authority in itself, without depending on anything outside the legislator's will to give the 'subjects' reasons to acknowledge its normative force. This is clearly not the case if the account of legislative authority bases the reasons for accepting the law in sanctions or other consequences attached to the law, or in any contingent connections between the legislator's will and desires which the subjects happen to have. If one takes the reasons for adherence to come from sanctions, then it is the imposition of sanctions rather than the legislator's willing, or enacting, the law that creates reasons for the subjects. They then act from self-interest, rather than from a recognition of the legislator's authority. This would also be true if one based the reasons for compliance on such motives as a desire for certain goods provided by a law, habits of obedience to, or a desire to please the legislator. In each of these cases, the reasons for adhering to the law are conditional on the existence of certain interests in the subjects, or on a fortuitous convergence of the interests of subjects and legislator. Thus, when the model of authority is developed in this way, the legislator's willing of the law would not carry its authority in itself and does not by itself create reasons for the subjects. The legislator may control or manipulate the behavior of his subjects, but he does not move them to act in the way that is characteristic of pure exercises of authority, by giving them binding reasons for action simply through the exercise of his will.

A different elaboration of the above schema would hold that the reasons to conform to the law come from the fact that it is enacted by an agent in a position of authority—roughly, that the authority of the law comes from the authority of the legislator's office. But even on this account, the legislator's will is not the ultimate source of reasons. The authority of the legislator's enactments will be explained by whatever puts that agent in a position of authority—say, from whatever gives the legislator the right to enact law, or from a prior duty of the subject to take the legislator's will as a reason for acting. In this sense, authority is conferred on his enactments by a source external to his will. Within this model, the legislator may have free reign to specify the content of the subjects' obligations; his enactments determine *what* they have reason to do. But the legislator's enacting a law creates reasons only against the background of his occupying a position of authority (e.g., in conjunction with a general obligation on the part of the subjects to take the sovereign's will as a reason). What creates reasons for the subjects to obey, and ultimately does the work of explaining their obligation, is the fact that he occupies a position of authority, rather than his particular acts of willing.

How then, can a legislator's act of will carry authority in itself? Kant's answer must be that a legislator creates authoritative reasons for others when her willing is guided by reasoning that any rational agent can recognize as authoritative. The reasoning underlying the legislator's adoption of a law must be sufficient to lead anyone to regard it as a good law to enact. But that is to say that the reasoning leading to the adoption of the law does not depend for its validity on any private or subjective conditions in the reasoner; the underlying reasoning must be valid unconditionally, and thus renders the principle valid without condition. What indicates that the legislator's willing is unconditionally valid is that it is able to gain the agreement of the members of a community of rational agents. Thus, if a legislator is to give law through her will—that is to say, if she is to act as a sovereign legislator—she must guide her legislative activity by the principle of willing in ways that can gain the agreement of all members of a community of ends.

To put the point another way, one gives law through one's will when one's willing a principle is sufficient by itself to give other agents authoritative reasons for actions. This will only be the case when the legislator's willing is guided by reasoning that any rational agent can acknowledge as valid and authoritative. Only then will other rational agents be moved to action in the way that is characteristic of the relationship of authority: by their taking the legislator's enactment of a principle as giving them binding reasons for conforming to it.

The analysis just outlined proceeds by asking what is presupposed for a legislator to give law through the exercise of his or her will, and argues that one gives law through one's will only when the reasoning underlying one's willing is unconditionally valid. When a model of legislative authority bases the authority of a legislative act either on the sanctions or desirable consequences attached to it, or by appealing to the sovereign's legislative position, one cannot claim that the legislator creates law through his or her will. In such cases, the normative force of a legislative enactment depends either on the consequences of the law, or on an external principle that confers authority on the legislator. Moreover, the subjects do not respond to the legislator in the appropriate way, since the normative force of the law comes from a source external to the legislator's will. The analysis to which I believe that Kant is committed locates the authority of a law in the deliberative procedure that the legislator follows in adopting it—that is to say, in the reasoning that goes into willing the law. Moreover, the deliberative procedure that a legislator must follow to create law through his or her will has its basis in the concept of authority. One 'enacts valid law' when one guides one's deliberation by the higher-order principle of willing principles that are supported by reasoning sufficient to lead any rational agent to accept them. When a legislator follows this basic principle, she gives law through her will, since her willing of a principle contains within itself reasons for any rational agent to accept it. She has given them reasons for action in the way that is characteristic of the relation of authority, since they can take her willing a principle as a reason to accept it.

In this way one can argue that the higher-order principle of willing principles that can gain the agreement of the members of a community of ends is constitutive of sovereign authority. It is the principle implicit in the concept of sovereignty, which, as we might say, states the 'form of lawgiving'. Think of it as the legislative procedure that an agent with autonomy must follow in order to create valid law. Since proper execution of this deliberative procedure confers validity on the resulting principle, it enables any agent with the capacity to employ this procedure to give law through his or her will.

This line of thought supports a conclusion about the deliberative procedure that a rational agent must employ in order to act as a sovereign. What does it tell us about the agents to whom law is given, or the community in which this power of sovereignty is exercised? We have seen that a sovereign legislator will give laws supported by reasoning that is unconditionally valid. But for the exercise of his sovereign powers to be effective, the subjects must recognize his willing of a principle as giving them reasons to accept it. If they are to accord immediate authority to the sovereign's willing, they must be moved to accept the sovereign's enactments through their understanding of the reasoning that goes into them. But then they must possess the same basic capacities to reason and to evaluate normative principles as the sovereign, and must also be able to carry out, and be motivated by, the deliberative process that guided the sovereign's enactment. Moreover, since the reasoning involved is valid without condition, they must have the ability to engage in, and be moved by, reasoning that is independent of private conditions in themselves. Thus, agents moved by their recognition of the authority of a sovereign's will must go through the same deliberative process in complying with his laws as he employed in enacting them. The law-following subject and the lawgiving sovereign will display the same volitional state.

The further conclusion to which we are led is that sovereign authority, as understood by Kant, is exercised among rational agents with the same basic capacities as the sovereign. The exercise of sovereignty presupposes agents who can respond in appropriate ways. In a word, one can only give law to, and exercise sovereign authority among, fellow sovereigns; a sovereign agent needs autonomous subjects and legislates to a community of equals.

As we also saw in the previous section, regarding authority as a specific kind of social relationship brings out the extent to which the exercise of sovereignty depends on the existence of agents with certain rational capacities who respond to the sovereign in specific ways. Since sovereignty is the power to move other agents through their rational capacities by one's use of one's own, its successful exercise is measured by the responses of other agents. In order to create law through the exercise of one's will, a sovereign's willing must be guided by reasoning that is unconditionally valid. The indication that this standard is satisfied is that one's underlying reasoning is sufficient to lead the other members of a community of rational agents to accept one's principles. One moves other agents through one's willing when they freely accept the principles that one wills on the basis of their understanding of one's underlying reasoning. In these respects a sovereign is bound to exercise this power in ways that can gain the agreement of all members of a community of ends. Their ability to agree with one's use of one's rational powers and to accept one's underlying reasoning is constitutive of sovereignty, establishing both the possibility of sovereign power and the limits within which it is exercised.

To forestall the complaint that this dependence of the sovereign on the agreement of other rational agents deprives her of her independence, it is worth citing (again) the power-conferring features of this principle. First, the sovereign agent remains free from constraint by any external standard or authority because the only limitations on the exercise of sovereignty are those implied by the principle that is constitutive of lawgiving. Second, guiding one's will by the principle of willing principles that can gain the agreement of a community of ends enables one to give law through one's will. It makes it possible to frame principles whose authority others must recognize, and to move them through one's willing. Thus, it gives one a power in relation to other agents, and a social status that entitles one to respect and dignity. These points illustrate the reciprocal nature of this constitutive principle. It is the common bond, the mediating principle that simultaneously binds the sovereign to his subjects, and obligates them to recognize his authority when he has followed its prescribed procedure.

This connection between autonomy and the idea of a realm of ends brings out the deeply egalitarian aspect of Kant's conception of the form that authority must take among agents with autonomy. True exercises of authority, and more generally, claims made in the name of reason, are not imposed from above, and cannot require blind submission or uncritical acceptance without an understanding of their underlying basis. Authority is exercised among equals, who are able to take a critical attitude toward any purported exercise of authority, and to acknowledge only those that they are led to accept by their own powers of reason. This authority, of course, that Kant hears in the claims of morality, is the non-dogmatic authority of reason. Reason may be pictured as an ongoing process of thought and discussion whose only constraints are those provided by its guiding regulative principle of the universal agreement of agents with autonomy. The final standards of rational thought and volition are not fixed substantive principles, but rather are rooted in the possibility of acceptance by rational agents who are bound by no constraints other than those constitutive of their rational powers, which enable them to be active participants in an ongoing process of critical thought and discussion, and to arrive at conclusions that can command the agreement of other sovereign agents like themselves.[19] A remark from the first *Critique* is worth quoting again here:

Reason must subject itself to critique in all its undertakings, and cannot restrict the freedom of critique through any prohibition without damaging itself . . . On this freedom depends the very existence of reason, which has no dictatorial authority, but whose claim is never anything more than the agreement of free citizens, each of whom must be able to express his reservations, indeed even his *veto*, without holding back. (*KrV* B766–7)

This remark indicates that the realm of ends is not simply Kant's ideal of a moral community: in so far as reason must be understood as an ongoing and open-ended critical process, in which any rational agent may participate and which preserves the autonomy of its participants, agreement among the members of a realm of ends is emblematic of the nature and authority of reason.

V. AUTONOMY AS A LEGISLATIVE CAPACITY

A principle aim of this essay has been to explore how autonomy is made possible by the capacity to think, act, and judge in ways that can make claims to universal validity. In particular, it has tried to show why the principle of willing in ways that can gain the agreement of other rational agents should be constitutive of autonomy, and its underlying regulative principle. Let us review how these aims have been accomplished.

The first step was to articulate Kant's substantive conception of autonomy as the freedom from constraint by external authority to engage in certain kinds of rational activities. The last section focused on Kant's understanding of autonomy as the capacity to give law through one's will (independently of external constraint). Kant adopts this conception of autonomy because he views reason as a lawgiving faculty. It is neither a body of given substantive principles for the regulation of thought and action, nor the capacity to discover such principles. Reason is, rather, in the first instance, the critical process by which authoritative normative principles are generated and established. What confers the authority of reason on any principle or conclusion is that it can be derived from, or supported by (or can survive), this critical process. Individual reasoners may be viewed as legislators, as opposed to discoverers or seers, because of their capacity to employ the procedure by which authoritative conclusions may be derived; they are able to carry out the process of critical thought and reflection that confers on its results the authority of reason. To make the parallel with legislation explicit, what makes a principle a law is that it has been enacted by the appropriate procedure; a legislator is an agent authorized to carry this procedure out. Similarly, what confers rational authority on a principle is that is established by the right process of critical deliberation.

Once autonomy is interpreted as a legislative capacity, certain things follow. Lawgiving is an activity that occurs in a community of agents, and a lawgiver is someone who exercises a certain kind of power, and occupies a certain status, in that community. A lawgiver has the capacity to move other rational agents through their reason by his use of his reason. One moves other agents in this way by engaging in reasoning (willing principles, judging, and so on) whose validity and authority does not depend on any private condition in the reasoner, and is thus general and unconditional. Reasoning that satisfies this standard is able to gain the agreement of the other members of a community of rational agents. One can thus hold that the higher-order principle of willing principles that can gain the agreement of a community of rational agents is constitutive of sovereign authority—in other words, that it is constitutive of autonomy. But as the principle that makes autonomy possible, it cannot be construed as a limitation on it. We have also seen that sovereignty, so understood, can only be exercised among sovereign agents with the same rational capacities as oneself. As a power to move other agents through one's reasoning, it must be exercised in relation to agents who can be moved by their understanding of the reasoning that goes into one's willing. Such agents must have the ability to engage in forms of reasoning that are unconditionally valid, and that ability confers on those who possess it the status of sovereign legislator.

This essay proposes changes in how we think about autonomy—both in the context of Kant's moral theory and generally. First, I have suggested that we need a substantive conception of autonomy that interprets it as a creative power or capacity of a certain kind. Kant, I have argued, understands it as the power of a rational agent to create reasons and values that can have authority for other rational agents, through one's employment of the deliberative procedures inherent in our shared rational capacities. Second, I have tried to show that autonomy, as much as agency itself, has an essential social dimension. We tend to think that autonomy renders agents independent of all uncritically accepted social influence and externally imposed standards; and it does. But that does not mean that the autonomous agent is an isolated atomic unit. Autonomy is meaningfully exercised among other autonomous agents, whose rational capacities serve as a constraint on, and confirmation of, its exercise. It presupposes a background of rules and social practices, or better, a system of reasoners able to exercise the same capacities, and limited only by the principle of using their reason in ways that other agents can accept while at the same time continuing to view themselves as autonomous.

This interpretation of autonomy also has implications for the shape that one might give to the Kantian account of the authority of morality. The main idea behind Kant's account of why moral requirements are demands of reason is, roughly, that conforming to moral demands makes one free, or autonomous, or the originator of one's actions; it makes one an agent in the fullest sense. The framework developed in this essay suggests a way to enrich this answer: having this status as an individual is inseparable from the ability to play an active role in a certain kind of public life. Kant's claim that the moral law is the law of a free will may be interpreted as the claim that it is the constitutive principle of an autonomous, or sovereign, will. It is the principle through which one occupies the status of sovereign legislator, bound to no external authority and with the power to give law to other rational agents through one's will. By conforming to this principle one overcomes private conditions in oneself and thinks from a universal point of view, to which others can give authority. It thereby makes one an active participant in a public life, and as such entitled to the recognition and respect of other legislating members of a realm of ends.[20]

NOTES

1. For Kant's views on these aspects of autonomy, see his discussions of freedom of thought and criticism. Cf. for example, *KrV* B766–B785; 'An Answer to the Question: What is Enlightenment?' and 'What is Orientation in Thinking?', in *Kant: Political Writings*, ed. Hans Reiss, 2nd edn., esp. 246–9; and *The Critique of Judgment*, § 40. For important discussions of these passages, to which I am indebted at several points, see the following essays by Onora O'Neill: 'Reason and Politics in the Kantian Enterprise' and 'The Public Use of Reason', in *Constructions of Reason*; 'Enlightenment as Autonomy: Kant's Vindication of Reason'; and 'Vindicating Reason'. She gives an overview of Kant's account of the authority of reason in 'Within the Limits of Reason'. For further discussion of autonomy in Kant, see also Thomas E. Hill, Jr., *Dignity and Practical Reason*, 83–8, 138–43 (esp. 141).

2. For the now standard triadic analysis of political liberty, see John Rawls, *A Theory of Justice*, 176–80; and Joel Feinberg, *Social Philosophy*, 4–14.

3. *The Concept of Law*, 24. See also his 'Positivism, Law and Morals', reprinted in *Essays in Jurisprudence and Philosophy*, 57–62.

4. *The Concept of Law*, 27–8. For further discussion by Hart of the concept of a power-conferring rule, see his 'Legal Powers', in *Essays on Bentham*.

5. Hart views power-conferring rules as 'secondary rules', which he distinguishes from 'primary rules' as follows. Under primary rules

   . . . human beings are required to do or abstain from certain actions, whether they wish to or not. Rules of the other type are in a sense parasitic upon or secondary to the first; for they provide that human beings may by doing or saying certain things introduce new rules of the primary type, extinguish or modify old ones, or in various ways determine their incidence or control their operations. Rules of the first type impose duties; rules of the second type confer powers, public or private. (*The Concept of Law*, 81)

6. For a classic discussion of constitutive rules, see John Rawls, 'Two Concepts of Rules', sec. III.

7. *The Concept of Law*, 28.

8. Again, this point is made by Hart:

   . . . possession of these [private] legal powers makes of the private citizen, who if there were no such rules, would be a mere duty-bearer, a private legislator. He is made competent to determine the course of the law within the sphere of his contracts, trusts, wills and other structures of rights and duties which he is enabled to build. (ibid. 41)

9. Just as linguistic rules govern the production of utterances and enable others to parse and interpret these utterances, there are cultural and social rules that govern the production of meaningful actions and which other agents use to 'parse' and categorize these actions. Their application is prior to assessment in terms of norms of rationality, morality, various kinds of social propriety, and so on, in that actions must meet these base level standards of intelligibility before they are candidates for further evaluation.

10. For another discussion of these issues, see Robert Brandom, 'Freedom and Constraint by Norms', esp. 192–6. I thank Lynne Tirrell for bringing this article to my attention.

11. Kantians seeking structural parallels between theoretical and practical reason should compare the progression of *form, matter*, and *community* found in the Analogies of Experience with that found in the formulas of the Categorical Imperative. The

Analogies take up the permanence of substance (the underlying ground that remains the same during change), the law of causality (the form of alteration or of interaction between substances), and the principle of coexistence in accordance with the law of reciprocity (mutual interaction between objects that is presupposed by coexistence in a world). One might think of the Formula of Humanity as concerned with the substance that is the subject matter of morality, the Formula of Universal Law as the law of interaction between such substances, and the Formula of the Realm of Ends as spelling out the principle of reciprocity presupposed by moral substances inhabiting a shared world.

12. See, e.g., *G* 4: 416, 419–20. The command model is appropriate for requirements and prohibitions, though less so for permissions. However Kant's examples suggest that the Categorical Imperative is used principally to determine the permissibility of proposed intentions or actions.

13. For examples of this approach to the social role of moral principles, see Rawls, *A Theory of Justice*, § 40, 'Kantian Constructivism in Moral Theory: Rational and Full Autonomy', esp. 516–19; and Lecture 2 of *Political Liberalism*. See also T. M. Scanlon, 'Contractualism and Utilitarianism'. For a recent discussion of this theme, see Samuel Freeman's discussion of public reasons in 'Reason and Agreement in Social Contract Views', and 'Contractualism, Moral Motivation, and Practical Reason'.

14. Here I elaborate on Thomas E. Hill, Jr.'s explanation of the sense in which practical reasoning for agents with autonomy is independent of inclination. See 'Kant's Theory of Practical Reason', (esp. sec. III), in *Dignity and Practical Reason*.

15. I associate (1) with the Formula of Universal Law, (2) with the Formula of Humanity, and (3) with the Formula of the Realm of Ends (act only from maxims that one could at the same time will as law for a realm of ends). Despite surface differences, I assume in this essay that (1) and (3) are at least extensionally equivalent.

16. It is worth noting that judgments that depend on an authority that is accepted uncritically, or without rational grounding, are conditionally valid in precisely the same way that hypothetical imperatives are. Take, for example, a belief whose acceptability depends on treating the pronouncements of a certain religious figure as authoritative, and a practical principle that states a desire-based reason. The normative force of the first will be restricted to those who regard the religious figure as an authority, that of the second to those who have the relevant desire. In each case acceptability depends on some condition in an individual that need not be shared by all others qua rational. I draw this point from Onora O'Neill; see *Constructions of Reason*, 34–6 and 58–9.

17. See *G* 4: 431, discussed at length in Chapters 4 and 5.

18. Cf. Joseph Raz, *The Authority of Law*, 16–19.

19. Though I cannot argue the point here, I suspect that Kant replaces the substantive first principles that provided the content for earlier dogmatic conceptions of reason with the idea of a plurality of reasoners whose primary resource is their own ability to reason and whose only restriction is the autonomy of others.

20. This essay was drafted in the Spring of 1992 at the National Humanities Center under a grant from the National Endowment for the Humanities (NEH). I am grateful to both the Center and to the NEH for their support. I would also like to thank Tom Hill, Jerry Postema, Chris Korsgaard, and Dan Brudney for their comments on earlier drafts of this essay.

This essay was written for a volume in honor of John Rawls, and is an occasion for expressing a very special sort of gratitude. In the spring of 1977, during my second year of graduate school, John Rawls was lecturing on Kant's moral philosophy. My interests in epistemology had led me to Kant's *Critique of Pure Reason*, in which I had immersed myself during the previous fall. Thinking that it might be useful to broaden my knowledge of Kant through some familiarity with his ethics, I decided to sit in on Rawls's lectures. There was also some talk around the department that Rawls might know something about this area of Kant's thought. The rumors were correct, and the lectures proved to be more than an interesting diversion. Reading Kant's moral philosophy reminded me of the reasons I had gone into philosophy in the first place, and Rawls's lectures showed me how to read Kant. More generally, these lectures were a model of how to approach any figure or text in the history of philosophy. I don't recall missing many of his lectures on Kant or any other subject in the years that followed. Rawls's lectures on Kant's moral philosophy set me on a path that I continue to travel, with no thought yet of turning back.

7

Agency and Universal Law

I. INTRODUCTION

A long-standing controversy about the universal law version of the Categorical Imperative is whether it can provide substantive guidance about choice and action. In response to the traditional Hegelian objection that it is purely formal and empty of content, a number of theorists sympathetic to Kant have ably made the case that the Formula of Universal Law (FUL), along with its variant the Formula of the Law of Nature (FLN), has important and substantive moral implications.[1] These theorists have not claimed that the FUL is a sufficient basis for a complete moral conception. Nor have they claimed that the criterion of universalizability expressed by the FUL provides anything like a mechanical procedure for testing individual maxims. They have argued, rather, that the FUL supports an account of a significant region of moral thought and that it may be used to frame instructive explanations of why certain maxims of action, formulated at a certain level of generality, are presumptively impermissible and others presumptively required.[2] In developing this approach, they have not thought that the FUL should be understood and employed without reference to the values of respect for humanity and autonomy that are the basis of the later formulations of the Categorical Imperative, and that are clearly the central values of Kant's moral theory. For example, they have tried to show how failures of universalizability in certain maxims reveal failures to respect humanity as an end and have regarded this result as one way to make out Kant's claims about the equivalence of the formulas.[3]

A version of the traditional debate between critics and defenders of Kant's moral theory can also be found within the circle of Kant's defenders. The issue here is not whether the Categorical Imperative is purely formal and empty of content, but whether the FUL is, and, in consequence, whether it is an adequate statement of the Categorical Imperative. Some theorists with equally strong Kantian sympathies have thought that emphasis on the FUL is misplaced and not the best approach to defending Kant's moral theory.[4] They have observed that the power and enduring contribution of Kant's theory comes from the values of respect for humanity and autonomy and from the ideal of moral community that are expressed by the later formulas. They rightly point out that Kant does not employ the FUL to arrive at conclusions about action outside of limited contexts in the *Groundwork* and the *Critique of Practical Reason*, and that when he does set himself the task of deriving particular duties in the *Metaphysics of Morals*, he tends to rely on the idea of the dignity of humanity.[5] They have suggested, again persuasively, that the viability of Kant's moral theory should not turn on the fortunes of the FUL.

Theorists in this latter group have acknowledged the force of the traditional Hegelian objections by raising questions about both the derivation of the FUL and its application. In the *Groundwork* Kant arrives at the FUL by moving from the general principle of conformity with universal law to the principle of acting only from maxims that one can will as universal law (*G4*: 402, 420–1). But it is unclear that these principles are equivalent, as Kant evidently assumes. Allen Wood has recently rehearsed the standard problems of application, including the problem of maxim description and the claims that the FUL classifies many innocent maxims as impermissible and is unable to rule out some that are clearly wrong.[6] Wood has given the 'empty formalism' issue a new dimension by arguing that the FUL should be understood as a purely formal, but merely provisional characterization of the moral law: 'The FUL and FLN are merely provisional and incomplete formulations of the principle of morality, which always depend for their application on other independent rational principles'. They provide a formal characterization of the moral law, that 'though necessary and entirely correct from a systematic standpoint, cannot provide us with a formulation well suited to be applied to particular cases'.[7] Since, in his view, the content of the moral law is given only by the entire system of formulas and not by any single formula in isolation, the purely formal nature of the FUL does not pose a problem for Kant's moral theory.[8] In essence, Wood accepts a version of the 'empty formalism' charge, but he argues that it misfires because it is directed against only a partial formulation of the moral law.

In this essay I offer some reflections about how the FUL has been understood by those who think that it can provide substantive guidance about choice and action. If the FUL were a purely formal criterion of universalizability, it would not reliably lead to any substantive moral judgments. What I want to point out is that these theorists have not, in general, understood the FUL as *purely* formal. Rather, they have incorporated a conception of rational agency into this formula, either explicitly or implicitly. As they have applied the FUL, a conception of rational agency plays a role in generating the contradictions that result from the universalization of certain maxims, and in this way determines whether a maxim can be willed as universal law without inconsistency. If so, an a priori conception of agency is a source of content in Kant's moral conception. Put another way, these theorists take the aim of the FUL to be that of determining whether a maxim can be willed as universal law for agents of a certain kind—namely, for rational agents with autonomy. Barbara Herman is quite explicit about this in her work on the Categorical Imperative, and I draw on her views extensively.[9] But it is implicit in the approach of other theorists in this group, and provides the best reconstruction of what Kant himself does in his examples. I do not think that it is controversial that these theorists have proceeded in this way, though at the same time it has not been generally recognized. My aim later in the essay will be to point to some of the ways in which a Kantian conception of agency produces the contradictions uncovered by the deliberative procedure associated with the FUL.

I will also connect these reflections with other textual and philosophical issues. Section II briefly discusses some of John Rawls's remarks about what he has called Kant's 'moral constructivism'—specifically his claim that a conception of the person plays a central role in specifying the content of a constructivist moral conception. My hope is that examining the role of a conception of rational agency in the Categorical Imperative will provide a better understanding of what it means to think of Kant as a constructivist. This section is somewhat of a digression, but I hope that it will put a few ideas on the table that focus attention on certain features of the overall structure of Kant's moral conception as we proceed. Section III asks how the FUL needs to be understood if it is to play its intended role in the extended argument of the *Groundwork*. Section IV shows why one is entitled to read a conception of rational agency into the FUL, and then considers some of the elements of this conception. In particular, it tries to make precise different senses in which rational agents with autonomy are independent spheres of judgment and choice and the sources of their own actions. Finally, Section V looks at various ways in which this conception of autonomous agency figures in determining whether a maxim can be willed as universal law without inconsistency.

II. MORAL CONSTRUCTIVISM

A constructivist moral theory holds that the content of a moral view may be specified by, or represented as, the outcome of a procedure of construction. In Kant's theory, the procedure of construction would be the deliberative procedure associated with the FUL—the so-called 'CI procedure'.[10] Rawls writes:

An essential feature of Kant's moral constructivism is that the particular categorical imperatives that give the content of the duties of justice and of virtue are viewed as specified by a procedure of construction (the CI procedure), the form and structure of which mirror both of our two powers of practical reason as well as our status as free and equal moral persons.[11]

He goes on to claim: 'It is characteristic of Kant's doctrine that a relatively complex conception of the person plays a central role in specifying the content of his moral view'. The 'basis' of the procedure of construction is 'the conception of free and equal persons as reasonable and rational' along with 'the conception of a society of such persons, each of whom can be a legislative member of a realm of ends', which conceptions are 'elicited from our moral experience and reflection'.[12] This procedure, when correctly laid out, incorporates all the requirements of practical reason and is shaped by 'the union' of the principles of practical reason with these conceptions of society and person.[13] By these remarks Rawls implies that the procedure of construction (the CI procedure) would not specify the content of a moral view unless a conception of persons as rational agents with certain powers and capacities (and related notions such as the conception of a society of such persons) were embedded in it.

Rawls's discussion of his own 'political constructivism' in *Political Liberalism* suggests a similar point. A rather opaque section in Lecture III of *Political Liberalism* begins:

I have said all along that political constructivism proceeds from the union of practical reason with appropriate conceptions of society and person and the public role of principles of justice. Constructivism does not proceed from practical reason alone but requires a procedure that models conceptions of society and person.[14]

The conceptions of society and person are the idea of society as a fair system of cooperation and the conception of free and equal moral persons moved by two higher-order moral powers. The public role of the principles refers to the fact that they are to serve as the public basis of justification of the major social institutions in a well-ordered society. The practical problem that Rawls's political constructivism is intended to resolve is to arrive at principles of justice for the basic structure that can play this public role in a society conceived of as a fair system of cooperation between free and equal moral persons.

It is less clear what Rawls means by saying the constructivism does not proceed 'from practical reason alone'. Context indicates that 'practical reason' here means the principles of practical reason, which include 'both reasonable principles and rational principles'.[15] The rational principles are the principles of rational choice that guide the deliberations of the parties. The 'reasonable principles' are not the principles of justice, since the latter are to be 'constructed using the principles of practical reason in union with political conceptions of person and society'.[16] Rather they are the 'reasonable conditions' on conceptions of justice represented in the original position—for example, that principles of justice set out fair terms of social cooperation, that arbitrary inequalities in individual life prospects created by the basic structure of society are unfair, that the principles treat all persons equally and specify an ideal of reciprocity, that the terms of cooperation be established by those subject to them, and so on. These 'reasonable and rational principles' are by and large formal, or not fully determinate, requirements. Even taken together (no matter how long we make the list), they are not sufficient to lead to a substantive conception of justice. Hence 'constructivism does not proceed from practical reason alone'. A procedure of construction that embodies all the relevant principles of practical reason leads to no substantive results until it incorporates further conceptions, such as a conception of the person (free and equal moral persons), of a society of such persons, and of the public role of principles of justice in such a society.

That Rawls says that Kant's 'procedure of construction' is shaped by the union of practical reason with a conception of the person and society indicates that he likewise does not take Kant's moral constructivism to 'proceed from practical reason alone'. That means roughly the following: practical reason, construed narrowly, is the source of formal constraints that apply to maxims of action. In addition to the principles of instrumental rationality, these constraints include a condition of universal validity, which is the condition that maxims conform to universal law or be suited to serve as universal law for a community of rational agents (e.g., as authoritative practical principles, or principles of justification, that all rational agents can accept and adopt). If the CI procedure incorporated only this condition of universal validity, it would not reliably have substantive implications when applied to maxims of action. It must also incorporate a conception of the agents for whom these principles are to serve as law, as well as related notions, such as a conception of a society of such persons, and of the social role of these principles within such a society.

It is important to note that, according to Rawls, constructivism holds that the content of a moral conception may be represented as the result of a procedure of construction 'once, if ever, reflective equilibrium is attained', or 'when, if ever, due reflection is achieved'.[17] Rawls writes: 'we interpret constructivism as a view about how the structure and content of the soundest moral doctrine will look once it is laid out after due critical reflection. We say that it will contain, in the manner explained, a constructivist procedure incorporating all the requirements of practical reason such that the content of the doctrine—its main principles, virtues and ideals—is constructed'.[18] There is no thought that the procedure of construction is a mechanical procedure for generating conclusions about duty without the need for judgment, or that one could devise a deliberative procedure to generate a moral conception from the ground up without relying on existing moral convictions at different levels of generality, both in laying the procedure out and in applying it.[19] Rather, constructivism makes a set of claims about the basis and overall structure that moral thought would be seen to have in our most adequate moral conception, and these claims lead to a distinctive conception of the objectivity of moral judgments. Constructivism holds that basic moral principles are grounded in and the result of an idealized process of reasoning that satisfies the relevant standards of practical reason. At the risk of oversimplifying, they are principles that are rationally willed as universal law for agents with autonomy by such agents. (I'll support this particular way of putting it in Section IV below.) What makes a claim about basic moral principles correct or justified is that it results from the correct application of the procedure of construction, which is taken to represent all the requirements of practical reason. There is no criterion for the truth or acceptability of basic moral principles outside of this (idealized) procedure. Objectivity is secured not through an independent order of moral values or facts, but through the standards of practical reason and the conception of the person that are incorporated into and represented in the procedure of construction—which standards and conception guide ordinary practical thought and are rooted in the standpoint of deliberation. The procedure of construction represents our own idealized reasoning—the conclusions that *we* (not perfectly rational agents) would reach after sufficient critical reflection.[20] But so understood this deliberative procedure is a standard of objectivity, since the actual conclusions about basic principles that individuals draw at any point in time are always subject to revision through further application, or from a more adequate conception of these procedures.

A constructivist theory is of interest because of the way in which it brings together different kinds of elements that go into a moral view—for example, both formal criteria of practical reason and more substantive (though still recognizably formal) conceptions, such as a conception of the person—by incorporating them into a 'procedure of construction' that can be used to specify the content of a moral view. Seeing how the conception of the person (i.e., a conception of rational agency) functions in this deliberative procedure may clarify one aspect of what it means to call it a constructivist moral conception. In the sections that follow, I sketch a reading of the overall argument of the *Groundwork* and then develop an interpretation of the Categorical Imperative that provides one way of seeing how a 'relatively complex conception of the person plays a central role in specifying the content of [Kant's] moral view'.

III. WHAT THE ARGUMENT OF THE *GROUNDWORK* NEEDS

One way to put the issue that divides Kant's defenders is whether the FUL can or should be given any kind of a privileged role in Kant's moral theory. It would be unwise to ignore the clear obstacles to doing so, such as the limited applicability of the FUL and the undeniable importance of the values of humanity as an end in itself and of autonomy. At the same time, there are (at least textual) reasons to look for a way to assign the FUL a privileged role of some kind.

First, Kant himself appears to. He regards the FUL as an abstract statement of the basic principle that we use to assess actions and make determinations of duty in ordinary moral thought.[21] The four examples in the *Groundwork* give us a range of cases in which Kant uses the FUL to support substantive moral conclusions (and there is general agreement that his arguments succeed in the last three of these examples). Indeed, Kant believes that the FUL supports the same practical conclusions as the Formula of Humanity (FH), which appears to be a more substantive principle. Although he believes that the formulas are equivalent—they are 'at bottom only so many formulae of the very same law' (*G* 4: 436)—he assigns priority to the FUL in moral judgment: 'One does better always to proceed in moral appraisal by the strict method and put at its basis the universal formula of the categorical imperative: *act in accordance with a maxim that can at the same time make itself a universal law*' (*G*4: 436–7).[22]

Second, the overall argument of the *Groundwork* seems to require that the FUL be privileged in some way as a statement of the supreme principle of morality. The aim of the *Groundwork* is to articulate the supreme principle of morality and to establish its authority as a requirement of reason. The FUL is initially introduced as a statement of the principle of morality and the ensuing arguments are aimed at establishing the authority of *this* principle (i.e., *this formula* of the Categorical Imperative).[23] The Second and Third Sections make different contributions to this project. After claiming to derive the FUL from the very concept of a categorical imperative or moral requirement (practical law), *Groundwork*, II goes through a sequence of reformulations of the Categorical Imperative that make explicit different features of the principle of morality.[24] The sequence of formulas is intended to advance, but not complete, the argument for the authority of this principle. (It cannot complete the overall argument since the reformulations result, for the most part, from conceptual arguments about what the idea of an unconditional requirement presupposes and such conceptual arguments stop short of showing that there really are any such requirements.) In introducing the FH, Kant makes the conceptual argument that if there is a categorical imperative, there is an end of absolute value that grounds determinate moral requirements. The argument that humanity is such an end seems to rely on concepts and substantive value commitments not yet encountered (and does not seem to be a conceptual argument).[25] But Kant believes that the FUL and the FH are just different ways of stating the same basic principle (*G*4: 436–40, esp. § 77). The FH advances the overall argument by bringing out the value that underlies moral thought. Humanity as an end in itself is a recognizable and compelling moral value. If that is what is at stake in moral conduct, we can begin to see why it makes sense to care about conformity to moral principle and to treat moral considerations as unconditionally binding.

Kant then argues that the FUL may be restated as a principle of autonomy, and this argument leads to the Formula of Autonomy (FA)—the principle of acting only from maxims through which you can regard yourself as giving law (for a realm of ends) (*G*4: 431–3, 434). This move signals a change in the self-understanding of the moral agent—that agents bound by moral requirements are not just subject to duty, but are a kind of sovereign lawgiver. Since moral requirements apply unconditionally, their authority cannot be based on appeals to contingent interests, but rather comes from the fact that they arise from one's will; that is to say, they have authority because they issue from a deliberative procedure that is rooted in the nature of rational volition. The agents subject to such principles are bound to them by the deliberative procedure that makes them laws, and accordingly, must have the capacity to carry this procedure out. The unconditional authority of moral requirements thus presupposes both that they issue from the rational will—that the will is a law to itself—and that moral agents possess a legislative capacity. The contribution of the FA to the overall argument of the *Groundwork* is to forge a connection between morality and autonomy that sets up a key argument in *Groundwork*, III.

Groundwork, III argues for the authority of the moral law by arguing that a free will is subject to moral laws and that we are free rational agents who inescapably identify with our free rational capacities. In order to establish that a free will is subject to moral laws, Kant argues that the positive conception of freedom of the will is autonomy, which he defines as 'the will's property of being a law to itself (independently of any property of the objects of volition)' (*G* 4: 440). A free will is a capacity to act independently of determination by external causes and external sources of reasons, but it must be governed by some law or principle. Thus a free will must involve the power to give itself laws and to act from such laws—it is a law to itself (in the sense that its essential nature is the source of a principle that can guide its own exercise). Kant then writes:

But the proposition, the will is in all its actions a law to itself, indicates only the principle, to act on no other maxim than that which can also have as its object itself as a universal law. This, however, is precisely the formula of the categorical imperative and is the principle of morality; hence a free will and a will under moral laws are one and the same. (*G* 4: 447)

For present purposes, two points about this argument are noteworthy. One is that it depends crucially on the identification of the FUL with the FA, which, as we have just seen, Kant tries to establish in *Groundwork*, II. (Kant is claiming in this passage that the principle of autonomy—that 'the will is in all its actions a law to itself'—just refers to the principle of acting only from maxims that can be willed as universal law.) The second point is that the FUL ('to act on no other maxim than that which can also have as its object itself as a universal law') is here taken to be 'the principle of morality'. In other words, the aim of this argument is to show that the basic principle of a free will is the FUL.

My purpose in sketching these familiar arguments is to point out that a very natural reading of the *Groundwork* assigns a privileged role to the FUL as a statement of the Categorical Imperative. This principle provides 'the formula' of the principle of morality, or the Categorical Imperative, and the sequence of formulas in *Groundwork*, II produces a restatement and more expansive understanding of this principle that enables Kant to argue for its authority in *Groundwork*, III. What does Kant's overall argument need if it is to succeed (or even come close to succeeding)? To bear out the claim that the FUL states the supreme principle of *morality*, Kant must connect this very abstract principle to the substance of common-sense morality by showing that it is the basis of familiar duties. Thus, the argument needs a working version of how the FUL supports substantive moral conclusions in some central cases. Further, since the argument moves forward through the sequence of reformulations of the Categorical Imperative, it also needs a working version of the equivalence of the formulas. This could consist in a story that shows that they are derived from the same basis or express the same fundamental requirement, or one that establishes analytical connections between them showing how the later formulas state ideas that are implicit in the initial formula. Any such story, once made out, would permit one to read the ideas expressed by the later formulas back into the FUL, with neither textual nor conceptual distortion.

The overall argument of the *Groundwork* as sketched above, however, does not require that the FUL by itself give a complete understanding of moral thought or that it yield either a generally applicable criterion of right action or an exhaustive method for deriving the content of a moral conception. Thus, while there are reasons to regard the FUL as a statement of the principle of morality (or Categorical Imperative), I do not suggest that it be assigned an absolutely privileged position, either in the argument of the *Groundwork* or in Kant's moral theory as a whole. Certainly the other formulas of the Categorical Imperative are needed to express aspects of moral thought that are not evident from the idea of conformity to universally valid principles by itself. And as far as the argument of the *Groundwork* is concerned, it would be perfectly acceptable if, for the purposes of moral deliberation and judgment, the FUL needs to be supplemented by ideas expressed through the other formulas, or if other formulas (e.g., the FH or the FRE) are needed to guide deliberation and judgment in certain contexts—acceptable, that is, as long as the other formulas have the kind of connection to the FUL that would be secured by a story about the equivalence of the formulas. In that case one could still maintain that the FUL is a statement of the principle of morality, even though it has limited application as an action-guiding principle.[26]

To tie these remarks together, the suggestion is that since the argument of the *Groundwork* treats the FUL as a statement of the principle of morality, the success of this argument requires that the FUL have some substantive implications in a central range of cases. But at the same time, its application as a general criterion of right action or as an action-guiding principle could be limited. Here it is important to bear in mind how narrow the aim of the *Groundwork* is. The project of its 'pure moral philosophy' is to present the purely rational elements of moral thought, in abstraction from everything empirical, and to establish the authority of the most fundamental and abstract principles and features of moral thought. These tasks require a statement of the principle of morality that brings out those formal features of moral thought that raise questions of justification—for example, that duties apply with necessity and have overriding authority. But in presenting the basic principle of morality in abstraction from empirical information, Kant also sets aside the kind of information needed to apply moral principles to the circumstances of human life. Action-guiding principles and applications are important, obviously (especially in ethics!), but they are not the project of this work.

IV. LAW FOR AGENTS WITH AUTONOMY

This essay will argue that the FUL (as employed by Kant and by various sympathetic theorists) relies on a conception of rational agents as autonomous to generate substantive moral judgments, so that the criterion that it embodies is whether a maxim can be willed as universal law for rational agents with autonomy. But it is fair to ask what entitles one to incorporate a conception of rational agency into the FUL. Kant claims to derive the FUL from the mere concept of a categorical imperative, which contains only the formal features of moral requirements. Even if a conception of autonomous agency does play a role in the deliberative procedure associated with the FUL, how does it get there, given the very spare basis from which the FUL is extracted?

This question is related to the issue of the so-called 'gap' in the derivation of the FUL.[27] A common objection to the arguments that introduce the FUL in *Groundwork*, I and II is that they lead only to the general principle that one ought to conform to universal law, and not, as Kant supposes, to the more substantive principle that one is to act only from maxims that can be willed as universal law. Kant begins from the concept of moral requirements as unconditionally necessary. His arguments from the concept of an unconditional requirement (or practical law) to the general principle of conformity to universal law are generally regarded as sound.[28] This principle may underlie the attitudes of conscientious moral agents, but by itself it provides no way to determine what universal laws there are. Thus the arguments lead to a principle that is purely formal and without substantive implications, and not to the FUL, which does appear to have some action-guiding implications. As Thomas E. Hill, Jr. has put it, the crucial transitions in Kant's argument appear to conflate two different readings of the first formula and he 'moves from an undeniable formal principle to a dubious substantive principle'.[29]

Even if Kant does jump from the general principle of conformity to law to the principle of acting only from maxims that one can will as universal law, the introduction of the FA suggests an argument that would fill this gap by showing that a certain conception of the moral agent is implicit in the idea of an unconditional requirement on action. This reasoning is also the justification for incorporating a conception of autonomous agency into the FUL. We have seen that Kant can argue from the concept of a practical law to the principle of conformity to universal law, whether or not he can go on to derive the FUL. Kant marks the transition to the FA by claiming that the will is 'subject to [the moral law] in such a way that it must be regarded as also giving the law to itself and just because of this as first subject to the law (of which it can regard itself as the author)' (*G*4: 431). The ensuing argument for this claim (the Sovereignty Thesis) is that it follows from the concept of a practical law that the agents subject to practical law must be regarded as legislating and thus have autonomy. This means that Kant finds (at least) two important notions in the very concept of a categorical imperative. One is the general principle of conformity to universal law. The other is the idea that the agents subject to such universal laws must be regarded as their legislators, and thus as agents with autonomy. This claim has been explored in earlier chapters, but there is an intuitive link between conceptions of law and rational agency that may help here: since laws are addressed to and govern the choices of rational agents, a conception of a kind of law can have implications for the kinds of agents to whom it applies. Agents subject to laws with certain features must have any rational and motivational capacities that these laws presuppose. Such laws should accordingly be understood as laws for agents with the requisite capacities.

If the agents subject to universal law must be regarded as autonomous legislators, these laws can only apply to agents with the legislative capacities that go into Kant's conception of autonomy. These laws—both particular substantive requirements and the higher-order principle that one should conform to universal law—must be understood as laws addressed to agents with autonomy. From this point, there are two routes to the conclusion that we may, indeed should, read a conception of autonomous agency into the FUL.

The argument is straightforward if one accepts Kant's step from the principle of conformity to universal law to the FUL. The fact that practical laws can only apply to agents with autonomy suggests that in asking whether a principle can be willed as universal law, the guiding deliberative question is whether it can be willed as universal law for agents with autonomy. And specifying the kind of agents for whom a principle is to serve as law sets constraints on what can be willed as law: a principle whose universal adoption in some way undermines the conditions of autonomous willing, or is inconsistent with any commitments that one has in virtue of having autonomy, is not coherently willed as universal law—for agents with autonomy.

But even if there is a gap in Kant's derivation of the FUL, one can still get from the concept of a practical law to this understanding of the FUL. Both the general principle of conformity to universal law and the idea that agents subject to practical laws must be regarded as their legislators follow (let us assume) from the concept of a practical law. Then it is reasonable to think that practical laws are addressed to agents with autonomy (legislative capacities), moreover, by those very agents themselves. This means, first, that the universal laws to which conformity is required are laws for agents with autonomy and that the principle of conformity to universal law should be specified as the principle of conforming to any universal laws that hold for agents with autonomy. Furthermore, if the laws in question are addressed to agents who must be regarded as their legislators (through whose will they get their authority), they are laws that they in some sense legislate or generate through their own rational volition. I take that to mean that they are principles arrived at through a deliberative procedure that is constitutive of their legislative capacities, and as such is internal to the nature of rational volition. So we should assess whether a principle can hold as universal law by asking whether it can be *willed* as universal law for agents with autonomy—that is to say, willed as laws for such agents by such agents (through a procedure that is constitutive of their legislative capacities). This is indeed the requirement stated by the FUL.[30]

Although Kant does not introduce this conception of autonomy until later in the argument of *Groundwork*, II, it is available to him as soon as he has the concept of a practical law. Since this conception of agency follows from the concept of a practical law, it is reasonable to hold that it is implicit in the FUL and built into it from the start.[31] In Chapter 3, I pointed out that Kant's derivation of the Categorical Imperative is marked by a movement from form towards content. What we see here is that this movement passes through, and is enriched by, a formal conception of autonomous agency. The formal features of practical laws lead to a formal characterization of the agents to whom such laws are addressed, and this in turn leads to a formal characterization of acceptable principles of conduct and relations between such agents (the ideal of acting from principles that can be willed as law for agents with autonomy by those very agents). We might expect this formal principle to lead to substantive limits on acceptable reasons and guidance about action when applied to a social world in which agents act on judgments of value and pursue their ends against a background of various social norms, practices and institutions, relations of power and dependence, expectation and need—that in such a world, certain principles of action fail to instantiate, and others are required by, the form of acceptable relations between agents. I believe that this is the case, but will argue (in the next section) that features of Kant's conception of autonomous agency play a role in producing these conclusions. That is to say, in addition to the empirical elements introduced by information about the social world in which rational agents operate, an a priori conception of rational agency makes a distinct contribution to these conclusions. But before turning to that question, however, we need to consider in greater detail some of the elements of Kant's conception of autonomy and his broader conception of rational agency.

Earlier chapters have argued for a circumscribed reading of Kant's conception of autonomy as the rational will's sovereignty over itself. Agents with autonomy are a kind of sovereign legislator bound only to their own will, with the capacity to give law through their willing (the legislative capacity to carry out and act from the reasoning that makes a moral principle a law). But agents with moral autonomy in this special sense will also possess other rational capacities and powers that are parts of Kant's inclusive conception of rational agency. All are in different ways powers of self-determination. What is important for our purposes here is that because they possess this range of capacities, rational agents with autonomy are independent spheres of judgment and choice and, in various senses to be explained, the sources of their own actions.

In a very general sense rational agents are the sources of their own actions because they are motivated to act by their own judgment of what they have most reason to do. Rational agents have 'the capacity to act *in accordance with the representation of laws*' (*G* 4: 412), or to determine their conduct by the application of various norms. They are motivated to act by the normative judgment that a given incentive or consideration is a good or sufficient reason for action. (The 'incorporation of an incentive into a maxim' (*Rel* 6: 24) may be understood as the normative judgment that the incentive is a good or sufficient reason for action leading to endorsement and adoption of the incentive.) A rational judgment is a free act that provides the spontaneity that is the essential element of agency.

Kant famously writes: 'Now one cannot possibly think of a reason that would consciously receive direction from elsewhere [*anderwärtsher*] with respect to its judgments, since the subject would then attribute the determination of his judgment not to his reason but to an impulse' (*G* 4: 448). The judgment is directed solely by, or better, just is the agent's grasp of reasons and drawing connections between various considerations to arrive at a normative conclusion; if directed by anything external to the agent's grasp and weighing of reasons it is not properly speaking a rational judgment but 'determination by an impulse'. And 'only under the idea of freedom can the will of a [rational] being be a will of his own [*ein eigener Wille*]' (*G* 4: 448): only as the spontaneous application and connecting of normative considerations that is not directed by anything external to the agent's normative capacities does the judgment represent the agent's own proper activity.[32] Presumably Kant held that rational agents conceive of themselves in this way in acting: it is part of their active self-conception that they think of themselves as the sources of their action through their own independent judgment.

Agents can be the source of their actions in the above sense without being the sources, that is, the 'legislators' of the norms and principles from which they act. Rational agents act on a wide range of normative considerations, including reasons based in formal norms of practical rationality, various social kinds of norms, and personal commitments and conceptions of value. Many of these, social norms in particular, are best viewed as externally given. Social norms and conventions may be devices that have evolved to serve various needs and interests—the work of human artifice in Hume's sense—and according to Kant's conception of free agency, agents are motivated to act from these norms by taking them to be sources of reasons. Still they are norms whose content and authority are externally given, neither self-legislated by the individual nor the work of pure practical reason. However, many rational capacities are, or are closely analogous to, normative powers—the power to create reasons and to change the normative situation of oneself and others through one's voluntary acts.[33] The possession of normative powers adds another dimension to the idea that agents are sources of their own actions, because they enable agents to create the reasons from which they act.

Since this is a very complex topic, I shall limit myself to simple examples of two kinds of normative powers. First consider norms and conventions that guide many ordinary forms of social interaction—those of promising and agreement, reciprocal exchange, gift, or exercises of authority, and so on. (A long list is possible here; for further discussion see Section II of Chapter 6.) Even if these norms are externally given, they confer powers to create reasons through one's willing. The 'willing' here is a voluntary act that follows a procedure or conforms to a shared understanding of what counts as an act of a certain kind (an agreement, a gift, an order, a legislative enactment). If I agree to meet you at the café at 3 p.m., I obligate myself; the fact that I have agreed is a reason for me to be at the café at 3. I also bring about a reason for you to be there by assuring you that I will be there; the fact that I have obligated myself to be there is a 'reason of assurance' for you to act accordingly. If, having authority over you, I order you to be at the café at 3, I give you a different kind of reason to go to the café; my (legitimate) order obligates you (creates a reason of authority) to go. There may be independent reasons for us to go to the café that exist prior to the agreement or to the command (the benefits of conversation, the stimulation of being in a lively place), but in both cases my voluntary act creates an additional reason that, by itself, is a sufficient reason for the action. Furthermore, the reasons that I create in each case have a certain structure. They are reasons that exclude or pre-empt the force of various reasons not to go to the café, for example that when it is time to leave for the café I would prefer to keep working in my office, or that you have wanted to keep to yourself lately and don't have much desire to go out. More generally, reasons of obligation preclude further deliberation on the merits of going to the café at the time of action and are taken to settle the question of whether to go. Powers conferred by such social norms enable individuals to enter into or modify normative relations with others, and to create informal rights and obligations. They give individuals the power to create reasons for themselves and others against the backdrop of shared social conventions, and so give them a role in shaping the normative landscape of the social world that they inhabit with others.

The capacity to set ends for oneself or to adopt values through reason is likewise a power to create reasons for oneself through one's will. In 'setting an end through reason', you judge that there are considerations that recommend its pursuit—in other words that the object has some value—and, by taking these considerations to be good or sufficient reasons, you make it your end. So far this is an instance of determining yourself to act by your judgment of what you have reason to do, and the reasons to which you respond could be the intrinsic value or the desirability that you discover in the object. It need not be a reason of your own creation or a value that you confer on the object. But by making it your end, you create an additional reason for pursuing the end over and above the reason that makes it worth adopting.[34] We may call this a 'reason of commitment'.[35] In adopting an end, you commit yourself to its pursuit and assign it a role or a priority in your overall system of ends and values. Your adoption of the end is now a reason to pursue the end, a reason that analytically contains reasons to take some of the necessary means that are within your reach. (The weight of these reasons relative to other reasons that you have will depend on the priority and overall role of the end.) A reason of commitment is desire-independent in the sense that its normative force is independent of your present level of interest or enthusiasm, even if your initial interest in the end is desire-based. In this respect, reasons of commitment are structurally similar to reasons of voluntary obligation and authority. The fact that I have made E my end is a reason for me to take steps toward the end when the occasion presents itself that excludes the force of certain kinds of reasons for not acting toward the end—for example, that my interest is lagging at the moment, or that measures that would further the end are tiresome, or that something else has my attention.[36] In other words, one's adoption of an end is a reason to act toward the end that rules out considerations such as present lack of interest, the effort required by the end, distraction by other interests, and so on, as legitimate reasons for inaction.[37]

The capacity to set ends through reason may be understood as a normative power in the technical sense. Whether or not it is constituted by social norms and conventions in the way in which the power to promise or the power to command is, there is a rational procedure through which it is exercised with analogies to the procedures through which agreements and commands are made. This 'procedure' defies explicit characterization (as, I expect, do the procedures and conventions constitutive of agreement and command), but, very roughly, it consists of some form of rational evaluation that supports the judgment that an end is good in some respect and that leads to the endorsement and adoption of it as one's end. This rational procedure will, of course, bring moral considerations to bear, since an 'end set by reason' must be morally permissible. Carrying out this procedure confers a new normative status on the end judged to be good or worth adopting by creating the reason of commitment to pursue it—just as the procedures for making agreements and promises, commanding, legislating, and so on make certain actions obligatory. The power to set ends for oneself adds another layer to the idea that rational agents are the sources of their actions because it makes them the source of some of their reasons for acting. It is a power to affect the normative landscape in one's own backyard, as it were, by creating reasons for oneself. In obvious ways this is a capacity to shape one's life around ends of one's own choosing. But more importantly, it is what Christine Korsgaard has called a capacity for 'self constitution'. By giving yourself reasons of commitment to pursue certain ends, you (in part) constitute yourself as a center of normative guidance over and above the various incentives in you that make claims on your attention. In this way you bring it about that there is a self over and above its various incentives that is the cause of its actions, and thus constitute yourself as an agent.[38]

Let me try to tie these remarks together. We have been considering some of the rational capacities and powers that can be ascribed to agents with moral autonomy in Kant's specific sense with an eye to detailing different ways in which such agents are independent spheres of judgment and choice and the sources of their own actions. Agents with autonomy are sovereign over themselves and have a share in legislating moral law, but they also possess a variety of other rational capacities and powers. Because rational agents have the capacity to determine their conduct by normative considerations (the capacity to act from 'the representation of laws'), their actions originate in their own (spontaneous) judgment of what they have most reason to do. This capacity makes them the sources of their actions in the ways we have seen, though by itself it does not make them the sources of their reasons for action. The normative principles and considerations by which rational agents guide their conduct are wide-ranging. They include various social norms through which agents take part in and support cooperative endeavors and interactions, form complex relationships with others, conform to normative expectations, recognize and honor rights and obligations (formal and informal), and so on, and thereby participate in a social world. Furthermore these capacities include an important range of normative powers, social and individual, possession of which makes them the sources of some of their reasons for action. Social normative powers enable them to create reasons for themselves and others and to play an active role in shaping their normative relations with others and their social world. The power to set ends for oneself is in similar ways a power to create reasons of commitment for oneself that is, in part, constitutive of rational agency.

Possession of these capacities and powers carries certain value commitments. Since their rational capacities enable agents to find reasons for action and value in the world, they value these capacities and the ability to exercise them. Rational agents that think of themselves as the sources of their action will value their capacity to initiate action through their own rational judgments. They are, in other words, committed to valuing the capacities and powers that make them agents. Finally, we may presume that they value the normative powers that enable them to play a role in shaping their normative worlds.

V. THE ROLE OF A KANTIAN CONCEPTION OF AGENCY IN THE CATEGORICAL IMPERATIVE

In this section I will trace some of the ways in which the Kantian conception of agency just sketched functions in the Categorical Imperative—specifically, how it generates the contradictions uncovered by the 'contradiction in conception test' and the 'contradiction in the will test'. Put another way, I will try to show how the contradictions identified by the FUL arise from willing certain maxims as laws for rational agents with autonomy. I'll briefly discuss some of the standard examples—deception, coercion, violence (contradiction in conception) and mutual aid (contradiction in the will). Throughout I will be considering what Barbara Herman has called 'generic maxims'—maxims of performing a certain kind of action for certain kinds of reasons—rather than the fully detailed maxims that characterize an agent's actual volition.[39] I will begin with Kant's example of deceptive promising, and will give two separate analyses, that, as far as I can see, are independent of one another.

First, we should note a minor complexity in the structure of the deceptive promise that holds generally for maxims of deception. In Kant's example, the deceptive promisor aims to get money through the agency of another—specifically, by employing the convention of promising to get the other to believe that he has a reason to give him the money. Obtaining money is the deceiver's end. But in context, getting the other to see reason to give him the money is a sub-goal in the service of this end. (Success in securing the victim's cooperation is not automatic and, for example, may require some skill.) The promise is the vehicle, or means, used to get the other to see a reason to offer his cooperation and contribute an action to the deceiver's end.

A promise can be used as the vehicle for this sub-goal because of standard ways in which a promise creates reasons for action that the agents do not have independently of this transaction.[40] The background to Kant's false promising example is that one agent, A, needs money and approaches another, B, who is in a position to help. We may assume that A's need is a reason for B to help—perhaps a reason of mutual aid or of friendship, depending on the circumstances—as long as B can do so without unreasonable loss. But this reason does not come into play while B believes that helping may incur a significant loss. This is where the promise comes in. A asks for the money and promises to repay. By promising, he binds himself to repay, and it is mutually understood that in promising A intends to bind himself. That means that when the time for repayment comes, the fact that A has promised will be (in light of the shared understanding of the social convention of promising) a sufficient reason to repay, and moreover a reason with special features: barring unforeseen circumstances and within limits set by the understanding between A and B, it closes off further deliberation on A's part as to whether to repay and it excludes the force of certain kinds of reasons not to pay that A may have at that time (e.g., that repayment does not serve A's self-interest, is burdensome, and so on). A has now given himself a reason for action that he did not have prior to his promise (the practice-based or social norm-based obligation to repay), and by incurring this reason he normatively alters B's reasons for action. By binding himself to repay, A assures B that he will repay; A leads B to believe that he will repay because it is their mutual understanding that A regards the obligation as a compelling reason to repay. With this assurance in hand, B now believes that he can help A without incurring a loss, and the reason of mutual aid applies. In this case, the reason of assurance created by A's promise is not a new reason for B to lend the money; rather it satisfies the rider that brings the prior considerations of mutual aid into play. All the same, B would not have reason to cooperate without the expectation of repayment created by A's promise.

Discussions of the maxim of deceptive promising often trace the failure of universalizability to the social conditions that support the existence and proper functioning of the practice, and they are certainly germane. But the operative point is that the maxim is self-defeating because if made a universal law, the intended 'victim' would see no reason to contribute an action to the deceiver's end. In willing the maxim as universal law, one wills that anyone be permitted to make promises which they have no intention of keeping in order to advance their own ends. But then promises would not bind, and so would create no assurance in others that the promised action will be performed. In situations in which the other's reason to cooperate is premised on this assurance, the other would see no reason to contribute his action to the promisor's end.

Two brief comments about this analysis. First, the universalization of deceptive promising for reasons of self-interest undermines the end of getting money by undermining the sub-goal of getting the other to believe that he has a reason to offer it. The contradiction in conception lies in the fact that the universalized maxim undermines the vehicle by which the deceiver gets the other to judge that he has a reason to cooperate.[41] Second, this analysis relies on features of an a priori conception of rational agency and the fact that a promise is a transaction between agents so conceived. It focuses on the fact that a promisor incurs a reason of obligation that creates assurance about his future conduct, that the promisor secures cooperation by getting the promisee to judge that he has a reason to cooperate based on this assurance, and that in the world of the universalized maxim, promises would not assure. Thus it assumes agents who guide their choices by various social norms and act on their judgment of what they have reason to do. The maxim is non-universalizable because of the way in which it tries to get the other to believe that he has a reason to cooperate (i.e., through the assurance that the promise purports to create). The failure of universalizability thus points to the way in which the deception manipulates the other through his agency, as it should.

Let me suggest as an aside, and all too briefly, that this analysis can be extended to the cases of lying and of breaking one's promises. Lying requires more complex treatment than deceptive promising, but lies are likewise attempts to further a goal through the rational agency of another. The immediate aim of a lie is to create a belief in another which serves the deceiver's ends—either because his end is simply that the other hold the belief or because the belief, if true, would be the basis of a reason for the other to act in a way that contributes to the deceiver's ends. While deceptive promises rely on the norms that govern promising, lies rely on various norms of language and communication to create the desired belief in another. Both promises and assertions are intended to lead others to form certain beliefs. A promise gives the other a reason to act in a certain way (lend the money) by assuring the other that the promisor will perform a certain action in turn (repay); it creates that assurance by indicating that the promisor is undertaking the obligation to perform that action. An assertion does not in the same way assure the other that you take what you say to be true, but it does create a normative expectation that you (on good grounds) take what you say to be true. Given these normative expectations, your assertion gives your listener a reason to believe that you take the assertion to be true and to accept it as true himself. If agents were universally free to lie for reasons of self-interest, convenience, and so on, assertions would no longer create these normative expectations.[42] As a result, an assertion would not give its recipient a reason for belief and a recipient would not take an assertion as a reason to form the belief that the speaker is trying to lead the recipient to form. These remarks clearly need further elaboration, but they suffice to make the point that a full analysis should support—namely, that maxims of deception for self-interest fail of universalizability because they use certain normative expectations to attempt to create a reason for the other to form a belief that will serve the deceiver's ends.

Breaking a promise is not the same wrong as making a deceptive promise, but can be handled within the same general framework. A promise enables an individual to further some end by securing the cooperation of another, and this end is the individual's reason for making the promise. When I break a bona fide promise for reasons of self-interest, either I ignore the reasons for action created by my promise or I take the inconvenience or burden of performing the promised act as a reason not to perform. But that is equivalent to acting as though a promise does not bind me. To be bound by my promise means precisely that my promise is a sufficient reason to perform the promised action that excludes as reasons the burden or inconvenience of performance, the fact that performance is no longer in my interest, and so on. If the maxim of breaking a promise for reasons of self-interest were universalized, agents would be free to break their promises. As a result promises would not bind, and thus would create no assurances about future conduct. But if promises did not assure, they would not be vehicles for securing the cooperation of others, and it would no longer serve one's purposes to make promises to others. Since the maxim fails of universalizability, it is morally wrong to break a promise and the practice-based obligation created by promising is also a moral obligation. Again, the failure of universalizability here is due to the way in which a promise secures cooperation by creating assurance about the promisor's future conduct.

In the analysis of deceptive promises just given, the contradiction in conception is produced by the way in which the deceiver uses a promise to get the other agent to judge that he has a reason to cooperate with his end. An alternate analysis focuses simply on the fact that deception, including both deceptive promises and lies, is an attempt to intervene in and to control the decision-making of another by attempting to lead the other to form certain beliefs that bear on the other's reasons for action. Such 'interventions' may be effected by appearing to bind oneself and to create an assurance about one's future action, as in the deceptive promise, or by deceptive statements that lead to false beliefs that bear on the other's reasons. Once deception is viewed in this way, one can argue that there is an incoherence in the universal adoption of the relevant maxim.

In universalizing a maxim of deception for self-interest, one wills that all agents be permitted to use deception to get other agents to see reason to cooperate with their ends. This is to will a state of affairs in which agents are permitted (for reasons of self-interest) to intervene in the decision-making of others by controlling the information and beliefs on which others base their judgments of what they have reason to do. Moreover, universal acceptance of this principle carries with it a certain conception of persons: since agents are free to substitute their own purposes and reasons for those of others and to attempt to direct their judgments from the outside in order to advance their interests, there is no inviolable boundary around agents. Agents are not regarded as separate spheres of decision-making and agency. In effect the universalization of this maxim supports a view of agents as potential extensions of oneself when it suits one's purposes. Because acting on this maxim is an attempt to control the agency of others, the universalized maxim is not coherent on its face as a law for agents with autonomy.[43] Agents with autonomy are in various ways the sources of their own actions. But in the world of the universalized maxim, the conditions of autonomous willing are undermined and agents are not conceived to be autonomous (as the sources of their actions through their own judgments about reasons).[44]

One feature that emerges from this second analysis is that the universalization of the maxim of deception for self-interest defeats a presupposition of the agent's adoption of the maxim. In the last section we saw that rational agents who 'cannot act otherwise than under the idea of freedom' (*G*4: 448) actively conceive of themselves as the sources of their actions through their own judgments about reasons. The agent who adopts a maxim of deception thinks of himself as minimally autonomous in this sense: he has his own purposes, which he regards as reason-giving for himself, and acts on his judgment of how best to advance them. His maxim has the intent of directing the other's choices for his own purposes. So in adopting this particular maxim, the agent regards his own judgment about reasons and purposes as the source of a sequence of actions, some of which are to be performed by the other. But since the universalized maxim leaves all agents free to attempt to control the judgments of others about their reasons, it undermines the conception of agents as the sources of their own actions. Thus, the universalization of the deceiver's maxim undermines the self-conception supposed in adopting this or any other maxim.

The role of a conception of autonomous agency in generating the contradictions in this analysis is quite evident—once deception is seen as an attempt to intervene in and control the willing of another. The maxim of deception for self-interest cannot coherently be willed as universal law for agents with autonomy since its universal adoption undermines the conditions of autonomous willing. And for the very same reason, in willing the maxim as universal law, the agent undermines, not the purpose of the maxim (getting the other to form a belief that gives him a reason to contribute an action to the deceiver's end), but a presupposition of his own adoption of the maxim—namely that he is the source of his own actions.

So far I have outlined what I take to be two distinct analyses of the maxim of deception for self-interest. Both focus on the fact that deception aims to achieve an end through the agency of another, but a conception of agency enters in different ways. The first analysis looks at *how* the deceiver tries to control the other's decision-making—that is, it looks at the use of deceptive promises and deceptive statements to get the other to see a reason to cooperate with the deceiver's ends. Here the contradiction in conception arises from the fact that universalization of the maxim undermines the vehicle employed to get the other to see a reason to cooperate. The second analysis focuses directly on the fact that deception is an attempt to control someone else's will, though without considering the vehicle of control. Here the contradiction in conception is due to the fact that universalization of a maxim of intervening in the decision-making of others undermines the conditions of autonomous willing, and therefore is not coherently willed as a law for agents with autonomy.

The second of these analyses, though not the first, as far as I can see, can be applied straightforwardly to maxims of coercion (and subtler maxims of manipulation).

It also has a less straightforward, though still plausible, application to maxims of using violence and aggression to further one's ends.[45]

Coercion involves the use of threat or intimidation to get another to act in a way that serves one's purposes. Like deception, it is an attempt to further one's ends through the agency of another, by giving the other a 'reason to cooperate' with one's ends that the other would not have apart from one's intervention; giving the other this reason to cooperate is a sub-goal in the service of one's larger ends. Coercion needs to be distinguished from other attempts to influence another person's actions, such as offers and non-coercive incentives, advice, persuasion, providing true information that bears on what it makes sense to do, and so on— here including attempts to influence another to act in a way that benefits oneself.[46] The defining feature of coercion seems to be that it seeks to control another's actions by attaching unacceptable consequences to the other's options, so that an action that the victim has reason to take in the absence of the threat is rendered ineligible or an action that the victim has independent reason to avoid is rendered eligible. The result is that the action sought by the coercer appears to the other to be the only, or the only acceptable thing to do under the circumstances. The following schema tries to make the notion a bit more precise; since coercion, obviously, can aim at getting the other either to perform some action or to refrain from some action, let X refer to both actions and omissions. A uses coercion against B when A threatens to bring about a consequence, S, unless B does X (if B does not do X), where X is some action that will contribute to A's ends that A wants B to perform. For example A threatens to fire B (S) unless B falsifies an accounting report for one of their firm's clients (does X). (Assume here that A will be rewarded by the clients if the report shows certain performance results that the clients desire.) A's proposal to B is a threat if the following conditions obtain: (i) apart from A's proposal, B finds X undesirable and either judges or would judge that he has good reasons not to do X (e.g., B believes that falsifying the report is wrong or would create a risk for him); and (ii) the consequence that A says that he will bring about makes, or is intended to make, refraining from X (not falsifying the report) substantially less desirable to B than it would be without A's intervention, to the point that B will judge that refraining from X is unacceptable or impossible, that he must do X despite his independent reasons for not doing X (e.g., being fired is sufficiently bad for B that he decides that falsifying the report is his best or only option, despite his belief that it is wrong or risky). What makes the use of the threat coercive is that A threatens to bring about S in order to get B to perform X (to get him to falsify the report). A's reason for threatening to bring about S is that A believes that attaching the threatened consequence to failure to do X will lead B to judge that not doing X is unacceptable; that B will take avoidance of the threatened consequence to be a reason to do X and will do X. The intuitive idea that this schema tries to capture is that the person being coerced has been subjected to the will of another. The victim may in some sense choose to do what the coercer desires, but his choice is controlled by the coercer.[47]

There are, of course, differences between deception and coercion. The coercer intervenes in the decision-making of the other by (roughly) attaching unacceptable consequences to the option of non-cooperation, rather than controlling the beliefs on the basis of which the other judges what he has reason to do. And coercion does not rely on the creation of normative expectations in order to give the other a 'reason to cooperate'; the reason is produced through the application of a credible threat. These differences aside, universalization of a maxim of using coercion to further one's ends is incoherent in essentially the same way. In willing the universalization of a maxim of coercion for self-interest, one wills a state of affairs in which all agents are free to control the decisions of others by attaching harmful consequences to certain of their options, so that the other will find cooperation to be the most viable or the only option.[48] Universal acceptance of this principle implies that there is no inviolable boundary around agents, so that persons are not viewed as separate spheres of agency. Since the universalized maxim undermines the conditions of autonomous willing, it is incoherent as a law for agents with autonomy. Likewise, the universalization of the maxim defeats the presupposition of the agent's autonomy. In adopting the maxim of coercion and the intention of controlling the agency of the other, the agent regards himself as the source of his actions. But by undermining the conditions of autonomous willing generally, the universalization of the maxim undermines the agent's presupposition of his own autonomy.

Violence—the use of aggression and killing to advance one's ends—can be accommodated within this framework if it is plausibly regarded as an attempt either to incapacitate or to eliminate the agency of another.[49] This is plausible where the use of violence is motivated by the fact that the other agent poses an obstacle to the aggressor's plans through his independence—that is, when he poses an obstacle because he is an independent agent with reasons to act in ways that will interfere with the aggressor's purposes. Violence responds to the independent agency and the difficulty of controlling another's willing by neutralizing it or eliminating it from the scene. It is not a way of directing another agent's will, but rather a method of managing someone whose willing one cannot effectively direct. But for that reason, it is a way of bringing someone else's agency under (one's) control. Maxims of violence are like deception and coercion in having the sub-goal of bringing the agency of another under one's control in the service of some end. If one accepts this view of violence, one can argue along similar lines that the universalized maxims of violence for self-interest cannot coherently be willed as universal law for agents with autonomy.

My suggestion then, is that maxims of deception and coercion to further one's ends share a common structure, and that at least some maxims of violence represent a variant of this structure. Deception and coercion attempt to achieve an end by intervening in and directing the volition of another—by in different ways giving the other a reason to act in a way that contributes to the end. Violence seeks to further an end, not by directing the agency of another, but by bringing it under control when the other's independence threatens the success of the aggressor's end. The sub-goal of the maxim is not to give the other a 'reason to cooperate', but to disable the other's capacity to act for his own independent reasons. The common structure is that all represent different ways of intervening in and controlling the agency of another for the sake of one's ends. As such, they cannot coherently be willed as universal laws for agents with autonomy.

Since the role of a conception of agency in contradiction in will arguments is fairly evident, let me close this section with a few brief comments on mutual aid. As is well known, Kant argues that willing a maxim of indifference (the maxim of respecting others' rights but never helping them when in need) as universal law conflicts with certain things that one necessarily wills as a rational agent. As end-setting agents, if we will any ends at all, we value the continued use of our agency, and are therefore committed to willing the conditions necessary for exercising our agency. Since the availability of assistance from others is one of these conditions, the universalization of the maxim of indifference produces a contradiction in the will. The argument shows that the policy of never taking the needs of others as reasons for assisting them is impermissible. From this it follows that one must adopt the policy of taking the needs of others as reasons for action and being willing to assist when the true needs and continued agency of another are at stake.[50] Given the general facts of human vulnerability, failure to adopt any policy about mutual aid is equivalent to holding the impermissible maxim of indifference.

Barbara Herman argues that Kant's argument for the duty of mutual aid depends on the claim that there are ends that it is not rational to abandon. Specifically, she notes that, given the facts of human need and interdependence, the irrationality of universalizing the maxim of indifference follows if either of two conditions holds. One condition is that there are 'necessary ends'—ends that one cannot give up. These necessary ends include the continued exercise of one's agency, and any ends or background conditions that are needed for the continued use of one's agency. A second is that an agent have some particular ends to which he is committed—that is, a set of personal ends no one of which is rationally required—whose value to the agent is greater than the value of non-beneficence, and which the agent cannot count on achieving unaided.[51] That there are ends that it is not rational to abandon is a general feature of rational agency; it is a normative claim established by appeal to a conception of agency and the value commitments that are built into the perspective of rational agency.[52] Kant's argument also depends on general facts about human limitations and social interdependence. But it is due to these features of rational agency that willing indifference as universal law produces a contradiction in the will. Without these commitments of rational volition, there is no contradiction in the will.

In this section I have tried to indicate some ways in which a Kantian conception of agency generates the contradictions uncovered by the deliberative procedure associated with the FUL. A conception of agency appears in different places within this deliberative procedure (both at the front and at the back, as it were). The universalizability of a maxim is determined partly by what one wills just in so far as one is rational and autonomous, and partly by the universal adoptability of the principle by a community of rational agents with autonomy. The first (its appearance at the front) is most apparent in the contradiction in will test. The universalization of the maxim of indifference produces a contradiction in the will because it conflicts with certain things that we necessarily will as rational agents with autonomy. The constraints imposed by the fact that one is willing a maxim as law for agents with autonomy are most apparent in the contradiction in conception test. For example, once deception, coercion, and violence are viewed as attempts to intervene in and to control the agency of another, the relevant maxims cannot coherently be thought of as universal laws for agents with autonomy. What is incoherent here is the universal adoption of these maxims by agents with autonomy, since universal adoption undermines the conditions of autonomous willing. These observations support the suggestion that the deliberative question underlying the FUL is whether an agent with autonomy can rationally will a maxim as universal law for a community of agents with autonomy.

Let me hazard a concluding remark: a concern often expressed about the use of the FUL is that, in order to deal with the problems of application, theorists have set up the CI procedure to yield the outcomes that we know in advance we want it to yield. Is the idea of universalizability then doing any independent work? One might worry that I have done something similar in the understanding of the FUL just sketched. I have chosen to look at maxims at a certain level of generality. Moreover, I have understood the maxims of deception, coercion, and violence in a very specific way as attempts to control the agency of others. So understood, these maxims lend themselves to treatment by the Categorical Imperative, which identifies the attempt to control as a wrong-making feature, in virtue of which they cannot coherently be willed as universal law for agents with autonomy. Haven't I just set up the procedure to yield results desired in advance, in which case the idea of universal law does no independent work?

To this objection, I would plead *nolo contendere*. First since on the view outlined here universalizability operates in conjunction with other elements, its work need not be 'independent'. More importantly, whether this should be a concern depends on what we expect a moral theory to do. It would be a concern if we think that a moral theory should provide a deliberative procedure that can generate a set of principles or judgments from the ground up. That would require that we base a procedure of moral deliberation on some set of moral notions, without having a clear idea of what its 'output' should be, and then use it to generate or identify a set of principles that, in virtue of being the output of this procedure, are correct or rationally authoritative. But this is not a plausible aim for moral theory, and this concern does not apply if one has a more plausible conception of the aim of a moral theory.

That aim, I suggest, is to articulate the basic elements and values, and to provide a systematic representation of the content and underlying structure of the moral outlook to the extent that it admits of systematization (acknowledging here that it is only possible to carry systematization so far). This aim would include at least three recognizably important tasks—an explanatory task, an action-guiding task, and a task of justification. (1) So understood, a theory can be expected to provide an explanation of why certain kinds of actions are wrong, required, or permitted (or whether certain kinds of reasons are adequate justification of certain kinds of actions). (2) It can be action guiding in a limited sense, by providing an overall moral orientation that can guide moral perception, judgment, and deliberation. (3) And it can provide a representation of a moral conception that permits one to carry out certain tasks of justification. This could include justification of the content, or establishing the authority of a moral conception whose content is in hand—that is, showing that this conception is reasonably endorsed. The *Groundwork* makes contributions to all three projects, but its primary aims are the tasks of justification.[53]

NOTES

1. See, e.g., Onora O'Neill, *Constructions of Reason*, ch. 5; Barbara Herman, *The Practice of Moral Judgment*, chs. 3, 6–7, 10; Christine Korsgaard, *Creating the Kingdom of Ends*, ch. 3; and John Rawls, *Lectures on the History of Moral Philosophy*, 'Kant, Lecture II'.
2. On the idea that the FUL should be applied to maxims at a certain level of generality, see O'Neill, *Constructions of Reason*, 83–9, where she argues that maxims are underlying practical principles by which an agent guides her more specific intentions. Likewise Herman claims that the CI procedure is suited to assess what she calls 'generic maxims' of the form 'to do an x-type action for y-type reason', rather than more detailed principles that represent an agent's actual volition. See *The Practice of Moral Judgment*, 147 ff., 217–24.
3. Cf. Korsgaard, *Creating the Kingdom of Ends*, 92–3, 100–1, 124–8; O'Neill, *Constructions of Reason*, 137–42; Herman, *The Practice of Moral Judgment*, 136–43, 154–8, 224–30.
4. Here I have in mind Thomas E. Hill, Jr. and Allen Wood.
5. For a useful enumeration of Kant's use of the idea of humanity as an end to derive specific duties, see Allen W. Wood, 'Kant's Formula of Humanity', 184–5. Kant often refers to versions of the FUL in considering questions of application, but it generally does little work in his actual arguments.
6. See Wood, *Kant's Ethical Thought*, 97–107. Wood's view is that, supplemented with suitable empirical premises, and in the third and fourth examples with independent rational (i.e., normative) principles, the contradiction in conception and contradiction in will tests support the impermissibility of the maxims in Kant's four examples (87–97, 108–9). But he argues that the FUL is inadequate as a general basis for moral deliberation, since, beyond these cases, it yields both false negatives and false positives. Moreover, he argues that since the FUL at best is a test of permissibility, it can never require the adoption of any particular principle and thus never establishes any positive duties (97–107).
7. Ibid. 91, 107
8. Ibid. 107, 183–7.

9. See Barbara Herman, *The Practice of Moral Judgment*, 120–7, 153–5, 225–30. Representative citations include: 'What I will argue is that without an account of rational willing or agency robust enough to deliver content, the CI cannot be an effective principle of moral judgment' (225). 'The successive formulations interpret the arguments of the CI procedure in terms that reveal the aspects of rational agency that generate contradictions under universalization' (227).

10. In referring to the 'CI procedure', as well as to the 'contradiction in conception' and 'contradiction in will tests', I use the idea of a 'procedure' or 'test' loosely to refer to an idealized representation of certain forms of moral reasoning that need to be supplemented by judgment. I believe that many other writers who employ these terms should be understood in the same way. For example, Onora O'Neill stresses throughout *Constructions of Reason* that the Categorical Imperative is not a moral algorithm; see pp. 18–19, 59 n., 128, 180. Even in the essay, 'Consistency in Action', where she refers often to Kant's 'universality test', she makes it clear that this is a criterion that applies to agents' underlying practical principles (i.e., maxims), that it is primarily a criterion of the moral worth of maxims rather than the rightness of action types, and that it is to be applied by agents to their own proposals for action and not by moral judges or spectators. These remarks indicate that she does not regard the Categorical Imperative as a mechanical procedure. See also John Rawls, *Lectures on the History of Moral Philosophy*, 166. As I try to make clear in this section, constructivism does not assume that we can devise a mechanical procedure for generating basic moral requirements from the ground up.

11. Rawls, *Lectures on the History of Moral Philosophy*, 237. See also 'Themes in Kant's Moral Philosophy', 97; and *Political Liberalism*, 89–90, 93.

12. Ibid. 240. Cf. 'Themes in Kant's Moral Philosophy', 97, 99.

13. Rawls mentions the 'union' of practical reason with conceptions of person and society at pp. 241 (twice) and 243 of *Lectures on the History of Moral Philosophy*.

14. *Political Liberalism*, 107.

15. Ibid. 107. Rawls continues here by saying that the principles of practical reason and the conceptions of society and person are 'complementary' and that they are different aspects of 'practical reason' (in a broader sense). He writes:

> Just as the principles of logic, inference and judgment would not be used were there no persons who could think, infer and judge, the principles of practical reason are expressed in the thought and judgment of reasonable and rational persons and applied by them in their social and political practice. Those principles do not apply themselves, but are used by us in forming our intentions and actions, plans and decisions, in our relations with other persons. This being so we may call the conceptions of society and person 'conceptions of practical reason': they characterize the agents who reason and they specify the context for the problems and questions to which the principles of practical reason apply.

> I take it that part of Rawls's point here is that principles of reasoning (both of logic and of practical reason) are normative principles that guide the thought and judgment of rational agents. One might also argue that these 'principles' and 'conceptions' are complementary in the further sense that these norms are constitutive of rational thought and volition and that one's capacity to follow and to apply such principles constitutes one as a rational agent.

16. Ibid. 109.

17. Ibid. 89; *Lectures on the History of Moral Philosophy*, 243.

18. Ibid. 274.

19. Allen Wood gives a gross mischaracterization of constructivism when he writes:

> . . . it is sadly fashionable in moral philosophy, both Kantian and non-Kantian, to think that moral theory must consist in some kind of rational decision procedure (such as some version of the principle of utility or Kant's FUL or FLN) . . . An ethical theory then becomes a kind of meat grinder into which we feed empirical facts, turn the crank, and out comes the series of acts we ought to perform, one after the next, like neat little sausages on a string. The position known as 'Kantian constructivism', which emphasizes the FUL (or FLN) and regards moral goodness or rightness [as] properties constructed through the application of a 'CI-procedure,' is a sad example of this repellent picture . . . ('What is Kantian Ethics?', 167)

Cf. also *Kant's Ethical Thought*, 337, 374–5.

I do not believe that the main idea of constructivism is that there is a procedure that enables us to 'test' maxims. Rawls's remark that constructivism is a view about the *structure* of the most adequate moral conception *after due reflection* makes it clear that it is not committed to any such moral decision procedure. (Wood, by the way, acknowledges in a footnote that Rawls rejects the picture of the Categorical Imperative as an algorithm; see 'What is Kantian Ethics?' 179–80.) Constructivism uses the idea of a procedure of construction in order to argue that objectivity is based in practical reason rather than in conformity to an independently given moral order (i.e., a moral order given independently of the principles of practical reason and the conceptions of person and society). Accordingly, one main feature of constructivism is its distinctive explanation of correctness in moral judgment. Rational intuitionism and related forms of moral realism hold that a moral judgment about basic principles is correct because it gets the independently given moral order right, and that a process of reasoning is correct (normally leads to correct results) because it tracks this moral order. Constructivism, by contrast, holds that a judgment about basic moral principles is correct because it issues from the correct procedure correctly followed—where the correct procedure is that which after due reflection best incorporates the relevant standards of practical reason and the conception of persons as rational agents that are rooted in the standpoint of deliberation. Here see Rawls, *Lectures on the History of Moral Philosophy*, 240, 242–3 and Christine Korsgaard, *The Sources of Normativity*, 36–7.

Constructivism is often termed a form of 'anti-realism' in ethics. While it is true that constructivism rejects the brand of moral realism found in rational intuitionism (both in its seventeenth, eighteenth, and early twentieth century versions), this label is misleading. First, it classifies constructivism with a number of views that reject the objectivity of moral judgment. Second, and perhaps more importantly, this label characterizes constructivism in terms of what it rejects (intuitionist brands of moral realism) and overlooks the fact that it offers its own account of what makes objective moral judgments possible.

20. The passage quoted at the beginning of this paragraph (cited at n. 18) continues: 'Here by full reflection is not meant perfect reflection at the end of time, but such increasingly critical reflection as might be achieved by a tradition of thought from one generation to the next, so that it looks more and more as if upon fuller reflection the moral view would be constructivist' (Rawls, *Lectures on the History of Moral Philosophy*, 274).

Here compare Charles Parsons's discussion of mathematical constructivism:

> We have suggested that the generation of a sequence of symbols is something of which the construction of the natural numbers is an idealization. But 'construction' loses its sense if we

abstract further from the fact that this is a process in time which is never completed. The infinite in constructivism must be 'potential,' rather than 'actual.' Each individual number can be constructed, but there is no construction which contains within itself the whole series of natural numbers . . . constructivism is implied by the postulate that no mathematical proposition can be true unless we can in a non-miraculous way *know* it to be true. ('Mathematics, Foundations of', 204)

21. See, e.g., *G* 4: 403–4, 421; *KpV* 5: 8, 8 n., 27–8, 44, 69–70.

22. Wood has argued that 'the universal formula' here refers to the Formula of Autonomy (or one of its variants) rather than the FUL; see *Kant's Ethical Thought*, 187–90. But I find these arguments unpersuasive.

23. See, e.g., *G* 4: 426–7. In the first passage, after deriving and illustrating the application of the FUL, Kant asks: 'is it a necessary law for all rational beings always to appraise their actions in accordance with such maxims as they themselves could will to serve as universal laws?' He asks, in other words, whether this principle really is rationally necessary. Likewise, at *G* 4: 449 Kant asks 'why ought I to subject myself to this principle and do so simply as a rational being?'—the principle being that 'maxims must always be so adopted that they can also hold as objective, that is hold universally as principles, and so serve for our own giving of universal law'. The phrasing of this principle is not unambiguous, but I take Kant to be posing the same question: whether the principle initially introduced by the FUL really has overriding normative authority.

24. Many commentators question whether Kant succeeds in extracting the FUL from the concept of a categorical imperative. Section III explains these doubts and suggests a way to address them.

25. Paul Guyer is right to hold that the proposition that humanity is an end in itself is synthetic a priori, that is, a substantive value claim established on a priori grounds. See *Kant on Freedom, Law, and Happiness*, ch. 5, esp. pp. 191–200. This seems to conflict with Kant's claim that the argument of *Groundwork*, II is analytic. But as is well known, this proposition is not actually established in *Groundwork*, III, since the argument contains a step that is affirmed only as a 'postulate', whose grounds are not provided until *Groundwork*, III (*G* 4: 429 n.) Thus while *Groundwork*, II may contain some synthetic strains, Kant is consistent in holding that it establishes no synthetic a priori propositions. For discussion of Guyer's views, see my review essay 'Value and Law in Kant's Moral Theory', 149–55.

26. Kant does seem to think that all moral requirements can be derived from the FUL once it is stated as the FLN; see the references in n. 12 above. So here I depart from Kant's understanding of how his view works.

27. The apparent gap in Kant's argument is discussed by many commentators. See Bruce Aune, *Kant's Theory of Morals*, 28–34, 42–3; Nelson Potter, 'The Argument of Kant's *Groundwork*, Chapter 1', 34–7; Thomas E. Hill, Jr., 'Kant's Argument for the Rationality of Moral Conduct', in *Dignity and Practical Reason*, 121–2; Henry Allison, 'On the Presumed Gap in the Derivation of the Categorical Imperative', in *Idealism and Freedom*; and Allen Wood, *Kant's Ethical Thought*, 47–9, 81–2. A recent book that focuses on this issue is Samuel J. Kerstein, *Kant's Search for the Supreme Principle of Morality*.

28. The argument in *Groundwork*, I (*G* 4: 401–2) proceeds from an analysis of the concept of a good will and is aimed at stating the basic principle on which a good will acts.

Briefly, and simplifying, a good will acts from respect for the moral law—that is to say, from an immediate recognition of the moral law as a source of authoritative reasons that exclude the force of and take priority over competing reasons for action based on desire and subjective ends. Thus the good will acts on the general principle of conformity to universal law as such—the general principle of acting from universally valid principles of conduct simply because they are required or make authoritative claims on us. In *Groundwork*, II (*G* 4: 421) Kant states explicitly that a formulation of the Categorical Imperative can be derived from the concept of a categorical imperative. He argues that we may infer that the Categorical Imperative simply states the necessity of conforming to universal law as such, which principle he then (without further argument) goes on to identify with the FUL. I discuss these arguments in further detail in Chapter 3, the first in Section II and the second in n. 32. Because both arguments rely on a conception of moral requirements as unconditional, I treat them in this section as different statements of Kant's 'argument from the concept of a practical law to the principle of conformity to universal law'.

29. Hill, *Dignity and Practical Reason*, 122. The substantive principle that Hill finds 'dubious' is that 'one must act on maxims which one can will as universal laws *in the sense* that it is (rationally) acceptable that everyone act on the maxim'.

30. In addition to arguing that the FUL does not follow from the idea of conformity to universal law, Allen Wood argues that Kant's derivation of the FUL fails to show how the idea of what we *can will* as universal law finds its way into the formula of the Categorical Imperative. He writes: '. . . it does not follow from the mere concept of a categorical imperative that *the will of a rational being*—what a rational being wills or consistently wills—has any role to play in determining the content of universal law'. He goes on to say that we could accept this criterion if we already knew that the moral law is a principle of autonomy, as Kant later argues (*Kant's Ethical Thought*, 81). My point here addresses this aspect of Wood's critique by pointing out that Kant's claims about autonomy follow directly from the concept of a practical law. So it is reasonable to think that it does follow from the concept of a categorical imperative that the content of universal law is determined by what a rational being can consistently will.

31. My suggestion for filling out Kant's derivation of the FUL has similarities to the strategy suggested by Henry Allison. Allison agrees with Aune and Wood that there is a gap in the *Groundwork* derivation of the FUL, but argues that the second *Critique* fills it by adding the assumption of transcendental freedom as a premise to the argument. This addition is supported by the version of the Reciprocity Thesis found in §§ 5–6 (*KpV* 5: 28–30), the general thrust of which is that an agent that can be motivated to act from a practical law, that is, to conform to such a law simply because it is a law, must be transcendentally free. See Allison, *Idealism and Freedom*, 150–4. I won't summarize Allison's proposed argument, but will simply note that it turns on the following idea: that since practical laws apply to and therefore presuppose transcendentally free agents, that conception of agency is available for the specification of the moral law.

32. For a nice discussion of the importance of spontaneity to Kant's conception of rational agency that links acting according to the representation of laws (*G* 4: 412), acting under the idea of freedom (*G* 4: 448), and the Incorporation Thesis (*Rel* 6: 24), see Henry Allison, 'Autonomy and Spontaneity in Kant's Conception of the Self', in *Idealism and Freedom*, 133–4.

33. For general discussions of the topic of normative powers on which I have drawn, see H. L. A. Hart, *The Concept of Law*, 27–33, 284–5, and *Essays on Bentham*, 169–70, 216–19; Neil MacCormick, 'Voluntary Obligations and Normative Powers, I'; and Joseph Raz, 'Voluntary Obligations and Normative Powers, II' (esp. 92–101), 'Promises and Obligations', and *The Morality of Freedom*, 173–4.

   In the paragraphs that follow, I also draw on Raz's notion of 'an exclusionary reason' as a feature of obligations and reasons of authority ('Promises and Obligations', 219–26; see also *The Authority of Law*, ch. 1). For discussion of related structural features of practical reasons, see T. M. Scanlon, *What We Owe to Each Other*, 50–5.

34. The point I am after in this paragraph is that an agent's adoption of an end creates an additional reason to pursue the end over and above the reasons that make it worth adopting in the first place. This position—that the adoption of an end creates a reason of commitment—is consistent with the view that the rational choice of an end is a response to value or desirability characteristics that are independent of our actual conative attitudes. There are a number of theoretical possibilities for understanding the values or desirability characteristics to which rational choice is responsive, and I won't develop a position on that question here. For now suffice it to say that in holding that rational choice confers a normative status on the end, one need not hold that the rational choice of an end is what makes it good. What makes the end good are its desirability characteristics or features that make it worth choosing. The normative status conferred on the end is akin to the status conferred on a principle of action when it is enacted as law by a duly constituted authority. More on this point in n. 36.

35. Reasons of commitment come into play most naturally in connection with ends, projects, relationships, values, and so on, that one is morally free to adopt or not to adopt. It is not clear that they come into play with ends that are morally (or rationally) required. Say that one adopts an end that one judges is morally required. The reasons that demand its adoption also demand that one pursue it and maintain it as one's end. Reasons of commitment do not appear to add much here.

36. Here compare Christine Korsgaard's view that willing an end is an instance of giving oneself a law, in 'The Normativity of Instrumental Reason', 245–7, 250–1 and *passim*. She writes:

   for the instrumental principle to provide you with a reason, you must think that the fact that you will an end *is a reason* for the end. It's not exactly that there has to be a *further* reason; it's just that you must take your act of will to be normative for you . . . It means that your willing the end gives it a normative status for you, that your willing the end in a sense makes it good. The instrumental principle can only be normative if we take ourselves to be capable of giving laws to ourselves—or, in other words, if we take our own wills to be legislative. (pp. 245–6)

   My suggestion (which I regard as a way of clarifying the position that she is after) is that the fact that you will, that is, commit yourself to, an end is indeed a 'further reason'. It is not a reason to adopt the end, but a reason to act toward the end over and above the reasons for adopting it, which analytically contains reason to take the necessary means. (The considerations that make the end worthwhile are reasons to pursue and to realize it; they indicate that it would be good if the end were realized. Your adoption of the end creates a further reason beyond these for you to realize the end.) Korsgaard's view that willing an end is an instance of giving yourself a law is right, but this way of putting it is preferable to saying that your willing the end 'makes the end good'. The normative status conferred on the end by one's volition is closer to that of law than to that of goodness or value, which, as these notions are commonly understood, do not carry implications of rational requirement. The concept of a reason of commitment seems to me to be a way to unpack Korsgaard's claim that willing an end is giving yourself a law because it spells out the structural features of the reasons that the agent creates for herself and brings out their similarities to reasons of obligation and authority. (In setting ends for ourselves through reason, we also 'give laws' and create reasons for other agents, e.g., to respect and to support our pursuit of the end. But that is another matter.)

It is worth noting that elsewhere in this essay Korsgaard refers to ends being good in this more ordinary sense. She notes that we must be able to say what makes our ends worthwhile in order to sustain our commitments in the face of the demands that they impose. 'To that extent, the normative force of the instrumental principle does seem to depend on our having a way to say to ourselves of some ends that there are reasons for them, that they are good' (p. 251) I take it that the reasons that make the end good here are considerations that guide its adoption, not reasons in any sense created by its adoption.

For an instructive discussion of these points, see David Sussman, 'The Authority of Humanity', esp. sects. II–III.

37. These points need to be worked out in greater detail. The idea that we adopt ends through discrete acts of commitment is one obvious simplification, but this way of talking is common and helps to illustrate the structural features of reasons of commitment. Reasons of commitment pre-empt the force of certain reasons not to act toward the end, but not others. They can themselves be limited or overridden by reasons from ends, values, and obligations that are more important, for example. Further, commitments are of course subject to revision and do not preclude reassessment of the end. Since you are the one in charge, the sovereign as it were, you can reconsider your commitment if you see reason to. Loss of interest in the end—or a change in your judgment about its value, a clearer picture of its costs, and so on—may be reasons to abandon the end, and if you abandon the end, you suspend the reasons for pursuing it that you created through your commitment. But until the commitment is rescinded, it gives you reasons to act toward the end that remain in force over time independently of changes in your attitudes, and rules out considerations such as current lack of interest as a good reason to forego some step toward the end on a suitable occasion. And again, this is the case even if it is a straightforwardly desire-based end that interests you because it gives you enjoyment. If the fact that you enjoy it is your reason for making it your end, the fading of enjoyment is a reason to abandon the end, but is still excluded as a legitimate reason for inaction while the commitment is in place.

38. For Korsgaard's development of the notion of self-constitution, see 'The Normativity of Instrumental Reason' (esp. 244–54) and 'Self-Constitution in the Ethics of Plato and Kant'. In the first of these essays, she emphasizes the role of the instrumental principle in self-constitution. Her view, greatly oversimplified, is that by conforming to the demands of the instrumental principle, I limit the influence of incentives that would derail me from my aims and I keep myself on track toward their realization. In that way I bring it about that there is a self over and above the various incentives in me that governs my choices, and thus I constitute myself as having a will.

She argues that the instrumental principle is in this way a principle that is internal to volition and constitutive of having a will. One might equally emphasize the importance to self-constitution of the power to set ends for oneself through reason and the rational procedures through which one issues reasons of commitment for oneself. Since taking steps to realize ends just is to follow the instrumental principle, it is by following the instrumental principle that one thinks of oneself as the cause of one's ends, thus of having a will (which Kant characterizes as a kind of rational causality). This is obviously central to rational volition. But the power to set ends for yourself has a prior role. There are reasons to take the means only if there are reasons to pursue the end, and reasons of the latter kind (I suggest) are supplied by the adoption of the end. However this is a minor modification to her conception of self-constitution, since the reasons created by committing oneself to ends analytically contain reasons to take the means. The power to set ends and the capacity to follow the instrumental principle obviously work in tandem. Focus on the structural features of reasons of commitment helps show how the capacity to give oneself such reasons constitutes the self as a center of normative guidance. Reasons of commitment exclude as reasons incentives that would hinder the realization of one's ends. This feature of such reasons mirrors the conception of the self as a center of normative guidance and direction over and above the various incentives in the self. Thus the capacity to issue this kind of reason is part of what is needed to constitute the self as a center of normative guidance.

39. See Herman, *The Practice of Moral Judgment*, 116–18, 147–50
40. In the discussion that follows I assume a normative power conception of promising. According to this view, a promise communicates an intention, by that very act of communication, to undertake an obligation to perform a certain action and to give the addressee a right that one perform that action, unless released by the promisee (here following Joseph Raz, 'Promises and Obligations', 211). What is significant for our purposes is that a promise is the exercise of a normative power to bind oneself through one's will and that the obligation initially created by a promise is not a moral obligation but a practice-based obligation, or a reason for action identified by the social norms that govern promising (social norm-based obligation). It depends on the shared understanding that if one promises, one's promise will function as a sufficient reason to perform the promised action. Practice-based obligations are properly termed 'obligations' because of their structural features—for example, the fact that one has promised is a reason to perform the promised action that excludes the force of certain kinds of reasons not to perform (as explained in the text). They are non-moral because their authority is not based in, say, respect for the moral law or respect for persons; rather it is based in the social justification for having the practice (or in the interests served by persons having this power) and in whatever socially instilled motives ground the disposition to comply with the relevant social norms (e.g., an understanding of the interests served by the norms, a disposition to comply with socially inculcated norms, concern for one's reputation, one's sense of honor, and so on). As I suggest below, however, the practice-based (or social norm-based) obligation to keep one's promises is *also* a moral obligation since the maxim of breaking one's promise for reasons of self-interest cannot be universalized and is thus morally impermissible.

Writers who have held that there is a non-moral obligation to keep one's promises (in addition to the moral obligation) include Rawls (see *A Theory of Justice*, 2nd edn., 303–5), Raz, and of course Hume. For recent discussions of different approaches to promising, see Scanlon, *What We Owe to Each Other*, ch. 7; Niko Kolodny and R. Jay Wallace, 'Promises and Practices Revisited'; and Michael Pratt, 'Promises and Perlocutions'.

My understanding of these issues has been helped by Gary Watson's unpublished paper, 'Promising, Assurance and Expectation'.

41. Discussions of the contradiction in conception test (CC) distinguish the 'logical contradiction' from the 'practical contradiction' interpretation of the contradiction. See Christine Korsgaard, 'Kant's Formula of Universal Law' in *Creating the Kingdom of Ends*. According to the first, universalizing certain maxims is logically inconceivable. This interpretation looks at the fact that acting on certain maxims would no longer be possible if they were universalized; for example, universalizing the maxim of deceptive promising would destroy the practice of promising, making it impossible to promise and thus to promise falsely. This interpretation of CC rejects maxims that would not be *possible* if universal. The practical contradiction interpretation holds that universalizing certain maxims leads to a practical inconsistency in the sense that the maxim would defeat its own purpose if universalized; it focuses on the fact that certain maxims could not be *successful* if universal. For example, if deceptive promising were universal, promises would lose their credibility and a false promise would not work as a means to one's end. According to this interpretation, the procedure rejects maxims 'whose efficacy in achieving their purpose depends on their being exceptional' (Korsgaard, 'Kant's Formula of Universal Law', 92). My discussion does not put much weight on this distinction, and I believe that either can be made to work. The first analysis of the deceptive promise given in the text is a version of the practical contradiction reading, but with this modification. The practical contradiction is that the universalization of the maxim frustrates the sub-goal of the maxim: under universalization, false promises would no longer be efficacious in getting another to see a reason to cooperate or to act as the deceiver desires. But this does make a difference to a disagreement between Korsgaard and Herman on the proper treatment of deceptive promises.

Korsgaard supports the practical contradiction reading of CC because both the contradiction in conception and contradiction in will tests then rely on the notion of rationality (within universalizability) seen in the Hypothetical Imperative. Because this reading of the CC test rejects maxims that are efficacious only if exceptional, she argues that it 'reveals unfairness, deception, cheating' and brings out a sense in which such maxims use others as means. 'If you do something that only works because most people do not do it, their actions are making your actions work. In the false promising case, other people's honesty makes your deceit effective' (ibid. 92, 93). The suggestion here seems to be that deception is a kind of free-riding. Herman has criticized this approach on a few counts. First, this reading of the CC test appears to reject morally innocuous maxims of coordination and thus fails to distinguish coordination from free-riding. That suggests that 'efficacious only if exceptional' is not in general a wrong-making feature. (I believe that the problem with maxims of coordination arises because the maxim is mischaracterized, but I won't elaborate here.) Second, she argues, quite plausibly, that Korsgaard's approach rejects deceptive promising for the wrong reasons. It incorrectly assimilates deception to free-riding and fails to capture the wrong done to the individual, namely that deception aims to manipulate and control its victim. (Free-riding involves taking advantage of other people's adherence to a mutually beneficial norm; but deception is a wrong done specifically to the person deceived.) Her conclusion is that the logical contradiction reading of CC correctly captures this wrong-making feature of deception (Herman, *The Practice of Moral Judgment*, 137–41).

The first analysis given in the text suggests a way that Korsgaard might reply. First, this analysis rejects maxims that, if universal, could not succeed in getting others to see reason to act in certain ways. So it does not imply that 'efficacious only if exceptional' is a general wrong-making feature. Second, by focusing on the sub-goal of getting the other to see reason to cooperate, this analysis does bring out the wrong done to the victim by aiming to manipulate and control. The second analysis that I go on to give in the text—which seems to me to be closer to the logical contradiction reading—also highlights as the wrong-making feature the fact that deception is an attempt to control another's agency.

42. That is, they would no longer create these expectations in circumstances in which a speaker might be inclined to lie. But since it might often be in a speaker's interest to lie, the universalization of the maxim would undermine the credibility of assertion generally, including in circumstances in which people lie for these kinds of reasons.

43. Cf. Barbara Herman, *The Practice of Moral Judgment*, 26, 154–6, 227–30, especially: 'A law of rational agency that entails the causal control of one will over another ... could not be a law of rational agency: a law describing the agency of ends-in-themselves. Under universalization, the maxim of deception produces a law of dissociated or dispersed and unfree agency ... universal deception violates the separateness of rational agents' (230).

44. Some of Onora O'Neill's discussions of contradiction in conception suggest this analysis; see *Constructions of Reason*, 96–7, 133–4. Cf. also some of her views in *Towards Justice and Virtue*, for example, pp. 56–9, 125–8, and 163–8, in particular her view that practical reason yields the basic requirement to reject as unreasoned principles that cannot be followed by all agents in the relevant domain.

45. Conversely, the first analysis, though not as far as I can see the second, can be adapted to cover maxims that involve free-riding of various sorts—but I won't pursue the point here.

46. My focus is on maxims of coercion for self-interest, but clearly not all attempts to influence another to act in a way that benefits oneself, so described, are coercive or morally suspect. There are also examples of coercion that are presumptively legitimate, such as threatening punishment for violations of a law or threatening to end a relationship with another unless that person alters certain patterns of behavior. A complete account of coercion is beyond the scope of this essay. The discussions of the nature of coercion which I follow are Robert Nozick, 'Coercion' and Harry Frankfurt, 'Coercion and Moral Responsibility' in *The Importance of What We Care About*.

47. Cf. Nozick, 'Coercion', 38.

48. I am not claiming that Kantian universalizability can be used to distinguish coercion from other attempts to influence, for example to distinguish coercive threats from offers. We need a grasp of this distinction before we think about universalizability. The intuitive difference that must be captured is that coercion attempts to control another's actions against his will by limiting his acceptable options. Offers, by contrast, enlarge a person's desirable options (so that people are generally willing to be made offers but not to be threatened); and since they leave the person space to decline, they are attempts to influence without controlling. (On these points see Nozick, 'Coercion', 37–44.) My claim is that given the ability to discriminate between coercion and other forms of influencing (such as offers), maxims regarded as coercive will be non-universalizable, while maxims understood to employ other forms of influence will be

universalizable and therefore permissible. What makes the difference is that coercion is an attempt to control another against the other's will. In other words, universalizability will sort coercive and non-coercive maxims differently once the maxims are understood in these terms (though universalizability will not give us an understanding of the difference between coercion and other attempts to influence). Thanks to Gideon Yaffe for prompting me to clarify these points.

49. Barbara Herman has argued that the contradiction in conception test is unable to reject maxims of violence and that the Kantian must here appeal to the idea of contradiction in will. Part of her point is that violence is not just a limiting case of coercion, which, she agrees, can be handled by the idea of contradiction in conception. See *The Practice of Moral Judgment*, 118–19. In this paragraph I sketch a way of thinking about violence that does make it amenable to treatment by contradiction in conception.

50. Here following Herman, 'Mutual Aid and Respect for Persons', in *The Practice of Moral Judgment*, esp. 55–7.

51. Ibid. 52 ff.

52. That rational agents who conceive of themselves as the sources of their own actions are committed to valuing their rational capacities is a normative claim, though not yet a moral claim. The idea needed by the contradiction in will argument is that it is built into the perspective of rational agency that each agent values his or her own rational capacities, not that they value rational nature in general. A second point worth noting here is that the claim that rational agents have some particular personal ends that they are not willing to abandon is not just a contingent or empirical fact about rational agency; it also has a normative dimension. Rational agents cannot act without an identity that they forge for themselves through commitments to various ends, projects, and values that endure over time. The need for a stable set of ends, some of which cannot be abandoned without cost, appears to be a constitutive feature of (finite) rational agency.

53. Earlier versions of this essay were presented to the Pacific Division of the American Philosophical Association, in March of 2000, and to the Beijing International Symposium on Kant's Moral Philosophy in Contemporary Perspective at Peking University, in May 2004. I am grateful to Houston Smit and to Xu Xiangdong for their respective invitations to present the paper, and to the audiences for their responses.

8

Self-Legislation and Duties to Oneself

I. INTRODUCTION

This essay considers some of Kant's 'foundational' remarks about duties to oneself and some of the problems that they raise. The problems that interest me lie more in what Kant says to clarify the basis of duties to oneself than in the idea of such duties themselves. I do not question the general coherence of duties to oneself, but instead am concerned with what such duties, as well as what Kant says about them, tell us about his general understanding of certain features of duty and obligation.

I see no special problems in understanding how one can have duties to oneself, especially in the context of a Kantian theory in which respecting humanity as an end in itself plays a defining role. Duties to oneself suppose that there are non-prudentially based reasons for adopting certain attitudes toward (certain aspects of) ourselves—for example, for valuing certain of our powers and capacities, our interests, our moral standing, and so on. The absolute value of humanity provides a perfectly general basis for respecting such capacities and interests in any human being. That we as agents are in a special position either to support or, on the other hand, to neglect or undermine the relevant capacities and interests in ourselves, and that we can and do act in ways that evidence failure to properly value these capacities and interests, gives us occasion to apply to ourselves the general reasons stemming from the absolute value of humanity. Of course, despite their common basis, we should not expect a precise correspondence between self-regarding and other-regarding duties, since the failures of self-respect to which we are liable do not always parallel the characteristic failures to respect others that occasion our duties to them. That aside, the general point is that merely having a share in the dignity due to persons in virtue of their humanity does not guarantee that one will respect its instantiation in one's own case.

The problems on which I focus emerge from Kant's attempt to dispel an apparent conceptual difficulty that he thinks attends the concept of duties to oneself. Essentially, he takes a fairly straightforward concept and, rather than shedding light on it, puts it under a cloud. But obfuscation gives commentators their work, and I will try to extract something of interest from Kant's fleeting remarks (perhaps more interest than he intended). I begin with a brief commentary on the introductory sections of Kant's treatment of duties to oneself. I then focus on the general model of duty that appears to be operative in these passages. Here I will be concerned both with how we should understand this general model of duty if we are to accommodate duties to oneself (as I think we should), and with how duties to oneself fit into a general model of duty that can be supported on independent grounds. As the essay proceeds, I also examine the connection, if any, between duties to oneself and Kant's notion of self-legislation—his thesis that the agents who are subject to moral requirements must be regarded as their legislators. Finally, I ask how duties to oneself fit into the social conception of morality and practical reason that I think we may attribute to Kant, and some variant of which is widely accepted among contemporary theorists who draw inspiration from Kant (constructivists, contractualists, and so on).

II. AN ANTINOMY IN THE CONCEPT OF DUTIES TO ONESELF?

In §§ 1–3 of the *Doctrine of the Elements of Ethics* (*MdS* 6: 417–20) Kant raises a foundational question about the concept of duties to oneself that takes the form of an antinomy: the concept of a duty to oneself at first seems contradictory (§ 1). But there are duties to oneself, since if there were not, there would be no duties whatsoever (§ 2). Like his other antinomies, this one is resolved by appeal to some distinction between noumena and phenomena, in this case a distinction between human beings viewed as natural beings with reason—*homo phenomenon*—and 'the same human being thought in terms of his *personality*, that is as a being endowed with *inner freedom* (*homo noumenon*)' (§ 3). This distinction is to dispel the initial appearance of contradiction, thus securing the possibility of duties to oneself, presumably by giving us two different senses in which to understand the agent in such duties. Going through these arguments in more detail will enable me to raise some of the questions and problems that I wish to address.

Here is the genesis of the (potential) contradiction that Kant sees:

> If the I *that imposes obligation* [*das Verpflichtende Ich*] is taken in the same sense as the I *that is put under obligation* [*dem Verpflichteten*], a duty to oneself is a self-contradictory concept. For the concept of duty contains the concept of being passively constrained [*einer passiven Nötigung*] (I am bound [*verbunden*]). But if the duty is a duty to myself, I think of myself as *binding* and so as actively constraining (I, the same subject, am imposing obligation [*Ich bin . . . der Verbindende*]). And the proposition that asserts a duty to myself (I *ought* to bind myself) would involve being bound to bind myself (a passive obligation that was still, in the same sense of the relation, also an active obligation), and hence a contradiction. (*MdS* 6: 417)

A noteworthy feature of this passage is Kant's adoption of an apparently voluntaristic and social model of duty according to which obligations are generated by some kind of interaction between agents, in which one agent makes a demand on another. This passage implies that in any duty there is an agent who is passively constrained and an agent who actively constrains the first through an act of volition. The passively constrained agent is the subject of obligation (*'subiectum obligationis'*)—the agent bound to act in a certain way. The active agent imposes the obligation on the subject through his will and (as indicated by a later remark at *MdS* 6: 442) is the agent *to whom* the duty is owed. Duties to oneself require that a single agent occupy both roles, but that appears to involve a contradiction when that agent is 'taken in the same sense'. The problem is not simply an inconsistency in the idea of a single agent both constraining and being constrained. Rather, the idea of constraint becomes meaningless or incoherent when a single agent occupies both of these roles, and that leads to a contradiction. Kant continues:

One can also bring this contradiction to light by pointing out that the one imposing obligation (*auctor obligationis*) could always release the one put under obligation (*subiectum obligationis*) from the obligation (*terminus obligationis*), so that (if both are one and the same subject) he would not be bound at all to a duty he lays upon himself [*der er sich auferlegt*]. This involves a contradiction. (*MdS* 6: 417)

When I occupy both roles, I (the active agent who imposes the obligation) am free to release myself when I (the passively constrained agent) am not inclined to fulfill the obligation, and that makes the idea of constraint meaningless. But a duty that one is not bound to fulfill (or where disinclination to fulfill the duty is a reason to be released from it) is self-contradictory.

The second prong of the antinomy, however, asserts that were there no duties to oneself, 'there would be no duties whatsoever, and so no external duties either' (*MdS* 6: 417). Since there clearly are some such duties, it follows that there are duties to oneself. There may be some temptation to read Kant as saying that duties to oneself are in some sense the foundation of all duty—for example, because a failure to live up to one's obligations to others shows an insufficient regard for one's own capacity for principled conduct (i.e., for one's personality), and therefore a failure of self-respect. (In literal Kant-speak, in violating your duty you would act in a way that is beneath your dignity as a moral agent and bring dishonor on your personality, thus displaying improper regard for that part of yourself.) For duties to oneself to be the foundation of all duty, one would have to hold that respect for one's own moral capacities is the fundamental reason for complying with any duty—so that, for example, the duty to respect the dignity of one's own personality provides the basic reason to fulfill one's other duties, or is in some way the reason why they are duties. However such a view seems untenable: the reason to treat others according to moral standards is that they make claims on us in virtue of their humanity, and such considerations should be sufficient to motivate our conduct.[1]

Moreover, while Kant's theory may allow for the view that respect for one's own personality provides supporting reasons for conscientiousness in one's duties to others, that is not the issue here. His argument (for the claim that if there were no duties to oneself, there would be no duties whatsoever) reads as follows:

For I can recognize that I am under obligation to others only insofar as I at the same time put myself under obligation, since the law by virtue of which I regard myself as being under obligation proceeds in every case from my own practical reason; and in being constrained by my own reason, I am also the one constraining myself. (*MdS* 6: 417–18)

Kant's point here is that the kind of self-constraint involved in laying down obligations on yourself is the foundation of all duty, so that any difficulty in the idea of constraining or binding oneself that vitiated the concept of duties to oneself would also undermine duty generally.[2]

In the *Groundwork*, Kant argues that all duties are in some sense self-imposed or self-legislated in that agents bound to moral requirements are bound in such a way that they must be regarded as legislating. As we have seen in previous chapters, Kant's thesis that rational agents legislate moral requirements for themselves needs to be stated with care. The basic idea is that moral requirements are rooted in principles that are generated by a deliberative procedure—the CI procedure[3]—that is grounded in or constitutive of the nature of rational volition, and which all moral agents are equally authorized to employ. '[T]he law by virtue of which I regard myself as being under obligation proceeds in every case from my own practical reason' (*MdS* 6: 417) in the sense that the deliberative procedure by which moral requirements are generated—the procedure that gives a principle the status of law—is constitutive of rational volition. My capacity to guide my own willing by this deliberative procedure (i.e., by the CI) invests me with agency in the fullest sense by enabling me to act as an autonomous sovereign agent, and when my willing does have the form of law, I maintain and express my sovereign status.

No matter how one interprets Kant's claims about moral agents giving law for themselves, it should be clear that legislating the moral law is not the special province of any one individual. Since moral principles are universal in scope, one legislates for moral agents generally, and not just for oneself. Moreover, the agents for whom one gives law have the same rational capacities and legislative status as oneself. From this it should follow that one can only will as moral laws principles that (it is reasonable to think) could command agreement among rational agents generally and that such principles are arrived at through a process of deliberation in which all agents have a share. It is for such reasons that the fundamental principle underlying this deliberative procedure may be understood as the higher-order principle of willing principles that can gain the agreement of all members of a community of ends.[4]

It is not widely recognized that it is a conceptual truth that moral requirements are self-legislated: this thesis is a node in the analytical argument of *Groundwork*, II, which unpacks what is contained in the ordinary concept of duty as an unconditional requirement on action. The fact that it follows from the concept of an unconditional requirement that they are legislated by those agents subject to them permits Kant to deny that there is any general incoherence in the idea of constraining or binding oneself through self-imposed principles. But if there is no general incoherence in the idea of being bound to self-given principles, then there should be nothing incoherent in the self-constraint at issue in the limited case of duties to oneself. Conversely, if an incoherence in the idea of binding oneself (imposing obligations on oneself) undermined the idea of duties to oneself, it would undermine all duties. Since there is no reason to think the latter, we can dismiss the prospect of the former.

The argument of § 2, if successful, indicates that the apparent inconsistency in the concept of duties to oneself should be resolvable, though without showing how. The 'Solution' in § 3 is supposed to fill this gap, suggesting that the contradiction dissolves when we understand the agent in duties to oneself in two different senses. Kant writes that when we are conscious of being subject to duty, we think of ourselves 'under two attributes', as sensible beings and as intelligible beings with 'the incomprehensible property of freedom' (transcendental freedom). This dual view of ourselves is evidently the basis of the distinction in the next paragraph between *homo phenomenon* and *homo noumenon*—between man as a natural being with reason who 'can be determined by his reason, as a *cause*, to actions in the sensible world' and 'the same human being thought in terms of his *personality*, that is, as a being endowed with *inner freedom*' (*MdS* 6: 418). However, a problem now arises because Kant seems to baldly assert rather than to argue that there is no contradiction in the idea that a being with personality or inner freedom can have obligations to himself: 'But the same human being thought in terms of his *personality* . . . is regarded as a being that is capable of obligation and, indeed, [of obligation] to himself [*ein Verpflichtung fähiges Wesen, und zwar gegen sich selbst*] (to the humanity in his own person)' (*MdS* 6: 418). In other words, Kant seems to simply claim that one who is capable of obligation has obligations to oneself.[5]

In fact, there is an argument that we can read into this passage that supports this response and shows that it is not vacuous. Agents who are subject to duties must view themselves 'under two attributes' because they are moved by different kinds of incentives. Agents who experience moral principles as duties are moved by sensible incentives that can conflict with reason. But since they have an interest in acting from moral principles, they may assume that they have a capacity to act from reasons that make no reference to empirically given desire-based interests; in other words, they ascribe transcendental freedom (personality) to themselves. Moreover, drawing on the argument of *Groundwork*, II just cited, agents subject to unconditional requirements are bound in such a way that they must regard themselves as their legislators. That is, not only do they ascribe transcendental freedom to themselves, they may also ascribe to themselves a special legislative capacity, a power to give supreme law through their willing. Furthermore, rational agents are committed to according supreme value to this legislative power, and it confers the special status of sovereign legislator, in virtue of which they possess dignity and are entitled to respect. Now agents with this legislative power can act in ways that do not acknowledge its proper value—for example, by failing to preserve or develop this power, by acting as though they did not possess it or were not entitled to the special moral standing that it confers, by exercising their power of choice in a way that is unworthy of someone invested with this legislative power, and so on. Accordingly there is occasion for this legislative power in oneself (call it one's 'personality' or 'humanity') to make claims on one's own attitudes and choices.

In this way Kant can in fact argue that those who have obligations have obligations to themselves. Briefly, those who are subject to obligations must also possess deliberative capacities of supreme value, and these capacities make claims on their choices and attitudes toward themselves. However, this reading of the passage introduces two further problems. First, it is unclear how appeal to the two aspects plays any role in dispelling the apparent contradiction. We expect the distinction between phenomena and noumena to rescue the idea of constraining or binding oneself from becoming meaningless by enabling us to think of the agent in two different senses. But in fact the agent as noumenon occupies both roles of binding and bound (*der Verbindende* and *der Verbunden*). Only the self regarded as transcendentally free can be subject to obligation; Kant is explicit that in thinking of man as a natural being (as phenomenon) 'so far the concept of obligation does not come into consideration' (*MdS* 6: 418). And the capacities that make special claims on our choices are those attributed to the self as noumenon. Crudely put, it is the legislative capacities of the noumenal self—our humanity or personality— that impose demands on the noumenal self's choices and attitudes toward itself. Intuitively it seems correct that duties to oneself require that we think of a single agent in two different senses, but the distinction between self as phenomenon and self as noumenon has not provided a way to do this. Second, if the basis of duties to oneself are the claims that one's own humanity makes on one's actions and attitudes, then the apparent contradiction in the concept of duties to oneself is removed not by viewing the subject under two different aspects, but, it would seem, by moving away from the voluntaristic and social model of duty that seems to have created the problem in the first place. Quite simply, if duties to oneself come from the fact that I am vested with certain capacities whose value I ought to acknowledge, it is unclear both how I bind myself to such duties through an act of volition and how I could release myself from any such obligations. The basis of duties to myself would be the perfectly general value of my humanity (or the capacity for humanity in me), in conjunction with my being specially positioned to either care for or neglect it in my own case, and there is nothing that I could do that would release myself from any duties that it imposes.

In the balance of this essay, I address a number of issues raised by these arguments. First, I will examine the suppositions about duty that lead to the apparent contradiction in the idea of duties to oneself—what I have been calling the 'voluntaristic and social model of duty' according to which obligations are imposed by one agent actively constraining another agent through his or her will. I think that it is fairly clear that this model does not represent Kant's considered view about duty in the simple form in which it appears to be employed in this passage. Still I think that Kant is a voluntarist about duty in a limited sense: one dimension of his view that moral requirements are self-legislated is that they are, in some sense, created through rational volition, indeed by the willing of those agents subject to duty. I also think that Kant's understanding of morality is essentially social in certain respects, in that the volitional process that gives rise to duties should ultimately be viewed as a deliberative process in which all rational agents have an equal share, the aim of which is to arrive at principles that all agents can endorse. So it is important to see what modifications may be needed in the model of duty that is operative in these passages. Here I want to draw on these remarks about duties to oneself to get clear about the general model of duty, specifically to get a model of duty that can accommodate duties to oneself; but also to see how duties to oneself fit into a general model of duty that can be supported on independent grounds.

I then want to assess the alleged kinship between the notion of constraining oneself at issue in duties to oneself and in self-legislation. If one were worried that the concept of a duty to oneself presupposed an untenable notion of binding or constraining oneself, then a gesture toward the idea of self-legislation (binding oneself through self-given laws) would seem appropriate. The same problems that Kant raises here for duties to oneself have been raised by others in regard to the idea of self-legislation. G. E. M. Anscombe, for example, dismisses Kant's notion of self-legislation as patently absurd (though I think that her objection misses its target).[6] So if one had shown that the idea of giving laws for oneself was not only coherent, but essential to an accurate understanding of moral requirement, it would be proper to allay these concerns about duties to oneself by noting their parallels with self-legislation. However, I will argue that duties to oneself and self-legislation have less in common than Kant supposes in that they involve different senses of constraining or binding oneself.

III. THE MODEL OF DUTY

Let me begin with two extended observations about the model of duty with which Kant operates in these and related passages in the *Doctrine of Virtue*. After exploring this model, I will suggest some modifications.

First, the opening of § 1 suggests the view that duties are standardly generated by a kind of volitional activity or interaction between rational agents, which, looking ahead (as well as back to *Groundwork*, 4: 433–4), I'll characterize as the reciprocal interaction and mutual influence of rational wills who co-exist as (equal legislating) members of a community of ends. As we have seen, in this passage (§ 1) Kant states that the concept of duty involves the idea of being passively constrained, but he also implies that in any instance of duty there is standardly an agent who actively constrains the first through his or her will, to whom the subject has the duty—hence the idea that duties are generated by some kind of volitional activity or interaction.[7]

This reading is reinforced by the assertion in § 16 that 'duty to any subject is moral constraint by that subject's will' (*MdS* 6: 442). To place this remark in context, note that what we might call the 'beneficiary' of the duty—the person (or thing) for whom the subject of duty is directed to care, who would benefit from the performance of the duty—is not always the person to whom one has the duty. Kant claims that the 'constraining subject' to whom one has a duty is always a person, indeed one 'given as an object of experience, since man is to strive for the end of this person's will and this can happen only in a relation to each other of two beings that exist' (*MdS* 6: 442). We can have duties not to destroy inanimate beauty, duties not to be cruel to animals, and a duty to regard all our duties as divine commands. But while these are, respectively, 'duties with regard to' (*in Ansehung*) animals, inanimate beauty and 'what lies entirely beyond the limits of our experience' (*MdS* 6: 443), they are not *duties to* these beings and entities. We can only have duties to beings with whom we can enter a certain kind of (reciprocal) relationship. In the case of animals and inanimate objects, this is precluded by their lacking wills; with transcendent entities (God and angels), the problem seems to be that we cannot interact or have relationships with them (at least not in ways that we know of). In each of the above cases, the duties are 'with regard to' these entities, but 'to ourselves'.[8]

What does Kant mean by 'moral constraint by a subject's will'? The 'moral constraint' readily connects to the familiar idea that limits on permissible conduct toward an individual are established by what that agent wills or can reasonably endorse. At the most general level, our duty in relation to others is to act only from principles that they can at the same time will, or to act toward others in ways that we can justify to them as agents with autonomy by appeal to jointly willed principles. If an agent affected by your conduct cannot reasonably endorse your conduct (or cannot will the general principle that would warrant it) then it is impermissible. How one is obligated to act in specific circumstances is thus a function of the particular principles that an agent can will or reasonably endorse.

There are different ways of understanding how another's will might be the source of these constraints, and these lead to different pictures of the form of activity by which agents might be thought to constrain or impose obligations on each other. Assuming that these constraints take the form of principles, one option is that they are principles that the agents with whom we interact explicitly voice or accept. A second option is that they are principles that it is reasonable for others to endorse, or which they are committed to accepting as rational agents with autonomy. A third option envisioning minimal activity on the part of the constraining agent is suggested by a reading of the absolute value of humanity or the capacity for rational volition. Moral constraint by a subject's will could be construed as the limits on conduct that are set by the absolute value of an agent's humanity—that in virtue of its absolute value, an agent's capacity for rational volition is a source of reasons that make claims on rational conduct. Of these options, the third is best folded into the second, since humanity has its absolute value in virtue of attitudes that rational agents have toward their humanity that are implicit in the nature of rational choosing. And I will simply suggest without argument that of the remaining two, it is preferable to opt for the second, according to which the standard of what an agent wills is ideal rather than actual acceptance of some set of principles. However, I would add this proviso: that the only reliable way that we have of ascertaining which principles agents with autonomy would find it reasonable to endorse in the ideal is through some kind of actual deliberative interaction with the kinds of agents we encounter under normal circumstances.

Moral constraint by a subject's will would accordingly be constraint by a principle or set of principles which that subject can reasonably will or endorse (or which the agent is committed to accepting as a rational agent with autonomy), which gives that agent a claim of some kind in the situation in question. But it should also be clear that (according to Kant) if the principle is reasonably endorsed by the agent to whom one has the duty, it is reasonably endorsed by any agent, including the passively constrained subject of duty. The principles by which we are bound in particular circumstances are not idiosyncratically willed by the agent advancing the claim, but are general principles that any agent can reasonably endorse. For that reason, these constraints should be understood as mutual and reciprocal limits and claims that agents jointly impose on each other through their willing.

The second general observation is that the interaction through which agents are thought to impose duties on each other has a kind of formal structure that is a function of the various *positions* or *roles* that agents can occupy within such interaction. If we succeed in articulating the various positions that make up this structure, we will have the model of duty that Kant employs. The two principal positions encountered so far are those of the passively bound agent, whom we may call the *subject* of duty (*subiectum obligationis*), and the active constraining agent, to whom the subject has the duty. Kant at one point refers to the latter as the *author* (*auctor obligationis*), but for reasons that will become clear, I will refer to the (agent in the) *source* position (the agent who is the source of the duty, to whom one has the duty). A third position is that of the *beneficiary* of a duty (the agent who would be the object of the subject's attention if the duty is fulfilled). As we will see, such positions represent roles that individuals can play in a complex normative structure, and are defined by specific deliberative questions and procedures for seeking to resolve them. They also represent different aspects of our relationship to moral principles. One potential advantage of developing this model is that it should provide a simple way to assess the coherence of the concept of a duty to oneself and to make plain the kind of self-constraint that it presupposes. Duties to oneself simply rest on the possibility of a single agent occupying both the subject and source positions (the 'to' position). However to see what this amounts to, we need to develop the model further, and in particular to see what the source position entails.

The idea of positions within a form of interaction should not strike us as strange given Kant's talk in the *Groundwork* (and elsewhere) of agents who legislate universal law through their maxims. Duties obviously have subjects—agents who are bound to act in certain ways under certain circumstances. Kant continues one line of the law tradition in ethics in thinking that duties are (in some sense) created by a process of volition and thus may also be understood to have a legislator. The language of moral legislation is appropriate due to Kant's belief that moral principles are generated and given authority by the application of a deliberative procedure that is acknowledged to be law-creating, much as positive civil laws are enacted by a sovereign carrying out a recognized legislative procedure. In addition, Kant's revolutionary insight that agents who are subject to duties must be regarded as their legislators is just the claim that the subject and legislative positions must be occupied by the same agents—in particular, that one who can occupy the subject position must also be able to occupy the legislative position.

Since Kant says that the agent to whom a subject has a duty actively imposes obligation on that subject through his will, one may be tempted to identify the source position suggested by these texts from the *Doctrine of Virtue* with the more familiar legislative position of the *Groundwork*. That is, one might think that the agent actively imposing obligation (*der Verbindende* or *der Verpflichtende*) is its 'legislator', and that the duty is owed to the agent in the legislative position. A legislator, after all, is an agent who actively imposes obligations on some set of subjects through the exercise of his or her will, and Kant appears to hold that a duty is to a particular agent in virtue of that agent's active role in imposing obligation or binding the subject. However identifying the source position with the legislative position would be a mistake, since that would lead to anomaly in the agent to whom the subject has the duty. Kant holds that the agent subject to a duty is also its legislator, 'since the law by virtue of which I regard myself as being under obligation proceeds in every case from my own practical reason' (*MdS* 6: 417–18). But if the agent in the legislative position is also the person to whom one has the duty, it would follow that all of one's duties are to oneself. That seems clearly wrong. Alternatively, we might make better sense of self-legislation by understanding moral principles as willed through a deliberative process in which all rational agents have an equal share. Again, if the person to whom one has a duty is the legislator, would it then follow that all duties are owed to all agents? That is equally unacceptable. If, as one might want to hold, the self that legislates is the impersonal self who could be any agent, and if the will of this impersonal self is the shared will of rational agents generally, to be constructed through a deliberative process in which all agents have an equal share, then these two options are not really distinct. Both make the idea that duties are standardly 'to' some distinct agent or set of agents quite idle in roughly the same way.

The general point is that if the agent who is the source of the duty is its 'legislator', then no particular agent is singled out as the person to whom the subject has the duty. If we agree that there is standardly some particular agent to whom the subject in any given situation has the duty, who is the source of the obligation (say, the source of the claim on the subject's conduct), then the source position must be kept distinct from the legislative position. Each may be a position from which agents can constrain or bind others in some sense, but if so, the kinds of constraint exercised will differ. This is because the agent to whom one has a duty is some specific individual, for example an individual who has some kind of claim on one's conduct. But no discrete individual is singled out as the legislator of a moral principle. While any moral agent must be able to identify with and to participate in the 'legislative process', it is not owned by any particular individual.

So far I have been treating the idea that there is an agent active in imposing obligation, to whom the subject has the duty (the source position), as basically unproblematic. But perhaps we need to rethink the source position. Is the idea that a duty is standardly to some specific agent or set of agents really a well-defined notion that we want to retain?[9] I think that we can define the source position through the idea that duties standardly are to some specific individual—for example, to the person who is the source of the claim on the subject's conduct. I also think that we should retain this idea, though circumspection is called for in characterizing this agent as active in imposing obligation. It may clarify things to note that there are different senses in which an agent might be the source of an obligation that Kant appears to conflate in the passages from the *Doctrine of Virtue*. A legislator is the source of binding norms by carrying out a legislative procedure. In a different sense, the agents with whom one interacts are a source of reasons for action, or claims on one's actions, in accordance with jointly willed principles. The source position amounts to the second of these notions. The distinction that Kant evidently fails to draw is that simply as occupant of the source position one is not the source of these general principles in the way that a legislator's will is the source of law.

Very generally, the individual to whom one has a duty in a given situation is the individual whose condition, interests, circumstances, or relationship or past dealings with oneself, and so on, give one reasons for action which make a special claim on one's conduct. That is to say that it is the person who, under the circumstances, is the source of reasons for one to act, or the source of some claim on one, in accordance with jointly willed principles. Put another way, the person to whom one has the duty is the person toward whom one is required to direct a certain kind of regard by some moral principle or set of moral considerations. That duties are standardly to specific individuals is a basic feature of Kant's moral theory because Kantian principles in effect tell us to direct certain forms of moral regard toward the individuals with whom we interact. The directionality and sense of the 'to' is given by the fact that the fundamental moral requirement (expressed in one way) is to adopt certain attitudes toward those with whom we interact. We have a general duty to show proper regard which is specified by substantive principles that pick out certain facts about a person's condition, needs, interests, circumstances, and so on, as the source of reasons for one to treat or view those individuals in certain ways.

We may safely maintain that duties are standardly to specific individuals as long as we recognize both that the way in which one can come to have a duty and what follows from one's having a duty to some individual (or group of individuals) vary widely from one kind of duty to another. Perfect duties of justice give one a clear understanding of what it is for a duty to be to another, and it is in this context that the phrase 'duty owed to an individual' is most appropriate. But we can hold that duties are standardly to specific agents without maintaining that they are owed to individuals in the way that duties of justice are owed.[10] Principles of respect for rights, of non-deception or non-manipulation, of promise and contractual obligations, of mutual aid, of beneficence, of gratitude, of loyalty, of respect, and so on, generate duties toward individuals in different ways. They single out different features of a person's condition or circumstances as giving rise to reasons for action, and what they give reasons to do (whether it is perform or refrain from some specific action, to adopt certain attitudes, etc.) will depend upon the principle—and often on the circumstances of action as well. Similarly whether performance of a duty can be demanded or enforced, what forms of complaint or censure may be voiced, and by whom, when a duty is not fulfilled will differ widely between duties of justice and duties of virtue, between perfect and imperfect duties, and so on (as specified by further jointly willed principles). It is unlikely that the 'to' (in the phrase 'duty to X') indicates any unique relationship beyond that sketched above in that there is no unitary account of how individuals come to have claims on others (are sources of reasons for action), or of what follows from the existence of such claims.

The agent who is the source of a duty, then, to whom the subject has the duty, is a claim-holder whose humanity constrains permissible conduct in some way specified by jointly willed principles. That agent is the source of reasons for action according to jointly willed principles, but is not, as such, the source of those principles. What, then, remains of the idea that an agent who is the source of a duty actively binds the subject of duty, or exercises 'moral constraint through his or her will?' What Kant says about this topic requires some modification. I have suggested that we interpret Kant's claim that duty presupposes an agent who actively constrains or binds the subject as the claim that duties are generated by the reciprocal interaction and mutual influence of equal legislating members of a community of ends. Both what Kant says and my reading of it fit the activity of 'moral legislation' better than they fit any activity of the agent who is the source of a duty. Is there indeed any interesting sense in which the agent who is the source of a duty is 'active' in binding the subject of duty through his or her will? Simply as the source of a duty an agent is not active at the 'legislative level' of willing or laying down principles that are generally binding, but there is room for activity and interaction between agents who are concerned to resolve normative issues by appeal to shared (i.e., co-legislated) principles—interaction at what we might call the 'level of agency'. For example, substantive principles that determine what the general demand for proper regard requires in specific circumstances enable individuals to advance certain kinds of claims and mutual demands. Settling what an individual may legitimately demand, or what constraints apply to some agent's conduct, by appeal to shared principles (determining the proper application of such principles) standardly involves some kinds of dialogue and interchange between agents. There are various ways in which jointly willed moral principles structure and mediate a kind of interaction between agents by putting individuals in a position (the source position) to express and to advance legitimate claims and to demand certain concrete forms of respect.

The conclusion that I want to draw in this section is that these pages of the *Doctrine of Virtue* employ a certain model of duty that needs to be expanded by adding a legislative position distinct from the positions of subject, source, and beneficiary. These positions are associated with different deliberative concerns and represent different roles that individuals may play in moral reasoning and deliberation. The concern of agents in the legislative position is to arrive at general authoritative principles that all can endorse, and they do so by use of the Categorical Imperative. The resulting principles require them, as agents, to direct certain forms of regard toward those with whom they interact, or who are potentially affected by their choices, and they determine individuals' duties in specific situations. In that way these principles specify situations in which agents are subject to duty and create various subject positions. Conversely they pick out certain facts about the condition and circumstances of agents as sources of reasons that make claims on permissible conduct. In so doing, they put individuals in a position to express and advance certain kinds of claims, thereby specifying various 'source positions' that agents can occupy in their interaction with others (or with themselves). Agents in the subject and source positions are concerned, respectively, with the duties by which one is bound and with the demands that one may legitimately place on the attitudes and conduct of agents generally. These questions are resolved by principles arrived at by the Categorical Imperative.

Finally, we should note that within this model there are different levels, as it were (or perhaps just different deliberative tasks), on which agents can interact and exert reciprocal influence on each other. At the legislative level there is deliberation guided by the Categorical Imperative, the aim of which is to settle on principles that any agent can endorse. At the level of agency there is a kind of give-and-take between individuals as subjects and sources of duties that is mediated by jointly willed principles. Here the concerns are to determine the bearing and proper application of jointly willed principles and to settle on the legitimate claims that they support and what they give individuals reason to do in specific situations.

IV. IMPLICATIONS

So far I have developed this model of duty primarily with duties to others in mind. Let me now return to the questions raised by Kant's so-called 'antinomy' in the concept of duties to oneself and consider what this model implies for duties to oneself. There are three specific points that I want to make. First, I comment on how this model supports the overall coherence of duties to oneself. Second, contrary to what Kant implies in the second prong of his antinomy, this model makes it clear that there is no special link between duties to oneself and self-legislation because different senses of constraining or binding oneself are at issue in each. Finally, it shows how duties to oneself fit into an essentially social picture of morality.

A. The coherence of duties to oneself

The model of duty outlined here makes it clear that a duty to oneself is one in which a single agent occupies both the subject and source positions—that is, is both the subject of duty and the source of the claim on that subject's choices. (As an aside, the same individual may, but need not be the 'beneficiary' of such duties. If we accept Kant's claim that lying violates a duty to oneself, we would have a case where other agents are the beneficiaries of a self-regarding duty. Here respect for one's own personality and for the natural purpose of one's capacity to communicate one's inner thoughts would give one reasons to be honest with others.) There is no particular bar to filling out the schema in this way (same individual as subject and source). It may not be easy to ascertain what these duties are, how we should react to those who, in our judgment, fail to fulfill them, and so on. But as long as there are reasonable principles that pick out certain facts about ourselves and our capacities for rational choice as the source of (non-prudential) reasons for us to regard or treat ourselves in certain ways, there are duties to oneself.

In § 3 (the 'Solution to this Apparent Antinomy'), Kant appears to suggest that the idea of a duty to oneself is sustainable only if, in thinking of a single agent as both the subject of duty and its source, we are taking that agent in two different senses. Earlier we saw that Kant's attempt to provide these different senses through the distinction between phenomena and noumena is misleading, since it is the agent as noumenon who is both the subject and the source of the duty (*der Verbunden* and *der Verbindende*). However the model of duty does give us different ways of viewing a single agent by setting out different positions that an agent can occupy within a complex structure or form of interaction that is sustained by the reasoning of a plurality of agents. It is an added benefit that the different senses of the agent are not provided by a distinction with distinctly metaphysical overtones but, roughly, by a distinction between different roles that an agent can occupy within a kind of social structure or form of social interaction.

B. Self-legislation and duties to oneself

Put in terms of this model of duty, Kant's claim that moral principles are legislated by those subject to them is the claim that the agents who occupy the subject position also occupy the legislative position. I noted earlier that the way in which agents bind themselves through their own legislation needs to be stated with care. The legislative position is not uniquely occupied by any single agent, but is shared equally with others. Moreover, the activity of giving law through one's willing is not carried out by individuals in isolation, but occurs in the context of and is made possible by a deliberative procedure that is social in nature—a procedure that all agents have equal authority to employ, the aim of which is to generate authoritative principles that all members of a community of ends (equal co-legislators) can endorse, whose successful employment by any individual requires confirmation by concurring judgments of others, and so on. Thus the claim that one is bound by one's own legislation refers to the active and shared role that any agent has in the deliberative procedure that generates the moral constraints on one's conduct.

A view commonly attributed to Kant is that one is bound to moral requirements *because* one legislates them (for oneself?)—as though one imposes obligation on oneself by simply exerting one's will in the form of a universal principle intended to guide one's own conduct. While it is strictly speaking correct that one is bound to moral requirements because of one's legislative role, this idea can be understood in a way that is misleading. Agents are not bound to moral principles simply by the fact of their share in the legislative process. Rather they are bound to moral requirements by what makes them valid moral principles, which is that they result from an authoritative deliberative process (i.e., the CI). What gives authority to this process is that it is the deliberative procedure that is constitutive of (autonomous) agency. As such it confers on any individual the power of (autonomous) agency—which is to say, confers the status of sovereign legislator on that agent—and gives any agent an equal share in the willing of universal law. To the extent that I am committed to my own agency, I am committed to guiding my will by this deliberative procedure (the CI), and my share in its employment allows me to accept the resulting principles through my understanding of the reasoning that stands behind them (from the inside, as it were). In a word, I am bound to moral principles by the fact that they result from an authoritative deliberative procedure, and what gives the procedure its authority is the legislative role that it confers on me.

By now it should be evident that self-legislation and duties to oneself involve different notions of constraining oneself that correspond to the senses of constraining or imposing obligation associated respectively with the legislative level and the level of agency. In self-legislation 'I am the one constraining myself' in that I am through my legislative role the source (with others) of the laws by which I am bound. I have argued that my binding or imposing obligation on myself should here be understood as my active role as a co-legislator in willing principles that apply to agents generally. In a duty to oneself, 'I am the one constraining myself' in that I am, in virtue of my humanity, a source of reasons or claims applying to my own actions in accordance with jointly willed principles. The constraints are claims that my own humanity makes on my conduct stemming from jointly willed principles concerned with how individuals should regard or treat themselves. In certain respects, the relationship that I have to myself in a duty to self is more individualized. In self-legislation one wills for agents generally, and this capacity to will principles that others can recognize as authoritative is what makes one an agent. In a duty to yourself, *your* humanity makes claims on you as an agent—though these claims are generated by a legislative process and the resulting principles that mediate between you as subject and you as the source of reasons for yourself.

C. Duties to oneself and a social conception of morality

It is often thought that a purely social conception of morality leaves no room for duties to oneself. Proponents of such conceptions of morality take that thought to argue against the existence of duties to oneself, and proponents of duties to oneself take it to argue against purely social conceptions of morality. However, I have (I believe) been assuming a conception of morality as social. I attribute to Kant (and endorse) the idea that duties are generated by a kind of volitional activity between agents, which I have characterized as the reciprocal interaction and mutual influence of rational wills who co-exist as members of a community of ends. So far, I see no reason to think that this conception of morality excludes the possibility of duties to oneself. Furthermore, I take it that this general conception of morality is accepted in some form by many contemporary Kantian theorists, many of whom are favorably disposed toward duties to oneself. So I will conclude with a brief suggestion as to how duties to oneself are consistent with and fit into an essentially social conception of morality.

What makes a conception of morality 'social' is a large issue, but what starts one in that direction might be the belief that moral principles in some way arise out of relations between individuals and presuppose some kind of interaction between individuals.[11] From here one can get different conceptions of morality as social in nature depending on whether the interaction that one has in mind occurs at the 'legislative level' or at the 'level of agency'. Characterizations of morality as social commonly focus on the latter. They think that such a conception takes moral principles (or the need for them) to be generated by a kind of interaction between individuals at the level of agency, for instance by demands that individuals make on each other as agents advancing their own interests in a social setting. According to such a view, the need for morality is created by the conflicting interests of largely self-concerned agents, and its purpose is to regulate interaction between agents in some impartial manner—for example, to establish limits on individual conduct, to set out legitimate demands that individuals may advance against each other, and so on. Such a conception of morality would appear to leave no room for duties to oneself, but only by begging an important question, since it defines morality in such a way as to exclude duties to oneself. It is fair to ask why we should accept such a definition of morality.

However, a conception of morality that takes moral principles to be generated by a deliberative process in which all agents have a share is equally a social conception of morality. I have suggested that we attribute to Kant the view that the legislative capacities that we possess as individuals are to be exercised with and among others, guided by the regulative aim of arriving at general principles that all members of a community of ends can endorse. This is a social conception of morality that takes moral principles to be generated by interaction between agents at the legislative level. If this legislative process generates principles concerning how individuals should treat themselves, then there is room for duties to oneself within a social conception of morality.

This suggestion raises an immediate question: what role does deliberation addressed to a plurality of agents play in generating duties to oneself, and why is this sort of mutual and reciprocal influence needed to generate such duties? One reason to assume a plurality of legislators in arriving at interpersonal principles is to ensure that the principles realize certain self-standing moral ideals such as equal consideration for the interests of all or equal respect for each individual considered as an agent with autonomy. A process of deliberation in which all members of some moral community have an equal share (among other things) considers the impact of potential principles on individuals from the perspective of each individual. In this context, that the resulting principles can be endorsed by all, or can be justified to each person (from his or her own perspective), reflects the fact that they give adequate weight to the interests of, or show equal respect for, each person. Equal respect and justifiability to each person (and so on) are central moral ideals that principles governing interpersonal conduct and attitudes should express. But they do not seem to be at issue in duties to oneself.

However in a Kantian context, that a principle is endorsable by any rational agent does more than indicate that it satisfies certain purely moral ideals. It shows in addition that the principle carries the authority of reason, and that points to a role for a plurality of legislators in generating principles of self-regarding duty.[12] The normative force of principles that are willed through a process of deliberation in which all individuals have a share will not depend on assumptions or values that not all agents must accept. A deliberative process whose regulative aim is general agreement among a plurality of agents will eliminate proposed principles of self-regarding duty that are purely personal in nature, or which have only partial authority that depends on values that are reasonably rejected. We might also want to say that it will uncover any considerations that are pertinent to the adoption of any proposed principle. All of this is to say that such principles bear the authority of reason. So a partial answer to this question is that it is through a deliberative process in which all agents have a share that a principle comes to have the authority of reason, and that any principles that ground genuine duties must have this imprimatur.[13]

NOTES

1. Even so, one might hold that duties to oneself play an important subsidiary role in moral thought. For example, one might hold that certain duties to oneself are morally central because they are duties to develop those rational capacities and sensibilities which enable one to fulfill one's duties generally. Or one might argue that self-respect provides a subsidiary reason, indeed a basic reason with the strength of duty, to fulfill one's duties to others, because you dishonor yourself by failing to do so. (For suggestions of this sort, see Nelson Potter, 'Duties to Oneself, Motivational Internalism, and Self-Deception in Kant's Ethics', sect. I.) However, there still must be reasons independent of one's attitude toward oneself that make these actions duties. You only dishonor yourself by acting in certain ways, for example, if there is an independent basis for regarding the action as wrong. (Here consider Hume on why regard for the virtue of an action cannot be the primary motive to virtuous conduct, *Treatise*, Bk. III, pt. II, sect. 1.)

2. As a point of clarification, we should note that all choice, prudential as well as moral, can involve the kind of self-constraint involved in controlling one's choices, setting aside motives that distract one from one's goals, and so on. The kind of self-constraint that appears problematic is not this kind of self-control, but that of imposing obligation on yourself through your own will.

3. The 'CI Procedure' normally refers to the deliberative procedure associated with the Formula of Universal Law. However I will use it very broadly to refer to some interpretation of the Categorical Imperative—that is, a deliberative procedure based in any of the formulas—that can be used to generate substantive moral principles. It is unclear how the Formula of Universal Law bears on duties to oneself, and it is generally agreed that Kant bases such duties on the Formula of Humanity. So for the purposes of this essay, it may be best to think of the 'CI Procedure' as a procedure of deliberation associated with the Formula of Humanity.

4. This claim is developed in Chapter 6.

5. I am grateful to Bernd Ludwig for pointing out a problem with Mary Gregor's translation, which I have altered in accordance with his suggestion. The claim that I suggest can be read into this passage, and which can be defended, is the claim that one who has obligations has obligations to oneself. However, what Kant says here is that the human being regarded as possessing personality is 'capable of obligation and, indeed, to himself . . . [*ein Verpflichtung fähiges Wesen, und zwar gegen sich selbst*]'. *Verpflichtung* does not specify whether the agent is *der Verpflichtende* or *der Verpflichtete* (the agent who obligates or the agent who is obligated), and presumably includes both. The assumption of beings who are 'capable of obligation' (*ein Verpflichtung fähiges Wesen*) is in fact sufficient for the argument, since all such beings presumably have obligations.

6. See G. E. M. Anscombe, 'Modern Moral Philosophy'.

7. Here note Kant's references to *das Verpflichtende Ich, der Verbindende, einer aktiven Nötigung, das nötigende (verpflichtende) Subjekt*, etc., at *MdS* 6: 417 and 442.

8. It is easy to provide examples in which the beneficiary of a duty is not the person to whom it is owed: you promise a dying friend that you will help his children get through college; or you agree to the organizer of a conference to get your paper to your commentator by a specified date: it would seem that the first duty created by the promise is to your friend/to the organizer, but that the beneficiary is the friend's children/the commentator (though one may have further duties to the beneficiary in each of these cases).

   Since Kant treats the distinction between duties to oneself and duties to others as exhaustive, we may assume his view to be that in every case there is an agent to whom a duty is owed, thus an agent who actively imposes the duty through an exercise of will. The presence of an agent who actively binds the subject of duty would accordingly be a general feature of duty within this model.

9. For another discussion of the idea that duties are to someone, see Thomas E. Hill, Jr., 'Servility and Self-Respect', in his collection *Autonomy and Self-Respect*, 16–18.

10. For this reason I have tried to use the phrase 'agent to whom one has the duty' rather than 'agent to whom the duty is owed' where stylistic considerations permit. When I have used the latter I intend it in a broad sense.

11. See Kurt Baier, *The Moral Point of View*, 215, 234. Baier is cited by Lara Denis in 'Kantian Ethics and Duties to Oneself'.

12. For further discussion of Kant's views about the authority of reason, see Onora O'Neill, *Constructions of Reason*, chs. 1–3 and *Towards Justice and Virtue*, ch. 2.

13. Thanks to Stephen Engstrom for his comments.

9

Agency and the Imputation of
Consequences in Kant's Ethics

I

In his notorious essay, 'On A Supposed Right to Lie from Philanthropy', Kant makes a set of claims that have greatly embarrassed many of his supporters. The Murderer in pursuit of the Friend whom you have taken into your house is now at your door, and has asked whether your Friend is there. Not only does Kant hold that it is one's duty to be truthful in this situation. He also states that the agent who does lie, and thus acts contrary to duty, may be held responsible for any bad consequences that might result. He writes:

That is to say, if you have *by a lie* prevented someone just now bent on murder from committing the deed, then you are legally accountable for all the consequences that might arise from it . . . It is still possible that, after you have honestly answered 'yes' to the murderer's question as to whether his enemy is at home, the latter has nevertheless gone out unnoticed, so that he would not meet the murderer and the deed would not be done; but if you had lied and said that he is not at home, and he has actually gone out (though you are not aware of it), so that the murderer encounters him while going away and perpetrates the deed on him, then you can by right be prosecuted as the author [*als Urheber*] of his death. For if you had told the truth to the best of your knowledge, then neighbors might have come and apprehended the murderer while he was searching the house for his enemy, and thus the deed might have been prevented. (*VRL* 8: 427)

To make things worse, Kant appears untroubled by the coincidental nature of the link between the agent's lie (violation of duty) and the bad outcome. In his view, neither the unforeseeability of the consequence nor the fact that its immediate cause was the wrongful act of another agent severs the link between the lie and the death of your friend. In this essay, Kant focuses on the legal responsibility (legal liability) of the liar for the bad consequences of a lie, but discussion of a similar case in *The Metaphysics of Morals* indicates that he would also hold the liar morally responsible for these consequences:

For example, a householder has ordered his servant to say 'not at home' if a certain man asks for him. The servant does this and, as a result, the master slips away and commits a serious crime, which would otherwise have been prevented by the guard sent to arrest him. Who (in accordance with ethical principles) is guilty in this case? Surely the servant, too, who violated a duty to himself by this lie, the results of which his own conscience imputes to him. (*MdS* 6: 431)

In these passages we find Kant relying on the following principles for imputing the consequences of an action to its agent: when an agent acts contrary to a strict moral requirement (a perfect or juridical duty which one may be compelled to perform), all of the bad consequences that occur as a result of that violation, whether foreseeable or not, are imputable to the agent.[1] Conversely, no bad consequences that result from an agent's compliance with strict moral requirements are imputable to that agent. In the latter case, bad consequences, including those that are imminent and foreseeable, are to be regarded as an 'accident', and compliance with duty blocks the imputation of any resulting harms to the agent (*VRL* 8: 428).

In this essay I analyze the structure and underlying rationale of Kant's principles of imputation (*Zurechnung*), with particular concern for his principles governing the moral imputation of bad consequences.[2] Among other things, I want to show how Kant's principles make the imputation of actions and consequences a question for practical reason, rather than a straightforward factual, causal, or metaphysical issue. For Kant the imputation of actions and consequences is made within the context of, and depends upon, the application of first-order moral norms governing conduct (those setting out strict moral requirements). In addition, I want to suggest that Kant's principles of imputation are generally sound, though they need to be qualified in important ways that I take up at the end of the essay.

Given what Kant says in 'On a Supposed Right to Lie', an attempt to take his views about imputation seriously may appear a dubious enterprise. Kant's conclusions in this essay are clearly flawed. But their defects are due to his accepting a rigoristic moral principle that makes no allowance for particularities of circumstance and gives insufficient weight to potential consequences and outcomes. The problems, in other words, stem from his conception of what one's moral requirements are in this situation. His essay illustrates the moral incoherence that results when principles basing the imputation of consequences on compliance with duty are applied in conjunction with first-order moral principles that are insensitive to consequences. But I do not see that it reveals any fundamental defect in Kant's principles of imputation. For Kant, questions of what is imputable can only be resolved after one has determined what an agent's moral requirements in a given situation are. For this reason, his principles of imputation will seem plausible only when applied in conjunction with moral principles which give adequate weight to foreseeable and potential consequences of actions and which assign responsibility for avoiding and preventing harms and bad outcomes in a reasonable way. For the purposes of this paper, I will assume without argument that Kant's moral theory may be understood in this way, and that his theory does not require the rigorism displayed in 'On a Supposed Right to Lie'.[3]

II

In the *Metaphysics of Morals*, Kant explains the concept of imputation in this way: '*Imputation* (*imputatio*) in the moral sense is the *judgment* by which someone is regarded as the author (*causa libera*) of an action, which is then called a *deed* (*factum*) and stands under laws' (*MdS* 6: 227).

Further elaboration is found in the *Lectures on Ethics*:

All imputation is the judgment of an action, insofar as it has arisen from personal freedom, in relation to certain practical laws. In imputation, therefore, there must be a free action and a law. We can attribute a thing to someone, yet not impute it to him; the actions, for example, of a madman or a drunkard can be attributed, though not imputed to them. In imputation the action must spring from freedom. The drunkard cannot, indeed, be held accountable for his actions, but he certainly can, when sober, for the drunkenness itself. So in imputation the free act and the law must be conjoined. (*MP-C* 27: 288)

Both actions and their consequences can be imputed. Whether one's action is to one's credit or demerit is determined by this principle:

If someone does *more* in the way of duty than he can be constrained by law to do, what he does is *meritorious* (*meritum*); if what he does is just exactly what the law *requires*, he does *what is owed* (*debitum*); finally, if what he does is *less* than the law requires, it is morally *culpable* (*demeritum*). (*MdS* 6: 227)

Kant's principles for imputing consequences to an agent are as follows:

The good or bad results of an action that is owed, like the results of omitting a meritorious action, cannot be imputed to the subject (*modus imputationis tollens*). The good results of a meritorious action, like the bad results of a wrongful action, can be imputed to the subject (*modus imputationis ponens*). (*MdS* 6: 228. Cf. *MP-C* 28: 289–90)

Briefly, no good or bad consequences are imputable to an agent who does neither more nor less than is strictly required. Bad consequences are imputed to an agent (as 'demerit') when the agent violates a strict moral requirement, and when the bad consequences would not have occurred but for the agent's violation. Conversely, when an agent does more than he or she is strictly required to do, any good consequences that occur are imputable as merit.

Legal and moral theorists commonly distinguish different levels of imputation. Imputation at the first level (*imputatio facti*) is the judgment that an action of a certain kind may be traced or assigned to the free agency of some person. It is thus concerned with what action an agent may be said to have (freely) done, or whether an agent has performed an action of a certain kind. Judgments at this level may be understood as primarily factual, rather than evaluative, though even then, as I will suggest, they are made against the background of sets of norms that pick out certain kinds of actions as salient for evaluative purposes. Imputation at the second level (*imputatio juris*) is concerned with the evaluation of an agent. Judgments of this second kind presuppose that the agent has performed (or failed to perform) a certain kind of action; they also presuppose a determination of the normative status of that action by the application of relevant norms or standards. Their aim is to assign to an agent (or to determine whether an agent deserves) praise or blame, credit or demerit, for having performed an action of that kind.[4] While these kinds of judgment are analytically distinct, and while it may be important in many contexts to maintain a sharp distinction between these two levels of imputation, they are commonly run together in ordinary moral contexts. A single judgment may contain an assessment of what an agent has done, an evaluation of the action, and an evaluation of the agent. ('Liar!') Indeed we have no particular interest in making judgments of the first kind except when they ground, or are relevant to, fully evaluative judgments. Our interest in imputability is not theoretical curiosity with what a person has done, but a concern with the moral appraisal of an agent.

From Kant's remarks on imputation it is evident, first, that he does not clearly maintain this distinction, and second, that for the most part he refers to imputation at the second level. That is, the judgments of imputation on which he focuses are a kind of moral appraisal of agents. I will approach Kant's principles of imputation in this light, and will assume that he has in mind a kind of evaluative judgment that attributes either actions or their consequences to an agent in a way that is to the agent's credit or demerit.[5] The imputation of actions is a part of the appraisal of an agent's character, while imputation of consequences to an agent—assigning them to an agent's 'account' or 'record', as it were—is the assessment of the difference which one's choices have made to what happens in the world, or to put it somewhat grandly, the difference which one has made to the course of human events. Both kinds of judgment concern ways in which one can do well or badly in the exercise of one's agency, and as such are part of the moral record of an agent's 'history of action'.[6]

Such retrospective judgments of merit and demerit are based on the principles that govern deliberation prospectively. Judgments imputing the consequences of actions become a possibility as soon as we recognize principles that direct us to deliberate with a concern for the ways in which our choices affect what happens (or fail to when they could have). Some of these principles forbid choices that will have bad consequences, or may direct one to perform an action that will achieve an important good or prevent a substantial harm. But in many cases the outcomes assigned moral significance by such norms are only indirectly connected to the aims and goals that we formulate on our own without moral prompting. If I am in a position to alleviate another person's suffering, or an unfortunate situation created by someone else's neglect, that may be a reason to do so. If an otherwise innocent choice that I favor will provide someone else with the means or the opportunity—or will simply allow—a cruel and malicious action to occur, that is probably a reason to choose differently. The fact that my exerting my influence will keep someone else from a self-destructive act may be a reason to intervene. Sometimes these reasons add up to duties. My point is simply that imputations of consequences (from a moral perspective) evince a concern for, and are attempts to assess, how we have done in relation to the reasons for action that arise out of our ability to make a difference to what happens.

Judgments of imputation are made against a certain background. Before analyzing his principles of imputation, I will show that judgments of imputability are judgments of practical reason, rather than simple factual or empirical judgments, by pointing out different things that Kant has in mind in saying that imputation presupposes both freedom and a law. ('In imputation, there must be a free action and a law . . . the free act and the law must be conjoined' (*MP-C* 27: 288).) First of all, the actions that may be imputed are the voluntary actions of free and responsible agents, which is to say, of agents who have the capacity to understand, apply, and follow relevant normative principles. Lunatics and drunkards when drunk are not 'free agents' in the relevant sense because they lack the psychological capacity to comply with various moral and legal norms.[7] Second, and more importantly, judgments of imputation apply to what Kant terms a 'deed' (*Tat* or *factum*).

A deed is a free action that is subject to the law. (*MP-C* 27: 288)

An action is called a *deed* insofar as it comes under obligatory laws and hence insofar as the subject, in doing it, is considered in terms of the freedom of his choice. By such an action the agent is regarded as the *author* of its effect, and this, together with the action itself, can be *imputed* to him, if one is previously acquainted with the law by virtue of which an obligation rests on these. (*MdS* 6: 223)

Actions that are candidates for imputation to an agent are those that are recognized as deeds by some set of norms, and the last remark suggests in addition that a necessary condition of imputing a consequence or outcome to an agent (regarding the agent as its 'author') is that it result from a deed of that agent. What, then, are 'deeds' and why does Kant think that only deeds and their consequences are imputable?

In defining a deed as a free action that falls under a law, what Kant must have in mind is that laws and normative principles, in addition to assigning acts their normative status, establish and define categories of actions that are significant for evaluative purposes. Before we can assess the normative status of an action, there must be some set of norms and social practices which establishes a category of action as a candidate for assessment and which determines what counts as performing or failing to perform that kind of action. In this way, what (if anything) an agent has done in some situation—or what, for evaluative purposes, we recognize an agent as having done—is determined by some set of norms. (And before we can say whether someone has acted well or badly, we must be able to say what the person has done, by bringing the action under descriptions available to us.) Law provides ready examples of what I have in mind. Traffic laws define certain ways of operating a vehicle as speeding, reckless endangerment, and so on, and thus as liable to penalty. Criminal laws categorize killings as murder, manslaughter, accidental death, and so on, and evaluate them accordingly. Obvious examples outside of the law are the sets of norms that determine what counts as making, breaking, and keeping promises, showing gratitude to a benefactor or failing to, or insulting someone and subsequently apologizing, and so on.

This general observation explains how certain inactions are recognized as omissions, or as actions which one fails to perform. A failure to do something which one could have done becomes an 'omission' when there is a set of norms which singles out that kind of action as potentially called for in that situation. It becomes a blamable omission when that action is morally required. But in the absence of some such norms, an inaction has no significance and is not recognizable as anything at all.[8] (In any given stretch of time there are an infinite number of possible actions that an agent 'did not do', most utterly insignificant.) For example, it only makes sense to say that I failed to help someone when I am in a situation in which helping is appropriate, as specified by norms of beneficence and mutual aid, and in which I am able to help. By Kant's principles, if helping is required and I do nothing, then my failure to help would be imputable to me. If a harm then results that my helping would have prevented, the harm is imputable to me. Likewise, passing the morning watching birds from my veranda is a noteworthy omission when it is my obligation to be lecturing at the university at that time.

A deed, then, is a kind of action recognized as potentially significant for the purposes of evaluation by a set of social, moral, or legal norms. Imputation of an action presupposes the judgment that the agent has performed such an action, as performance is defined by the relevant norms and practices. Since imputation is a kind of appraisal of how one has exercised one's agency, it makes sense to hold that we impute actions and the consequences of actions that have been picked out in this way as morally significant.

An implication of this theory is that voluntary actions within an agent's control not recognized as significant by any set of norms would not count as deeds (relative to those norms), and would not be the kind of thing that it makes sense to impute. For example, my walking down my street to put a letter in the mailbox is something I do. But neither my walking nor my way of walking are the kinds of thing which we have an interest in imputing to me (as Kant understands the concept), since they have no moral significance. Of course if, on my way, I notice that my elderly neighbor has collapsed on his front porch and I keep walking, the situation changes: what I have done now falls under a different description. As I idly skip stones in the ocean on a summer evening, no one would impute to me (as a consequence of my action) the ripples that form in the water or the sinking of the stones, though it is certainly true that I have caused them. Again, the situation changes if they are rare stones that my niece has collected for her geology project, which I am thoughtlessly throwing away. In that case, I may be held responsible for ruining her science project, for her subsequent expulsion from school, and for the life of drugs and crime that followed.

To summarize, there are at least three different respects in which imputation presupposes some set of laws or practical principles. First, the agents to whom things can be imputed must have the psychological capacity to follow the relevant norms, as well as the knowledge that enables them to apply them properly. In other words, whether an agent is free and the action voluntary depend upon whether the agent is able to apply the relevant norms to his or her circumstances. Second, the candidates for imputation are deeds and their consequences, where deeds are categories of actions and omissions that are recognized as significant by a set of norms. Third, whether an action or one of its consequences is imputable to an agent in a given situation turns on what the agent's moral requirements are and whether or not they have been satisfied. An action is imputed (as blamable) when it is a deed that violates a duty; the bad consequences of an action are imputed to an agent when they result from such a violation of duty. (Finally, to these points we might add that such judgments are a moral appraisal of an agent.)

III

The account given so far makes it clear that imputations of consequences are not the same as causal ascriptions. There is a 'factual requirement' that the outcome imputed be a consequence of an agent's action or inaction. But (1) only some of the things that one causes may be imputed, and (2) outcomes may be imputed of which one is not the cause (or the primary cause) in any ordinary sense. To give an example of the first, if a harm is caused either by an action that is morally required or by one that is morally permissible, the harm is not imputable to the agent since he has complied with all applicable moral requirements. Kant gives the example of a general whose orders lead to the death of enemy soldiers. Since he is doing what he is required to do, he is not morally accountable for their deaths. Or take a creditor who causes hardship to a debtor in exercising his right to collect the debt. On the assumption that his actions are fully permissible, the resulting harm would not be imputed to the creditor (though his action may be viewed as its cause).[9]

The second possibility is illustrated by situations in which an action or omission of an agent, A, that violates a moral requirement leads to a situation in which B harms C. Here are some examples: (a) Imagine that A speaks truthfully to the Murderer (B) and gives him the information needed to locate and kill the Friend (C). But let's depart from Kant and classify A's truthfulness as a foolish violation of his duty to preserve the Friend's life. (b) A crafts instructor at a prison (A) carelessly (unintentionally but negligently) includes a sharp knife in the equipment brought to a class. Without the instructor seeing it, a prisoner (B) hides the knife in his clothing, takes it from the class, and later uses it to assault and seriously injure a guard (C). (c) I take my neighbor's power-boat without his permission, while he is away. My neighbor (C) would have lent it had I asked, but would not have approved of my using it without asking. While the boat is tied to my dock, someone (B) steals the outboard motor. (To complicate this example, assume that the same thief would have stolen the motor if I had left the boat at its owner's dock where it belonged.) (d) In Bernard Williams's well-known example, Jim (A), while touring in a Central American country, encounters Pedro (B), a colonel in the right-wing army, who has assembled and is about to execute twenty villagers (C) suspected of having rebel sympathies. Pedro generously offers Jim the opportunity to shoot one of the villagers, and assures him that he will shoot all twenty if Jim passes this opportunity up.[10] Assume for purposes of argument that Jim is morally required to accept Pedro's offer in this situation, but that he declines. In each case, A has violated a moral requirement, and A's doing so leads to a situation in which B wrongfully harms C. Common sense would hold that it is B, not A, who is the primary cause of the harm to C, but on Kant's principles the harm is also imputable to A.

To put the point in general terms, a judgment of imputation asserts a relationship between an agent and a set of bad consequences that may be expressed as follows: it is the relation that one bears to those bad consequences that result from one's violation of a moral requirement. This relation is not the same as 'being the cause of' (though, of course, both relations will obtain where one is the cause of the harm imputed).

Let me add (without argument) that the conclusions supported by Kant's principles strike me as generally acceptable in these cases, though this kind of example indicates the need for certain qualifications. Some of Kant's remarks suggest that in imputing an action or consequence to an agent, we regard the agent as its 'author' (*Urheber*), so that A would be regarded as author of the bad results in each of the above (cf. *MdS* 6: 223, 227). This is acceptable as long as we recognize that 'author' is not the same as 'cause', and allow that an outcome can have several authors. There may be a number of agents who 'authorize' an undesirable outcome by, variously, causing or contributing to its production, by creating the conditions that make its occurrence possible, by failing to take measures in their power to avoid or prevent it, and so on (in each case, in violation of some strict duty). Their role in contributing to the outcome may render them blamable to varying degrees. Moreover, imputing an outcome to one agent does not preclude also assigning blame to others.[11] The bad consequences in these examples are also straightforwardly imputable to B, since B acts wrongly, and since his wrong action is necessary for the occurrence of the harm.

IV

We need consider the underlying rationale of Kant's principles. As we have seen, he appears to hold that all bad consequences that result from a violation of a strict moral requirement may be imputed to the agent, even when they are directly caused by other agents, are unforeseeable, or in some way result from accident or bad luck. Conversely, compliance with duty guarantees the agent immunity from imputability, even when bad consequences are imminent and foreseeable. Why should one accept these principles?

A response is suggested by Kant's claim that 'the key to all imputation in regard to consequences is freedom' (*MP-C* 27: 290). This remark amounts to the claim that we may impute the consequences resulting from actions that are 'freely done' in the sense that the agent is the ultimate source of authority under which that action is undertaken—that is to say, 'its author'. In this particular context, when Kant refers to an action as free or freely done, he means that an agent acts on reasons that are independent of those laid down by an external authority, which one recognizes as reasons at one's own initiative or discretion—as we might say, when you act on your own authority. This goes beyond what is ordinarily meant by 'free action'.[12] But Kant connects free agency to autonomy, and whether an agent is autonomous, as he understands this concept, is a question of whether the agent is subject to requirements laid down by an external authority, or which derive from an external source of reasons. When Kant says that 'the key to all imputation in regard to consequences is freedom', the idea is that the subject to whom an action or its consequences may be imputed is the individual agent on whose authority the action is undertaken: we impute to you the actions and consequences of actions that you do on your own authority.[13] This principle can be used to explain why compliance with duty renders an agent immune from blame while violation puts the agent at risk, as well as why good consequences are imputed as meritorious to an agent who does more than duty requires.

We can clarify what Kant means by free actions in this context by contrasting them with actions that are not free. The primary case of an agent who does not act freely is an agent who is subject to, and complies with, an authoritative requirement that leaves no latitude or discretion in how to act. Examples would be an agent subject to a strict moral requirement (someone who is duty-bound to be truthful and thus not free, or at liberty, to lie), an agent bound by a law or legal arrangement (an agent who is not free to give a good to a someone who needs it because he is contractually bound to give it to another, a judge who is not free to give a lenient sentence to an offender who may be morally deserving of it, and so on), or an agent who is 'under orders' from another agent who has authority over him and has issued a legitimate command.[14] If you act 'under the authority of the law' by complying with a legitimate requirement, you should not be viewed as the 'author' of the action or of its consequences. If you are not at liberty to refrain from an action that foreseeably leads to a harm, it makes no sense to impute that harm to you. It would be imputable to the agent on whose authority you act. And if no such agent can be found—say because the requirement is a moral requirement that does not originate in the will of any individual agent—then the bad results are not imputable to anyone, and must be regarded as an 'accident'.

A different way of 'acting under the authority of a law' represents a secondary class of actions that are 'not free', in this special sense. These are actions permitted by an authoritative law or principle, which can be justified by citing their permissibility. Examples would be the creditor exercising his right to collect his debt; or someone who takes advantage of a loophole in a legal system to benefit himself at the expense of others, who can justify his action by citing the fact that the law permits it. Kant gives the example of an agent who fails to aid another person in need, who can justify his non-beneficence by noting that giving aid is not strictly required in the circumstances.[15] In general terms, one who does neither more nor less than a law requires acts under the authority of that law (rather than on one's own authority), because one allows the law to limit one's conception of what one has reason to do. In doing no less than the law requires, you acknowledge the authority of the constraints that it sets. In doing no more than is required, you allow its strict requirements to exhaust your conception of what you have reason to do in the way of good actions. To justify this limited conception of what good actions you have reason to do, you can cite the fact that no more is strictly required by the law. In doing neither more nor less than is required, you act under authority of the law because you act in a way that is fully authorized by the law. If it turns out that your actions lead to bad outcomes, the consequences should not be imputable to you but to the authority on which you act. And again, if that authority is the moral law, there is no agent to whom the consequences are imputable, and they must be viewed as an accident.

According to this interpretation, the two cases of actions that are free in this special sense are actions that are contrary to strict duty and actions that do more than duty requires. This explains why Kant holds that only the consequences of such actions are imputable. In acting contrary to a strict duty, you depart from the law and do something that you are not authorized to do. Since you can claim no justification for what you do, you act 'under your own authority', and by the principle just stated, are the agent to whom any bad consequences are imputable. Similarly, when you do more than you are strictly required to do, you have broadened your conception of what you have moral reason to do beyond what is narrowly required by the law. Thus, you also act at your own discretion, and it seems fitting that you should get credit for the good that results. In both cases you are the agent on whose authority your actions are taken. Accordingly, it makes sense to view you as the author of the consequences, which is to say, to impute the bad consequences of wrongful acts and the good consequences of meritorious acts.[16]

V

Kant's principles appear to yield plausible and unproblematic results in the range of cases in which what one is required to do is determined by the harms (or other bad consequences) that will foreseeably or may potentially result from one's actions or omissions. The obvious examples are situations in which one has a duty to refrain from a harmful action (because it is harmful); a duty to refrain from an otherwise permissible action that will foreseeably result in an unintended harm in that situation; a duty to avoid creating a risk or a danger to others; a duty to provide aid that would prevent a harm from occurring, and so on. Assume that an agent in such a situation violates or fails to comply with the duty, and that as a result, the harm providing the reason for the duty then occurs. By Kant's principles, the harm would be imputable to the agent, and that seems reasonable. In some cases it may be difficult to determine what one's strict requirements are, especially when it is a question of aiding another or intervening to prevent a harm that will be caused by the wrongful action of a third agent. Presumably there are situations in which one can have a duty to prevent a serious harm, even though the risk or threat of harm is created by others. That, however, is the first question. What is potentially imputable is settled by how such questions about the content of our strict requirements are resolved.

However there are other kinds of cases in which Kant's principles of imputation seem problematic. Kant's discussion of the Murderer at the Door indicates his willingness to impute bad outcomes that were not foreseeable by the agent at the time of action and bad outcomes that appear accidentally connected to the agent's violation. As we might say, Kant's principles require that the agent be 'at fault' by violating a strict moral requirement, but not that the imputable outcome be 'the agent's fault' in the sense that it is caused by the agent's action (or omission) and results from that feature of the action (or omission) that makes it a violation of duty.[17] While it helps to bear in mind that imputation is not intended to be straightforward causal ascription, it is still troubling that Kant's principles appear to allow the imputation of consequences that were not fully within an agent's control (because unforeseeable, or due to the actions of another) and in which the link between the agent's choice and the resulting harm is accidental.

To illustrate the point about accidental harms, let's return to my unauthorized use of my neighbor's boat and consider each of the following outcomes occurring while the boat is under my control: (a) While securely moored at my dock, the boat is destroyed by a storm (which would have destroyed it while moored at my neighbor's dock). (b) The boat is damaged beyond repair when I strike a submerged log while operating it safely in normally good water (where my neighbor might also have taken the boat). (c) The boat sinks because of the worsening of a pre-existing defect in the boat, which is due to my neighbor's failure to maintain it properly. (Assume that the existence of the problem was not evident to me, and that I had no reason to expect it.) (d) The boat is destroyed in an accident with another boat, where I am operating safely and the other is clearly at fault. (e) While operating the boat in a normally busy channel in which swimming is both foolish and forbidden, I strike and kill a swimmer.

These examples bring out a noteworthy feature of Kant's principles. A violation of a moral requirement in the past can ground the imputation of bad consequences to an agent even when there is nothing faulty in the conduct that immediately precedes and leads to the bad consequences in question. In each of these examples I am at fault (violate a strict moral requirement) in taking the boat, but beyond that, there is nothing objectionable in my conduct. Had I been using the boat with permission, there would be no grounds for imputing anything bad to me. More generally, there would be no grounds for imputing the bad consequences to me if, in similar circumstances, I had acted in the same way and with same results, but no violation of duty on my part led to my being in those circumstances. In this sense, the violation of a duty can make all the difference to whether or not a bad outcome is imputable to the agent. It is because of this feature of Kant's view that it will sometimes impute bad outcomes that are accidentally linked to an agent's violation. In these examples, the features of my action that make it a violation of duty are not what lead to the bad results. The harms and damages do not result from any carelessness in the way in which I care for and operate the boat, and in that sense, follow from my violation of duty by accident. However, Kant's principles would appear to impute these bad outcomes to me. Is that reasonable?

I will address this question by laying out the retrospective reasoning in which Kant's principles might lead one to engage. The background is that one is under a strict moral requirement in some situation. I assume that in deciding what one's requirements are, one must deliberate with a view to the potential and foreseeable outcomes that might follow on various choices, and that consideration of these possibilities plays a role in determining what one is required to do. I stress potential outcomes here, because, given the limits on our abilities to predict and to control the outcomes of our actions, it is rational to give weight to kinds of outcomes that sometimes result in situations similar to the one we are in (possibilities within the normal course of events), even if we have no reason to think them at all likely in our actual circumstances. If one reasons conscientiously and satisfies all applicable requirements, then one has done as well as one can. One acts blamelessly, and there are no grounds for imputing any bad results that may then occur. But someone who violates a strict requirement might engage in the following assessment of what he has done after the fact: 'In acting contrary to duty I did something that I should not have done, and moreover, something that I had compelling reason not to do. Since I can act on my judgment of what I have compelling reason to do, I did something from which I could have refrained in the circumstances. Had I acted as I ought, the bad outcome would not have occurred. But since the bad outcome was a consequence of my choice—a choice which in the circumstances I had compelling reason to and was able to refrain from— I must view it as part of the difference that my exercise of my agency has made to the world. That is, I impute it to myself'.

The problem with imputing unforeseeable or accidental harms to an agent is that one appears to be blaming a person for something that was beyond his control, which he could not have prevented in the circumstances. But it is improper to hold someone accountable for an occurrence that he could not have avoided, or could not be expected to have avoided. If that is the objection to Kant's principles, then the line of reasoning just sketched suggests a defense. We could grant that these are cases of unforeseeable or accidental harms, but note that one could have prevented these harms from occurring by complying with one's duty. Moreover, the existence of the duty gave one decisive reason to refrain from the action that in fact led to the harm. Thus one could have acted in a way that would have avoided the bad outcome, and there was a compelling reason in the circumstances to have acted in that way.

This reply fits well into a general analysis of the conditions of responsibility. We commonly hold that a basic condition of holding an agent accountable, either for an action or for its consequences, is that the agent have the ability in the relevant circumstances to refrain from that action (or the action that leads to the undesirable consequences). Showing that the agent, at the time of action, was unable to avoid performing the action (and that this inability is not culpable) precludes imputing it to the agent. What does having the ability to refrain from or avoid an action amount to in this context? It involves at least two things. First, the agent must have the general capacity to reason from factual information and ordinary normative principles to conclusions about how to act, and the capacity to act on one's judgment of what one has most reason to do. Second, the agent must, at the time of acting, be in a position to see that there is reason to refrain from the action. What makes one able to see reason to refrain from the action is, of course, quite complex; but roughly, various factual information and normative principles must be available to the agent, and ordinary reasoning from these facts and principles must support the conclusion that the agent should refrain from the action.

The standard excusing conditions come into play when an agent is unable to avoid or refrain from an action that there is compelling reason not to perform. Certain forms of excuse focus on an agent's capacity for practical reason. Various psychological and physical incapacities excuse either because they render an agent unable to deliberate properly or unable to act on one's judgment of what one ought to do. Coercion, threat, or duress can excuse because they place an agent in a situation in which the reasons that favor an action (wrongful action) outweigh the moral considerations that normally tell against it. Other forms of excuse focus on an agent's state of knowledge. Culpability may be blocked, for instance, when one acts in ignorance, either of fact or of moral principle or law, when the bad consequences are completely unforeseeable by the agent, or when they occur by accident. These factors excuse (when they do) because they are conditions of an agent, or facts about the agent's circumstances, that prevent the agent from seeing that there is reason to refrain from that action in those circumstances. (Here we could say either that there is no reason for the agent to refrain from the action in the circumstances, in the sense that there is no chain of practical reasoning from generally available evidence that leads to the conclusion that the action should not be performed; or we could say that there is no reason which the agent can see.) When I can see that my action is likely to cause some harm—as I am starting to back my car out of my driveway, I notice the five year old from down the street racing down the sidewalk with his tricycle at full throttle—I see reason not to do what I had intended to do. But if I am unable to foresee the likely harm, it cannot figure in my practical reasoning. For example, it is after dark and I do not see the child even after I look up and down the sidewalk, as I normally do because of the ubiquity of neighborhood children. The information that I have provides me no reason not to move my car. Information that I do not have—that little Frank is speeding down the sidewalk in my direction—would lead me to conclude that I should wait; but since I do not have that information, I cannot reach that conclusion.

Briefly stated, then, one can refrain from or avoid an action when one has the capacity to act on one's judgment of what one has reason to do and when considerations available to the agent show that there is reason to refrain from the action. This line of thought helps explain why it is reasonable that a violation of duty make all the difference as to whether or not a consequence is imputable to an agent. When the action that leads to the undesirable outcome is contrary to duty, there is a compelling reason in the circumstances, available to the agent, for refraining from the action. An agent who can see reason to refrain from an action, and can act on his judgment of what he has reason to do is able to avoid the action. By this route one satisfies the common-sense condition of responsibility that the agent to whom a wrongful action or bad outcome is imputed have opportunity to refrain from the action. The unusual feature of this analysis is that it allows this general condition to be satisfied in certain cases where the bad consequences imputed to the agent are unforeseeable and unexpected. An agent can have a compelling reason for refraining from an action that leads to harm, and is thus able to avoid it, even without any knowledge, precise or otherwise, of the bad consequences that are ultimately to be imputed. When the harm resulting from an action is foreseeable, the ability to avoid the action is directly tied to one's ability to foresee its harmful consequences. That factual information, along with relevant normative principles, supports the conclusion that there is reason not to perform the action, and thus puts the agent in a position to avoid it. When the harm cannot be foreseen or predicted, or is completely unexpected in the circumstances, comparable factual information cannot figure in the agent's reasoning about how to act. But since the agent is under a requirement not to do the action, the moral considerations available to the agent are sufficient by themselves to support the conclusion that there is reason not to perform the action. Since, as it were, the moral considerations put the agent in a position to have avoided the action that led to the undesirable consequences, imputing them to the agent is warranted.[18] Thus, the line of reasoning sketched above can apply to bad consequences that an agent was not in a position to see: one did something that one should not have done, and as a result, something bad happened. One could have avoided whatever contribution one made to its occurrence, in the sense that one had a compelling reason in the circumstances to refrain from that action.

I find that this line of thought supports imputing the bad results to me in (b) through (d). I wrongly took the boat, and as a result of my doing so, it was damaged. For all I can see, I could have avoided the harms by leaving the boat where it belonged, as I had compelling reason to, and could have done. (c) and (d) add the complication that negligent or reckless acts of others were also necessary for the occurrence of the bad outcome. But, as noted above, imputation of a harm to one agent does not imply that it may not also be imputed to others, or that no other agents are blamable. (a) is problematic because the same result would likely have happened even had I not taken the boat. But there is an epistemological barrier to citing that possibility to show that the conditions for imputability have not been satisfied. For all I know, things might have turned out differently had I left the boat where it belonged. Since I cannot rule that possibility out, it seems that I am not in a position to disclaim responsibility.

But our reaction to (e) is likely to be different, and examples with this structure point to the need to limit what is imputable to an agent. By what principle should we limit the consequences that an agent may be regarded as authorizing through a violation of duty? The fact that a bad outcome is directly caused by the actions of another agent need not limit imputability, since (I have suggested) there can be strict duties to take measures to prevent harms that may be caused or created by other agents. (Here the limits on our duties to prevent this kind of harm will set limits to what is imputable, presumably on the principle that requiring more than a certain degree of aid and intervention would be unreasonable.) Nor must imputability be limited to outcomes that are foreseeable at the time of acting. It is reasonable to expect agents to take into account the possibility of kinds of outcomes that can result in the normal course of events, even if there is no reason to think them likely (and no way to know that they are likely) in their actual circumstances.

The problem in (e) is that the reasons for action that I have in virtue of standing under the requirement do not extend to the kind of outcome that actually results. The duty in question does not give me a reason to act in ways that generally avoid that kind of result. (That is, the duty to respect another's property does give me a reason to act in ways that will avoid damage to another's property, but not a reason to act in ways that standardly prevent accidental death. Accidental death is not the kind of occurrence that falls within the scope of that duty.) It would seem that the imputation of bad consequences by Kant's principles should be limited along the following lines: an outcome resulting from a violation of duty is imputable to an agent when the requirement under which the agent stands provides a reason to act in ways that will standardly, or under normal circumstances, prevent or avoid (not result in) outcomes of that general kind. There might be different reasons why compliance with the duty would normally prevent that kind of outcome. It could be because that kind of outcome is not an unexpected result of violations of this duty, within the normal course of events. Or it could be because it is the kind of outcome that it is the (or an) aim of the duty to prevent. Or it could be because it is the kind of outcome whose potential occurrence within the normal course of events figures in the explanation of what one's requirements are, or whose potential occurrence as a result of certain kinds of actions figures in the explanation of why those actions are contrary to duty. To illustrate these possibilities in terms of the above examples, the duty not to use another's property without authorization does give me a reason to act in a way that will standardly avoid damage to that property because: (1) it is not unusual for unauthorized use of another's property to result in damage to that property; (2) damage to another's property (resulting from its use by another) is a kind of outcome which property rights aim to prevent; and (3) the possibility of damage while being used by another figures in the explanation of why use by others is wrong.[19] Here are three different ways in which compliance with a duty will standardly prevent certain kinds of consequences; perhaps there are other possibilities as well. This is a complex question that is important for the assessment of Kant's principles, and it deserves more discussion than I am able to give it here.[20]

NOTES

1. In the *Lectures on Ethics*, Kant holds that bad consequences are only imputable when they result from violation of a juridical duty which an agent may be compelled to perform, that is, a violation of a law of the state. Here his concern is with imputation in a legal sense. 'So if I merely do what is requisite, nothing can be ascribed to me in demerit, or merit either . . . For insofar as a man has done what he has to, he is not free, because he has done the action in that he was necessitated by the law. But if he acts contrary to his obligation, it is imputed to him, because there he is acting freely, and contrary, indeed, to the law that necessitates him to . . .' (*MP-C* 27: 1438). See also the next section 'Of the Grounds of Moral Imputation', where Kant says that 'the violation of juridical laws, and the observance of ethical laws must at all times be imputed *in demeritum* and *in meritum*' (*MP-C* 27: 290). However, I assume that his theory may be extended to cover imputation in a broader moral sense, and under 'strict moral requirements', I will be including perfect duties, non-performance of which is wrong and blamable, though not legally punishable. If this is not Kant's meaning, then I am suggesting a modification. As will become clear, I also believe that strict moral requirements can include some duties to give aid, or to intervene to prevent harm to others.

2. That is, I am concerned specifically with imputation of consequences in moral, rather than legal contexts. In most of Kant's discussions of this topic, he appears to be concerned with legal contexts, but I believe that Kant adopts the same basic principles for both. And I limit myself to imputation of bad consequences and related judgments of culpability and demerit, and will not take up meritorious imputation.

3. Many writers sympathetic to Kant have argued that his basic principles do not require the position on lying taken in this essay. For discussion of this and related issues, see Christine M. Korsgaard, 'The Right to Lie: Kant on Dealing with Evil', in *Creating the Kingdom of Ends*; Thomas E. Hill, Jr., 'Making Exceptions without Abandoning the Principle: Or How a Kantian Might Think About Terrorism', in *Dignity and Practical Reason* and 'A Kantian Perspective on Moral Rules', in *Respect, Pluralism and Justice*; and Barbara Herman, *The Practice of Moral Judgment*, ch. 7, esp. 151–7.

4. For a clear presentation of these distinctions see Joachim Hruschka, 'Imputation', esp. 672–86.

5. That is to say that in the rest of this essay, I will be discussing judgments of imputation at the second level. Throughout I am supposing that the imputation of bad

consequences of an action to an agent presupposes imputation of the action at both levels. That is, one must ascertain that the agent has performed an action of a certain kind that violates a moral requirement, and is culpable for having done so. Any bad consequences of the action may then be imputed to the agent (subject to the limitations introduced in Section V).

6. For discussion of the concept of moral 'record-keeping' see Joel Feinberg, *Doing and Deserving*, 124–8. Cf. also Tony Honoré, 'Responsibility and Luck', esp. 531, 537–45, who argues that responsibility for the outcomes of our actions is essential to an agent's personal identity and character.

7. Presumably ignorance of the facts also renders one unable to properly apply and act from the norms governing one's circumstances. For a good general discussion of the concept of voluntary actions and moral responsibility, see Alan Donagan, *The Theory of Morality*, ch. 4.

8. Kant registers this point in the following passage: '. . . but those consequences that arise from the non-performance of ethical action cannot be imputed, since it cannot be regarded as an action when I leave undone what I had no liability to do. So ethical omissions are not actions; but juridical omissions are, and can be imputed, for they are omissions of that to which I can be necessitated by law' (*MP-C* 27: 290). I presume that regarding something as an action (*Handlung*) in this context is the same as regarding it as a deed.

9. Here again one must take into account the foreseeable and potential harms in determining what the general's duties are and what the creditor is morally permitted to do. When the creditor's collection of the debt would cause severe hardship to the debtor, that may impose moral limits on his rights to collect. I assume that Kant's conclusions about the imputability of consequences in such cases will be reasonable when based on a conception of duty that gives proper weight to imminent harms and other sorts of undesirable outcomes.

10. Bernard Williams, 'A Critique of Utilitarianism', in *Utilitarianism: For and Against*, 98–100.

11. Note that in the case of the servant who lies at the householder's request, Kant says that 'the servant too' is guilty: 'die Schuld fällt auch auf den [Dienstbote]' (*MdS* 6: 431). The fact that he made it possible for his master to commit the crime does not diminish the master's guilt.

12. This remark introduces a different sense in which actions and consequences may only be imputed to agents who act freely from that discussed above. In the first sense, agents acting freely are responsible agents acting voluntarily; in this sense, they are agents who act outside the range of any moral requirements, or who act 'on their own authority'. To combine these conditions, potentially imputable actions are those voluntary actions of responsible agents that are deeds undertaken at the agent's own authority.

13. We may also impute to you actions, and consequences of actions, done by others at your authority. So some actions that are not done freely (i.e., whose agents do not act freely) are still imputable. If I act under your authority, I do not act freely. But my action, or its consequences, could still be imputable to you. The principle determining when an action or consequence is imputable is that there be some agent on whose authority it is done; this need not be the agent who actually executes the action.

14. Thus, of the agent who speaks truthfully to the Murderer at the Door, Kant says that it was 'merely an *accident* (*casus*) that the truthfulness of the statement harmed the

resident of the house, not a free *deed* (in the juridical sense)' (*VRL* 8: 428). The deaths of the enemy soldiers are not imputed to the general because, given that his action is coerced by the law, it is not considered to be free: 'It is the question whether one may impute to someone what he had to do in virtue of the law, to a general, for example, the death of so many foes left on the battlefield. Their death, to be sure, not their murder. But here he is considered insofar as his action was not free, but compelled by law, and in that sense it cannot be imputed to him. As a free action it would be ascribed to him, but as a legal action not to him, but to whoever gave the law' (*MP-C* 27: 289). Someone who fulfills an obligation is not free, that is, not at liberty to act otherwise. Someone who acts against a law, though he misuses his freedom, acts freely, and the consequences of his actions may be imputed to him: 'For insofar as a man does what he has to, he is not free, because he has done the action in that he was necessitated by the law. But if he acts contrary to his obligation, it is imputed to him, because there he is acting freely, and contrary, indeed, to the law that necessitates him to the action; he is thus misusing his freedom, and here all the consequences can legitimately be imputed to him' (*MP-C* 27: 1438).

15. *MP-C* 27: 1438. It seems a distortion to say that actions of this sort that are permitted or authorized by morality or law are 'not free'. The principles in question do not require, but simply leave the agent free to undertake the action in question, and it is up to the agent whether or not to do it. But the point is that actions permitted in this way may be performed under the authority of the principle that permits them, rather than under the agent's own authority. The existence of the permission or authorization allows an agent to shift responsibility for the action away from himself and onto the principle that permits it. The agent might perform the action because, and only because, it is permitted (i.e., would not perform it were it not permitted), and can cite the principle for justification. Someone who profits from a legal loophole might say that since he is doing what the law permits (and would not do it were it not permitted), there is nothing wrong with what he does. The problem, if there is one, must lie in the law that permits his act. There is a clear sense in which someone who in this way acts within the scope of a moral or legal principle takes his reasons for action from that principle, and thus 'acts under the authority' of that principle.

16. In this section I have suggested that agents who act on a moral requirement (and in a secondary sense, on a moral permission) do not act on their own authority but on the authority of the moral law, and that one acts on one's own authority when one does either more or less than duty requires. But this reconstruction of Kant's theory would appear to conflict with his view that the agents who are subject to moral laws must also be viewed as their legislators. In other words, if moral agents legislate the moral law, as Kant holds, agents who act on moral requirements do act on their own authority. One way to resolve this problem is to note that moral agents do not legislate the moral law as individuals. It is more accurate to say that the 'legislation' that produces moral principles is the collective use of human reason, in which all rational agents participate equally. When an agent acts on moral principles, the action is authorized by those uses of reason that are universally valid (universally justifiable), and the agent is no more or less its author (i.e., the authority on which it is undertaken) than any other moral agent. An agent who does more or less than duty requires acts on his or her own personal authority in virtue of having gone beyond the limits on action established by those uses of reason that are universally valid in the ways pointed out. That is the

ground for imputing the consequences of these actions to the agent. But when bad consequences result from actions that are either morally permissible or morally required, responsibility must be shared equally by all moral agents. Either no particular agent is blamable, or no one agent more than any other.

17. Here I draw on Joel Feinberg's analysis of 'his fault' judgments—judgments to the effect that a bad outcome was 'his (or her) fault' (*sua culpa*). See Joel Feinberg, 'Sua Culpa', in *Doing and Deserving*, 187–221. Feinberg's initial analysis holds that a harm is a person's fault when (1) the person's action or omission was at fault (violates a duty or is otherwise morally defective); (2) the faulty act (or omission) caused the harm; (3) the act caused the harm in virtue of its faulty aspect. The third, or 'causal relevance', condition is designed to rule out accidental connections between a faulty act and the resulting harm, such as a situation in which an unlicensed driver operating a vehicle 'in an (otherwise) faultless manner causes an edgy horse to panic and throw his rider' (ibid. 195). We would not say that it was the driver's fault that the horse threw his rider. Though the driver was at fault in driving without a license, his being unlicensed (the faulty aspect of his conduct) is not what caused the horse to panic. To handle further complications that I will not go into, Feinberg's final analysis of *sua culpa* is this: (1) the person's action or omission was at fault, and is at fault in virtue of creating an unreasonable risk of harm; (2) the faulty act (or omission) caused the harm; and (3) the harm that resulted falls within the scope of the risk of harm in virtue of which the act was at fault. In other words, the action is at fault in virtue of creating the risk of a certain kind of harm, and the harm that resulted from the action is a harm of that kind (ibid. 199).

My point above is that while Kant's principles of imputation require both that an agent violate a strict duty and that the violation be necessary for the occurrence of the bad results, as stated so far, they do not seem to require that the harm be 'the agent's fault' in the sense just given. The issue that needs to be addressed is whether Kant's principles of imputation must be supplemented by some kind of causal relevance condition, and how best to do so within a Kantian framework.

18. The fact that these accidents occur as a result of a violation of duty does set them apart from accidents resulting from permissible actions, because the duty provides reason to refrain from the action that led to the harm. Imagine that the boat that I damage in example (b) by striking a submerged log is my own. It is true that I could have avoided the accident if I had not taken the boat out that afternoon. But if I felt like taking the boat for a spin, there was no reason not to. Nothing in my circumstances gave me any reason to refrain from the action that eventually led to the accident. Part of what places an accident or completely unforeseeable consequence beyond an agent's control, or renders it unavoidable in the circumstances, is that the agent in that situation had (i.e., could see) no reason to refrain from the action that in fact led to the harm. The existence of the requirement changes things by giving the agent a compelling reason not to perform the action that leads to the bad results. In this sense, accidents resulting from a violation of duty are 'avoidable' in a sense in which accidents resulting from permissible actions are not.

19. To return to the Murderer at the Door, the scenario that Kant imagines may not be as improbable as it seems. If you believe that truthfulness is unconditionally required in all circumstances, and your Friend knows this, it is not surprising that he would sneak out the back door, since he would expect you to reveal his whereabouts if asked.

Common knowledge that people accept certain principles can ground expectations about how they will act in various situations. In a context where most people take truthfulness to be required without exception, the well-intentioned lie could represent a departure from what is normal that could lead to the conjunction of events that Kant imagines. Thus, given Kant's conception of what is required, the kind of outcome that he imagines would not be an unexpected departure from the normal course of events. It is the kind of possibility that the deliberating agent has a reason to consider (even if there is no way to know that it is likely in the actual circumstances), and the duty to be truthful would give the agent a reason to act in ways that would normally avoid that kind of outcome.

20. This essay was first presented at a conference on 'Zurechnung von Verhalten in Recht und Moral' at the Institüt für Strafrecht und Rechtsphilosphie, Universität Erlangen-Nürnberg in October 1993, and later given to the Department of Philosophy, University of North Carolina, Chapel Hill. I am indebted to members of both audiences for their comments. In particular, I would like to thank Thomas E. Hill, Jr., Gerald Postema, Cheshire Calhoun, and Friedrich Toepel.

Bibliography

Allison, Henry E. *Kant's Theory of Freedom* (New York: Cambridge University Press, 1990).
—— *Idealism and Freedom* (New York: Cambridge University Press, 1996).
Anscombe, G. E. M. 'Modern Moral Philosophy', in G. E. M. Anscombe, *Collected Philosophical Papers, Vol. III: Ethics, Religion, and Politics* (Minneapolis: University of Minnesota Press, 1981).
Aune, Bruce. *Kant's Theory of Morals* (Princeton: Princeton University Press, 1979).
Baier, Kurt. *The Moral Point of View* (Ithaca, NY: Cornell University Press, 1958).
Bauch, Bruno. *Immanuel Kant* (Berlin and Leipzig: de Gruyter, 1921).
Beck, Lewis White. *A Commentary on Kant's Critique of Practical Reason* (Chicago: University of Chicago Press, 1960).
Bittner, Rüdiger. *What Reason Demands* (New York: Cambridge University Press, 1989).
Brandom, Robert. 'Freedom and Constraint by Norms', *American Philosophical Quarterly*, 16/3 (1979), 187–96.
Broadie, Alexander, and Elizabeth Pybus. 'Kant and Weakness of the Will', *Kant-Studien*, 73/4 (1982), 406–12.
Christman, John, ed. *The Inner Citadel* (New York: Oxford University Press, 1989).
Clarke, Samuel. *A Discourse of Natural Religion*, in D. D. Raphael, ed., *British Moralists, 1650–1800*, i (Oxford: Clarendon Press, 1969. Reprinted by Hackett Publishing, 1991).
Cohen, G. A. 'Reason, Humanity and the Moral Law,' in Christine Korsgaard, *The Sources of Normativity* (New York: Cambridge University Press, 1996).
Cohen, Joshua. 'The Natural Goodness of Humanity', in Andrews Reath, Barbara Herman, and Christine M. Korsgaard, eds., *Reclaiming the History of Ethics* (New York: Cambridge University Press, 1997).
Darwall, Stephen L. *Impartial Reason* (Ithaca, NY: Cornell University Press, 1983).
Denis, Lara. 'Kantian Ethics and Duties to Oneself', *Pacific Philosophical Quarterly*, 78/4 (Dec. 1997), 321–48.
Donagan, Alan. *The Theory of Morality* (Chicago: University of Chicago Press, 1977).
Dworkin, Gerald. *The Theory and Practice of Autonomy* (New York: Cambridge University Press, 1988).
Engstrom, Stephen, and Jennifer Whiting, eds. *Aristotle, Kant, and the Stoics* (New York: Cambridge University Press, 1996).
Feinberg, Joel. *Doing and Deserving* (Princeton: Princeton University Press, 1970).
—— *Social Philosophy* (Englewood Cliffs, NJ: Prentice-Hall, 1973).
Foot, Philippa. *Virtues and Vices* (Berkeley and Los Angeles: University of California Press, 1978).
Förster, Eckart, ed. *Kant's Transcendental Deductions* (Stanford, Calif: Stanford University Press, 1989).
Frankena, William K. *Ethics* (Englewood Cliffs, NJ: Prentice-Hall, 1973).
Frankfurt, Harry G. *The Importance of What We Care About* (New York: Cambridge University Press, 1988).

Freeman, Samuel. 'Reason and Agreement in Social Contract Views', *Philosophy and Public Affairs* 19/2 (1990), 122–57.

—— 'Contractualism, Moral Motivation, and Practical Reason', *The Journal of Philosophy*, 88/6 (1991), 281–303.

Gauthier, David. *Moral Dealing: Contract, Ethics, and Reason* (Ithaca, NY: Cornell University Press, 1990).

Green, T. H. *Collected Works*, ii, ed. R. L. Nettleship (London: Longman, Green & Co., 1886).

Griffiths, A. Phillips. 'Kant's Psychological Hedonism', *Philosophy*, 66 (1991), 207–16.

Guyer, Paul, ed. *The Cambridge Companion to Kant* (New York: Cambridge University Press, 1992).

—— *Kant's Groundwork of the Metaphysics of Morals: Critical Essays* (Totowa, NJ: Rowman and Littlefield, 1998).

——*Kant on Freedom, Law, and Happiness* (New York: Cambridge University Press, 2000).

Hart, H. L. A. *The Concept of Law* (Oxford: Oxford University Press, 1961; 2nd edn., 1994).

—— *Essays on Bentham* (Oxford: Oxford University Press, 1982).

—— 'Positivism, Law, and Morals', in H. L. A. Hart, *Essays in Jurisprudence and Philosophy* (Oxford: Clarendon Press, 1983).

Herman, Barbara. *The Practice of Moral Judgment* (Cambridge, Mass.: Harvard University Press, 1993).

—— 'Rethinking Kant's Hedonism', in Alex Byrne, Robert Stalnaker, and Ralph Wedgwood, eds., *Fact and Value: Essays on Ethics and Metaphysics for Judith Jarvis Thomson* (Cambridge, Mass.: MIT Press, 2000).

Hill, Thomas E., Jr. *Autonomy and Self-Respect* (New York: Cambridge University Press, 1991).

—— *Dignity and Practical Reason* (Ithaca, NY: Cornell University Press, 1992).

—— *Respect, Pluralism, and Justice* (New York: Oxford University Press, 2000).

Honoré, Tony. 'Responsibility and Luck', *The Law Quarterly Review*, 104 (Oct. 1988), 530–53.

Hruschka, Joachim. 'Imputation', *Brigham Young University Law Review* (1986), 669–710.

Hume, David. *A Treatise of Human Nature*, 2nd edn., ed. P. H. Nidditch (Oxford: Oxford University Press, 1978).

Irwin, Terence. 'Morality and Personality: Kant and Green', in Allen W. Wood, ed., *Self and Nature in Kant's Philosophy* (Ithaca, NY: Cornell University Press, 1984).

—— 'Kant's Criticisms of Eudaemonism', in Stephen Engstrom and Jennifer Whiting, eds., *Aristotle, Kant, and the Stoics* (New York: Cambridge University Press, 1996).

Kerstein, Samuel J. *Kant's Search for the Supreme Principle of Morality* (New York: Cambridge University Press, 2002).

Kolodny, Niko, and R. Jay Wallace. 'Promises and Practices Revisited', *Philosophy and Public Affairs*, 31/2 (Spring 2003), 119–54.

Korsgaard, Christine M. *Creating the Kingdom of Ends* (New York: Cambridge University Press, 1996).

—— *The Sources of Normativity* (New York: Cambridge University Press, 1996).

—— 'From Duty and for the Sake of the Noble: Kant and Aristotle on Morally Good Action', in Stephen Engstrom and Jennifer Whiting, eds., *Aristotle, Kant and the Stoics* (New York: Cambridge University Press, 1996).

Korsgaard, Christine M. 'The Normativity of Instrumental Reason', in Garrett Cullity and Berys Gaut, eds., *Ethics and Practical Reason* (New York: Oxford University Press, 1997).

—— 'Self-Constitution in the Ethics of Plato and Kant', *The Journal of Ethics*, 3 (1999), 1–29.

McCarty, Richard. 'Kantian Moral Motivation and the Feeling of Respect', *Journal of the History of Philosophy*, 31/3 (1993), 421–35.

—— 'Motivation and Moral Choice in Kant's Theory of Rational Agency', *Kant-Studien*, 85/1 (1994), 15–31.

MacCormick, Neil. 'Voluntary Obligations and Normative Powers, I', *Proceedings of the Aristotelian Society*, suppl. vol. 46 (1972), 49–78.

Nagel, Thomas. *The Possibility of Altruism* (Princeton: Princeton University Press, 1970, 1978).

—— 'Rawls on Justice', in Norman Daniels, ed., *Reading Rawls* (New York: Basic Books, 1975).

—— *The View from Nowhere* (New York: Oxford University Press, 1986).

Nozick, Robert. 'Coercion', in Robert Nozick, *Socratic Puzzles* (Cambridge, Mass.: Harvard University Press, 1997); originally published in Sidney Morgenbesser, Patrick Suppes, and Morton White, eds., *Philosophy, Science, and Method: Essays in Honor of Ernest Nagel* (New York: St Martin's Press, 1969).

O'Neill, Onora. *Constructions of Reason* (New York: Cambridge University Press, 1989).

—— 'Enlightenment as Autonomy: Kant's Vindication of Reason', in Peter Hulme and Ludmilla Jordanova, eds., *The Enlightenment and its Shadows* (London and New York: Routledge, 1990).

—— 'Vindicating Reason', in Paul Guyer, ed., *The Cambridge Companion to Kant* (New York: Cambridge University Press, 1992).

—— *Towards Justice and Virtue* (New York: Cambridge University Press, 1996).

—— 'Within the Limits of Reason', in Andrews Reath, Barbara Herman, and Christine M. Korsgaard, eds., *Reclaiming the History of Ethics: Essays for John Rawls* (New York: Cambridge University Press, 1997).

—— *Bounds of Justice* (New York: Cambridge University Press, 2000).

Parsons, Charles. 'Mathematics, Foundations of', in Paul Edwards, ed., *The Encyclopedia of Philosophy*, (New York: Macmillan Publishing Co., 1967; repr. 1972).

Paton, H. J. *The Categorical Imperative* (Philadelphia: University of Pennsylvania Press, 1971).

Pogge, Thomas. 'The Categorical Imperative', in Paul Guyer, ed., *Kant's Groundwork of the Metaphysics of Morals: Critical Essays* (Totowa, NJ: Rowman and Littlefield, 1998).

Potter, Nelson. 'The Argument of Kant's *Groundwork*, Chapter 1', in Paul Guyer, ed., *Kant's Groundwork of the Metaphysics of Morals: Critical Essays* (Totowa, NJ: Rowman and Littlefield, 1998).

—— 'Duties to Oneself, Motivational Internalism, and Self-Deception in Kant's Ethics', in Mark Timmons, ed., *Kant's Metaphysics of Morals: Interpretive Essays* (Oxford: Oxford University Press, 2002).

Pratt, Michael. 'Promises and Perlocutions', in Matt Matravers, ed., *Scanlon and Contractualism* (London and Portland, Ore: Frank Cass Publishers, 2003).

Raphael, D. D., ed., *British Moralists, 1650–1800*, Vol. I (Oxford: Clarendon Press, 1969; reprinted by Hackett Publishing, 1991).

Rawls, John. 'Two Concepts of Rules', *The Philosophical Review*, 64/1 (1955), 3–32; repr. in Rawls, *Collected Papers*.

—— *A Theory of Justice* (Cambridge, Mass.: Harvard University Press, 1971; rev. edn., 1999).

—— 'Kantian Constructivism in Moral Theory: Rational and Full Autonomy', *The Journal of Philosophy*, 77/9 (1980), 515–34; repr. in Rawls, *Collected Papers*.

—— 'Themes in Kant's Moral Philosophy', in Eckart Förster, ed., *Kant's Transcendental Deductions* (Stanford, Calif.: Stanford University Press, 1989); repr. in Rawls, *Collected Papers*.

—— *Political Liberalism* (New York: Columbia University Press, 1993; rev. paperback edn., 1996).

—— *Collected Papers*, ed. Samuel Freeman (Cambridge, Mass.: Harvard University Press, 1999).

—— *Lectures on the History of Moral Philosophy*, ed. Barbara Herman (Cambridge, Mass.: Harvard University Press, 2000).

Raz, Joseph. 'Voluntary Obligations and Normative Powers, II', *Proceedings of the Aristotelian Society*, suppl. vol. 46 (1972), 79–102.

—— 'Promises and Obligations', in P. M. S. Hacker and Joseph Raz, eds., *Law, Morality, and Society: Essays in Honor of H. L. A. Hart* (Oxford: Oxford University Press, 1977).

—— *The Authority of Law* (Oxford: Oxford University Press, 1979).

—— *The Morality of Freedom* (Oxford: Oxford University Press, 1986).

Reath, Andrews. 'Kant's Theory of Moral Sensibility', *Kant-Studien*, 80/3 (1989), 284–302.

—— 'Hedonism, Heteronomy, and Kant's Principle of Happiness', *Pacific Philosophical Quarterly*, 70/1 (1989), 42–72.

—— 'The Categorical Imperative and Kant's Conception of Practical Rationality', *The Monist*, 72/3 (1989), 384–410.

—— 'Intelligible Character and the Reciprocity Thesis', *Inquiry*, 36 (1993), 419–29.

—— 'Legislating the Moral Law', *Nous*, 28/4 (1994), 436–64.

—— 'Agency and the Imputation of Consequences in Kant's Ethics', *Jahrbuch für Recht und Ethik*, 2 (1994), 259–82.

—— 'Legislating for a Realm of Ends: The Social Dimension of Autonomy', in Andrews Reath, Barbara Herman, and Christine M. Korsgaard, eds., *Reclaiming the History of Ethics: Essays for John Rawls* (New York: Cambridge University Press, 1997).

—— 'Introduction to the *Critique of Practical Reason*', in Kant, *Critique of Practical Reason*, tr. and ed. Mary J. Gregor (Cambridge: Cambridge University Press, 1997).

—— 'Self-Legislation and Duties to Oneself', in Mark Timmons, ed., *Kant's Metaphysics of Morals: Interpretive Essays* (Oxford: Oxford University Press, 2001).

—— 'Constructivism', in Lawrence C. Becker and Charlotte B. Becker, eds., *The Encyclopedia of Ethics*, 2nd edn., vol. i (New York and London: Routledge Publishing, 2001).

—— 'Value and Law in Kant's Moral Theory', *Ethics*, 114/1 (Oct. 2003), 127–55.

Reath, Andrews, Barbara Herman, and Christine M. Korsgaard, eds., *Reclaiming the History of Ethics: Essays for John Rawls* (New York: Cambridge University Press, 1997).

Reiner, Hans. *Pflicht und Neigung* (Meisenheim: Verlag Anton Hain, 1951).

Ritter, Joachim. *Historisches Wörterbuch der Philosophie* (Stuttgart: Schwabe & Co. Verlag, 1971).

Rousseau, Jean-Jacques. *The Discourses and Other Early Political Writings*, tr. and ed. Victor Gourevitch (New York: Cambridge University Press, 1997).

—— *The Social Contract and Other Later Political Writings*, tr. and ed. Victor Gourevitch (New York: Cambridge University Press, 1997).

Rousseau, Jean-Jacques. *Oeuvres Complètes*, III: *Du contrat social, Écrits Politiques* (Paris: Gallimard, 1964).

Scanlon, T. M. 'A Theory of Freedom of Expression', *Philosophy and Public Affairs*, 1/2 (Winter 1972), 204–26; repr. in T. M. Scanlon, *The Difficulty of Tolerance* (New York: Cambridge University Press, 2003).

—— 'Contractualism and Utilitarianism', in Amartya Sen and Bernard Williams, eds., *Utilitarianism and Beyond* (New York: Cambridge University Press, 1982).

—— 'Kant's *Groundwork*: From Freedom to Moral Community' (unpublished lectures, delivered at Johns Hopkins University, 1983).

—— 'The Significance of Choice', in Sterling McMurrin, ed., *The Tanner Lectures on Human Values* (Salt Lake City: University of Utah Press, 1987).

—— *What We Owe to Each Other* (Cambridge, Mass.: Harvard University Press, 1998).

Schneewind, J. B. *The Invention of Autonomy* (New York: Cambridge University Press, 1998).

Sussman, David. 'The Authority of Humanity', *Ethics*, 113/2 (Jan. 2003), 350–66.

Timmons, Mark, ed. *Kant's Metaphysics of Morals: Interpretive Essays* (Oxford: Oxford University Press, 2002).

Watson, Gary. 'Promising, Assurance and Expectation', unpublished manuscript (2005).

Wiggins, David. *Needs, Values, Truth* (Cambridge, Mass.: Blackwell, 1987, 1991).

Williams, Bernard. 'A Critique of Utilitarianism', in *Utilitarianism: For and Against* (Cambridge: Cambridge University Press, 1973).

—— *Moral Luck* (New York: Cambridge University Press, 1981).

—— *Ethics and the Limits of Philosophy* (Cambridge, Mass.: Harvard University Press, 1985).

Wolff, Robert Paul. *The Autonomy of Reason* (New York: Harper & Row, 1973).

Wood, Allen W., ed., *Self and Nature in Kant's Philosophy* (Ithaca, NY: Cornell University Press, 1984).

—— 'Kant's Formula of Humanity', in Paul Guyer, ed., *Kant's Groundwork of the Metaphysics of Morals: Critical Essays* (Totowa, NJ: Rowman and Littlefield, 1998); originally published in Hoke Robinson, ed., *Proceedings of the Eighth International Kant Congress*, vol i, part 1 (Milwaukee: Marquette University Press, 1995).

—— 'Self-Love, Self-Benevolence, and Self-Conceit', in Stephen Engstrom and Jennifer Whiting, eds., *Aristotle, Kant, and the Stoics* (New York: Cambridge University Press, 1996).

—— *Kant's Ethical Thought* (New York: Cambridge University Press, 1999).

—— 'The Final Form of Kant's Practical Philosophy', in Mark Timmons, ed., *Kant's Metaphysics of Morals: Interpretive Essays* (Oxford: Oxford University Press, 2002).

—— 'What is Kantian Ethics?' in Kant, *Groundwork for the Metaphysics of Morals*, ed. and tr. Allen W. Wood (New Haven: Yale University Press, 2002).

Index

Index of Passages